Building State and Security in Afghanistan

The Liechtenstein Institute on Self-Determination at Princeton University

The Liechtenstein Institute on Self-Determination at Princeton University's Woodrow Wilson School of Public and International Affairs supports teaching, research, publication, and negotiation about issues pertaining to the state, self-determination, self-governance, sovereignty, security, and boundaries with particular consideration of socio-cultural, ethnic, religious issues, and related legal, diplomatic, economic, strategic, and environmental matters involving state as well as nonstate actors. The institute was established in 2000 through the generosity of H.S.H. Prince Hans Adam II of Liechtenstein.

Building State and Security in Afghanistan

edited by
Wolfgang Danspeckgruber
with Robert P. Finn

Liechtenstein Institute on Self-Determination
at Princeton University

First reprint in 2010

Liechtenstein Institute on Self-Determination at Princeton University
Woodrow Wilson School of Public and International Affairs
Princeton University
Princeton, New Jersey 08544
USA
Telephone: 609.258.6200
E-mail: lisd@princeton.edu
www.princeton.edu/lisd

Distributed throughout the world by
Lynne Rienner Publishers, Inc.
1800 30th Street
Boulder, CO 80301
USA
www.rienner.com

Printed and bound in the United States of America
ISBN: 978-0-9773544-4-3

Contents

Acronyms

ACSF	Afghan Civil Society Forum
AFN	Afghani (National Currency of Afghanistan)
AIA	Afghan Interim Authority
AIHRC	Afghan Independent Human Rights Commission
AMF	Afghan Militia Forces
ANA	Afghan National Army
ANBP	Afghan New Beginnings Program
ANDS	Afghanistan National Development Strategy
ANP	Afghan National Police
APM	Antipersonnel Landmine
ASP	Afghanistan Stabilization Program
ATA	Afghan Transitional Authority
CAT	Civil Affairs Team
CDC	Community Development Council
CERP	Commanders Emergency Response Program (US Department of Defense)
CLJ	Constitutional Loya Jirga
CMOC	Civil Military Operations Center
CTC	Counter-Terrorism Committee
CTED	Counter-Terrorism Committee Executive Directorate
CVR	Civil Voter Registry
DDR	Disarmament, Demobilization and Reintegration Process
DFID	Department for International Development (United Kingdom)
DIAG	Disbandment of Illegal Armed Groups Program
DoD	Department of Defense
DSRSG	Deputy Special Representative of the Secretary-General
ELJ	Emergency Loya Jirga
ESF	Economic Support Fund (US Department of State)
FCO	Foreign and Commonwealth Office (United Kingdom)
GTZ	Deutsche Gesellschaft für Technische Zusammenarbeit (German Agency for Technical Cooperation)
iANDS	interim Afghanistan National Development Strategy

ICRC	International Committee of the Red Cross
IDLO	International Development Law Organization
IDP	Internally Displaced Persons
IEC	Independent Election Commission
IFES	International Foundation for Election Systems
ISAF	International Security Assistance Force
ISI	Inter-Services Intelligence Directorate (Pakistan)
JCMB	Joint Coordination and Monitoring Board
JEMB	Joint Electoral Management Body
JRC	Judicial Reform Commission
KFOR	NATO Kosovo Force
KhAD	Khadamat-e Etela'at-e Dawlati
LOTFA	Law and Order Trust Fund for Afghanistan
MOD	Ministry of Defense
MOI	Ministry of Interior
MSF	Médecins sans Frontières
NCCTs	Non-Cooperative Countries and Territories
NPP	National Priority Program
NSP	National Solidarity Program
OECD	Organization for Economic Cooperation and Development
OHDACA	Overseas Humanitarian Disaster and Civic Aid
ONUC	United Nations Operation in the Congo
OSCE	Organization for Security and Cooperation in Europe
PRO	Provincial Reconstruction Office
PRT	Provincial Reconstruction Team
PSF	Provincial Stabilization Fund
QIP	Quick Impact Project
RDZ	Regional Development Zone
SNTV	Single Non-Transferable Vote
SRSG	Special Representative of the Secretary-General
SSR	Security Sector Reform Process
UNAMA	United Nations Assistance Mission in Afghanistan
UNAMIR	United Nations Assistance Mission for Rwanda
UNDP	United Nations Development Programme
UNFICYP	United Nations Peacekeeping Force in Cyprus
UNHCR	United Nations High Commissioner for Refugees
UNICEF	United Nations Children's Fund
UNIFSA	United National Islamic Front for the Salvation of Afghanistan
UNODC	United Nations Office on Drugs and Crime
UNSMA	United Nations Special Mission to Afghanistan
UNTAC	United Nations Transitional Authority in Cambodia
USAID	United States Agency for International Development
USG	United States Government

Acknowledgements

WHEN I VISITED KABUL FOR the first time in 2003 I was impressed with the immaculately clean and beautifully colored burqas, bustling construction activity, and the work intensely going on all around me in a society which had suffered so much for so long. I experienced the serenity and the historical foundation of a highly cultured society when I had the opportunity to call on King Zahir Shah in his palace. I was impressed by his profound devotion to the future of his country and fellow citizens, and with his interest in connecting with a Euro-American visitor and learning about possible projects that could ameliorate the economic situation in Afghanistan and link it more firmly to Europe and America. When I left Kabul, activity in construction, agriculture, small business, and industry was visible everywhere. Still, the horrendous destruction and the absence of any basic form of infrastructure for water or power supply was also plainly clear. I saw countless invalids and injured wherever I visited and saw many a widow with young children clearly without a father. This juxtaposition of progress and depravation was all experienced amidst a stunning mountainous topography, which challenges the Alps in its beauty.

Fate was such that I was in the region dealing with Kashmir and visiting Islamabad when the two Buddhas of Bamiyan were destroyed, turning into rubble icons of cultural history which had no comparison. The political shockwaves which ran through Islamabad and its international community at that moment will be forever with me. It became clear in those days of March 2001 that somehow something dramatic was developing. Six months later the world experienced global terrorism at its worst and Afghanistan's fate would experience yet another momentous development. On September 9 assassins targeted and killed Ahmed Shah Massoud, on September 11 terrorists attacked the United States, and weeks later the international Coalition operation "Enduring Freedom" based upon Article V of NATO and with UN Security Council support commenced.

In November 2001, the Liechtenstein Institute on Self-Determination (LISD) hosted eight senior Afghans under the leadership of former Vice-President Sarabi at Princeton University to discuss with them variants of federalism versus centralization, experiences of Austria and Switzerland with their respective constitutions, and self-governance of rural communities. In September 2003, a special event in the LISD Afghanistan project that had started in 2001 was the unforgettable visit to Princeton University by President Hamid Karzai. His talk and presence with students and faculty demonstrated the demands of a statesman in search of the best for his people at home and abroad, and of one who wants to educate those abroad about the challenges his country has to master and opportunities it can offer.

Several of my students and collaborators became involved early on in LISD's work on Afghanistan that continues today, particularly my associate Rani Mullen, as well as Knut Hammarskjöld, Karim Thomas, Rishma Thomas, and international experts Wolfgang von Erffa, Hans-Ulrich Seidt, Volcker Stanzl, Amin Saikal, Olivier Roy, Paul Bucherer, Claudia Fritsche, and Christian Wenaweser. Soon Robert Finn joined our activities as well, then from his post as the first US ambassador to post-Taliban Afghanistan and later as a senior research associate and collaborator at LISD. Robert's connections, gained through his years of government service, as well as his deep knowledge of the region's culture, literature, and history, have enriched the project immensely.

In close partnership with Rani Mullen, our expert group evolved into a team: Tarek Ghani, Sarah Lister, William Maley, Andrew Reynolds, Anne Tully, Larry Sampler, Eckart Schiewek, Michael Schmunk, Barbara Stapleton, J Alexander Thier, Marvin Weinbaum, Andrew Wilder, and more recently Lieutenant General Karl Eikenberry, Ahmed Evin, and Ambassador Francesc Vendrell. Our group also benefited from the participation in several of our colloquia of then Afghan foreign minister, Dr. Abdullah Abdullah, then vice-president, Hedayat Amin Arsala, minister of reconstruction, Amin Farhang, as well as the presence of senior Afghan ambassadors and experts, especially Ambassadors Ravan Farhadi and Said Jawad, and M. Masoom Stanekzai, who helped to provide a personal link with Afghanistan.

I would like to express my appreciation to Anne-Marie Slaughter, dean of the Woodrow Wilson School, who attended our very first Afghanistan meeting in 2001 and has since been a staunch supporter of and actively engaged in the institute's work on Afghanistan and the region. Special thanks go as well to colleagues at Princeton University, including former Princeton president Robert Goheen, Jennifer Widner, Nancy Bermeo, Thomas Christensen, James Doig, Sükrü Hanioglu, Michael Barry, Atul Kohli, and Deborah Yashar, as well as to my LISD associates and collaborators Dorothy Hannigan and Lilo Berner-Dettwiler, my conference coordinators Ciara Knudsen and Miriam Schive, and my wonderful students Arthur Boutellis, Shelly Culbertson, Natasha Gopaul, Babur Habib, Amy Paro, Prerna Singh, Kayvon Tehranian, Maya Tudor, and Yusufi Vali.

Thank you very much also to Jonathan Elist and Constance Wilhelm for their work on the index and appendices for the book.

Much of the LISD's Afghanistan project work has been graciously financed by the Carnegie Corporation of New York, with particular support from Stephen Del Rosso. Some conferences were supported by the Government of Liechtenstein, and the project also has enjoyed the full interest of Prince Hans Adam II of Liechtenstein, who from the onset engaged deeply in this rapidly expanding endeavor and participated in meetings on both sides of the Atlantic. Hereditary Prince Alois of Liechtenstein also took part in memorable colloquia, including in March 2003 the first-ever video link connecting Triesenberg, Liechtenstein, Washington, DC, and Kabul.

On a personal note, this indeed is the first project in which my beloved daughters Carolina and Mariella have been involved, hosting senior Afghans in our home in Princeton, helping with meetings in Istanbul and Vienna, and engaging in discussions with project participants. Their mother and my wife, Annegret Dettwiler-Danspeckgruber, while also greatly interested in Afghanistan, has supported me in innumerable ways while excelling in her own demanding career.

This present volume is the result of all these efforts. It stands for the involvement and vested interests of everyone mentioned in making state- and security-building in Afghanistan a success for the Afghans, for their children, and, indeed, for our own. It is for the future that we try to remedy the mistakes of the past and deal with the problems of today. It is for the individual man, woman, and child in Afghanistan, their security and prosperity, that we have taken to this task.

This book is, therefore, dedicated to the many Afghan and international heroes who have dedicated themselves to the untiring effort of creating a secure, just, and prosperous Afghanistan.

—*Wolfgang Danspeckgruber*
Princeton University
Princeton, New Jersey

Foreword:
Afghanistan as a Land Bridge Country

Hamid Karzai,
President of the
Islamic Republic of Afghanistan

THE VISION FOR A PROSPEROUS, peaceful, stable, and democratic Afghanistan is the wish of every man, woman, and child in this country, who have suffered for more than two decades from severe destruction and the trauma of war and conflict.

The process of state-building in Afghanistan started with the Bonn Conference while the Interim Administration in December 2001 inherited a state that had been torn by years of conflict, ignorance, and several waves of manmade and natural disasters. We started to rebuild the country on the ashes of war in a fragmented and divided society.

To achieve our vision, one can see in the development of Afghanistan the most difficult challenges that a country can face. The source of inspiration to shoulder such overwhelming challenges is the resilience, willingness, and participation of the Afghan people, while our confidence springs from international supporters who share this vision with us. The incident of September 11 is the proof of our argument that peace and stability in Afghanistan means peace and stability in the region that will contribute to global security.

Many have participated with us in our struggle, in helping us to achieve our vision, and have contributed in different ways and through different means to the process of state-building in Afghanistan. Some of these efforts were more successful than others but some were less so or failed. One of the most important contributions has originated from the activities of think-tanks, institutes, and colloquia in the form of analysis, fresh ideas, and recommendations, whether presented as separate papers or books such as this present one, which combines expert views from within and outside Afghanistan. This can play an important role in raising the awareness of our partners to the complexity of state-building and stability in Afghanistan and gives food for thought.

Building peace and stability in Afghanistan is both an opportunity as well as a global challenge. If the internal dynamics are not well understood this unique opportunity will be lost. In contrast, if the Afghan people, the government, and our international partners work together around a common agenda and effectively use the resources that produce long-lasting results without imposing conditions that are not appropriate or relevant to our social and cultural context, Afghanistan will be stable and the world will be safer.

The topics discussed in this important book cover a wide range of issues, from the challenges of building a democratic state, security, rule of law, and national institutions to social and economic reconstruction including the engagement of the international community. These are all relevant topics.

Even though Afghanistan is facing enormous challenges, a lot has been achieved over the past five years. Afghanistan has made significant progress toward democracy while reconstructing the country's political, social, and security institutions. These include adopting an enlightened constitution and holding successful presidential and parliamentary elections while creating a national army and a national police force, dismantling major factional militia units, and building a national economy from ground zero. One of the early successes was in education, in getting more than six million children back into schools. According to recent survey results, access to basic health services has increased from 9% to 80%. The importance of this is not only access to the services but the broader impact of these services. There have been some dramatic improvements with regard to child mortality. Tens of thousands of children (i.e., 85,000) who would have died are now alive, which gives me a great sense of happiness and pride.

I do not want to portray a rosy picture. The ground realities in Afghanistan are always changing and there is no simple solution for a wide range of problems and challenges. They are difficult but not impossible. Stability and development in Afghanistan need to take their course and pace and must be adopted and internalized throughout the system but not by imposed models copied from elsewhere. Such initiatives would be difficult to integrate and even impossible to sustain once international assistance is reduced.

Frustration of Afghans and the international community could be addressed effectively by making focused investment on national capabilities to deliver services to the public, in particular in sectors such as security and the judiciary, and by creating an efficient, effective, and clean public administration. Creating sustainable employment opportunities and effectively addressing rural poverty is an area of significant importance for investing in a stable Afghanistan.

The issue of decentralization at this point and time is a premature idea; first we need to consolidate the country and our political system. Transferring power to the people is already happening and it will continue until it will create a good balance of power between the center and the subnational level in accordance to our constitution.

It is also critical that the international community avoid creating parallel administration systems for the delivery of security and reconstruction services that undermine the credibility as well as the ability of the Afghan government. My experience shows that the national budget is the most useful tool to coordinate the effective use of resources and ensure transparency and accountability among all stakeholders. We do know that in areas where good coordination and cooperation exists our efforts were more fruitful.

Afghanistan is located at the meeting points of the Middle East, the Indian subcontinent, and East Asia. Historically, the strategic position of Afghanistan has been important as a trade corridor. Afghanistan has seen a vast range of goods, peoples, and ideas being exchanged along the famous Silk Road. Today once again Afghanistan has the potential to be changed into a land bridge country. To achieve this, three things are needed: more investment in infrastructure (transport, energy, communication, trade, and transit), ensuring security, and keeping our impartiality in our relations with our neighboring countries. The recent Peace Jirga between Afghanistan and Pakistan, our joint efforts for good relations with Iran and other Central Asian countries—including all other regional powers—are part of our efforts to sustain and further build regional consensus on peace and stability in Afghanistan and to reduce tensions through building trust.

Finally, I would like to thank the Liechtenstein Institute on Self-Determination at Princeton University for its tireless efforts focusing on Afghanistan and for the publication of this important and valuable book, which will help many to learn more about Afghanistan and to think with depth about the problems we face in this country. I have full confidence that we will achieve our vision but it will take time, resources, and long-term commitment.

—President Hamid Karzai
Kabul
Islamic Republic of Afghanistan

Preface: Can Afghanistan Become the Switzerland of Asia?

Prince Hans Adam II of Liechtenstein

AT FIRST GLANCE THIS NOTION of Afghanistan becoming the Switzerland of Asia is a provocative idea, but Afghanistan and the international community need an ambitious vision if this great country, destroyed by decades of war, wants to have a bright future. The similarities between Switzerland and Afghanistan cannot be discounted: both countries are landlocked and mountainous, their populations are ethnically and religiously mixed, and they are both surrounded by much larger countries which have to a certain degree a population with very similar ethnic and religious backgrounds.

Like Switzerland in Europe, Afghanistan can offer important trade routes for north-south, east-west trade to South Asia and Central Asia. The construction of motorways and railroads through the mountains costs a lot of money. The poor Afghan state should not be burdened with this task but rather look for foreign investors who will build toll-roads for the international traffic through Afghanistan. Luckily for Afghanistan, a modern infrastructure with transportation, telecommunication, and water supply can now be outsourced to private enterprises that have the know-how and the capital.

What has been the success of Switzerland? The rule of law, democracy, and a very open market economy. The most challenging task for the new Afghanistan will be to establish the rule of law, for without the rule of law there is no democracy and no market economy. No serious businessperson will invest in a country where there is no rule of law or will at least ask for a very high profit margin to cover the risks. To establish the rule of law in Afghanistan will require the support of the international community because the only commodities with surpluses in Afghanistan are weapons and drugs. A program to buy those weapons and those drugs will need the financial support of the international community, but it would bring money to the local people as long as the program is in place.

To establish the rule of law you need a constitution and laws, an efficient police force, state prosecutors, and independent judges. Here again the support of the international community will be vital. In writing down the constitution and the laws, you do not have to invent the wheel again but you have to look at what has worked efficiently in other countries and what has not worked. Countries which were quite successful in their modernization at the end of the nineteenth century and the beginning of the twentieth century, like Japan and Turkey, copied to a large extent laws which proved to be successful in Europe. Such an approach makes it so much easier to train a police force, prosecutors, and judges who can profit from the experience already gained from these kinds of laws.

Experience shows that the rule of law will only survive over longer periods of time if it is based on democracy and therefore accepted by the majority of the population. A stable democracy cannot be built only top-down but it has also to be built bottom-up. If it is only built top-down it runs the risk of becoming the dictatorship of the majority. The question that has to be solved is what community is the basic unit for the democratic state in Afghanistan, is it the village and the city or the province? Smaller units are generally better because people have a better knowledge of the representatives they elect and the problems they have to deal with. Smaller units also encourage the cooperation between those units, and they can form alliances on a regional basis depending on their needs. One has to take into account that traditional borders between provinces or regional states might not be relevant after the displacement of so many people. Hopefully the millions of refugees who have lived many years outside of Afghanistan can return. They might not settle where they came from but rather where they find a job. If Afghanistan is successful with its economic development, large numbers of people will probably move from the countryside into cities or villages, which will rapidly grow into new and important cities. This is at least what happened in countries which were economically successful. With a rapidly shifting population inside Afghanistan, old borders between provinces and regional states might soon become irrelevant and might bring new tensions if there is not enough flexibility in this respect.

Many states which are politically decentralized—and Afghanistan has to be, like Switzerland, a politically decentralized country—have a parliament consisting of two chambers, a lower house where the parties are represented according to their popular vote nationwide, and an upper house where regional states or provinces are represented on an equal basis. It is questionable if it would be a wise decision to introduce such a system into Afghanistan, at least for the moment. It adds to the cost and complexity of the system and might create new tensions during a time when the borders of provinces and regional states are ill-defined. It would be much better to give the basic political unit much autonomy, whatever this unit might be—village, city, or small province—and to restrict the central government to very few but important tasks which only the central government can do efficiently.

One task under the purview of the central government would be foreign relations and defense. But, instead of building up an expensive army it would be much better for Afghanistan to declare its neutrality and to have this neutrality guaranteed for a longer period of time by the international community. Much more important for the central government is to maintain the rule of law and there, a well-trained police force is more important.

Transportation and communication are also tasks which have to be regulated by a central government in order to be efficient. That does not mean that the central government has to own the infrastructure. On the contrary, for a poor country like Afghanistan it is much better to have this infrastructure built, owned, and operated by a private enterprise.

Education and health are other tasks which have to be regulated by the central government but not owned and operated. Experience has shown that in those developing countries where the central government owned and operated education and health services, the tendency was to concentrate the resources on a small elite by building universities and hospitals whereas basic education and health services were neglected. The economically successful developing countries, mainly in Asia, concentrated on good primary and secondary education and a basic health service, leaving university education for those who could afford it. Basic education today should not only concentrate on reading, writing, and calculation in the native language but also offer English as a second language and some computer literacy.

This, with an efficient communication system, should give the next generation in Afghanistan access to the whole world even from a remote village. Afghanistan, like Switzerland, should be in a good position to attract tourists from all over the world, but to be attractive in this business today you need, beyond a secure and stable environment, English speakers, communications, and transportation.

To build an open and efficient market economy with high growth rates in a developing country you need not only the rule of law, and democracy if you want to sustain the rule of law, but also an efficient system of taxation. For local governments to be efficient and fiscally responsible they have to have their own tax authority and have to compete against other local governments in taxation and efficiency. Experience shows that it is better to leave direct taxation authority with the local government and indirect taxation with the central government. Most experts agree that the value added tax as introduced in the European Union is today the most efficient indirect taxation. The European Union could probably be convinced to technically support the introduction of such a value added tax in Afghanistan. To give the local governments an incentive to fully support the application of the value added tax, it would be wise to give them a small share of the taxes they have raised locally. The tendency within the World Trade Organization and elsewhere is to eliminate custom taxes over a certain period of time. To build up a real open market economy it will be better for Afghanistan not to tax imports or exports but to rely only on the value added tax.

Central governments prefer to have central banks and their own currencies because then they can print their own money to finance their expenses. It is a dangerous concept and has destroyed many economies, not only of developing countries but also of developed ones. For a small country, if you are not Switzerland, to have your own currency in a globalized, economically integrated world is much more a liability than an asset. This is also one of the reasons why most members of the European Union have decided to give up their own currencies and to build up a new common currency with the euro. If you want to build up an open market economy you need a currency which is fully convertible. If you want to have your own currency which is fully convertible you need very high reserves in foreign currency or gold, as are Switzerland's assets, but which Afghanistan does not have and will not have in the foreseeable future. For Afghanistan, by far the best solution is to take over one of the big fully convertible currencies like the dollar, the euro, the yen, or perhaps the pound. Besides having a fully convertible currency from the beginning, the interest rate and the inflation rate will be much lower over a longer period of time than in a local currency. Probably most of the economic aid will come from the European Union, and the European Union will probably also be the largest trading partner of Afghanistan in the future. Former members of the Soviet Union, like the Baltic States, will become members of the European Union and one cannot exclude that one day even Russia might become a member. Thus, for Afghanistan the euro might be the best choice of all the convertible currencies now available.

For Afghanistan to become the Switzerland of Asia is an ambitious goal but not an impossible one. The European Union has many different models of association depending on how developed a country is and the nature of its economy. Perhaps one day even a membership in the European Union might be possible. But long before that, Afghanistan could become a very important base for the European economy inside the Asian market. At the same time, Afghanistan would also be a very important base for Asian companies into the European market. European, American, and Japanese companies would invest in Afghanistan, as would companies from India, Pakistan, Iran, China and other Asian countries. To turn Afghanistan into the Switzerland of Asia might be less crazy than many people might today think.

—*Prince Hans Adam II of Liechtenstein*
Schloβ Vaduz
Principality of Liechtenstein

Introduction

Wolfgang Danspeckgruber
and Robert P. Finn

AFGHANISTAN REPRESENTS ONE OF THE most unique combinations a country and its society may offer. It is a country with a challenging and unforgiving but majestic geography which favors independence both to the central authorities in the capital but also to potential intruders from the outside. It holds a unique geopolitical location south and east of the Hindukush connecting Central Asia to South Asia, and the Middle East to each of them. It is home to a proud, independent people with a history of ages-old religions and diverse cultures, but also of conflict and war. The Afghans and their country stand out in terms of drama, disadvantages and sometimes even simple suffering, witnessing nearly three decades—an entire generation—of warfare and civil strife. Afghanistan too is home to one of the most archaic societies north of the Indian Ocean. It has very little transportation or energy infrastructure, one of the world's highest rates of poverty, and some of the lowest levels of literacy, health care and GDP per capita. However, Afghanistan is today the world's most important opium producer and is centrally located in a region marked by high population and poverty with tendencies toward fundamentalist religious expression. Afghanistan itself became a base of Islamic militancy.

As a reaction to the September 11, 2001 Al Qaeda terror attacks on the United States, an international coalition of more than fifty states under US leadership intervened in Afghanistan with the objectives to depose the Taliban, destroy Al Qaeda, and capture Osama Bin Laden dead or alive. The Coalition operated under UN Security Council authorization and under the activation of NATO Article V. Five years after that sudden international presence in Afghanistan and the establishment of a true government by free and fair elections, there remains no semblance of "normality." On the contrary, it seems that while new dynamics take hold of Afghanistan itself, the scope and character of the influences of neighboring states is in a continual state of flux. New challenges posed by drugs and terrorism loom large and become ever more demanding. It may well be that western nations and the wider international community will in the future repeat some of the critical missteps that helped create the situation confronting Afghanistan today.

Background

From its time-shrouded origins as the land of Aryana, the territory of Afghanistan has hosted conquerors as diverse as Alexander the Great and Babur the Mogul Conqueror of India, defeated the armies of the British Raj and the Soviet Union, and produced some of the finest world masterpieces of art and literature including the world-renowned Buddhas of Bamiyan. The exigencies of politics and sociology have created a mosaic of peoples and languages whose economic and ethnographic imperatives form much of the understructure that informs the current situation in Afghanistan and the region.

Conflicts among Pashtun, Tajik, Hazara, Uzbek, Kizilbash and Baluch long predate the existence of Al Qaeda and the Taliban. Similarly, regional relations among Afghanistan and its neighbors reflect a complex history that goes back to the very beginnings of recorded history. Alexander's armies conquered Afghanistan and left their imprint as part of a campaign through a familiar geography that stretched from west to east until finally daunted by the strange flatness and heat of the Punjab plain. Through the centuries, warriors swept down from the mountains of the Hindukush to raid and finally conquer the rich agricultural society of India. The tide has never been just one way, however, and Babur, the first Mogul Emperor, is buried not in Delhi, but in his garden overlooking Kabul. Afghanistan contains layers of culture and religion: Greek, Buddhist, Nestorian Christian, Hindu and finally Islamic. The problems of Afghanistan and the possible solutions lie not just in the politics of post-September 11, but in the close weave of a tapestry that has existed for centuries. Ignorance, conscious or unconscious, of these factors has helped to contribute to the current situation in Afghanistan.

More is known about the Great Game. This nineteenth-century rivalry between Russia and the British Empire resulted in the delineation of Afghanistan's borders to a problematic degree. The recognition of the de facto government suited the needs of both parties but the government had the admonitory advantage of having destroyed several British armies sent to conquer it. Thus the Afghanistan created by default contained diverse and often antagonistic ethnic groups that were constantly augmented by discontented fellow tribesmen from the north and east as the two empires, British and Russian, established their suzerainty and began to implement their respective views of civilization.

The resentments and memories those tribesmen brought with them are one more strand in the fabric of the contemporary situation. When the fighters of the Islamic Movement of Uzbekistan were expelled from the former Soviet Union, they took refuge in Afghanistan and later Pakistan, in a movement that was perfectly familiar to residents of the area. The specifically Islamic rendering of the struggle in Afghanistan is real, but it is also in many cases a code for resistance and the desire to maintain traditional values and life patterns in the face of an encroaching environment that clearly would alter them. The fact that the diversity of Islam does not support this is irrelevant in a traditional environment, hence the active resistance to education, particularly for girls. There is much underneath the actively Islamic surface of Afghanistan.

In 1979 during the Cold War, the Soviet Union intervened in Afghanistan in order to topple an unwanted government and to ascertain the taking of power by a leadership under Moscow's control. The Soviet intervention took place at the same time when Shah Reza Pahlevi, the ruler of neighboring Iran, was toppled in Tehran by a theocratic revolution under Ayatollah Khomeini. The Soviet occupation of Afghanistan lasted until 1990 when Mikhail Gorbachev decided to withdraw the troops in part as a signal to soften the Cold War tensions, but also because the human, financial and military costs of the occupation had become unacceptable for the Soviets. The heroic resistance offered by the Afghans, with the support of the Pakistani ISI and at least indirect US sponsorship caused tens of thousands of Soviet casualties and became key to Moscow's decision to withdraw.

However, the decades of guerilla warfare and the enhanced influence by foreign intelligence and military support also created a new class of warriors in totally impoverished Afghanistan who built their identity onto ethnic-cultural dimensions and increasing religiousness. Kabul was not capable of exerting control over the country and in this post-occupation power vacuum, Afghan civil war broke out. Mujahideen fought the most bloody and destructive battles against one another, causing bloodshed, suffering and destruction even greater than ten years of Soviet occupation. While the Afghan people descended into the abyss, the United States and western nations remained otherwise occupied. The Berlin Wall fell, Germany united, Saddam Hussein annexed Kuwait, and Yugoslavia began to unravel in bloody civil war under the instigation of the Serbian, Croatian and Bosniak leadership. Years of fighting and mayhem left hundreds of thousands of Afghans dead and injured, millions of invalids and orphans, and totally ravaged the already very backward country. It was from within this con text that the Taliban came to power, a new radical and ruthless kind of organization which brutally established seeming tranquility through the most archaic and suppressive male interpretation of Islam.

The attacks in the United States on September 11, 2001 were the galvanizing events that finally made the world community realize it had to deal with the threat of Islamic fundamentalism and with a movement that chose terror as its weapon in attempting to re-create its vision of the early years of Islam and to free Islamic lands from the domination of unbelievers or heretics. These attacks were neither the first, nor sadly the last, as terrorist acts have occurred in many countries. In the spring of 2006, Islamic rebels virtually took over the state of Somalia and immediately began implementing Islamic codes and punishments. Somalia was the place where Bin Laden claimed his first victory over the US when American troops withdrew from there in 1993. Forced by US pressure on the government to leave his safe haven in Sudan, he had moved back to Afghanistan where his Al Qaeda organization had worked successfully with the Taliban to take over the state and establish a fundamentalist regime. Spring

2001 saw the destruction of the two giant Buddhas of Bamiyan, symbols of highest cultural value, through the forces of the Taliban. It appeared that the last fragments of resistance to the Taliban would soon be eliminated and officials in Tajikistan to the north made preparations to receive the final influx of refugees from northern Afghanistan. The assassination of Ahmed Shah Masood, the charismatic Northern Alliance leader, on September 9, 2001—two days before the attacks on the United States, on its World Trade Center and Pentagon—utterly changed that.

Within weeks, the Coalition's multinational forces had started to attack Al Qaeda's installations in Afghanistan, and troops from some fifty nations entered Afghanistan under the auspices of the United Nations to liberate the country from the Taliban and Al Qaeda. For the first time, the US established a physical presence in Afghanistan and the region through its military forces, with important political and strategic ramifications. One of the consequences of the "light footprint" advocated by US Secretary of Defense Donald Rumsfeld and supported by the UN Secretary-General's Special Representative, Lakhdar Brahimi, was the establishment of alliances with the very local commanders and militia leaders whose internecine fighting had paved the way for the takeover of Afghanistan by the Taliban and Al Qaeda in the first place. A quick overall military victory led to the takeover of Kabul by troops, supported by the Coalition, from the Tajik-dominated Northern Alliance and to the withdrawal of Taliban forces to the Pashtun heartland in the east and southeast to strongholds from which they create security problems with surprising ferocity even in 2007.

In November of 2001, an international conference convened under UN auspices in Petersberg-Bonn brought together representatives of virtually all Afghan groups, domestic and in the diaspora, except the Taliban. In sometimes cantankerous meetings, a plan was drawn up for an interim Afghan government and a step-by-step return to elected self-government in Afghanistan. Some lessons contained in the plan were derived from previous UN operations in the Balkans and in East Timor. The plan, approved at the meeting on December 5, 2001 and the next day by the United Nations Security Council in New York, set up a coalition interim government headed by Hamid Karzai, a Pashtun tribal leader who was recognized for his ability to deal impartially with all factions. Indeed, he became known afterwards as "Mr. Afghanistan," a sobriquet which has since fallen into desuetude. His cabinet contained many of the same military commanders, such as then General (later Marshall) Fahim, Hazara leader Khalili, Hazret Ali of Jalalabad and others who were principally responsible for Afghanistan's civil wars. Their actions then, and actions taken during the fighting against the Taliban that have led to serious accusations of human rights abuses, are among the basic issues that continue to haunt Afghanistan. Similarly, other leaders, such as Ismail Khan of Herat and Gul Agha Sherzai of Kandahar, returned to areas where they had been powerful before the Taliban takeover.

The plan laid out by the Bonn Agreement was for an initial period of setting up an Afghan government, which would then, in about six months, hold a

Loya Jirga to affirm the support of the people for the government. This would be followed a year later by a Constitutional Loya Jirga, to draft a constitution and then proceed to the registration and election of the president and a new national parliament. Caveats were laid down for minority representation and gender issues. The system functioned, albeit imperfectly. The first Loya Jirga was held in June 2002, and remarkably assembled in a rambunctious group everyone from ex-king Zahir Shah to Pacha Khan, one of the more truculent warlords on the Afghan border. Amid much complaining, lots of private cabals, and a surprisingly strong showing by Dr. Masooda Jalal, a female candidate, Karzai was affirmed as president. An eleventh hour effort to bring back Zahir Shah failed when he announced that he did not want to be king and then followed with a showing on the podium that demonstrated clearly that he was beyond the age of actively governing. He was given the title "Father of the Country" and first place in national protocol. At the end of the conference, in true Afghan fashion, Pacha Khan managed to disappear before Coalition forces could get their hands on him.

The second Loya Jirga was more problematic, as members were chosen in a series of jirgas nationwide, with many claims of pressure and manipulation. The constitution they produced, with much help from foreign experts, envisioned a strong central government and a presidential system. It contains a number of problems, both in terms of religious and judicial issues and in terms of governance that are only now beginning to appear.

The third phase was that of elections. Over a year was lost in questions of registration and the nature of the elections, until a decision was finally made to separate presidential and parliamentary elections. Both were finally held, although voting in the presidential elections took place along ethnic lines and several losing candidates initially disputed the outcome. Parliamentary elections were highly successful despite Taliban attempts to disrupt them. The voting system used resulted in a parliament that includes many militia commanders and some former Taliban. The lower house is now headed by Abu Sayyaf, a fundamentalist, and managing the Parliament will be a difficult task for President Karzai.

Responsibility for assistance was divided between the new Afghan government and the international community, thus setting up a problem area which has become an increasingly significant issue in Afghan reconstruction, or as some would have it, construction. The Afghan government vocally complains that the failure of the international community to give it control over assistance funds has led to mismanagement, overspending and the undermining of its efforts at governance. International participants, for their part, charge the Afghans with rampant corruption and an inability to manage or govern. Sadly, there is truth to all of the charges. In addition, the UN mandated system of lead nations, where nations are assigned responsibility for coordinating assistance and, more importantly, managing development, has failed in certain areas and has been only partially successful in others. Most fingers point towards the justice area, the responsibility of the Italians, but there have been significant problems in many other areas as well. One reason for this is the lack of a significant monitoring system that could oversee programs and recommend changes.

The inability of the international Coalition to secure a complete victory over the Taliban and Al Qaeda and in fact, the growth of those forces in at least part of the country, has completely overshadowed the many successes in Afghanistan. The opening of a second war in Iraq, led by the United States, has had many repercussions for Afghanistan. From numbers of troops to amounts of aid, Afghanistan has become attached to Iraq in many ways. Allegations that the Iraqi regime was somehow involved in the September 11 attacks resulted in the conflating of the two wars in a macabre equation that wound up fulfilling itself, as Al Qaeda became a powerful force in Iraq and the techniques of that war, such as suicide bombing, spread to Afghanistan. Support in the international community for the war in Afghanistan has in many cases lessened as a reflection of the unpopularity of the war in Iraq. The international effort in Afghanistan has to deal with this fact.

Content

The chapters contained in this volume represent the results of the work on the respective subjects since 2001. The authors met in a series of international meetings and colloquia sponsored by the Liechtenstein Institute on Self-Determination at Princeton University's Woodrow Wilson School of Public and International Affairs as part of its interdisciplinary project undertaken with funding from the Carnegie Corporation of New York, "Building State and Security in Afghanistan," and continued in the subsequent project, "State, Security and Prosperity: Afghanistan, Its Neighbors and the Region." They deal with some of the key institutional, structural and historical problems of Afghanistan. Together they provide a unique lens for viewing Afghanistan and, perhaps, also a light for seeing further in seeking solutions for the problems they discuss.

The first section of the book focuses on state-building. William Maley's chapter deals with the issues of state-building and the idea of a strong state, which has been suggested as the model for Afghanistan. He first treats security for the state, then focuses on the nature of the state itself. After this, he addresses the issues in designing state structures, the practical problems which arise from those structures, and then conclusions on the nature of building a state, strong or not. In the second chapter, Marvin Weinbaum gives an overview of the history of security in Afghanistan, explaining how security was provided disparately by both tribes and the government. He looks at the quest for security on both the local and national level since the formation of Afghanistan, underscoring the positive and negative effects of regional concerns for security and how they translate into the national arena. Similarly, he discusses the regional security issues of Afghanistan, pointing out both how problematic Afghanistan is for the area and how, given the right circumstances, Afghanistan can in fact make a specific positive contribution to regional security issues.

In the third chapter on state-building, Andrew Reynolds addresses the question of how political institutions shape the chances for democracy and stability in an emerging multiparty state like Afghanistan. He explains that although the Afghan constitution sets up a powerful presidency and a unitary state, entrenching liberal democracy remains fraught with difficulties. His analysis highlights key problems with the use of the Single Non-Transferable Vote system in Afghanistan, and offers a perspective on where the constitution bolsters democratization and where it inhibits the likelihood of a new stable democratic order in Afghanistan. In the final chapter of the first section, J Alexander Thier grapples with the difficult matter of Afghanistan's judiciary sector. He engages with security issues, the deplorable physical state of legal institutions such as courthouses and jails, the equally deplorable state of a judiciary dominated by religiously motivated appointments, and the differences between sharia and secular law and how they may play out in Afghanistan's future. In his analysis, he deals with Italy's efforts as lead nation and those of the United States, particularly USAID's role in helping judicial reform, and raises interesting questions about the nature of the reform process, and the perils of disregarding non-state, community law.

The broad theme of centralization versus decentralization frames the six chapters in the second section of the volume. Rani D. Mullen provides a study replete with comparative analysis from other post-conflict situations and other South Asian countries to support the argument that the central-periphery development debate in Afghanistan is not an enigma but a problem that can be solved by a systematic effort expressed in rationalized sequencing and timing. It may seem to outsiders that everything must be done at once in Afghanistan, but a careful reading of Afghanistan's historical and structural issues can provide a methodology for a sophisticated sequencing that will enable both sides of the equation, the center and the periphery, to develop and mature in cohesion with one another. The chapter by Andrew Wilder and Sarah Lister deals with the question of how political institutions shape change for democracy and stability. Wilder and Lister give a history of the Bonn Agreement and its implementation, and they provide unique observations about the many discrepancies between goals, actions and ideals. Susanne Schmeidl's chapter provides an extensive essay on civil society in which she discusses the differences between civil society in Afghanistan, as it has developed in the context of Afghan society, and the concept and idea of civil society prevalent in western democracies. She shows the involvement of Afghan civil society in specific detail throughout the process of the implementation of the Bonn Agreement based on her own first-hand observations of the process and how it took place.

The fourth chapter in the second section is by the volume's editors and focuses on the economic potential as well as the economic problems that face Afghanistan. The authors argue that Afghanistan cannot stop being a problem until it can support itself, and that this is in fact possible. Highlighting the serious threat posed to development by ongoing security problems, the chapter explores both the problems and potentials for human and economic development in Afghanistan, noting some of the progress that has been made and directions in which movement could take place. Barbara Stapleton's contribution significantly increases the understanding of the security debate which took place over Afghanistan from 2001 to 2004. The chapter is more than a history of the Provincial Reconstruction Teams (PRTs) in that it also provides the reader with a vivid recounting of the various debates that took place as the international community tried to set up internal security within Afghanistan and deal with the twin problems of warlords and the Taliban and at the same time maintain a "light footprint" on the ground.

Finally, Eckart Schiewek discusses the unique security situation in northwest Afghanistan in the period from the fall of the Taliban until mid-2004 as security waxed and waned. His chapter explains the establishment of a Security Council of the north under the auspices of the United Nations Assistance Mission in Afghanistan (UNAMA) to deal with ongoing security problems between the forces of Jumbush leader General Dostum and those of Commander Muhammad Atta. The commission succeeded for some time in maintaining stability in a very volatile area without having any significant security presence or enforcement power of its own.

The final section of the book includes two chapters focusing on the international perspective. Amin Saikal's study of Afghanistan's border issues focuses on Afghanistan's borders in toto and the issues they involve, issues dealing with the Afghanistan-Pakistan border that are centered on but not limited to the Durand Line, and options for dealing with the issues for both sides. He concludes that the problem of the unresolved border presents a critical block for dealing with the security issues that are vital to Afghanistan and that only the United States can bring the necessary pressure on Pakistan to solve this issue. Anna Seleny's chapter rounds out the volume, appropriately taking the discussion beyond the border of Afghanistan to bring focus to the central question that precipitated the international intervention in Afghanistan—the question of Islamism and its relation to other ideologies. Seleny traces the history of thought and expression throughout the realm of Islam and through its history, showing that pragmatism, pluralism and expression rather than repression have been vital concepts of Islamic states. She also points out that modernism produced secularism in many Islamic countries, and argues that the methodology to win the war against Islamic fundamentalists is to seek out and work with myriad other, more moderate voices of Muslim thinkers, many of whom reside in western countries.

Afghanistan appears more problematic today than it did in 2001. Then, the Bonn Agreement set out a program for transition that seemed practicable. In fact, much of that program has been implemented. What this volume addresses are the problems that developed along the way, the problems that were overlooked at the outset, and the problems that are lasting. Indeed, the real struggle for Afghanistan is just beginning.

Part I
State-Building

1

Building State and Security

William Maley

THE RECONSTITUTION OF A POLITY which has experienced as much trauma as Afghanistan has over the last twenty-five years is a daunting exercise and grounds for pessimism abound. Those who hold office as a result of the Bonn process and its constituent elements are confronted with the task of attempting more-or-less-simultaneously to reestablish a functional political system, cope with the dysfunctional dimensions of an economy with a substantial criminalized component, satisfy the expectations of a population emerging from decades of unadulterated misery, and reintegrate millions of returnees[1]—all in the context of a drift of attention in the wider world to the new theatre of operations in Iraq. Few leaders in recent times have inherited such a grim bequest.

Where the instrumentalities of the state have been severely disrupted, as in Afghanistan, ordinary citizens often experience insecurity of diverse kinds, reflecting threats to their livelihoods of both physical and economic varieties, and from both foreign and domestic sources. The construction of a "strong" state might seem the obvious solution to this problem of insecurity. This chapter suggests that the problem is more complicated, and draws on a range of examples to suggest that a number of issues in "state-building" must be carefully addressed if harsh unintended consequences are not to ensue. These issues relate to the scope of state activity, the processes by which the state is to be legitimated, and the effectiveness of checks and balances to ensure that power is not abused. State-building needs the durable support of committed friends and cannot be rushed. This is one key reason why the recent record of state-building under international supervision has proved so patchy.

The chapter is divided into five sections. The first examines various senses of the word "security," and argues that adequate security is essential for any meaningful state-building process. The second discusses the nature of the state, and notes the way in which state capacity depends upon both coercive capacity and generalized normative support. The third draws on a range of examples to identify some of the key issues of principle which arise in designing and establishing new state instrumentalities, and the fourth examines some practical problems which pose obstacles to success. The fifth offers some brief conclusions. I have relatively little to say directly about Afghanistan, but the specific matters which I do discuss are rich with implications for the present Afghan situation.

Concepts of Security

"Security" is an expression with a checkered history. In writings on world affairs, it has long been associated with realist theories which emphasize the "anarchical" character of international relations, and depict the territorial state as the focus of security calculations. Armed forces capable of deterring or repelling the threat or use of force against the territorial integrity or political independence of a state figure as the principal instruments with which security is assured, although such approaches also recognize the importance of alliance as a device by which the objectives of a threatening power can be thwarted. Realism of this sort is not by any means the only approach to understanding international relations, but it retains staunch and sophisticated defenders,[2] and its emphasis on security of the state probably resonates more strongly with ruling elites in major powers than more recent and diverse usages. And the dangers of external attack have long been apparent to Afghans, for whom the legacies of the Soviet invasion in December 1979, and Pakistan's "creeping invasion" via the Taliban movement from 1994 onwards, remain concrete and immediate.

Nonetheless, the purely realist approach has long been under challenge. For example, in the late 1960s, peace researchers such as Johan Galtung argued that the notion of direct violence that underpinned realist accounts of war and peace should be augmented by the notion of "structural violence" (measured by variations in life expectancy between the populations of different states) which treated human wellbeing rather than territorial integrity or political independence as the central criterion according to which one should determine whether "peace" had been realized. This new approach proved to be a fleeting distraction, not least because the notion of "structural violence" was poorly developed, and because in certain circumstances the alleged evils of structural violence could be cited to defend the use of physical violence to achieve a higher "peace."[3] However, it did open the door to a much more effective challenge to state-centric realism, which came with the advent of human security discourse in the 1990s.

As a point of focus, "human security" was much less alarming in its implications than the radical posture of the early peace researchers. It shared their focus on human wellbeing, but did not lend itself to the justification of revolutionary violence along lines anticipated by writers such as Sorel and Fanon. One school of human security thinking, associated with the 1994 United Nations Development Programme (UNDP) Human Development Report, grounded human security in seven values: economic security, food security, health security, environmental security, personal security, community security and political security.[4] Sudden threats to these constituted human security threats. Another school of thought, associated with former Canadian Foreign Minister Lloyd Axworthy, focused more on threats to human security resulting from violent conflict rather than underdevelopment,[5] with such perils as antipersonnel landmines (APMs) and the explosive remnants of war receiving considerable attention. Around these schools a degree of contestation has developed. For some, a human security approach necessarily provides scope for an interrogation of existing political structures; for others, the UNDP's values are too broad and vague. In a careful recent study, Kerr, Tow and Hanson have argued that the adoption of a human security agenda is particularly facilitated by a "strong perception among key policy-makers that a particular issue presents both a normative challenge and a threat to their national security." However, where Afghanistan is concerned, they also argue that "there is ample evidence that the US is continuing to use the rhetoric of human security but failing to take enough action to ensure the safety of the Afghani people from political violence, which now comes from a variety of sources."[6] Even self-interest need not carry the day.

Some analysts of human security have pointed to the agencies of the state as a source of insecurity,[7] and the twentieth century provides abundant grounds for caution. But there is a further type of insecurity which haunts the daily existence of many ordinary people: that which arises when they are exposed to the predations of armed forces which operate without the constraint of any law because the state has collapsed or is ineffectual. Here, it is the lack of security guarantees that a well-functioning state can offer which contributes to their misery. This can be seen as a failure to deliver "human security," but it is a problem that has been recognized for centuries, and it is one with which Afghans are all too familiar. Thomas Hobbes captured it exquisitely in his famous account of war: "For as the nature of Foule weather, lyeth not in a showre or two of rain; but in an inclination thereto of many days together: So the nature of Warre, consisteth not in actuall fighting; but in the known disposition thereto, during all the time there is no assurance to the contrary."[8] This remains a huge problem in Afghanistan, which is why effective state-building—to provide the necessary "assurance to the contrary"—is central to the country's prospects.

The State

The evolution of "the state" as a set of political and administrative instrumentalities has been a key focus of research in both history and political science, and attempts to identify the defining features of the state have demonstrated the extreme complexity of the concept.[9] Very few "states" have emerged as a consequence purely of deliberate design; rather they have reflected an admixture of conscious "construction activities" with cumulatively-significant adjustments to structure and function in response to a range of factors influencing the behavior of political actors.

Of course, an immediate question which arises is what distinguishes "the state" from *other* concentrations of power that might be found within a particular territory. This matter was addressed head-on by the German sociologist Max Weber, who in one of the most widely-quoted passages in social science described the state as a "compulsory organization with a territorial basis," and argued that the "claim of the modern state to monopolize the use of force is as essential to it as its character of compulsory jurisdiction and of continuous operation."[10] States, unlike other power centers, advance claims of sovereignty. While the notion of sovereignty is itself highly textured and multi-layered, Krasner has usefully distinguished four senses of the term: *domestic sovereignty* refers to the existence of internal political authority; *interdependence sovereignty* refers to "the ability of public authorities to control transborder movements;" *Westphalian sovereignty* is based on "the exclusion of external actors from domestic authority configurations;" and *international legal sovereignty* refers to "mutual recognition."[11] Afghanistan can claim high marks for the last of these, but otherwise its sovereignty claims have been severely undermined in recent decades.

To understand specifically how this is the case, it is useful to turn to some of the central capacities that any state worthy of the name needs to display. This in turn opens a window onto what a "state-building agenda" might address. Migdal identifies these as "capacities to *penetrate* society, *regulate* social relationships, *extract* resources, and *appropriate* or use resources in determined ways."[12] These are indispensable if the state is to be a distinct actor, that is, a locus of decision and action. Premodern polities often lacked the capacity to exercise these capacities in a systematic and continuous fashion, with the ruler's power firmly established in walled fortresses and citadels, but subject to rapid erosion once one passed the outer walls. Modern states are marked by more diversified structures. Migdal has distinguished four different types. First are the *trenches,* consisting of "the officials who must execute state directives directly in the face of possibly strong societal resistance." Second are the *dispersed field offices,* that is, the "regional and local bodies that rework and organize state policies and directives for local consumption, or even formulate and implement wholly local policies." Third are the *agency's central offices,* the "nerve centers" where national policies are formulated and enacted and where resources for implementation are marshaled. Fourth are the *commanding heights,* the "pinnacle of the state" where the "top executive leadership" is to be found.[13] At the level of trenches and dispersed field offices, Afghanistan has historically been rather weak, although with notable variety over space and time. At present, there is a notable gulf at this level between de jure and de facto states.[14]

Jean-Jacques Rousseau wrote in 1762 that the "strongest is never strong enough to be always master, unless he transforms strength into right, and obedience into duty."[15] This is why the idea of "legitimacy"—generalized, normative support—is at the heart of any serious discussion of state-building. Of course, power can be exercised on non-legitimate bases such as coercion or exchange, but on their own these tend to generate prudential compliance rather than durable commitment, in a way that is both fleeting and fragile. The lack of foundations grounded in legitimacy helps explain why communist regimes collapsed so rapidly in Eastern Europe in 1989 when the threat of a Soviet intervention to bolster local elites lost all credibility.[16] It equally helps explain why the Taliban regime unraveled so swiftly in November-December 2001. Legitimacy is important not only as a source of mass support but also in ensuring elite harmony, for as Weber put it, "organized domination requires control of the personal executive staff and the material implements of administration."[17]

Thus, the bases upon which legitimacy might develop are neither simple nor straightforward. Weber, who wrote extensively on the subject of "legitimate domination" (*legitime Herrschaft*), famously pointed to traditional, legal-rational and charismatic grounds for legitimacy, and in the Bonn Agreement of December 2001, one can see how elements of these were woven into an elite settlement in the hope of giving the Afghan Interim Administration as solid a foundation as possible.[18] But other grounds can be identified. For religious leaders, it may well be that what T. H. Rigby has called "goal-rational" legitimation is more salient,[19] whereas for ordinary people emerging from societal disarray, it may simply be the ability of a new "state" to perform certain long-neglected tasks that succeeds in winning it generalized normative support. Unfortunately, the obverse also applies: *failure* to perform can rapidly erode such support. In the actions of princes, as Machiavelli suggested, one judges by results.[20] If a new regime is not in a position to perform certain basic functions effectively, it is more likely to attract scorn than generalized normative support—although it may be given the benefit of the doubt as long as the preceding era is remembered as even worse. The lesson is that capacity and legitimacy are integrally connected.

Design of the State

When the state has largely collapsed, there is no magical formula for rebuilding it.[21] The wreckage of the old state may offer little in the way of building material for the new. Some of the most successful of the consolidated democracies—for example the Anglophone parliamentary democracies, and the Scandinavian states—thrive on the basis of institutions with venerable histories, which have acquired the support they enjoy by proving their utility in good times and bad. Effective institutions are like spider webs, in that they work best when built by the spiders themselves. However, a disrupted state is not a blank sheet on which a new future can be painted in a carefree fashion. On the contrary, both the international system and local society constrain what can be attempted in the realm of institutional design.[22]

In recent years, a relatively new phenomenon has appeared, namely that of the "Transitional Administration," typically set up under United Nations auspices. While international organizations have a much longer history of involvement in internal political conflicts than is often appreciated,[23] the Transitional Administration is very much an outgrowth of so-called "complex peacekeeping," which began to take shape as the end of the Cold War extracted the United Nations Security Council from the stalemate, created by Soviet and American veto powers, in which it had long languished. The establishment of the United Nations Transitional Authority in Cambodia (UNTAC) to conduct elections in that country pursuant to the 1991 Paris Peace Accords was a landmark exercise,[24] and succeeded in resolving a troubling "regional conflict." However, UNTAC's success in bringing "democracy" to Cambodia was much more ambiguous, given that the results of the impressive 1993 election were progressively thwarted by communist "salami tactics," culminating in a July 1997 coup and an election in 1998 which was run by the forces which had lost in 1993.[25] Transitional Administrations have since been used in various parts of the Balkans and in East Timor after the local population voted for independence from Indonesia at a UN-run "popular consultation" in 1999, an event which triggered mayhem and ultimately an international intervention with the consent of the Indonesian president.[26]

Afghanistan, interestingly, did not go down this path, and even at the time it was clear why. On the ground, those anti-Taliban forces which had long resisted a Taliban takeover of the entire country found themselves in secure control of Kabul from mid-November 2001, and it was unthinkable that they would thereafter settle for anything less than *central* roles in an *Afghan* administration. This led directly to the establishment of a United Nations *Assistance* Mission in Afghanistan (UNAMA), complemented by an International Security Assistance Force (ISAF).[27] This "light-footprint" approach has earned some criticism, inter alia on the ground that it has been at the expense of the export to Afghanistan of effective means of securing compliance with internationally-accepted human rights standards,[28] but it was realistic in the light of the need identified in the 2000 Brahimi Report to match mandates to available resources.[29]

Shaping the contours of the new Afghan state has thus been an activity very much at the mercy of Afghan intra-elite politics, although with somewhat heroic attempts by UNAMA to affect things positively from the sidelines. The arduous process by which Afghanistan's new 2004 constitution (*Qanun-e Asasi*) was drafted has distracted attention from other important developments relating to the reestablishment of state structures. The imperative to offer offices to a range of forces represented at the Bonn meeting in 2001 had one very regrettable outcome, namely the establishment of far more ministerial positions than made any sense. Crass politics thus preempted careful reflection on what structures of central administration might be most appropriate for a country with a recent history resembling Afghanistan's. Yet such reflection exposes a range of options. States can vary in both their *scope,* the ambit of activities which they seek to undertake, and their *strength,* their ability to give effect to laws and policies.[30] Debate over the scope of state action lies at the heart of modern political theory. Some states limit themselves to minimalist "night watchman" responsibilities such as supply of defense and police; others embrace in addition the supply of a "safety net" to prevent gross suffering on account of poverty; still others commit themselves to a more thoroughgoing dirigisme in which the state claims overall responsibility for resource allocation and income distribution, at the expense of market relations.

With the failures of the Soviet command economy and of socialist experiments in Third World countries such as India and Tanzania, this last approach has lost most of its shine. Nonetheless, there is often a residual "statist" mood to be found in countries where the state has broken down, and it is therefore important to ensure that certain choices be clearly delineated. In particular, it is important to distinguish between coordination of the activities *of* the state, and coordination *by* the state of social activity more generally. Attempts at the latter should be treated with some caution. Many forms of social activity of course need to take place within an appropriate framework of law. However, that provides no justification for a drift to central planning. As James C. Scott has put it, a "village, city or language is the jointly created, partly unintended product of many, many hands. To the degree that authorities insist on replacing this ineffably complex web of activity with formal rules and regulations, they are certain to disrupt the web in ways they cannot possibly foresee."[31] In particular, it is important that rulers of recovering states avoid going down the paths which their predecessors trod to disastrous effect. They must avoid long-term dependence on rentier income; they must avoid the temptation to sink scarce funds in grandiose "display projects;" they must guard against the outbreak of corrupt, predatory or extractive behavior in their midst. But that said, there are also dangers associated with the emergence of what in the Afghan context the World Bank has called a "Second Civil Service" of "NGOs, consultants, advisors and employees of UN and other international agencies, including expatriate consultants and Afghans attracted by relatively high salaries."[32] This, of course, has political ramifications: the ability of the government to boost its standing by being seen to be doing good is limited if other actors in effect claim the credit, and good governance is not enhanced when the "Second Civil Service" is not transparent.[33]

This brings us to a further point of some importance. Approaches to state-building can vary according to whether they assume a general disposition towards *altruistic* behavior, which the state should facilitate, or a general disposition towards *selfish* behavior, against which it is necessary to take precautionary measures. The former approach looks for guardians, the latter asks who will guard the guardians themselves. The most prosperous and stable states are in general those which have followed the latter course. They display the positive effects of constitutionalism and its two key elements, the doctrines of the separation of powers and the rule of law. A basic separation of powers stands in the way of tyranny by making it more difficult to coordinate and execute repressive actions.[34] Montesquieu, the great proponent of the classical doctrine, argued that "there is no liberty, if the judicial power be not separated from the legislative and the executive."[35] The importance of this condition cannot be overstated. One of India's great strengths, which contrasts profoundly with the situation in its neighbor Pakistan, is the robust independence of an apolitical higher judiciary. However, an independent judiciary on its own does not guarantee the rule of law. For this, it is necessary also that rules be general in character, prospective only, be applied in accordance with accepted norms of interpretation, and bind rulers as well as ruled. In Afghanistan, Article 3 of the 2004 constitution gives some cause for concern. By providing that laws shall not contradict the "beliefs and provisions" of Islam, it virtually invites religious extremists to seek positions on the Supreme Court, where, as Barnett R. Rubin puts it, "one may safely predict that political rather than purely interpretive considerations will shape the outcome."[36] This came to a head in March 2006 when conservative jurists supported an apostasy charge against an Afghan convert to Christianity, prompting a major international crisis for the Karzai government. One reason why this happened was that the president had too readily allowed conservatives to obtain a foothold in the judiciary, where at least they did not bother him on a day-to-day basis. Fortunately, a series of fresh appointments to the Supreme Court in 2006 put paid to this trend.[37]

Given the state's claim to monopolize the use of force, and given the institutional requirements for the effective discharge of even minimal state activity, it is virtually inevitable that meaningful state-building will require the reconstitution of the security sector—in most cases, both an army and a police force. "Security sector reform" has generated a great deal of discussion in recent times,[38] not least because of its uneasy relationship in post-conflict settings to the highly-charged activities of disarmament, demobilization and reintegration (DDR) of combatants, and the even more uneasy relationship of these activities to the rebuilding of trust. All too often, those charged with developing new, professional armed forces experience pressure to absorb fighters from liberation forces active in a prior phase of a country's politics. This runs the risk of giving the new army a distinctly factional appearance; the alternative, unhappily, may be the survival of substantial, well-armed militias in the service of "warlords." Thus in Cambodia, the post 1993 "Royal Cambodian Armed Forces" came to be the armed wing of the ruling party,[39] while in East Timor, well after independence in 2002, the army was confronted with serious institutional problems "including a poorly understood definition of its role, low morale, uncertain respect for discipline and authority, insufficient training of personnel, and unresolved relations with former combatants,"[40] something which gave rise to a crisis in Dili in March 2006 when soldiers who had been dismissed after going absent without leave then took to the streets in protest. Any young state finds itself confronted with a dilemma: to secure disarmament it is necessary to create a climate in which people are not impelled to retain their arms for fear of their fellows; yet without overwhelming force at the state's disposal it is difficult to create such a climate. Unless outside powers are prepared to help, the custodians of the state can look forward to a long period of tension and insecurity, which of course does little to assist their wider quest for legitimacy.[41] In Afghanistan, security sector reform has made some progress, but the achievements have been patchy and there is still a long way to go, especially in the areas of police reform and disarmament of illegal armed groups.[42]

Obstacles to Success

While all transitions are different, there are certain common obstacles to success which deserve specific mention. These relate to inadequate security, a shortage of resources, spoiler behavior, and a loss of wider commitment to make a transition work.[43]

The importance of a neutral security force in complex transitions can hardly be overestimated. As Charles King has argued, "In civil wars, external powers are often the only available generator of trust between the contesting parties. . . . Trust among the belligerent parties thus depends on each side feeling sufficiently secure in its own position to accept the legitimacy of contending interests and to discuss ways in which those interests might be accommodated in a final settlement."[44] A substantial neutral security force also symbolizes a serious international commitment, and can help induce local political actors to shift to more constructive modes of behavior. Without a neutral security force, there is little to protect ordinary citizens if a peace agreement or transition process unravels badly. The cases of Rwanda and East Timor are extreme, but they highlight the heavy costs of miscalculation. In Rwanda, the force which was deployed to support the Arusha Accords of 1993, known as UNAMIR, was too weak to be effective, and was unable to halt the genocidal slayings which broke out in April 1994, not least because key major powers were unwilling to back its expansion.[45] In East Timor there was no international security force, for the May 5, 1999 Accords on East Timor signed by Indonesia and Portugal had left the maintenance of security in the hands of Indonesian state agencies which were actually in league with the very militias that ran amok in early September 1999.[46] In Afghanistan, the immediate effects of the slim international military presence were not so dire, but the lack of a widely-deployed, neutral security force did contribute significantly to the loss of momentum which the Afghanistan transition experienced in early 2002, when it became very clear that the US Administration did not support ISAF expansion.[47]

Resources to kick-start a process of state-building are also important, and in the initial stages almost unavoidably must come from external sources in order to rebuild the state's extraction capacity. Here, there is a healthy balance that needs to be struck: too few resources, and the state will remain enfeebled; too many, and it runs the risk of losing any sense of accountability to its own citizens, a victim of what has been called the "resource curse." The most chilling contemporary example of a victim of the resource curse is the Republic of Nauru, which at its independence in 1968 had abundant supplies of valuable and exportable phosphate, but which thereafter totally squandered its assets, to the point that at the beginning of the twenty-first century, it was notorious for its toleration of money-laundering through shell banks with no presence in Nauru itself, and subject to "countermeasures" arising from its being included on the List of Non-Cooperative Countries and Territories (NCCTs) maintained by the OECD Financial Action Task Force on Money-Laundering.[48]

At present, Afghanistan is not confronted with an oversupply of resources, although its capacity to absorb resources in certain sectors is limited. On the contrary, it is faced with a considerable gap between the rhetoric of states and their actual commitments. In preparation for a major meeting with donors held in Berlin from March 31 to April 1, 2004, the Afghan government circulated an extremely detailed set of proposals which were directed, in Finance Minister Ashraf Ghani's vivid phrase, to lifting the people of Afghanistan to the level of "genteel poverty." The central conclusion of the report was that "Afghanistan will require total external assistance in the range of US$27.6 billion over 7 years on commitment basis. A minimum of US$6.3 billion of external financing will be required in the form of direct support to the national budget—preferably more, since budget support helps build the State and its legitimacy."[49] Donor promises fell far short of this, totaling only $8.2 billion for the period March 2004–March 2007, and $4.4 billion for March 2004–March 2005. In early 2006, in preparation for a major conference in London from January 31 to February 1 to endorse a new Afghanistan Compact, the Afghan government published a new Afghanistan National Development Strategy, building on the detailed analysis which had been prepared for the 2004 Berlin meeting. The conclusions of the summary report of the strategy were stark. Over five years, Afghanistan would require $18.865 billion to cover development needs; domestic revenue was anticipated to amount to $4.489 billion, not enough even to cover non-development recurrent costs of $5.453 billion; and therefore $19.829 billion, or just under $4 billion per year over five years, would be required in the form of assistance from the wider world.[50] Yet future donor commitments at the conference from March 2006 totaled a mere $10.5 billion, barely half the figure Afghanistan needed.[51]

A further obstacle to success in transition can be the presence of well-equipped and determined spoilers, who are often the single main source of instability in transitional phases. One of the most unfortunate asymmetries in transitions is that it is cheaper and easier to be a spoiler than a builder. Spoilers come in different shapes and sizes.[52] *Total spoilers* will settle for nothing less than total power, while *partial spoilers* engage in spoiling activity as a way of pressing some claim. Some may be driven by a desire for revenge, which seems to have been at the heart of the vicious destruction mounted by pro-integration militias in East Timor in 1999. Ideology can be a potent addition to the mindset of the spoiler, as the crude racialism of the *génocidaires* in Rwanda in 1994 made clear. However, a craving for total power can also derive from an individual's personality traits: the rocketing of Kabul from 1992–1995, a classic example of spoiler activity, owed much to the ruthlessness of the leader of the Afghan Hezb-i-Islami (Party of Islam), Gulbuddin Hekmatyar.[53] Spoiler behavior can also occur at the behest of an external patron. There is no doubt that Hekmatyar enjoyed strong backing from Pakistan's Inter-Services Intelligence Directorate (ISI); and the ISI was subsequently to become, in the words of the 9/11 Commission, "the Taliban's primary patron."[54] Southern Afghanistan remains deeply insecure, again as a result of spoiler activity apparently backed by circles in Pakistan.[55] Dealing with spoilers is an intrinsically difficult undertaking. Because total spoilers approach politics in a zero-sum way, there is little scope for dealing with them. In principle it may be possible to accommodate partial spoilers, but the price they demand for ceasing to spoil may itself be high. It may also be the case that the perceived success of one set of spoilers in advancing their agenda may encourage others to undertake spoiler activity as well, creating a serious problem of moral hazard.

Perhaps the greatest problem of all for states emerging from chaos is to retain the attention of the wider world. Some state behavior is driven by altruistic considerations, but arguably not much. The Rwandan case is by far the most tragic recent example of the perils of appearing peripheral to the interests of major powers, but it is hardly novel. The notorious comments made on September 27, 1938 by British Prime Minister Neville Chamberlain as Hitler threatened the destruction of Czechoslovakia—"How horrible, fantastic, incredible it is that we should be digging trenches and trying on gas masks here because of a quarrel in a faraway country between people of whom we know nothing"—remain a classic indicator of the dangers, as Telford Taylor put it, of "not facing up to unpleasant realities."[56] Unfortunately, disrupted states struggle for attention in a world in which conflicting forces vie for the attention and support of the leaders of the major powers, and the leaders in turn vary in their insight, wisdom and judgment. By 2003, Afghanistan was no longer the focus of attention which it had been in the months following the September 11, 2001 attacks.[57] Although (or perhaps *because*) Osama Bin Laden had not been tracked down and captured, the gaze of US policy-makers shifted to Iraq. This led to a transfer of intelligence assets to the Iraq theatre of operations, but more seriously, it signaled to the remnants of the Taliban that they might have a future after all. And as the US and its allies found that stabilizing Iraq in the aftermath of Saddam Hussein's overthrow was not as easy a task as had seemingly been thought,[58] Afghanistan remained sidelined.[59]

Conclusion

In conclusion, I would simply offer two observations. The rebuilding of state and security takes *time,* and it is not clear that the wider world is prepared in all cases to make the necessary commitment. While one can find some encouraging examples of long-term support—postwar Germany and Japan, as well as peace operations in Cyprus (UNFICYP) and Kosovo (KFOR)—there are other cases, such as the Congo from 1964 after the ONUC operation, of relapse because the foundations for future stability were insecure. There is a danger that the successful elections in Afghanistan in October 2004 and September 2005 will end up providing the international community with a pretext for a premature exit.

Of course, not all is bleak. Afghanistan is no Iraq. Transition processes may bring disappointment in numerous ways while at the same time societies nonetheless muddle through. Confronted with state disruption and insecurity, ordinary people develop complex coping strategies. Those who live to be witnesses of "democratic transitions" are often tough survivors. Given Afghanistan's problems, it is a tribute to the spirit of the Afghan people that large numbers do still remain committed to the transition process. A survey conducted for the Asia Foundation in February-March 2004 found that 64% of respondents felt that the country was heading in the right direction.[60] While this had fallen to 44% when the question was again asked in 2006, only 21% of respondents answered that things were heading in the wrong direction.[61] These data capture rather well the nature of Afghanistan's dilemma: it has made progress, but it is not yet out of the woods.[62]

Notes

1. See William Maley, "The Reconstruction of Afghanistan," in Ken Booth and Tim Dunne, eds., *Worlds in Collision: Terror and the Future of Global Order* (London: Palgrave Macmillan, 2002), 184–193 at 184.

2. For a distinguished example, see John J. Mearsheimer, *The Tragedy of Great Power Politics* (New York: W. W. Norton, 2001).

3. See William Maley, "Peace, Needs and Utopia," *Political Studies,* vol. 33, no. 4 (December 1985): 578–591.

4. See Kanti Bajpai, "The Idea of Human Security," *International Studies,* vol. 40, no. 3 (July-September 2003): 195–228 at 203–204.

5. Ibid., 212. See also Rob McRae and Don Hubert, eds., *Human Security and the New Diplomacy: Protecting People, Promoting Peace* (Montreal and Kingston: McGill-Queen's University Press, 2001); and Andrew Mack, ed., *Human Security Report 2005: War and Peace in the 21st Century* (Oxford: Oxford University Press, 2005).

6. Pauline Kerr, William T. Tow, and Marianne Hanson, "The Utility of the Human Security Agenda for Policy-Makers," *Asian Journal of Political Science,* vol. 11, no. 2 (December 2003): 89–114 at 93 and 99.

7. See for example Alex J. Bellamy and Matt McDonald, "'The Utility of Human Security': Which Humans? What Security? A Reply to Thomas & Tow," *Security Dialogue,* vol. 33, no. 3 (September 2002): 373–377.

8. Thomas Hobbes, *Leviathan* (Cambridge: Cambridge University Press, 1996), 88–89.

9. See S. N. Eisenstadt, *The Political Systems of Empires: The Rise and Fall of the Historical Bureaucratic Societies* (New York: The Free Press, 1969); Gianfranco Poggi, *The Development of the Modern State: A Sociological Introduction* (London: Hutchinson, 1978); Gianfranco Poggi, *The State: Its Nature, Development and Prospects* (Stanford: Stanford University Press, 1990); Martin van Creveld, *The Rise and Decline of the State*

(Cambridge: Cambridge University Press, 1999); Graeme Gill, *The Nature and Development of the Modern State* (London: Palgrave Macmillan, 2003).

10. Max Weber, *Economy and Society: An Outline of Interpretive Sociology,* volume I (Berkeley and Los Angeles: University of California Press, 1978), 56.

11. Stephen D. Krasner, *Sovereignty: Organized Hypocrisy* (Princeton: Princeton University Press, 1999), 9. There is, of course, nothing magical about the idea of sovereignty; it is simply one organizing principle out of many upon which global political society might be based. See Christian Reus-Smit, *The Moral Purpose of the State: Culture, Social Identity, and Institutional Rationality in International Relations* (Princeton: Princeton University Press, 1999), 159.

12. Joel S. Migdal, *Strong Societies and Weak States: State-Society Relations and State Capabilities in the Third World* (Princeton: Princeton University Press, 1988), 4.

13. Joel S. Migdal, "The State in Society: An Approach to Struggles for Domination," in Joel S. Migdal, Atul Kohli, and Vivienne Shue, eds., *State Power and Social Forces: Domination and Transformation in the Third World* (Cambridge: Cambridge University Press, 1994), 7–34 at 16.

14. See Anne Evans, Nick Manning, Yasin Osmani, Anne Tully, and Andrew Wilder, *A Guide to Government in Afghanistan* (Washington, DC and Kabul: The World Bank and the Afghanistan Research and Evaluation Unit, 2004), 12–14.

15. Jean-Jacques Rousseau, *The Social Contract and Discourses* (London: J. M. Dent, 1973), 168. Edmund Burke made a similar point in his 1775 *Speech on Moving Resolutions for Conciliation with the Colonies:* "the use of force alone is but temporary. It may subdue for a moment; but it does not remove the necessity of subduing again: and a nation is not governed, which is perpetually to be conquered." See *Select Works of Edmund Burke,* volume I (Indianapolis: Liberty Fund, 1999), 236.

16. See Jan Pakulski, "Eastern Europe and 'Legitimacy Crisis'," *Australian Journal of Political Science,* vol. 25, no. 2 (November 1990): 272–288; Timur Kuran, *Private Truths, Public Lies: The Social Consequences of Preference Falsification* (Cambridge: Harvard University Press, 1995), 261–288.

17. Max Weber, "Politics as a Vocation," in H. H. Gerth and C. Wright Mills, eds., *From Max Weber: Essays in Sociology* (London: Routledge and Kegan Paul, 1948), 77–128 at 80.

18. S. Frederick Starr, "Sovereignty and Legitimacy in Afghan Nation-Building," in Francis Fukuyama, ed., *Nation-Building: Beyond Afghanistan and Iraq* (Baltimore: The Johns Hopkins University Press, 2006), 107–124 at 109, claims that at Bonn, "the international community . . . believed that the main and essential measure needed to establish legitimacy was the holding of national elections." This is a serious oversimplification of what was a much more nuanced approach. See William Maley, *Rescuing Afghanistan* (London: Hurst and Company, 2006), 33.

19. See T. H. Rigby, "Introduction: Political Legitimacy, Weber, and Communist Mono-Organisational Systems," in T. H. Rigby and Ferenc Fehér, eds., *Political Legitimation in Communist States* (London: Macmillan, 1982), 1–26.

20. Niccolò Machiavelli, *The Prince* (Harmondsworth: Penguin, 1978).

21. See Sebastian von Einsiedel, "Policy Responses to State Failure," in Simon Chesterman, Michael Ignatieff, and Ramesh Thakur, eds., *Making States Work: State Failure and the Crisis of Governance* (Tokyo: United Nations University Press, 2005), 13–35 at 30.

22. This point has been elaborated by Barnett R. Rubin, *The Fragmentation of Afghanistan: State Formation and Collapse in the International System* (New Haven: Yale University Press, 2002), 12–15.

23. See Linda B. Miller, *World Order and Local Disorder: The United Nations and Internal Conflicts* (Princeton: Princeton University Press, 1967); Lawrence T. Farley, *Plebiscites and Sovereignty: The Crisis of Political Illegitimacy* (Boulder: Westview Press, 1986); Simon Chesterman, *You, The People: The United Nations, Transitional*

Administration, and State-Building (Oxford: Oxford University Press, 2004); Richard Caplan, *International Governance of War-Torn Territories: Rule and Reconstruction* (Oxford: Oxford University Press, 2005).

24. For perspectives on this exercise, see Michael W. Doyle, *UN Peacekeeping in Cambodia: UNTAC's Civilian Mandate* (Boulder: Lynne Rienner, 1995); Trevor Findlay, *Cambodia: The Legacy and Lessons of UNTAC* (Oxford: Oxford University Press, 1995); Sorpong Peou, *Conflict Neutralization in the Cambodia War: From Battlefield to Ballot-Box* (Kuala Lumpur: Oxford University Press, 1997); MacAlister Brown and Joseph J. Zasloff, *Cambodia Confounds the Peacemakers 1979–1998* (Ithaca: Cornell University Press, 1998).

25. See John M. Sanderson and Michael Maley, "Elections and Liberal Democracy in Cambodia," *Australian Journal of International Affairs,* vol. 52, no. 3 (November 1998): 241–253.

26. See Jarat Chopra, "The UN's Kingdom of East Timor," *Survival,* vol. 42, no. 3 (Autumn 2000): 27–39; Ian Martin, *Self-Determination in East Timor: The United Nations, the Ballot, and International Intervention* (Boulder: Lynne Rienner, 2001); Astri Suhrke, "Peacekeepers as Nation-Builders: UN Dilemmas in East Timor," *International Peacekeeping,* vol. 9, no. 4 (Winter 2001): 1–20; Michael G. Smith with Moreen Dee, *Peacekeeping in East Timor: The Path to Independence* (Boulder: Lynne Rienner, 2003).

27. Emphases added.

28. Norah Niland, "Justice Postponed: The Marginalization of Human Rights in Afghanistan," in Antonio Donini, Norah Niland, and Karin Wermester, eds., *Nation-Building Unraveled? Aid, Peace and Justice in Afghanistan* (Bloomfield: Kumarian Press, 2004), 61–82.

29. See *Report of the Panel on United Nations Peace Operations* (New York: United Nations, A/55/305–S/2000/809, 21 August 2000).

30. See Francis Fukuyama, *State-Building: Governance and World Order in the 21st Century* (Ithaca: Cornell University Press, 2004), 6–14.

31. James C. Scott, *Seeing Like a State: How Certain Schemes to Improve the Human Condition Have Failed* (New Haven: Yale University Press, 1998), 256.

32. *Afghanistan—State Building, Sustaining Growth, and Reducing Poverty* (Washington, DC: The World Bank, 2005), 47. See also Astri Suhrke, *When More is Less: Aiding Statebuilding in Afghanistan* (Madrid: Working Paper no. 26, Fundación para las Relaciones Internacionales y el Diálogo Exterior, 2006).

33. On implications for legitimacy, see Ashraf Ghani, Clare Lockhart, and Michael Carnahan, *Closing the Sovereignty Gap: An Approach to State-Building* (London: Working Paper no. 253, Overseas Development Institute, September 2005), 11. On transparency, see Ashraf Ghani, Clare Lockhart, and Michael Carnahan, "An Agenda for State-Building in the Twenty-First Century," *The Fletcher Forum of World Affairs,* vol. 30, no. 1 (Winter 2006): 101–123 at 120.

34. See F. A. Hayek, *The Constitution of Liberty* (London: Routledge and Kegan Paul, 1960), 184–185. It is, of course, necessary to guard against fragmentation to a dysfunctional degree. See Andrew Macintyre, *The Power of Institutions: Political Architecture and Governance* (Ithaca: Cornell University Press, 2003), 23–26. On the idea of separation of powers more generally, see M. J. C. Vile, *Constitutionalism and the Separation of Powers* (London: Oxford University Press, 1967); Geoffrey Brennan and Alan Hamlin, *Democratic Devices and Desires* (Cambridge: Cambridge University Press, 2000), 211–254.

35. Baron de Montesquieu, *The Spirit of the Laws* (New York: Hafner Press, 1949), 152.

36. Barnett R. Rubin, "Crafting a Constitution for Afghanistan," *Journal of Democracy,* vol. 15, no. 3 (July 2004): 5–19 at 15. For more detailed discussion of this provision,

see Mohammad Hashim Kamali, "Islam and its Shari'a in the Afghan Constitution 2004 with Special Reference to Personal Law," in Nadjma Yassari, ed., *The Shari'a in the Constitutions of Afghanistan, Iran and Egypt—Implications for Private Law* (Tübingen: Mohr Siebeck, 2005), 23–43 at 36–38.

37. Robert I. Rotberg, "Renewing the Afghan State," in Robert I. Rotberg, ed., *Building a New Afghanistan* (Washington, DC: Brookings Institution Press, 2007), 1–21 at 5–6.

38. See William Maley, "International Force and Political Reconstruction: Cambodia, East Timor and Afghanistan," in Albrecht Schnabel and Hans-Georg Ehrhart, eds., *Security Sector Reform and Post-Conflict Peacebuilding* (Tokyo: United Nations University Press, 2005), 297–312.

39. See Dylan Hendrickson, "Cambodia's Security-Sector Reforms: Limits of a Downsizing Strategy," *Conflict, Security and Development,* vol. 1, no. 1 (2001): 67–82.

40. *Report of the Secretary-General on the United Nations Mission of Support in East Timor* (New York: United Nations, S/2004/333, 19 April 2004), paragraph 7.

41. On the importance of security generally, see Kimberly Zisk Marten, *Enforcing the Peace: Learning from the Imperial Past* (New York: Columbia University Press, 2004), 158–165.

42. See Amnesty International, *Afghanistan: Police Reconstruction Essential for the Protection of Human Rights* (London: Amnesty International, ASA 11/003/2003, March 2003); Michael Bhatia, Kevin Lanigan, and Philip Wilkinson, "Minimal Investments, Minimal Results: The Failure of Security Policy in Afghanistan" (Afghanistan Research and Evaluation Unit, Briefing Paper, June 2004); International Crisis Group, *Afghanistan: Getting Disarmament Back on Track* (Kabul and Brussels: ICG Asia Briefing no. 35, 23 February 2005); *Afghanistan Security: Efforts to Establish Army and Police Have Made Progress, but Future Plans Need to Be Better Defined* (Washington DC: Report to the Committee on International Relations, House of Representatives, GAO-05-575, United States Government Accountability Office, June 2005); Mark Sedra, "Security Sector Reform in Afghanistan: The Slide Towards Expediency," *International Peacekeeping,* vol. 13, no. 1 (March 2006): 94–110; Tonita Murray, "Police-Building in Afghanistan: A Case Study of Civil Security Reform," *International Peacekeeping,* vol. 14, no. 1 (January 2007): 108–126.

43. For a more detailed discussion, see William Maley, "Democratic Governance and Post-Conflict Transitions," *Chicago Journal of International Law,* vol. 6, no. 2 (Winter 2006): 683–701.

44. Charles King, *Ending Civil Wars* (Oxford: Oxford University Press, for the International Institute for Strategic Studies, Adelphi Paper no. 308, 1997), 77 and 78. See also Barbara F. Walter, *Committing to Peace: The Successful Settlement of Civil Wars* (Princeton: Princeton University Press, 2002); William Maley, "Institutional Design and the Rebuilding of Trust," in William Maley, Charles Sampford, and Ramesh Thakur, eds., *From Civil Strife to Civil Society: Civil and Military Responsibilities in Disrupted States* (New York and Tokyo: United Nations University Press, 2003), 163–179.

45. See Michael Barnett, *Eyewitness to a Genocide: The United Nations and Rwanda* (Ithaca: Cornell University Press, 2002); Roméo Dallaire, *Shake Hands with the Devil: The Failure of Humanity in Rwanda* (Toronto: Random House, 2003).

46. See William Maley, "The UN and East Timor," *Pacifica Review,* vol. 12, no. 1 (February 2000): 63–76; James Cotton, *East Timor, Australia and Regional Order: Intervention and Its Aftermath in Southeast Asia* (London: Routledge Curzon, 2004).

47. See Alan Sipress, "Peacekeepers Won't Go Beyond Kabul, Cheney Says," *Washington Post,* 20 March 2002.

48. *See Financial Action Task Force on Money Laundering: Annual Report 2001–2002* (Paris: Organization for Economic Co-Operation and Development, 2002).

49. *See Securing Afghanistan's Future: Accomplishments and the Strategic Path Forward* (Kabul: Government of Afghanistan, Asian Development Bank, United Nations Assistance Mission to Afghanistan, United Nations Development Program, and The World Bank Group, 17 March 2004), 11.

50. *Afghanistan National Development Strategy: An Interim Strategy for Security, Governance, Economic Growth and Poverty Reduction* (Kabul: Islamic Republic of Afghanistan, 2006), 61.

51. Beth Gardiner, "World Pledges $10.5B for Afghanistan Aid," *Washington Post,* 1 February 2006.

52. See Stephen John Stedman, "Spoiler Problems in Peace Processes," *International Security,* vol. 22, no. 2 (Fall 1997): 5–53.

53. See William Maley, *The Afghanistan Wars* (London: Palgrave Macmillan, 2002), 194–217.

54. *The 9/11 Commission Report: Final Report of the National Commission on Terrorist Attacks Upon the United States* (Washington, DC: National Commission on Terrorist Attacks Upon the United States, 2004), 123.

55. On Pakistan's ongoing connections with the Taliban, see Laura King, "Pakistani City Serves as Refuge for the Taliban," *Los Angeles Times,* 21 December 2006; Paul Watson, "On the Trail of the Taliban's Support," *Los Angeles Times,* 24 December 2006; Carlotta Gall, "At Border, Signs of Pakistani Role in Taliban Surge," *New York Times,* 21 January 2007; Seth G. Jones, "Averting Failure in Afghanistan," *Survival,* vol. 48, no. 1 (Spring 2006): 111–128; Amin Saikal, "Securing Afghanistan's Border," *Survival,* vol. 48, no. 1 (Spring 2006): 129–142; Barnett R. Rubin, "Saving Afghanistan," *Foreign Affairs,* vol. 86, no. 1 (January-February 2007): 57–78; and William Maley and Daoud Yaqub, *A Long Hot Summer: Crisis and Opportunity in Afghanistan* (Sydney: Lowy Institute for International Policy, Policy Brief, March 2007). On Pakistan's longer-term entanglements in Afghanistan, see Mariam Abou Zahab and Olivier Roy, *Islamist Networks: The Afghan-Pakistan Connection* (London: Hurst and Company, 2004); Rizwan Hussain, *Pakistan and the Emergence of Islamic Militancy in Afghanistan* (Aldershot: Ashgate, 2005); Daniel Byman, *Deadly Connections: States that Sponsor Terrorism* (Cambridge: Cambridge University Press, 2005), 187–218.

56. Telford Taylor, *Munich: The Price of Peace* (New York: Doubleday, 1979), 1004.

57. See Seymour Hersh, "The Other War," *New Yorker,* 12 April 2004; Richard A. Clarke, *Against All Enemies: Inside America's War on Terror* (New York: Free Press, 2004), 263–279.

58. See Anthony Cordesman, *Iraq: What Is to Be Done* (Washington, DC: Center for Strategic and International Studies, 2004); *Iraq's Transition: On a Knife Edge* (Baghdad and Brussels: ICG Middle East Report No. 27, International Crisis Group, 2004); Toby Dodge, *Iraq's Future: The Aftermath of Regime Change* (New York: Routledge, 2005); David L. Phillips, *Losing Iraq: Inside the Postwar Reconstruction Fiasco* (Boulder: Westview Press, 2005); William R. Polk, *Understanding Iraq* (New York: HarperCollins, 2005); George Packer, *The Assassins' Gate: America in Iraq* (New York: Farrar, Straus and Giroux, 2005); and Ahmed S. Hashim, *Insurgency and Counter-Insurgency in Iraq* (Ithaca: Cornell University Press, 2006).

59. For an excellent overview, see *Afghanistan Reconstruction: Deteriorating Security and Limited Resources Have Impeded Progress; Improvements in U.S. Strategy Needed* (Washington, DC: United States General Accountability Office, 2004).

60. *Democracy in Afghanistan 2004: A Survey of the Afghanistan Electorate* (Kabul: The Asia Foundation, 2004), 21.

61. *Afghanistan in 2006: A Survey of the Afghan People* (Kabul: The Asia Foundation, 2006), 9.

62. See Gilles Dorronsoro, *Revolution Unending: Afghanistan, 1979 to the Present* (New York: Columbia University Press, 2005), 354.

2

Security in Afghanistan: A Historical Perspective

Marvin G. Weinbaum

DEEP DEFICITS IN SECURITY ARE familiarly associated with developing societies and weak states. For Afghanistan, the added handicap of almost a quarter century of civil war and nearly a decade of foreign occupation left the country without the defenses offered by legitimate authority, a functioning economy or a coherent society. In the post-Taliban era, domestic security remains a paramount concern for the Afghan people. Together with the country's reconstruction, with which it is intimately tied, domestic security is the measure by which most Afghans judge their government and its international benefactors. An understanding of popular expectations and demands about security require that they be viewed in reference to experience with custom and history. Without context, security goals for the Afghan state and society could be unrealistic and important lessons ignored.

Traditionally, security in Afghanistan has been elusive and tenuous. Institutions of the state have afforded few identifiable, dependable protections for the individual. To the extent that protections against threats of lawlessness, injustice and economic deprivation were realized, solidarity groups (*qawms*) to which individuals belonged provided what little recourse was available. Family, clan, tribe or ethnic groupings were themselves mostly limited to their own resources for protection. The wellbeing of such communities often depended on keeping their distance from a state viewed as predatory and oppressive. The state and its institutions have also been continuously vulnerable. Tribal and religious forces brought down a reformer king in 1929. A successor monarchy that yielded more than four decades later to a republican government was a victim of ideological forces spawned from external influences. Over the 1980s, a foreign-assisted Islamic resistance wore down communist Afghan regimes and their foreign protector, the Soviet Union. Inheriting power in 1992, contesting political factions surrendered the capital of a withered state in 1996 to a more cohesive Islamic force, the Taliban, which in turn, succumbed to an American-led military intervention in 2001.

This chapter looks at the quest over time among individuals, groups and the Afghan state for security, and the means they have used to advance it. The discussions take note of the striving by individuals for basic justice and economic survival, the efforts of solidarity groups and communities to guard their interests and integrity, and the state's struggle for ascendancy over its domestic and foreign adversaries. The chapter takes particular note of the regional nature of threats to Afghanistan's political stability and economic welfare. But it also considers how the country can contribute to prosperity and peace in a difficult, if not dangerous neighborhood. A concluding section draws from Afghanistan's past some guides for addressing contemporary challenges and for managing its security future.

Individual and Communal Security

As in virtually any traditional society, personal security, justice and economic protections for the individual in Afghanistan were likely to be sought in solidarity groups and patron-client relations rather than through government institutions, national or local. An individual's membership in a clan, tribe, religious, ethnic or occupational group (usually more than one) was indispensable to survival. Any sense of investment or attachment to institutions of the state was consequently minimal. More often than not, government actions affecting individuals were seen as arbitrary, even tyrannical. Most people resisted the state bureaucracy when possible, usually by evading its authority. In general, security was found in not calling attention to one's self or community.

Still, few Afghans could get the state entirely out of their lives. When forced to come to terms with its presence, they devised ways to deal with its agents. For the individual, this was usually impossible without the assistance of khans and other local influentials acting as intermediaries with the government's sanctioned village chief (*malik*) or higher authority. They could perform such services as helping individuals avoid military service or gaining for them a hearing for their grievances and claims.

Unlike a feudal society where protection is obligated through deferential status and behavior, Afghan society is more egalitarian and less stable. Power that accrues to a local leader has traditionally been the result of a consensus within the community and is ultimately based on the individual's ability to show that he is worthy of respect. The khan often demonstrates this by his hospitality, his ability to arbitrate individual disputes, as well as his defense of the qawm when it comes into conflict with agents of the state.[1]

The Afghan individual has been at the same time separated from the state in the usually secure space provided by the *ulema* (Islamic scholars) and *qazis* (religious judges). Aided by the presence of the local *mullah* (cleric) and *pir* (spiritual leader), certain sectors of life have traditionally been kept insulated from the intrusion of the state. While Islam was largely symbolic in Afghanistan's constitutions, at the community level it provided an alternate, at times countervailing set of rules. Tribal codes (*pashtunwali*) among rural Pashtuns also provided a means by which most local disputes and interpersonal issues were kept out of the government's purview.

For most Afghans, the basic security of sufficient food, adequate shelter, and freedom from disease occupies the highest priority.[2] The protections afforded by public laws or constitutional guarantees are abstractions next to the realities of achieving physical and economic wellbeing. Issues that are the concern of urban elites and foreign groups, including women's and human rights issues, are not only poorly understood but are frequently viewed as unwelcome intrusions into private affairs or religious beliefs. Those who in the past have tried incautiously to free individuals from ties and obligations that effectively imprisoned them socially and economically not only failed but also provoked a fierce conservative reaction.

Respect for individual rights and the legitimate representation in courts enforcing secular law emerged only with the constitutional period beginning in 1964. Until then there was no private bar to represent individual defendants and even with this development, the function of private attorneys was poorly understood both within the legal community and the wider public. Nor could the individual feel comfortable with the country's jurists and judicial system. The judge, despite his higher social status, was poorly paid and, seeking personal gain, was widely viewed in the community with suspicion and even contempt as a result of incidences of arbitrariness, incompetence and personal corruption. Justice from the courts also suffered where the jurists placed ethnic, tribal and family loyalties ahead of professionalism.[3]

Historically, the central government has had to coexist in ruling at the local level with village and tribal structures. When the state dealt with the village it usually acted in an aggregate fashion. Thus taxes were levied collectively, and those fines imposed for rebellions and crimes were applied against the community as a whole.[4] Rather than the state offering physical and social security and defense of communal rights, Afghan leaders were more likely to use communities as an instrument of state control over the people. By employing divide-and-rule tactics with the country's ethnic groups, the state weakened the ability of these groups to stand up to central authority. As such, governments aggravated the structural problems in Afghan society and diminished the ability of these groups to defend their interests.

Only occasionally did the normally passive resistance of provincial and local groups to the central government become broadly confrontational with a resort to violence. Locally originating armed insurrections were narrowly based and not sustained. This of course most dramatically changed with the Islamic resistance to the 1978 communist coup. A countrywide opposition mobilized, by most accounts, in reaction to specific socio-economic policies fostered by the Kabul government. Another view finds the resistance a direct challenge to the authority of the communist state. While Olivier Roy concedes that the two explanations are interlinked, he describes the recent history of Afghanistan to be one of "revolts against central power, and of resistance to the penetration of the countryside by state bureaucracy."[5]

In general, groups usually found ways to work outside the government channels, defending their own interests, free of central government administration. It was traditionally the inability of the central government to provide security that induced tribes to look after themselves, forming in effect their own tribal militias. Most solidarity groups such as clans were not linked to the government through institutional arrangements so much as through personal relationships. But a psychological gap was often observed between government officials and people of the village, as the former were far more oriented to urban areas and had difficulty adjusting to their rural constituencies.[6]

Even if they shared the same ethnic and tribal membership, local officials exhibited different lifestyles and usually failed to gain respect. As Thomas Barfield has written, an official was usually more interested in maintaining his communication with Kabul than in developing good relations with local groups and individuals.[7] Consequently, ordinary people were often disappointed in using these lower officials as intermediaries with higher authorities. The larger ethnic communities—Pashtuns in the south and east, Uzbeks in the north central areas, Tajiks in the northeast and far west, and the Hazaras in the central highlands—were able to establish access to regional power centers for petitioning on behalf of their interests.

The relationship of solidarity groups with government authority has nevertheless been ambiguous. As Nazif Shahrani has written, despite a latent hostility among the ethnic minorities, there is neither active support nor active hostility toward government. Ethnic minorities in the north, he observes, are more accustomed to a strong government presence than Pashtun southerners.[8] Still, traditionally, it was the Pashtuns who prospered most by the relationship with the state, the Hazaras least. Certain elements of the Pashtun community and urban Tajiks were favored in economic opportunities.

The more powerful the groups, the greater their access to state resources for themselves and the better their ability to succeed against their adversaries in a competition mostly over land and water. Meanwhile, the interests of an expanding urban middle class increasingly diverged from the rest of urban dwellers as well as from the rural masses. That which bureaucrats, merchants, students and military officers sought as necessary for their protection was far different than from the rest of Afghan society. By and large, these urban groups had a greater dependence on the institutions of the state for their security and prosperity.

While security for the state and the society are distinct, they are also often interdependent. If security in one seriously deteriorates, the other cannot escape its effects. Most civil and social bodies face greater difficulties in guarding their interests without a state capable of mediation and enforcement. At the same time, where the society undergoes a breakdown with the failure of constituent groups to exercise mutual toleration and a reasonable level of cooperative behavior, state instruments are likely to become valued prizes in destructive competition.

The Insecure State

Poor performance and failure to gain legitimacy have regularly plagued instrumentalities of the Afghan state. Usually lacking in resources and beset with corruption and nepotism, the country's institutions have seldom delivered services demanded of a modern state. They have all too frequently alienated those who came in contact with them, and, as already mentioned, have paled in the competition for allegiance with primordial solidarity groups. Only in Kabul was there a reasonably high degree of identity with state institutions. For much of the country's rural population, which until recent years meant most of Afghanistan, the state could at best hope to reach some minimal accommodation with the society.

Aside from the Soviet invasion in 1979, the security of the modern Afghan state has, then, been threatened from within, not without. At the critical moment in 1929 when King Amanullah tried to defend Kabul against conservative religious leaders and rural khans, the army refused to fight. After his abdication, the national army dissolved, leaving a reactionary Tajik bandit to try to consolidate power. When several months later a military campaign by an exiled critic of Amanullah, Nadir Khan, restored the monarchy, he owed his crown to British-sponsored Pashtun tribesmen. Although the cooptation of traditional leadership became a goal for the new regime, it was also determined to build a reliable army that could counter tribal power.

The royal court understood the importance of a professional army, one with modern training organization and equipment.[9] A centrally controlled system of military conscription was intended to assure the national government's ascendance over the tribes that continued to be viewed as the major threat to Kabul's rule, though security against a foreign enemy was used to justify maintaining a large force. By the 1960s, the army was in many respects the country's most modern institution. But financing the army took a large portion of the budget and placed the government in a position of considerable reliance on the Soviet Union, to which Afghanistan was in debt for equipment, spare parts and training. From 1955–1978, the Soviet Union provided $1.2 billion in military aid. It helped to recruit and equip in this period an army, officially 100,000 strong.[10]

Members of the Musahiban royal family also sustained their rule by adopting the divide-and-rule policies, mostly by pitting Pashtuns against non-Pashtuns. In general, they chose secular nationalism over trying to legitimize their rule through an Islamic idiom. In this as well as the monarchy's essentially urban character, there was a disconnection with most of the society. Much of the time the king—Zahir Shah succeeded his assassinated father in 1933—and his governments seemed out of touch with the countryside, unable to cope with the growing Islamic political consciousness and the ideological polarization among the educated classes. Organized Muslim youth, whom authorities had repressed in the years before Afghanistan adopted its democratic constitution of 1964, grew bolder and more disruptive. Dedicated communists, even better organized, challenged the regime from the ranks of students and the military.

The loyalty of the officer corps to the national government was critical to the survival of the monarchy. This was to prove ultimately its undoing. Supposedly, the army and air force were insulated from politics. But in fact the military's higher ranks were being ideologically radicalized largely as a consequence of their intimate relationship to the Soviets. By the 1970s the military had, in effect, become largely autonomous of government authority, as it demonstrated with the coup of July 1973.

A strongly pro-Moscow faction of the Afghan communist party, in collaboration with the army and in partnership with former Prime Minister Sardar Mohammad Daoud, overthrew the monarchy. Daoud, a cousin of the king, assumed the presidency of the new republic. Subsequently he distanced himself from communist influences and sought to balance Afghanistan's dependence on the Soviet Union with financial assistance from wealthy Muslim states. Like the monarchy, the more authoritarian Daoud government worried more about possible threats from domestic Islamists than from local communists. Daoud was brought down by another faction of the communist party in a 1978 coup organized by mid-level military officers.

On coming to power the communist leadership moved, often ruthlessly, to introduce far-reaching social and economic reforms. Their policies and the ideological arguments to justify them were intensely alien to most Afghans and drew the angry opposition of tribal and religious figures. By the summer of 1978, Islamic militants had mounted a rural resistance to Kabul. The communist government called on the regular army and police, backed by a brutal intelligence organization, to put down the rebellion. But there followed the near total breakdown of the national army through desertions, leaving much of the countryside to the mujahideen. A purge of the officer corps following the coup that removed Daoud helps to explain the virtual collapse of the Afghan army.[11]

The main goal of the Soviet invasion in December 1979 was to bolster the Afghan army with new communist leadership that could carry the fight against the insurgency once the Red Army withdrew. But the ability of communist governments in the 1980s to stand on their own against internal enemies was, as earlier, compromised by continuing factional and ethnic conflict in the army's officer corps. Resistance to conscription, leading to evasion and desertions, also adversely affected the army's operational capacity. To try to compensate for the military's shortcomings in securing the regimes of Babrak Kamal and Mohammad Najib, the intelligence organization, known by its acronym KhAD, was greatly enlarged to possibly as many as 30,000 members, and an estimated 100,000 informers.[12] The introduction of Revolutionary Courts enhanced the repressive powers of the intelligence service.

A concerted effort was also undertaken to strengthen state institutions. But the best the communist regimes could do was to overwhelm, never absorb, those social structures that challenged the state. Differences within the Afghan communist party also weakened its ability to bridge societal differences. Under Soviet occupation, there was never much effort to try to transform the rural society; it sufficed merely to control it. Although repression always played the dominant role, more subtle strategies were also employed, such as playing social elements against one another by exploiting group differences. To defend itself, the communist regime sought to protect the state by wresting control away from traditional power sectors. Only in the late 1980s, before the departure of Soviet troops in early 1989 and the ousting of the Najib regime in 1992, did thc Kabul government opt for a strategy that attempted to co-opt local power figures and networks, and promised representation to other ideological persuasions.

The 1990s saw a decade of civil war, first among the victorious mujahideen parties, and then between the Taliban and its northern adversaries. Mujahideen ascendance introduced turf wars among the warlords' private militias driven by personal ambitions and reinforced by long-simmering struggles for ethnic ascendancy. The years between 1992 and 1996 mark the nadir in modern Afghan history for both state and society. With much of the country in virtual anarchy, its discredited rulers became easy prey to a force of Afghan student activists emerging from the leading religious seminaries in Pakistan. Aided by Pakistani military handlers and Arab financial supporters, these mostly young, pious Afghans easily prevailed over their widely hated adversaries.

In power, the Taliban showed little talent for and less interest in governing. Occupied with fighting and praying, the movement and its leaders almost entirely ignored the country's recovery and relied in the main on nongovernment organizations and international relief agencies for meeting people's basic needs. Under Taliban rule, a war-weary population became increasingly desperate to see the country's physical rehabilitation and economic improvement, even while it continued to welcome the movement's ability to maintain public order.

The Taliban era would also seem to suggest that the leadership was tapping into a deep vein of Afghan society. Mostly ethnic Pashtuns, the Taliban professed highly doctrinaire interpretations of Islamic law. Ordinarily, the Afghans, including those in the conservative Pashtun tribal belt, are not readily drawn toward radical political Islam.[13] To the extent that ideological extremism motivated conflict during the Taliban years, it was imported by Afghans as refugees in Pakistan, brought up and schooled under the influence of militant Diobandi Islamic orthodoxy. Most Afghans, though personally consumed by their religion, do not conceive of their religious obligations in political terms. The non-ideological character of these Afghans helps to explain why they can so easily break alliances, changing loyalties when circumstances dictate. Afghans at first largely welcomed the mujahideen after many had adjusted to communist rule, and were then able to cooperate with the Taliban before later embracing the presidency of Hamid Karzai.

Security and the Region

State security in Afghanistan is bound up with the country's relations within the region and especially with its immediate neighbors. The solutions to many of Afghanistan's problems are plainly regional in character and scope.[14] At stake along with territorial and regime integrity is Afghanistan's economic viability as a landlocked state. Cultural penetration, including religious fanaticism, represents to some another form of invasion. Without the cooperation and assistance of regional powers, history has shown that Afghanistan's prospects for domestic stability and a measure of prosperity are sharply diminished. Economically, Afghanistan is entirely dependent on its neighbors for access to imports and its ability to export to near and distant commercial markets. Another kind of cooperation across borders in recent years impinging directly on Afghanistan's stability and economic security is the interdiction of anti-regime militants and the need for regional assistance in curtailing poppy production and drug trafficking.

Afghanistan's national interests have been most at risk when regional states compete for influence and try to carve out spheres of influence. Because of Afghanistan's multiethnic character and existence as a crossroads of West, Central and South Asia, the country is liable to become a pawn in the struggles among stronger powers. The classic example is the long period when Afghanistan was treated as a buffer state in the colonial Great Game between Czarist Russia and Britain, each seeking its proxies within the country. The Cold War brought another form of competition that sought to keep the country out of either the Soviet or western orbit. But as both these competitions demonstrated, external powers may be willing to show forbearance so long as none seem intent or capable of assuming a position of dominance in Afghanistan. For insurance, however, neighboring countries have regularly been patrons to subnational leaders and particularly championed ethnic and regional populations. All of Afghanistan's ethnic groups have cross-border cousins with whom they have some degree of cultural and economic affinity and with whom they have created economic interdependencies and strengthened cultural ties. Yet despite this, as is frequently pointed out, none have acquired separatist tendencies, and Afghanistan has no history of separatist movements.

Afghan leaders have demonstrated how carefully crafted foreign policies are able to capitalize on the country's strategic position to enhance the country's ability to survive and prosper. Notably during the Cold War years between 1955 and 1978, Afghanistan was able to gain immunities and attract badly needed development assistance when courted by outside powers. In what is referred to as bitarafi, it cleverly played the two sides, the United States and Soviet Union, against one another. President Sardar Mohammad Daoud's (1973–1978) efforts at a different diplomatic strategy were aborted, however, when he sought financial aid from Iran and the Arab countries to balance Moscow's influence on Afghanistan.

Politically, relations with Pakistan have been problematic from the time of Pakistan's founding in 1947, mostly because of the colonial division of a shared Pashtun ethnic population, and Islamabad's serious designs on Afghanistan for strategic planning against India. Over the 15 years following the Soviet Union's 1979 intervention on behalf of its communist clients in Afghanistan, Pakistan became a poorly disguised, indispensable participant in a jihad against the Soviets and their Afghan communist junior partners. With the financial backing of the United States and Saudi Arabia, Pakistan served as the principal patron to the mujahideen parties based within its territory.

The active promotion by Afghan governments beginning in the mid-1960s of an independent Pashtun ethnic state to be carved from northwest Pakistan brought retaliation in the form of periodic border closings that denied access to Afghanistan from Karachi, the major port of entry for imports. Possible confrontation between the countries over Kabul's alleged backing of an insurgency in Pakistan's Baluchistan in 1975 was averted only though regional good offices and despite Soviet instigation. A year earlier the government of Prime Minister Z. A. Bhutto had supported a brief, failed Islamic insurgency against the Daoud government and had given sanctuary to its fleeing leaders.

Between 1994 and 2001, Pakistan was no less instrumental in assisting the Taliban in a civil war that pitted the Islamic movement against the Kabul government of Burhanuddin Rabbani, and then against its remnants fighting under Ahmed Shah Masood constituted as the Northern Alliance. Although there is no evidence that regular Pakistani forces ever fought alongside the Taliban, it is indisputably true that Pakistan loaned individual military personnel to assist in the planning and logistics that made Taliban victories possible. It also facilitated the movement of arms to Kabul financed mainly by private sources in the Gulf.

Iran's involvement in Afghanistan over time has also had a threat dimension. A dispute over a further diversion of the waters of the Helmand River in Afghanistan's southwest brought tensions in the 1960s but never progressed to where armed confrontation seemed likely. An agreement between the countries, criticized by Afghan nationalists and Marxists alike, was reached before the fall of the Afghan monarchy in 1973. Even while Iran admitted more than two million refugees from Afghanistan during the 1980s and 1990s, unlike Islamabad, Tehran never hosted jihadi groups fighting the Soviets. The capture by the Taliban of Herat and western Afghanistan in 1995 unnerved the Iranians. They chose to believe that this unforeseen force was a Sunni plot involving Saudi Arabia and Pakistan, along with the United States, designed to cause problems for Iran. When the Taliban captured the northern city of Mazar-i Sharif in 1996 and a number of Iranians with diplomatic status were massacred in the attack, Tehran threatened military retaliation against the Taliban. Iranian forces were mobilized for an offensive intended to occupy the western part of Afghanistan. But after considerable debate in Tehran, the politically isolated and economically hurting Iranian revolutionary government decided against an attack that could have brought international condemnation and a possible armed confrontation with Pakistan. Although Iran provided exile to key mujahideen leaders ousted by the Taliban and became the main supplier to anti-Taliban forces of the Northern Alliance, its territory never served as a staging ground for attacks on the Taliban.

Later in the decade Iran joined Afghanistan's other neighbors, the Russians and the Americans in the formation of a Six Plus Two grouping that sought through economic sanctions to weaken the Taliban and induce its leaders to sever ties with Osama Bin Laden and his Al Qaeda organization. The Tehran government stood by in October and November 2001 as the American military, now backed by all Afghanistan's neighbors including Pakistan, launched air attacks against a Taliban government in control of almost all of the country's territory. Post-Taliban, Iran cooperated with the international community in establishing a government framework and timetable at Bonn, Germany, in December 2001 and subsequently refrained from taking a spoiler role in the writing of a constitution and the holding of presidential and parliamentary elections. Just the same, Iran's leadership remains anxious about American military forces operating in western Afghanistan and the possibilities of permanent basing in a strategic partnership between Kabul and Washington. But for the time being, Iran has sought to assert its interests economically through a flourishing export trade and infrastructural development assistance, and exports its culture, especially to western Afghanistan. Iran also contributes directly to Afghan security by imposing its often out-gunned security forces against drug traders en route for Iran's domestic market or Persian Gulf transit points.

Among those noncontiguous regional states, India and Saudi Arabia have participated most in post-communist developments in Afghanistan, mostly with strategic objectives in mind. Saudi Arabia was an equal partner with the United States in financing the anti-Soviet jihad of the 1980s. It remains committed to propagating its own brand of Islamic belief, both as part of its self-appointed missionary zeal and to counter Iranian influence in the country. As such, the Saudi government maintains close ties with elements in Afghan civil society and several of its aspiring leaders. Saudi Arabia, which plays a minor role in the post-Taliban recovery, could assume a critical position should the West lose interest in Afghanistan.

India has traditionally held a large presence in Afghanistan. Before the communist regimes it had been a significant trading partner, and many in the governing elite had strong personal ties with Indian institutions. New Delhi's refusal to condemn the Soviet occupation drew strong criticism among the mujahideen leaders in exile in Pakistan, but relations warmed once many of these same figures replaced the communists in 1992. India played a secondary but not insignificant role in the anti-Taliban coalition that emerged late in the 1990s and, following the fall of the Taliban, has moved decisively to assert its influence with the Karzai government. Much to the displeasure of Islamabad, the Indians have established consulates in Afghanistan's major cities and allocated support to several high profile development projects. Many interpret Indian assistance as linked to its ambitions to assume the responsibilities of the region's preeminent power. Others credit New Delhi's broadening involvement in Afghanistan as a renewed effort to assure that the country does not offer Pakistan its once sought strategic depth against India. For Kabul, the availability of India as a counterbalance to Pakistan has historically given Afghan regimes important leverage against a Pakistan often viewed as overbearing and exploitative.

Afghanistan can also be jeopardized by political developments internal to countries in the region. The insurgent movements in neighboring states and the radicalization of their politics have had strong spillover effects on Afghanistan. Anti-regime militants in Tajikistan, Uzbekistan and China took refuge in Afghanistan during the 1990s and became participants in its civil conflicts. Concern about the resurgence of domestic insurgencies continues to define the policies of these countries toward Afghanistan. Increasing political repression in Uzbekistan and its estrangement from the United States along with a still enigmatic Turkmenistan could have implications for projected extensions to Afghanistan of an electric power grid and gas pipeline. Loss of the American air base in Uzbekistan has complicated logistic support for military operations on behalf of the Karzai regime. The indulgence of jihadi groups and their institutions in Pakistan by the Islamabad government that sustains the Kashmiri separatist cause gave birth to the Taliban and fuels the neo-Taliban insurgency against the current government in Kabul. In Iran, the doctrinaire Islamic government may pursue a less nuanced foreign policy and conceivably more assertive policies in Afghanistan, especially should Kabul's strategic partnership with Washington be seen in Tehran as posing a military threat from Afghanistan. Additionally, American-promoted sanctions on Tehran over its nuclear policies could lead Iran to forego its support for the Karzai government in favor of instigating client leaders in the western provinces to seek greater autonomy from Kabul. The temptation to provide material assistance to various insurgent groups fighting the US and its allies may also be difficult to resist.

Chances for peace and prosperity are thus interrelated and interdependent. Many of the current suspicions and disagreements regionally have clear historical antecedents. Prospects for overcoming these differences and achieving long-term stability seem dim across the region without cooperation among states that is focused on open markets and free trade. It may require that Afghanistan's neighbors appreciate fully how pivotal a stable and more developed Afghanistan can be in furthering regional trade. Economic progress along with greater respect for people's rights and wellbeing is often believed to offer the best opportunity to suppress tendencies toward extremism.

The Security Legacy and Challenges

Years marked by civil war, occupation, displacement and ideological penetration have left imprints on individuals, their communities and the Afghan state.

Over and above the more traditional insecurities, new ones have appeared, as have ways to cope with them. People have come into contact with state institutions in ways far different than previously, and their expectations of those in authority have in many respects changed. The Kabul government has also had to redefine its relationship with regional and local authorities, searching for sources of legitimacy and finding better ways to manage long-standing tensions between the country's center and the periphery. Additionally, in defining its security responsibilities, the Afghan state has had to make adjustments to circumstances so that it has become more reliant on international benefactors than ever before.[15]

While recent trends in anti-regime activities are worrisome, several ingredients for stability and security in the post-Taliban era still compare favorably with those in the past, including the supposed halcyon days that preceded the communist takeover in 1978. Although ethnic differences remain politically salient, the stakes are relatively low and differences negotiable as they mostly involve the distribution of offices and externally provided resources. Absent are disputes over possession of great sources of wealth, such as oil, emotionally charged sectarian conflicts, or ideological divisions reflected in radically divergent agendas for Afghanistan. The deep left-right cleavage that was so ruinous to the country from the 1960s through the 1980s is gone. So too is the Cold War competition that, for all the development assistance that Kabul was able to extract, placed the country clearly in the strategic sights of the major powers.

The prevailing international commitments to Afghanistan are also broader and more generous than ever before. They are unlikely to quickly dissolve as they did after the Soviet military's departure in 1989. And in light of the political discontinuities with which Afghanistan is familiar, the current leadership can mark with pride the achievements that began with creating an interim governing structure, writing a constitution, and holding presidential and parliamentary elections. In contrast with the most recent decades, present-day Afghanistan is also free from the kind of dominant personality who, whether through ideology or charisma, would try to wield authoritarian rule. Usually the strongest criticism of Karzai as a leader is that he is not decisive enough.

Despite its gains, Afghanistan is likely to remain for some time a highly insecure state and society. For most Afghans, the fruits of internationally funded development have barely impacted their lives. Humanitarian relief efforts have succeeded in staving off predicted hunger crises, especially among the returning refugees. But impressive statistics on economic expansion disguise the uneven progress across the country and the hardship that continues to exist. More than 50% of the population lives below the poverty line, 40% are unemployed, and only a small fraction has access to clean water and electricity. Health care has seen very little progress for a society where life expectancy, drawn down by high juvenile mortality rates, stands at 43 years of age.

The deep deficits that exist in the economy and society are often traced to the conditions of underdevelopment that have been Afghanistan's historic lot as a landlocked, resource-poor country. More than a generation of conflict that devastated the countryside and destroyed towns and cities drove at least one-third of the population into exile. State institutions and an economic infrastructure, never well developed, have been slow to recover since 2001. So too, improvement of the security environment has lagged behind expectations. At least part of the disappointing progress in reconstruction and security has been the delay among both Afghans and their foreign benefactors in appreciating the interrelationship between these two goals. As much as better security can be a precondition for those engaged in the recovery efforts, without progress in creating employment and building confidence in the future, it becomes difficult to reorient those actively engaged in criminal activities to change their behavior. Moreover, both the rebuilding process and security are undermined by the absence of responsible, responsive governance, and the presence of the kind of authority that indulges corruption and incompetence.

For the great majority of Afghans, crime in the absence of the rule of law is the chief security concern, more so than anti-regime terrorism. Smuggling, banditry and corruption are of course endemic to the country. But all forms of criminality are believed to have increased since 2001, leading to unfavorable comparisons between the current leadership and the Taliban in maintaining order. While traditional means will continue to be important for adjudicating differences among people, few people doubt the importance of formal judicial institutions and a workable legal framework for extending the state's authority and laying the basis for a modern economy. To date, little progress has occurred in building an infrastructure of courts, judges and jails. Moreover, a largely unresponsive, often corrupt bureaucracy is unable to deliver vital services. Its decisions are frequently discriminatory and arbitrary. The national police, the force most directly charged with providing internal security, are poorly trained and distrusted.

The source of much of the country's criminality and abuses of rights are the hundreds of local militia commanders. Warlordism, as it is frequently called, does not have deep roots in Afghanistan. Armed groups, territorially powerful, are mostly a product of the anti-Soviet jihad and, even more so, the political vacuum created in the wake of the Afghan communists' defeat in 1992. Most were swept away with the arrival of the Taliban only to return as local authority disintegrated with the Taliban's departure. These groups can be a substitute for absent government in defending a community. More often they prey upon a local population, employing extortion and intimidation. Karzai's presidential victory in 2004 is believed owed in many areas to the support of voters who had hoped that a strong leader would hasten the dismantling of the oppressive private armies.

A UN-sponsored program managed during 2005 to remove weapons from the largest militias and to begin the demobilization and reintegration of their members into the society. Yet most of the smaller illegally armed groups continue to operate. Reintegration has been a difficult process, as it is deeply contingent on progress in reconstruction, creating alternative livelihoods that can replace what has been for many militia members the only employment they have ever known. While some gains have occurred in co-opting and suppressing several of the country's most prominent regional warlords, Karzai has been increasingly criticized for the appointment of these same individuals to high positions in the Kabul bureaucracy and the provinces. Many commanders and their close associates acquired legitimacy with their election in September 2005 to a newly created parliament.

Importantly, while the central government appears to have a tenuous writ outside of the capital, it is nevertheless not directly challenged by provincial powerbrokers. Whatever their degree of cooperation with the Karzai government, none of those identified as regional warlords have sought formal autonomy or taken up arms against the Kabul government. For the time being, all seek to benefit from the largesse of international donors. Karzai is generally acknowledged as instrumental to attracting foreign assistance, and can count on American and NATO troops to ensure his government's survival. The only meaningful confrontation with the state comes from the reconstituted Taliban and those militants associated with two former mujahideen leaders who have never accepted Karzai or a western presence in the country.

The illegal production and trafficking of opium poppy is closely linked with most forms of criminality and represents the greater peril to the country's development, stability and security. With the growth of the drug economy during the last decade—providing income for as many as two million Afghan farmers—Afghanistan has attracted worldwide attention for fear that the country is headed toward becoming a narco-mafia state. At present, the Karzai government is helpless to prevent traffickers, cooperative militia commanders, corrupt government officials and anti-regime elements from profiting off the drug trade.

Afghanistan does not have a long history as a principal source of high-value drugs, but the past may offer some guide as to how best to deal with the problem. A key to successful central government intervention has been its capacity to enforce its will on issues deemed to be of critical importance to the state and at the same time have the wisdom to use this power selectively and within limited scope. This suggests that a broad, heavy-handed attack on the narcotics problem is prone to fail and, worse still, is likely to be politically destabilizing in turning large numbers of farmers—with no other way of eking out a livelihood—against the government. In drug enforcement as in military operations more generally, programs that are carried out indiscriminately and insensitively are almost certain to turn away those whose cooperation is essential for compliance. The Afghan communists and their Soviet army sponsors offer the model on how not to initiate difficult social and economic change.

A nuanced approach would be an eradication program that begins with those farmers in the best position to switch to alternative crops, and one that takes aim primarily at drug labs and traffickers, along with others who profit from the trade. Proposals to subsidize traditional and new crops as a means to wean growers from poppy cultivation while minimizing losses of income and farmers' indebtedness may have merit. An effective, sustainable eradication program also demands gains in judicial reform and comprehensive agricultural sector development. Success may also require the assistance of religious leaders in making the case, as did the Taliban in 2000, that poppy growing is un-Islamic. In any case, government and international policy should leave no doubt as to a determination to succeed, while also signaling a readiness to settle for steady, gradual progress.

The Afghan National Army (ANA) and national police force are the centerpieces for extending central authority and creating an improved security environment. Both are expected to give the Karzai government its best chance of gaining an upper hand over warlords and drug barons. Government officials and their international advisors have pinned their hopes on deploying a future ANA force of 70,000, of which nearly 35,000 had been trained by mid-2007.[16] Although improved, there have been difficulties to date in recruitment, training and retention of soldiers. Some outside observers have argued that a smaller, better-trained army makes more sense and that funds for the expensive program should be used instead for a more competent and better-paid national police force. Neither the military or police, will, in any case, be able to assume any time soon the major responsibilities in defending the regime, now carried by international forces.

A controversial new approach to security comes in recognition that neither the army nor police is as yet up to the job of securing districts in the south that have felt the brunt of the intensified insurgency. While the training of an army has shown increased capability after a poor start, the nationally directed police have been slow to cast off their reputation for corruption and ineptness. In response, the Kabul government began in 2006 to recruit auxiliary or community police to supplement the regular local police in several southern provinces. This involves rearming many with local militia connections, an approach that is seemingly at odds with an internationally supported policy designed to disarm illegal armed groups across the country. The greatest concern is that these less-trained cadres will fall under the sway of local influentials and conceivably the drug dealers. The government counters with the argument that recruits are being carefully screened and will be closely monitored. In either case, the policy represents a retreat from the kind of state-building that has been a principal goal of the central government and its international patrons.

Today, as historically, military actions alone cannot ensure security and stability, and if used disproportionately or indiscriminately in counterinsurgency can alienate affected communities. The past also suggests that a strengthened military can pose a threat to legitimate state authority. A large national army will be an institution over which there is an increased likelihood of competition for control among various regional and ethnic elements. And while the professional military envisioned by its sponsors can possibly insulate itself against capture by a single set of interests, it can also lead, as in Pakistan, to the undoing of democratic government. This likelihood increases as the military's claims on the national budget grow and its self-confidence rises. Eventually its officer corps may conclude that generals are more qualified to govern than are elected politicians. As previously suggested, during civilian rule from 1965 through 1978, the military was mostly preoccupied with plotting the overthrow of regimes. Similarly, the final blow to the communists' hold on power in 1992 came with the defection of key military figures to the mujahideen. The accountability of the Afghan army as well as other institutions in the security sector is thus a concern of long standing in the country. The development of the appropriate mechanisms and culture of accountability, as in obedience to the law and civilian ascendancy, seem especially critical as Afghanistan strives to create a more robust state authority.[17]

A new obstacle to state power comes ironically from one of its presumed successes. The parliament that was elected in September 2005 provided a test of whether the increasing violence, especially in the south and east, would permit a credible set of contests to be conducted. Minimal voter education with a confusing ballot increased the possibilities of abuse. As it were, turnout declined sharply from the presidential elections the previous year; and a large number of elections to the lower house were contested because of irregularities. The lower turnout probably reflected a growing cynicism over unappealing candidate choices and growing doubts about the value of voting as a means to improve their economic circumstances and address their grievances. The threats of anti-regime insurgents seemed to play a minor role in discouraging participation.

Afghanistan's earlier experiences with elected parliaments leave reason for concern for the present. The national elections of 1965 and especially of 1969 were widely accepted as mainly free and fair. Even while voters had a poor sense of what was meant by democracy, they saw the electoral process as offering an opportunity to improve their lives and advance their own interests and those of their solidarity groups. But the refusal of the royal court to legitimize political parties precluded the emergence of sufficiently disciplined factions to mobilize majorities for legislating.[18] The ensuing paralysis of the policy making process brought discredit on this earlier experiment in democracy and paved the way for the overthrow of the monarchy. A similar denial of party participation in the 2005 elections by a Karzai-supported law has produced a fractious, largely independent-minded parliamentary membership that has already found its greatest unity in opposing the president and his government. A legislative-executive standoff, as seems increasingly probable, would not only produce a central government incapable of addressing the country's problems but could lead to a constitutional crisis. In reducing the public confidence in the national government, disintegrative political forces would gain ground, and, as in the past, increase the appeal of a Taliban-like solution.

Conclusion

A resurgent Taliban, with or without its Al Qaeda allies, attracts speculation both outside and within Afghanistan. As already noted, the movement, as a purveyor of an extremist Islamic ideology, carries little attraction today in Afghanistan. A religious agenda is not seen as addressing those problems to which most Afghans give highest priority. Above all, the Taliban in power had demonstrated an inability to lead a national recovery from years of conflict and devastation. To the extent that Taliban forces remain a threat, it is only as a default alternative to repudiated or vacated national authority. The prospects for these militants have grown with their ability to capitalize on grievances, namely the belief among Pashtuns that they are being denied the benefits of reconstruction that others are seen as receiving. These feelings have intensified with misdirected and culturally insensitive military operations, whether by foreign or Afghan troops. Even then, recent history instructs that to succeed, an Islamic insurgency in Afghanistan depends on the active collaboration from extremist groups in Pakistan and the connivance of Pakistani authorities, both of which are alleged by the Afghan leadership to be occurring.

None of Afghanistan's neighbors is directly engaged in trying to destabilize the Karzai regime or undermine the country's recovery. All have had their quarrels with policies of the Kabul government, but the likely alternatives are unattractive. Disintegration of the Afghan state would again unleash a tide of refugees across its borders. Renewed conflict would certainly end region-wide aspirations for accelerated trade and energy transfers between Central and South Asia. Several of Afghanistan's neighbors also remember that the Taliban, while in power, had openly boasted of intentions to export their own Islamic beliefs and to lend assistance where insurgencies were aimed at installing new regimes across the region. As such, all of the regional powers are likely to show restraint toward Afghanistan as long as the others in the neighborhood also refrain. But should the current experiment in constitutional government in Afghanistan fail or the international community loses its interest in the country, these states can be expected to lay claim to time-honored spheres of influence. None have shed their earlier client groups and capacity to meddle in Afghanistan.

Assessing the future security environment calls for a strong dose of realism grounded in an appreciation of Afghanistan's past. Insecurities have always loomed large as features of Afghan society, polity and economy, and there is little reason to believe, in view of the country's limited physical and human resource base, that any dramatic transformation is in the offing. A safe society, viable economy and functional government were never features of the national landscape and may have to remain as distant goals. Perhaps the most that the country can aspire to in the foreseeable future is what its own leaders have referred to as reaching the status of a "normal developing country." Failure to temper expectations could evoke popular disappointments that pose dangers for any regime and weaken international resolve to assist.

Still, there remain reasons for optimism. Above all, Afghans have demonstrated their capacity to endure, a determination to survive circumstances that might have broken the will of other peoples hoping to recapture and rebuild a nation. The last quarter century has very likely created a more politically conscious population, one less accepting of social discrimination and economic and political exploitation, and desiring more from their rulers. Despite their deep class, ethnic, regional and sectarian affinities, the Afghan people's unwavering determination to remain a single nation also gives hope that they will find the patience and mutual accommodation that national stability and development demands. These strengths are buttressed by international recognition—even if not yet sufficient commitment—that effective control over large portions of Afghanistan by the Taliban and its allies would revive the civil war, end the neighboring states' forbearance, and again provide international terrorism with an ideal home base. For all the disappointments to date, it is probably still possible to buy Afghanistan enough time to build the national institutions and extend the legitimate authority that can deliver reasonable security and welfare to Afghanistan's citizens. In any long-term commitment to achieve greater security, the country's leaders and international benefactors must be prepared to draw lessons from and also strive to overcome much that marks Afghan history.

Notes

1. Olivier Roy, *Islam and Resistance in Afghanistan* (Cambridge: Cambridge University Press, 1985), 23.

2. For a discussion of the various dimensions of security, that also include environmental security and freedom from violent conflict, see William Maley, *Rescuing Afghanistan* (London: Hurst and Company, 2006), 57–60.

3. Marvin G. Weinbaum, "Legal Elites in Afghan Society," *International Journal of Middle East Studies,* vol. 12 (1980): 42.

4. Roy, *Islam and Resistance,* 23.

5. Ibid., 10.

6. Barnett Rubin, *The Fragmentation of Afghanistan* (New Haven: Yale University Press, 1995), 20.

7. Thomas Barfield, "Weak Links on a Rusty Chain: Structural Weaknesses in Afghanistan's Provincial Government Administration," in M. Nazif Shahrani and Robert L. Canfield, eds., *Revolutions and Rebellions in Afghanistan* (Berkley: University of California Press, 1984), 173.

8. M. Nazif Shahrani, "Marxist Revolution and Islamic Resistance in Afghanistan," in Ibid., 7.

9. Richard Newell, *The Politics of Afghanistan* (Ithaca: Cornell University Press, 1972), 72.

10. Rubin, *The Fragmentation of Afghanistan,* 20.

11. Ibid., 120–121.

12. Ibid., 133.

13. Thomas Barfield, "Radical Political Islam in an Afghan Context," in *Political Transition in Afghanistan: State, Islam, and Civil Society* (Woodrow Wilson International Center, Asia Program Special Report, no. 122), 15–17.

14. See S. Frederick Starr, "A 'Greater Central Asia Partnership' for Afghanistan and its Neighbors," (Johns Hopkins School of Advanced International Studies, Central Asia-Caucasus Institute, A Silk Road Paper, March 2005). Also see Weinbaum, "Afghanistan and Its Neighbors: An Ever Dangerous Neighborhood," (United States Institute of Peace, Special Report 162, June 2006).

15. For a comprehensive study of security issues, see Michael Bhatia, Kevin Lanigan, and Philip Wilkinson, *Minimal Investments, Minimal Results: The Failure of Security Policy in Afghanistan* (Afghan Research and Evaluation Unit, June 2004).

16. "Afghanistan: Post-War Governance, Security, and U.S. Policy," (Washington, DC:The Library of Congress, Congressional Research Service Report for Congress, 17 March 2006), 26.

17. Maley, Rescuing Afghanistan, 76.

18. Marvin G. Weinbaum, "Afghanistan: Nonparty Parliamentary Democracy," *The Journal of Developing Areas,* vol. 7, no. 1 (October 1972): 57–74.

3

Constitutional Engineering and Democratic Stability: The Debate Surrounding the Crafting of Political Institutions in Afghanistan

Andrew Reynolds

THE NEWLY ELECTED ADMINISTRATION IN Afghanistan may be considered an off-spring of the terrible events in America of September 2001. But after creating the space for something to be born, the parents who shepherded in the new order have proven themselves to be suspect when it comes to nurturing the fledgling's growth, providing security for its future, or disciplining its wayward ways. What love there is has been tough, while parental understanding has been in short supply.

Nevertheless, Afghanistan continues to dramatically illustrate that the question of how to establish democracy in a plural society after conflict is today as salient to American foreign policy as at any time since the end of the Second World War. A stable state is most likely to be (at least pseudo) democratic, and a stable Afghanistan is good for Afghans, Americans who need reliable allies in regions of great instability, and for other western governments who want to eliminate the petri dishes of anarchy from which terrorism grows and festers.

But today's Afghanistan is a highly complex mosaic of power plays, age old enmities, battles over religion and nation, and struggles over wealth, which teems through the political discourse, and in essence these conflicts are expressed through debates about new constitutions and political institutions. Who has power, how are they chosen, and how is that power restrained? The playing field has become the field of democratic design, which makes sense as political institutions do more than anything else to shape the chances for democracy and stability in any emerging multiparty dispensation.

There were a handful of people in Afghanistan whose work in 2003 was instrumental in determining their country's long-term future, but few people inside or out of the country knew their names. As part of the Bonn Accords, signed in December 2001 by the victorious factions formerly opposed to the Taliban, a small "constitution technical drafting committee" was established by Interim President Hamid Karzai to report to a "constitutional Loya Jirga" (national assembly) at the end of 2003. The Accords laid out a highly optimistic timetable with a new constitution being in place by December 2003 and national elections held by the following June (ultimately postponed to October 2004). The Afghan "experts" were given an impossible brief: write for us a constitution which will keep the teacher, farmer and warlord happy, which will right the wrongs of the past and make all ethnicities feel secure. They were urged to go into the cities and mountains to ask the people what they thought and reminded that the power brokers of today must still approve of what they write when it is presented tomorrow. Indeed, in one crucial respect—that of the legislative electoral system—the choices made by the constitutional drafters and ratified by the Loya Jirga were ultimately swept aside by a presidential decree.

This chapter poses the question: how do political institutions shape the chances for democracy and stability in an emerging multiparty state like Afghanistan? It is almost redundant to say that a viable constitutional order in Afghanistan has to surmount and survive ominous obstacles. How does one entrench multiparty, multilayered liberal democracy in a country that has no secure infrastructure to speak of, a history of violent ethnic fragmentation and warlordism, and where the state has nowhere near a monopoly of legitimate force or power of implementation? Throughout the transition, President Karzai, the shepherd of the new constitutional order, only had limited control of the capital, Kabul, and only there because of the support of foreign occupying troops. Outside Kabul, in the hinterlands of the south and east, is bandit country. Large swathes of territory are controlled by Taliban-leaning militias or warlords hostile to Karzai and the US presence. In the supposed "friendly" areas of the west and north factional infighting and localized strongman extortion deeply injure the president's claim of a "national mandate."

Before a democratic order can be established in any state there needs to be disarmament and demobilization, and a functioning national army and police force. Before democracy can endure in Afghanistan the drug trade has to be eradicated, jobs need to be created, and farmers must be able to provide food for their families and communities. But before any of this foundational work occurs, a new constitution needs to become manifest, shoving front and center the thorny issues of human rights in a post-conflict milieu, crafting a secular justice system where religious justice has been the recent norm, and allocating legislative and executive power in the new order.

But the difficulties faced by foreign and domestic planners in crafting a new Afghan order can be directly linked to a pervasive lack of appreciation of how transitions from authoritarianism succeed and how institutions can be designed to enhance the chances of democracy.

The Transition and Constitutional Design Process in Afghanistan

In the face of a Northern Alliance invigorated by American air power and military muscle, the Taliban fell like a house of cards in November and December 2001 and Hamid Karzai was anointed as chairman of a six month interim government by the

UN on December 22, 2001. Six months later, on schedule, a tribal grand council "Loya Jirga" was convened to install and perpetuate the mandate of Karzai's Interim Administration through the period leading up to elections planned for June 2004. But the Loya Jirga set an antidemocratic precedent which has bedeviled the constitutional design process and evolution of multiparty politics ever since. The Loya Jirga was deeply undemocratic in both its selection and function[1]: 1,051 delegates were indirectly elected as representatives with varying degrees of electoral fairness and transparency from major parts of the country but the interim authority got to appoint another 600 delegates thereby ensuring Karzai's election and keeping a lid on organized dissent. To further ensure that the US-Karzai view of how the state should be crafted was victorious, the Loya Jirga discussions were chaotic and unfocused, power was ceded to strongmen who had been co-opted into the Karzai camp, and very little was on the table for discussion and decision to begin with.[2] Ultimately southern and eastern Pashtuns felt left out of a process they saw as essentially Northern Alliance Tajik/Uzbek driven.

Through 2003 various committees worked on drafting a new constitution which was then presented to a second Loya Jirga in December 2003. The "technical experts" received much solicited and unsolicited advice from outside the country but as a group they were closely aligned with the interim president and were believed to be strongly swayed by his views on how the new state should be politically structured. Civil society received barely a look-in during the 2003 drafting process and even more telling was the lack of recognition of marginalized political groups in the process: the moderate Taliban, local power bases outside of the Karzai camp, and Northern Alliance interests not persuaded by the Pashtun from Kandahar. The selection of the Constitutional Loya Jirga (CLJ) may have been slightly more inclusive and democratic than the first Loya Jirga but its workings were decidedly not. The constitutional drafters had come up with a highly majoritarian presidential system, devoid of federalism, with much local administration or other focal points of power. CLJ delegates received the large printed draft on their arrival in Kabul and were given little time to reflect on the implications or alternatives. There was immediate and widespread unease with such a winner-take-all presidential system but again the format of the CLJ was managed to preclude significant alteration to the document as presented.

Anti-state and anti-Coalition violence in Afghanistan has remained fairly constant during the five years since January 2001. The figures for civilian deaths are notoriously inaccurate but relatively reliable figures put Afghan deaths during

Political Transition Timeline

War End	Interim Authority	Loya Jirga	CLJ	Presidential Elections	Legislative Elections
0 Hour	1 Month	6 Months	24 Months	34 Months	40 Months

the October war at 2,500 with a further 700 dying in the following two and a half years. Events on the road to democracy have, if anything, exacerbated the violence. Deaths from political violence fell after the first Loya Jirga but then steadily rose in the run-up to the Constitutional Loya Jirga, spiked in the months leading up to the original June 2004 date for elections, and rose again before the actual presidential election in October 2004. These raw death figures only tell part of the story as attacks on aid workers, UN workers, election officials, Coalition and ISAF troops have continued unabated over the last year. Furthermore, sporadic internecine warfare in Herat and the north have added to the fragility of the overall security picture.

A Lens of Analysis: Seeing State Health in Afghanistan through the Eyes of Medicine

When it comes to democratic design broadly conceived it is useful to don the white coat of a doctor and see the failing state as ailing patient. The metaphor encompasses how political institutions and constitutional designs can be seen as medicines which can contribute to stabilizing a nation and invigorating a just, free and inclusive state. Of course such an approach requires asking some tricky opening questions: how can we tell that society is stable? How does one define, conceptualize and measure "democratic health?" How do we assess these very "symptoms of sickness?" Do we use measures of political violence, democratic robustness and socio-economic indicators of development, or are other issues equally prescient? And then when seeking to address the illness that beguiles a weak state how can we appropriately diagnose a nation's malady? On what cultural, historical and political factors do we need to focus? After the diagnosis, one applies the medicine, so what is in the medicine chest of political institutions and how might we expect them to ameliorate conflict?

There are many ways in which this analogy has resonance, not merely in Afghanistan but in other troubled parts of the world. Failed political settlements are often born of poor diagnosis or inappropriate treatment. In Liberia, for instance, at the end of the 1990s, the diagnosis was simply that elections needed to be held and consequently the treatment was a simplistic winner-take-all race which did nothing to alter existing power structures already heady with their own corruption. The missteps of US policy in Iraq in the first half of 2004 were characterized by a flailing search for a transition mode which would give the appearance of Iraqi influence but in reality retained US control. The Coalition diagnosis of what ailed Iraq and what would stabilize the nation appears to have been that Saddam Hussein ailed Iraq and his removal was the cure. This proved to be far from the whole case and after the catastrophic failure of a series of US-led governance proposals—an appointed council, followed by elite based caucuses, and then a hollow transfer of sovereignty—the transition and election details were ultimately punted to the United Nations.

What "ails" Afghanistan? A weak center posed against a strong, corrupt and unruly periphery? Or a ticking ethnic bomb where the largest group has only a minority of the people but has ruled the nation pretty much uninterrupted since 1747? Does Afghanistan need modern infrastructure and a middle class before democratic institutions, or is the real sickness the dominance of tribal hierarchies backed up by the law of the gun? A well considered diagnosis is highly complex and thus designing the right political institutions is a fine art, but the endeavor is made even more complex by the lack of clarity over what the goal is. Is a healthy Afghanistan one with a fully fledged and robust liberal democracy, or an incipient democracy with the conditions which might allow participatory and accountable forms of government to grow? Or is a healthy Afghanistan one of internal political stability, the absence of violence, with or without democracy? One might cynically suggest that the US and British interest in a healthy Afghanistan is not about domestic niceties in Kabul but rather a state which ceases to be a haven for those who would attack Americans and Europeans. While these aims can get confused and may not be mutually inclusive, in fact there are clearly tensions between promoting each of the goals.

One of the most overlooked truisms of all political transitions is that designing political institutions, just as applying medicine, is a temporally defined task. When there is conflict, the institutions negotiated or imposed are about triage and first aid—keeping the patient alive in the field (e.g., Bosnia in the 1990s, Sierra Leone since 1995, or indeed Afghanistan over the last two years). Then emergency medicine takes over—encompassing enhanced provisions for power sharing, decentralization or varying degrees of minority autonomy (e.g., South Africa and Kosovo, or secession as in the case of East Timor and Indonesia). The next steps, medically, are convalescence and long-term care. However, it is rare that the institutions are then adapted and reinvented to promote the long-term health of the nation-state and its political stability, addressing the underlying socio-political divisions and helping to consolidate democracy. There is strong evidence that the institutions so crucial at the time of triage (e.g., ethnic power sharing and simplistic elections) actually retard the prospects for democratic growth in the medium term. The Dayton Accords, signed in November 1995, finally brought a type of closure to the civil war which had raged throughout the territory of the former Yugoslavia since 1992 costing over 100,000 lives and the violent expulsion of over half of the Bosnian population from their homes. But the hopes for peace born in Dayton, Ohio, came at the cost of political structures which did all they could to separate, segment, delimit and ultimately make all politics in Bosnia about ethnic identity and political-physical separation. Virtually no space was left for the evolution of moderate multiethnic parties which might lay seeds of a return to shared nationhood in the Balkans. The failure to adapt institutions to new realities partially explains why so many nations never complete their treatment regimens/transitions to consolidated democracy.

It has been argued that the political first aid Afghanistan required at the time of triage after 2001 was a fully ethnically inclusive structure of governance backed but by a monopoly of force provided for the Kabul government by Coalition and NATO forces. The Interim Administration was inclusive on some levels but as mentioned earlier it swayed towards the inclusion of the powerful rather than the representative. Most warlords were let into the tent but embryonic civil society movements of Afghans without armies and private agendas were not as encouraged. That perhaps is a political design question best left for the post-triage period but the Interim Administration was not even given a basic monopoly of force to back up its tenuous rule. US and British troop numbers were inadequate and the scope of peacekeeping was paltry. It is also clear that very little scope for political reform has been built into the new constitution to allow for different needs and realities 10, 20 or 50 years hence. As I shall describe below Afghanistan has a triage constitution which is largely set in stone and may not be appropriate for an emerging democratizing but divided nation-state.

Afghanistan's first national elections of October 2004 alluded to the problem that all too often international power brokers rush a patient to surgery (elections) before it is stable enough to survive such a shock to its system. President Karzai was a full partner in the headlong rush to elections in 2004 but without adequate registration, planning and security the recipe for disaster was always present. While it is true that the "development first, democracy later" argument is empirically flawed, at the same time rushing to elections can be dangerous when: 1) the infrastructure to facilitate legitimate elections is lacking and a climate which allows for free campaigning is often non-existent; 2) the electoral administration is under-prepared and lacks capacity (problems such as mislabeling the indelible ink can arise); and 3) early elections reinforce and replicate the existing power structures before alternative forms of democratic mobilization have had the space or time to assert themselves. This usually means that politics resets to the default, and the default is ethnic polarization.

That the presidential elections came off without massive instability and a declamation against the final results by losing candidates was more due to serendipity and skillful political wheeling and dealing than the integrity of the process (see below). Oftentimes the run to the operating theater and the trauma it causes the patient is exacerbated by discharging too early—withdrawing aid, expertise and attention before the political institutions are able to stand on their own feet. Cambodia was such a case in the 1990s and Afghanistan may suffer the same fate if resources are not made available, at least at the electoral level, for subsequent national elections.

The medical metaphor also speaks to the way in which political institutions in new democracies are rarely considered in the whole and with reference to their interaction with other institutions and elements of state-building. Just like medicines, political institutions need to be "holistically designed," i.e., they need to work in concert with each other to be successful. Different institutional prescriptions can work against each other in a harmful way (and exacerbate the illness) if the treatment regimen is not complementary for the whole. In medicine, one drug may react with another and retard the patient's progress, or the treatment of one ailment may create new problems in other parts of the body.

In constitutional design, for instance, a seemingly inventive electoral system may combine with a power laden presidential executive to cause gridlock and polarization.

In the Afghan case, holistic also means that political design needs to work in concert with other keys to a transition to stability. It is not enough to have the skeleton of a good constitution in place if demobilization and demilitarization have not been addressed, if regional power remains in the hands of ethnic strongmen, if the economy continues to be infested with an illegal opium trade, and if basic infrastructure does not facilitate the building of a national economy or identity.

Nevertheless, medicine is not always miraculous. There are limitations as to what degree a well designed constitution can save a deeply divided society. Political institutions can be used as medicines for a nation's maladies but other socio-political networks need to be in good working order to facilitate long-term political health. A fully functioning judiciary, a progressive education system, high levels of employment, economic development, and internal security will provide the foundation for a stable polity. At times of sickness appropriate medicines have to be taken, and they may need to be taken for a considerable length of time, but the society also needs to eat well, exercise fully and avoid stepping in front of the proverbial bus. While it is true to say that while the very best constitutional package cannot save a state from the slings and arrows of violent conflict or economic misfortune, a badly designed set of institutions will exacerbate, exaggerate and generally feed creeping fragmentation and instability in a plural society.

The October 2004 Afghan Presidential Election

There are at least two distinct pillars of a successful election. The first is that administratively the mechanics of the election run smoothly and everyone who wants to vote is given reasonable access to the polls and that the day itself is peaceful and free from widespread disruption. The second pillar is that the election and the subsequent results are accepted as legitimate and by various audiences: in the eyes of voters, in the eyes of the candidates/political elites, and last in the eyes of the international donor community. While these pillars of a successful election are clearly related they are not mutually dependent. There have been many cases of deeply flawed elections which have produced results which were broadly acceptable not just to the political elites and international watchers but to some extent to the bulk of voters as well. Nevertheless, there have also been elections which were administratively pretty good, which led to results which were an accurate reflection of the system as it was intended, but were ultimately rejected as being illegitimate by voters or losing candidates.

The momentous October 9, 2004 presidential elections in Afghanistan fit more into the first category than the second. While there were significant challenges to freeness and fairness during the election process and its aftermath, the slim majority first-round victory for Hamid Karzai was quickly ratified by foreign powers (led by the US), grudgingly accepted by the leading losing candidates, and led to no significant mobilization against the integrity of the process by voters. In many aspects the election was a huge success and has pushed Afghanistan much further up the mountain towards democratization and stability. However, those successful aspects did not include the holding of a free or fair election which could have been said to be an accurate reflection of the free will of the electorate.

The successes ledger of the October election was not unsubstantial. The Joint Electoral Management Body recorded that just over 8.1 million votes were cast which represented 70% of the voters supposedly registered and an even greater proportion of the estimated voting age population. The huge majority of the 4,900 polling stations in country and 2,800 in Iran and Pakistan were free from violence promoted by the Taliban or any other localized anti-election groups. Estimated turnout in the most fragile southern and eastern provinces was not dissimilar to the country as a whole, although in the province of Zabul turnout was less than 40%. There was a reasonably significant number of women voters outside of the conservative Pashtun south which led to 40% of the voters overall being women, a not unimpressive performance in a country where women's rights have been so suppressed for so long that separate polling places were needed to even allow for their chance to vote.

In many aspects the flaws of the presidential election process occurred well before election day. The registration process was characterized by dubious figures inflated by multiple registrations, underage registrations and the buying and selling of voter IDs.[3] The extent of the over-registration was impossible to gauge but anecdotal evidence, bolstered by the actual election results in some provinces, indicates that over-registration was a significant issue in some areas. Campaigning in the run-up to the presidential vote consisted of some large Qanoni, Mohaqiq and Dostum rallies in their Tajik, Hazara and Uzbek heartlands, respectively, and two Karzai campaign speeches outside of Kabul, one of which to Ghanzi was called off after a rocket was fired at the landing presidential helicopter. But overall both major and minor candidates did not have access to areas in which they were not likely to be dominant. The playing field for the campaign was also skewed heavily in favor of the incumbent interim president who had name recognition and international backing. While the media did not explicitly promote Hamid Karzai to the detriment of other candidates, the state media was instrumental in establishing his name over the previous three years.

On the day itself there were insufficient international or domestic monitors to take more than a cursory glance at the integrity of polling but those who were in the field witnessed a host of administrative hiccups (incorrect procedures for securing ballot boxes, stations running out of ballots, poor security, etc.) and a number of political manipulations. These ran the gamut of intimidation of voters, posters of candidates in polling places and "example" ballots displayed inside polling booths, to the extreme of election officials being given hundreds of voter IDs by tribal heads and filling out ballots for a single candidate. These are just anecdotal examples of fraud and as such it is difficult to tell how systematic such manipulations were or whether they would have effected the final result significantly. The independent expert panel constituted to analyze complaints ultimately found that the problems highlighted to them did not substantially affect the final result. The most severe problem on election day was confusion around which marker pens were the indelible ink ones. This led to widespread and valid complaints that the only block on multiple voting was ineffective in many parts of the country. Combined with the fact that multiple registrations were commonplace, this leaves the possibility that there was multiple voting in some areas.

As noted above, the legitimacy of an election result in a fledgling democracy is a multifaceted question. Hamid Karzai's coronation was always going to be legitimized in the eyes of most of the international donor community because that was the pathway they had chosen. The OSCE and American decision not to observe the election was part and parcel of avoiding the embarrassing position of having to criticize as flawed the election of the only candidate who stood any chance of stabilizing the nation. The fact that Karzai won over 50% on the first round and led his nearest rival by almost 40% ensured that the majority of voters "believed" in the final victory even if they felt there were shortcomings in fairness at the margins.

The Pashtun community was the delivery vehicle behind Karzai's victory. Indeed, his victory on the first round would have been much more in question if Afghans in Pakistan (who were overwhelmingly Pashtun) had not been allowed to vote. The Pashtuns clearly felt the result was legitimate but in much of the Hazara center and Uzbek and Tajik north, Karzai was roundly defeated by ethnic entrepreneurs. Mohaqiq swept the mountainous Hazara center, Dostum dominated Uzbek areas in the north, and Qanoni did well (although not quite as dominant) among the Tajiks of the north and west. President Karzai must reach out to such non-Pashtun constituencies, especially in the forthcoming legislative elections. Last, legitimacy is in the eyes of the losing candidates and their backers. At first it looked as though the majority of the losing candidates were going to cry foul and argue that the election was too flawed to be legitimate. But strong arm-twisting brought Dostum, Qanoni and Mohaqiq back into the fold and they were the only losers who mattered. It will be interesting to see what these politicians and militia leaders were offered for their acquiescence.

Afghan Democracy: Institutions in the New Constitution

Rather than opting for a decentralized and federalized state the new Afghan constitution gives a huge amount of power to the central state in Kabul. The constitutional drafters diagnosed the ailment of Afghanistan through the ages as one of a weak center thwarted in its reform and modernization efforts by a powerful,

Afghan Presidential Election Results: October 2004

Hamid Karzai	Independent	4,443,029	55.4%
Yonous Qanooni	Hezb-e-Nuhzhat-e-Mili Afghanistan	1,306,503	16.3%
Haji Mohammad Mohaqiq	Independent	935,325	11.7%
Abdul Rashid Dostum	Independent	804,861	10.0%
Abdul Latif Pedram	Hezb-e-Congra-e-Mili Afghanistan	110,160	1.4%
Massooda Jalal	Independent	91,415	1.1%
Syed Ishaq Gilani	Nuhzat-e-Hambastagee Mili Afghanistan	80,081	1.0%
Ahmad Shah Ahmadzai	Independent	60,199	0.8%
Abdul Satar Serat	Independent	30,201	0.4%
Hamayon Shah Asifi	Independent	26,224	0.3%
Ghulam Farooq Nijrabi	Hezb-e-Istiqlal-e-Afghanistan	24,232	0.3%
Syed Abdul Hadi Dabir	Independent	24,057	0.3%
Abdul Hafiz Mansoor	Independent	19,728	0.2%
Abdul Hadi Khalilzai	Independent	18,082	0.2%
Mir Mohammad Mahfouz Nedaee	Independent	16,054	0.2%
Mohammad Ebrahim Rashid	Independent	14,242	0.2%
Wakil Mangal	Independent	11,770	0.1%
Abdul Hasseb Aryan	Independent	8,373	0.1%
Valid Votes		8,024,536	100.0%
Invalid Votes		104,404	
Total Votes		8,128,940	

unaccountable, corrupt and fragmented periphery. This led to the creation of a powerful presidency atop a very centralized state, with severely limited provincial and local government roles. Despite the intuitive validity of the diagnosis the prescription flew in the face of wisdom drawn from other fragmented societies in conflict. The comprehensive powers of the president are also able to be wielded by a single actor/party without formal reference to other voices. Unlike some other post-conflict political dispensations, Afghanistan's executive is not required to be a multiparty, multiethnic reflection of majority and minority opinion. There may well be cosmetic ethnic balancing in the office of the presidency and his deputies and in the cabinet but this is not constitutionally mandated and exists or not, effective or not, at the whim of the sitting president. The legislature is bicameral but it has a highly restrained role in crafting and approving legislation, and the upper house is stacked with presidential appointees filling a third of the seats.

The September 2005 Legislative Elections

In September 2005, nearly 6.5 million Afghans voted in the freest and most competitive legislative elections they had ever experienced; 2.75 million women cast votes for the Wolesi Jirga (lower house) and had a significant impact on the

Constitutional Arrangements in Afghanistan and (Interim) Iraq

Afghanistan		Iraq (Interim)
Strong Presidency	*Executive Type*	Parliamentary-Presidential
Executive Can Overwhelm Legislative Power	*Separation of Powers*	3 Person Presidency Retains Some Powers of Appointment and Legislative Veto
Unitary-Centralized	*Federal or Unitary*	Asymmetrical Federalism with Enhanced Kurdish Powers
Bicameral: Lower House popularly Elected; Upper House Elected by District and Provincial Governments and Appointed by President	*Legislative Type*	Constitutional Assembly Acts as Interim Legislature and Constitution Writing Body
246?	*National Assembly Size*	275
Single Non-Transferable Vote in Multi-Member Provinces	*Legislative Electoral System*	National Closed List PR
Each Province Must Elect a Minimum of Two Women to National Assembly—There Were Two Women in the Transitional Cabinet	*Gender Diversity Mechanisms*	The National Assembly Must Be 25% Women—6 of the 31 Ministers of the Interim Government Were Women
None	*Minority Veto*	Any Three Provinces (Kurds Are a Majority in Three) Can Veto the New Constitution by a Two-Thirds Majority Vote
Highly Limited	*Decentralization*	Limited
Islamic	*Legal Basis*	Islamic/Secular

power dynamics of the new legislature. Elections were also successfully conducted for local councils and indirectly to the Meshrano Jirga (upper house). On December 18, 2005 the new parliament convened and the international community claimed a substantial part of the 2001 Bonn Agreement fulfilled: "the establishment of a broad-based, gender sensitive, multi-ethnic and fully representative government through national elections."

For legislative elections, initial discussions in Afghanistan alighted upon a provincially based List Proportional Representation system as most appropriate for elections to the Wolesi Jirga. The provinces were to be multimember districts ranging in size from around three members to nearly forty. Such a system would have allowed parties and independents to run, with voters making a mark by their party or independent of choice. However, the electoral law decreed in 2004 announced that voters would choose between individual candidates rather than voters (in the same multimember provincial districts). Thus a Single Non-Transferable Vote (SNTV) was created, a system used in Japan from

1948 to 1993, but today used only in Jordan, Vanuatu, the Pitcairn Islands and (partially) in Taiwan.

Simply stated SNTV gives the voter a single vote to cast for a single candidate, but multiple seats are elected at the same time from a given district. The system is believed to lose its efficacy if the districts are too large in size, for that reason in Japan, Jordan and Vanuatu the average district was four members in size. But in Afghanistan the districts ended up being based on provincial boundaries and ranged from two to 33 members in size (with one-third of the districts being over nine members in size). Under SNTV, candidates are elected by simply winning the most votes—if four MPs are to be elected from a district then the top four vote getters are elected—regardless whether they have a majority or minority of the votes or how far ahead of the next candidate they are. In theory one candidate could be elected with 90% of the votes while three others could be elected with 3% each.[4]

How Was SNTV Expected to Work in Afghanistan?

The received wisdom of the consequences of SNTV based on 40 years of evidence in Japan and a decade of use in Jordan was that the system was manageable in specific circumstances, but it was not desirable as a means of translating votes into seats in a democracy. The system had been part of the institutions "gifted" to the Japanese in 1948 and was the product of King Hussein's manipulation of the former block vote system in Jordan in 1993.[5]

The chief flaws of SNTV in theory (and in practice in Japan) were the difficulties of strategic coordination for parties and their candidates. How many candidates should you stand within a given constituency, and how can you discipline your voters to share their votes across your candidates equally? The lottery nature of the system led to high disproportionality between votes and seats won, a tendency to exclude minority parties, the encouraging of clientelism and corruption among those MPs elected, and ultimately the fragmentation of the ruling party.

In 2004, Andrew Wilder[6] and I speculated on how SNTV might work if it were to be used under the conditions that existed in Afghanistan.[7] We argued that the negative consequences of the system centered on five themes: representation, establishing a stable party system, a clear and effective vote, allowing the executive and legislature to govern, and promoting dynamic women in parliament.

Representation

First-time elections in post conflict fledgling democracies need to do a particularly good job of fairly translating votes cast into seats won for majorities, minorities and independents. Elections results are particularly susceptible to challenge if the "losers" feel that the voting system has discriminated against their core constituency. There should also be a reasonable expectation on the part of political actors that if they do relatively well in the vote they will win representation. We believed that in Afghanistan SNTV could violate these assumptions. Because the relationship between votes and seats is capricious, seat share would depend more on how many candidates stood in a province and how voters distributed their votes across those candidates. In the largest districts the results would be a lottery when it came to independents and minority fragments.

Establishing a Stable Party System

The experience of many post-conflict democratizing states is that the promotion and encouragement of a stable party system is a prerequisite for democracy and stability. Even in former "no-party" systems, like-minded interests gravitate together and movements, blocks, lists and alliances are formed because of the necessity of governing. Manipulating electoral systems to try to eliminate parties merely makes such blocks unaccountable, less democratic and less able to respond to voters' interests. We speculated that while the electoral law did not bar political parties running candidates, the fact that such party affiliations were not on the ballot and that the SNTV was designed to weaken parties meant that the system would mitigate the growth of a dynamic and accountable party system. Any factions/alliances formed in the legislature were likely to be fragmented and personality driven, beholden to regional power bases rather than national interests. SNTV would promote a multitude of independents and small political factions making government formation and legislative politics exceptionally difficult.

A Clear and Effective Vote

As noted by Johnson et al., we believed it was crucially important that the Afghans were able to cast their votes easily and express their political preference clearly on the ballot paper. If the ballot was too complex voters would be alienated and unable to appreciate the relationship between their vote and government formation. It was clear that the incentives of large district SNTV would encourage a large number of candidates making ballots long and confusing. Such ballots where hundreds of candidates were listed, without party names or symbols, would be particularly confusing for illiterate voters, and individual candidates would have a difficult time in publicizing their own unique symbol. Last, because of the vagaries of SNTV, the fragmented parliament produced, and the lack of transparency in government formation, voters would have little feel for how their single vote had accounted for the government of the day.

Allowing the Executive and Legislature to Govern

Conventional wisdom has it that in fledgling democracies which balance power between a directly elected executive and a legislature, it is important to facilitate a parliament which is likely to work in harness with the president and not block his or her will at every turn. Gridlock in government, at a time of pressing need for effective policy making, is particularly dangerous. We noted in 2004 that if parliamentary elections had been held at the same time as the presidential elections, the SNTV system might have been more likely to produce a block to support Hamid Karzai but the near year-long gap was bound to weaken his base in the Wolesi Jirga. In a memo written for President Karzai in January 2005 I argued that:

> The system [SNTV] will advantage those parties/movements most able to mobilize and manipulate votes. While the President has broad multi-ethnic support he does not have the level of party "machines" that Commanders and provincial power brokers have in the North, East and West. Thus if anti-Karzai forces are a tune to the winning strategy of SNTV they are likely to win many more seats than their vote share would suggest.[8]

A simulation, based on the assumption that a "pro-Karzai" forces party had somewhat less ability to discipline and control their candidate nomination and vote distribution strategy than the oppsition "Qanooni," "Mohaqiq" and "Dostom" parties, gave "pro-Karzai" forces 41% of the Wolesi Jirga, based on the 55% vote share he received in the presidential election.

Promoting Dynamic Women in Parliament

Last, we were troubled that SNTV, in combination with the gender provisions of the electoral law, may breed concentrated resentment against the election of women candidates who had received dramatically fewer votes than their male counterparts. Evidence from elsewhere suggests that affirmative action mechanisms (quotas) give a fillip to the advancement of women's interests when: 1) they are not seen as overtly manipulative by voters; 2) they facilitate the election of women to some degree independent of traditional power structures; 3) those women elected have some degree of electoral base and legitimacy; and 4) it serves the "male parties" interests to stand progressive women candidates that will appeal to both male and female voters. Clearly Afghanistan is a political environment not known to be friendly to the involvement of women in political leadership positions or even visible social and professional positions. The registration of women was particularly challenging in the southeast, and just finding an adequate number of women candidates proved difficult in the provinces of Zabul, Uruzgan and Nangarhar. The election law was to reserve an average of two seats per province (a total of 68 seats) which could only be filled by women candidates. We felt that the likelihood of women winning such reserved seats with dramatically fewer votes than male candidate losers was high throughout the entire country. It should be noted that this fear was, of the five areas of concern, perhaps the least born out by the election results themselves.

The Real-Life Consequences of SNTV in 2005

Representation

The question of whether SNTV produced a legislature in 2005 broadly representative of the political cleavages within Afghan society is a difficult one to judge. First, the party system is so embryonic that one cannot simply assess the number of votes won by political movements and their strength in parliament. There are approximately 33 identifiable parties/factions/alliances in the Wolesi Jirga but few presented ideological platforms, rather they are individuals allied with regionally and nationally powerful strongmen. One significant proxy for opinion and balance is the degree of ethnic diversity in the new legislature. Indeed, there were concerns that partisan politics would devolve into a Tajik/Uzbek/Hazara opposition block, versus a collection of Pashtun representatives who are presumed to be supportive of the Pashtun President Hamid Karzai. Andrew Wilder's analysis of the proportions of ethnic representation in the new Wolesi Jirga are very close to the estimated range of ethnicities within the country as a whole (although these estimates vary and are highly controversial—there has not been a government census for over thirty years).[9]

But ethnicity may not necessarily be the sole driving force behind disputes in the legislature. Wilder finds that while 40% of the Pashtuns can be categorized as "pro-government," 14% are in the opposition camp, and nearly half are "non-aligned"—including many of the new women MPs. Tajiks are similarly split almost equally between "pro-government," "anti-" and "non-aligned" camps, and only the Hazaras and Uzbeks can be classified as being overwhelmingly on the opposition benches. When it comes to policy, both pro-government and opposition factions can unite on a conservative interpretation of Islam and are likely to push hard for legislation rooted in such interpretations. Factions/parties led by Sayaf and Rabbani (pro-Karzai) and Qanooni (anti) are at the forefront of over 65 MPs who are fundamentalist, who will be supported by many of the 47 MPs in the more moderate traditionalist camp (led by the Hazara Shiites). The smallest group (of 43) can be classified as more progressive, dominated

Ethnicity	Legislative Seats	%	Estimated Population Share (%)
Pashtun	118	47	40–45
Tajik	53	21	20–25
Hazara	30	12	10–13
Uzbek	20	8	8–10
Others	28	12	NA
Total	249	100	

Source: Wilder 2006 and Reynolds 2006

by Dostum's secular Junbesh party and the 13 liberal democratic and leftist MPs.

It is also important to stress that the new MPs are not the individuals who the majority of Afghans voted for in September 2005. Just over two million of all the votes cast were for winning candidates (32%), and thus over two-thirds (four million) of all votes were cast for candidates who lost. This 68% "wasted vote" level is remarkably high. In the Iraqi general elections of January 2005 only 5.3% of votes were wasted, and less than 1% in the first democratic elections in South Africa in 1994.

It is also hard to believe that a legislature where nearly half the members were mudjahideen fighters against Soviet occupation in the 1980s is in touch with the concerns of everyday folk who live in a very different Afghanistan to that of a quarter of a century ago. It is also troubling to see credible analysis from human rights groups in Kabul which identify among the Wolesi Jirga membership 40 commanders still linked to militias, 24 who belong to criminal gangs, 17 drug traffickers, and serious war crimes allegations outstanding against 19 new MPs.

The expected lottery nature of SNTV was demonstrated. The first seat in each region was won with an average of 11.5% of the vote but the last seat was taken on average with only 5.7% (the lowest being just 0.5% in Kabul). On average there were only 864 votes between the lowest polling elected candidate and the highest polling (male) runner up. Such tiny margins not only bring into dispute the results in areas tainted by vote fraud and campaign manipulation but they make wild swings of legislative power likely from election to election. Despite incumbency (perhaps because of it) most of the current Wolesi Jirga MPs can be very easily ousted next time around.

Establishing a Stable Party System

In the run-up to parliamentary elections SNTV was expected to retard the development of a stable party system, accentuate the fragmentation of politics in Afghanistan, and leave national legislation beholden to parochial regional warlords and religious fundamentalists. The results gave credence to each of these concerns. Only 16% of the over 2,800 candidates were from registered political parties and "party" candidates won less than a third of the seats in the lower house. As noted earlier, Wilder identifies 33 various slates/alliances/factions of which the very largest group is comprised of the 25 members of Yunus Qanooni's New Afghanistan party (only 10% of the total). The new and liberal democratic alliance of 14 parties—the National Democratic Front—won only seven seats, with the old leftist parties winning just six. The block supporting President Karzai is a motley collection of small bands led by powerful individuals: Rabbani, Ismail Khan, Wali Masood, Gailani, Ahadu, Sayaf and Khalili. Each of these interests will need to be assuaged to guarantee a voting block for the president's legislative agenda.

A Clear and Effective Vote

There is substantial evidence to suggest that voters did find the SNTV system and the poster-sized ballots confusing. Each candidate had to communicate to the voters either their face, or a neutral symbol which had been assigned to them by the electoral commission.[10] Many candidates, especially new entrants to the political scene, found this immensely difficult. The fragmentation of the vote points to a large number of voters unsure of which blocks were likely to be influential in the new parliament. There were over 2,800 candidates for only 249 seats and over 400 in Kabul alone. Craig Charney, who conducted an October 2005 poll in Afghanistan, believes that the main reason that Afghans did not vote was that they could not find a candidate to support. He argued that this was compounded by the ballot, associating "the low turnout in Kabul [with] the electoral system there, where people, often of low literacy, were confronted with pages and pages of ballots."[11]

Overall turnout in Afghanistan dropped from 69% to 50% between October 2004 and September 2005, going as low as 29% in the south. In contrast, turnout increased from 58% to 70% between January and December 2005 in Iraq. The level of invalid or "spoilt" ballots was also very high in the SNTV Wolesi Jirga election. A total of 5% of all ballots were rejected—2.9% because they were marked in error, or for disqualified candidates; 2.1% which were just blank. This 5% compares to less than 1% in the 1994 South African elections, 1.1% in the January 2005 Iraqi elections, and 2.4% in the Liberian election of November 2005.

Allowing the Executive and Legislature to Govern

The new legislature is likely to make the passage of President Karzai's reform agenda difficult. The fragmentation and vested interests mean that each executive bill will have to be backed by a majority cobbled together with piecemeal promises and pork-barreling.

From having a comfortable majority in the presidential election, Karzai now has a block sympathetic to him which makes up less than a third of the Wolesi Jirga (and this block is by no means monolithic). Wilder identifies another 84 MPs (34%) who can be considered "pro-opposition" and 84 MPs who are either non-aligned or have no clear factional alignment. The strength of the "opposition" to Karzai was demonstrated by Yunus Qanooni's success in December 2005 in winning the coveted chairmanship of the Wolesi Jirga (by 122 to 117 over Karzai's favored candidate, Abdul Rasul Sayyaf). Qanooni subsequently resigned from his de facto position as "leader of the opposition" in favor of Burhanuddin Rabbani who confusingly had been seen as within the president's camp.

Women in the Wolesi Jirga Election

There were significant signs of success in the special mechanism for electing women to the new Wolesi Jirga. The 68 women members represent the highest

		Presidential (% Votes)	Parliamentary (% Seats)
Pro-Karzai		55	32
Anti-Karzai		45	34
	Qanooni	16	10
	Dostum	10	8
	Muhaqeq	12	7
	Others	7	9
Non-Aligned		—	34

Source: JEMB elections results and Wilder 2006

female percentage in Asia and the special quota mechanism—ensuring on average that two women were elected from each of the 34 provinces—was largely unchallenged by all sides during the elections. It almost goes without saying that the progress of women in Afghan politics is remarkable when considering the suppression that women endured under the Taliban just a few years ago. In the election results women showed themselves to be able to go head to head with male candidates and in some cases to be successful in the face of substantial disadvantages. Nineteen women (or just under 10% of all parliamentarians) were elected in their own right without the aid of the affirmative action mechanism, most notably Fauzia Gailani who topped the poll in the large western province of Herat against strong local and warlord-backed male candidates. Another significant success story was Malalai Joya who came in second in the province of Farah. Her election illustrated the way in which many voters, alienated from traditional, corrupt and warmongering candidates, found something of a protest vote in the small but impressive wave of women entering the fray. Malalai Joya had bravely denounced the warlords at the Constitutional Loya Jirga.[12] Fawzia Kofi, who had been elected as of right in the eastern province of Badakhshan, was elected by the new Wolesi Jirga as their second deputy chairperson. The 68 women in the Wolesi Jirga form a highly significant voting block which is for the most part unaligned with traditional interests.

But while the 2005 election did see dramatic strides in the representation of women, their actual influence on future legislative power-plays remains unclear. Forty-nine of the female MPs owe their positions in parliament to the quota mechanism and the 422 male candidates they leapfrogged to get there (an average of twelve higher-polling men in each district) will not let them forget that fact. The 19 women elected without the aid of the quota only won an average of 3% of the vote each—as much a consequence of the fragmenting SNTV system as their popularity. The 68 women elected averaged just 2.3% each. The highest percentage vote for a woman was 9.2 in the Panshjer Valley (the heartland of the Northern Alliance) and the highest vote, 9,092 for Safia Sidiqi, who came in third in Nangarhar. Malalai Joya, the top vote getter in Herat, only received 3.6% of the vote. While the fear of many women being elected with dramatically lower vote shares than unsuccessful male candidates was not born out, in Zabul the woman who claimed the reserved seat only polled 751 votes (the highest "losing" male polled 1,816).

By and large the electoral system of SNTV in large districts did what academics expected it to do, and not what Hamid Karzai's advisors hoped it would do. The president's team hoped that the electoral system would retard the emergence of new parties, fragment the existing opposition blocks and weaken the ability of regionally powerful strongmen to drag into parliament followers on their coattails. In their dream scenario a core loyal Pashtun majority block would emerge, upon which the executive could rely upon for legislative support. While the system did indeed serve to fragment opposition and retard the emergence of new parties it also fragmented the president's Pashtun base and translated a majority of popular support in the presidential election into only around one-third of a parliamentary block predisposed to support the president's agenda.

As predicted, the new Wolesi Jirga has already shown itself to be a place of wheeling and dealing, of clientelism and shifting alliances, and an arena where men with tainted pasts hold significant sway over the future. Liberal democratic and progressive new parties were faced with high hurdles to get their messages across and candidates elected. As a result, many of the hopes for moderation and non-violent change are now vested in the 68 women MPs who are less tied to transitional patterns of commander or clan parochialism.

The SNTV electoral system came about by a path of muddled missteps and was a disservice to the millions of Afghans who deserved a clear and transparent tool to craft their first truly democratic parliament. If the system is retained for subsequent elections there is every reason to believe that the fragmentation and parochialism of the legislature will grow and politics will continue to be detached from the masses. SNTV in Afghanistan is destined to reinforce incumbents who strong arm and bribe their way into office. If the reserved women's seats are ever abolished, the space for democrats would be even further constrained. No electoral system can ever transform an illiberal polity to representative democracy without a raft of supporting social, economic and institutional transformations. But it is also true that an appropriately crafted system of proportional representation might encourage the emergence of new political parties and avoid the great anomalies that were so apparent in the Wolesi Jirga elections of 2005.

The Prospects for Democratic Stability

First and foremost the prospects for democratization and political stability in Afghanistan hinge upon much more than just the political institutions. The demobilization of private militias, significant infrastructure development and schooling, and a breaking of the political-elite dependence on drug money will go some way to ensuring that democratic electoral competition is the paramount mechanism for making decisions and resolving conflicts in the new Afghanistan. But the specifics of the political game set up by the current constitution will shape the new state in significant and perhaps dramatic ways.

What are the likely outcomes of the political arrangements described in this chapter? In the short term President Karzai will face a popularly elected legislature which, while not powerful, will carry democratic legitimacy and irritant power. The SNTV electoral system in conjunction with the inchoate party system and lack of a "Karzai organization" on the ground means that the new Wolesi Jirga is likely to be highly fragmented with a few organized "warlord" type parties and a gaggle of independents. These independents might coalesce around the power and patronage of the presidency and provide Karzai with enough legislative votes to sweep away opposition (i.e., the Jordanian parliamentary dynamic). Conversely, they may form satellites of Islamic fundamentalism, regional militia blocks (the Northern Alliance), and ethnic wedges which are only united in their desire to extract as much as possible from Kabul and make Karzai's life as difficult as possible. The highly centralized nature of the state makes the national allocation of power the only game in town and as such majorities and minorities will focus their efforts to win favor there.

Are the arrangements found in the new constitution the best arrangements? They may not have been the "best" if one had conducted a proper diagnosis of what ails Afghanistan and prescribed a holistic package of institutional medicines but they were perhaps predictable. De jure power now rests largely in the hands of one man but de facto power is much more complex and the recognition of that reality is the informal executive and economic power sharing exemplified by the president's continuing need and willingness to include some of the most powerful warlords and ethnic entrepreneurs in his cabinet and ranks of governors. The question becomes: is this de facto power sharing relationship between the elected but weak and the unelected but strong the best way to grow popular support for democracy and legitimize the state in the eyes of regular Afghans? Is it the best way to nurture the various strands of a vibrant civil society and encourage democratic and robust political parties? If not, then what would be or would have been better?

Even a cursory exam of the patient suggests that a federal system of decentralized but accountable power is key to the chances of incorporating democratic elements outside of the capital. As Goodson argues, a symmetrical, multiethnic form of federalism bolstered by local structures was a much better option than buying-off provincial warlords in back room deals.[13] Indeed, there are difficulties in decentralizing power without reducing the country to a patchwork of regional fiefdoms[14] but the alternative is an unaccountable pact behind a smoke screen of "minority inclusion." Perhaps what is needed are more formal power-sharing arrangements at the executive level using Swiss-type regional movements as proxies for ethnic interests, but at the same time leaving space for those identifiers to break down and multiethnic movements to emerge, compete for, and share power. It is also apparent that a stronger legislature, one not so controlled by the executive, might be a crucial constraint on any president bent on domination. The historical precedent of Afghan leaders possessed of too much self belief, too much de jure power, but not enough legitimacy or humility to recognize the limits of their mandate to govern is not good.

Notes

1. Larry Goodson, "Afghanistan's Long Road to Reconstruction," *Journal of Democracy,* vol. 14, no. 1 (2003): 83.

2. Ibid., 94.

3. Andrew Reynolds and Andrew Wilder, *Free, Fair or Flawed: Challenges for Legitimate Elections in Afghanistan* (Kabul: Afghanistan Research and Evaluation Unit, 2004).

4. For a discussion of how Afghanistan ended up with SNTV, see Reynolds, "The Curious Case of Afghanistan," *Journal of Democracy,* vol. 17, no. 2 (April 2006): 104–117.

5. Hussein believed that limiting a voter to a single vote in a multi-member constituency would injure the capacity of the Muslim Brotherhood to win seats. Subsequent elections gave some credence to this notion. See Andrew Reynolds and Jorgen Elklit, "Jordan: Electoral System Design in the Arab World," *The International IDEA Handbook of Electoral System Design* (Stockholm: International IDEA, 1997), 53–54.

6. Formerly the Director of the Afghan Research and Evaluation Unit, based in Kabul.

7. Reynolds and Wilder, *Free, Fair or Flawed.*

8. The memo was solicited by Zalmay Rassoul, the National Security Minister, and was discussed with Dr. Amin Farhang, Minister of Reconstruction, and Ashraf Ghani, Finance Minister, before reaching President Karzai.

9. Andrew Wilder, *The 2005 Elections in Afghanistan: Case Studies from Herat and Kandahar* (Kabul: Afghanistan Research and Evaluation Unit, 2006), http://www.areu.org.af/publications/A%20House%20Divided.pdf.

10. Candidates were given a choice of three symbols drawn at random. These included representations of animals, forms of transport, cell phones, oil rigs, and weather patterns. Thirty-five MPs were elected with animal symbols (with birds leading the way with 16); 32 won with planes, trains, automobiles (including bizarrely four boats in this land-locked nation); while there were 14 fruit and vegetable MPs.

11. See http://www.tcf.org/afghanistanwatch/charneyresearchpoll.pdf.

12. See Wilder, *The 2005 Elections in Afghanistan.*

13. Larry Goodson, "Afghanistan's Long Road to Reconstruction," 89.

14. Ibid., 91.

4

A Third Branch?: (Re)establishing the Judicial System in Afghanistan

J Alexander Thier

TWO EVENTS ILLUSTRATE THE CHALLENGES in establishing a competent, independent and accountable judiciary in Afghanistan. Only ten days after the close of Afghanistan's Constitutional Convention, Afghanistan's Supreme Court violated the word and spirit of Afghanistan's new constitution. Without any case before the court, and based on no existing law, the court declared on January 14, 2004 that a performance by the Afghan pop singer Salma on Kabul television was un-Islamic and therefore illegal. The video featuring the modestly dressed Afghan woman singing about rural life was recorded in the 1970s. "We are opposed to women singing and dancing as a whole and it has to be stopped," said then Deputy Chief Justice Fazl Ahmad Manawi.[1] This ruling was consistent with past behavior of the court and its chief justice, Mawlavi Fazl Hadi Shinwari, an Islamic fundamentalist and former head of a religious school, or madrassa, in Peshawar, Pakistan. Shinwari also tried to ban cable television and coeducation using similar tactics.

Although appointed by former President Burhanuddin Rabbani in the chaos that gripped Kabul in fall 2001, Mr. Karzai kept Justice Shinwari on the bench, giving him virtually unchecked appointment powers, until his reappointment to the court was rejected by the new Afghan parliament in the spring of 2006. The five year reign of Shinwari marred attempts at legal, professional and administrative reform of the judiciary. Shinwari put scores of unqualified mullahs on the bench at all levels, and created a "fatwa council" in the Supreme Court to issue religious edicts—an entity with no legal basis. Shinwari, who was simultaneously the head of Afghanistan's Ulema Council, a quasi-official national council of religious leaders, represented a deep threat to the integrity of the Afghan judicial system by imposing fundamentalist interpretations of the Koran rather than enforcing Afghan law.

The second story concerns the travails of the chief justice of the Provincial Court of Herat, Mullah Khodaadad. As chief justice of the courts in Herat, Mullah Khodaadad labored under the heavy-handed rule of Ismael Khan, the de facto ruler of western Afghanistan until mid-2004. In 2002, Khodaadad described a murder case in an outlying village wherein the alleged perpetrator was convicted by the eyewitness testimony of several villagers. Two days after his conviction, the convicted was released by order of Ismael Khan. Khodaadad complained of intimidation and the lack of independence. In 2003, Khodadaad was hit by a car, an act many suspected was political violence for his allegiance to the central government. Then, factional fighting erupted in Herat in March 2004 during which Ismael Khan's son, a central government minister, was killed and the central government appointed military commander chased out of the province. Following the fighting, supporters of Ismael Khan burned down Khodaadad's house.

Afghanistan is, for the moment, set on a course of nation-building that promises to create security, government and the rule of law. Its new constitution creates a blueprint for a modern Islamic state, replete with a powerful central government; checks and balances between its president, bi-cameral legislature and independent judiciary; neat administrative boundaries and elected provincial councils. A national army and national police force will provide security, with a courthouse in every district to enforce the law and protect citizens' rights. The problem, of course, is that none of these things yet exists.

Reestablishing a legitimate justice system in this context presents enormous, if not insurmountable, challenges. Every aspect of the picture of a functioning judiciary is presently absent. There are few buildings to house judges, prosecutors, attorneys, police and prisoners. There are equally few skilled professionals to fill the buildings. There is no communications infrastructure or libraries, and few files. It remains unclear which laws are in force—but even those approved by Kabul are not in the hands of officials in the provinces. Fundamentally, a political culture that respects the rule of law is also missing.

There have been important advances, however, with the support of the international community. In 2006, the entire Supreme Court was replaced through the legislative approval process required in the Afghan constitution. Shinwari's successor, Chief Justice Abdulsalam Azimi, is known as a thoughtful and moderate jurist with strong Islamic legal credentials who came out strongly in favor of reform and anti-corruption efforts at his inauguration. And Ismael Khan was ultimately removed from his governorship in Herat (and made a minister in Kabul), somewhat reducing his ability to influence events there. Such changes at the top are important, but progress on governance and the rule of law throughout the country remains slow. Although in both cases their power has been diminished, the likes of Shinwari and Ismael Khan remain the rule, rather than the exception.

This chapter first discusses the broader political situation in Afghanistan, including ongoing security issues and the status of state institutions. It then focuses specifically on the state of the judiciary, and its legal and historical underpinnings. Finally, the chapter addresses the key challenges in building a justice system in Afghanistan and the role of the international community in this process.

Security and State-Building in Afghanistan

The international community is making a significant investment in the future of Afghanistan.[2] Over five years into the intervention there, the return on investment is much less than what it should be. The primary reason is continued insecurity throughout the country, and failure to deliver good governance. As a result, support among Afghans for the Karzai government and the international presence in the country have waned and the forces opposed to the international intervention and the government in Kabul have been emboldened.

Building functioning, legitimate and accountable state institutions is essential to reestablishing a stable and prosperous Afghanistan. These institutions must exist at the central, provincial and local government level. At present, there is not a coherent set of institutions functioning in Afghanistan that is able to meet the basic requirements of a state: to provide security, to enforce the law, to deliver services. The Afghan government lacks the personnel and physical infrastructure needed to carry out these functions. The US and its partners are working with the government to develop national institutions, and to weaken those elements that challenge the primacy of the state. However, insecurity is the greatest impediment to the successful creation of a state apparatus in Afghanistan.

Political and security control of most of Afghanistan remains atomized, with political, military and economic resources in the hands of regional power brokers, commanders and a nominally pro-government bureaucracy. Acts of terrorism and attacks against international military forces and the Afghan government by anti-government forces remain a daily reality. Much of the country, including key ministries in Kabul, remains under the sway of volatile factional forces. Despite pro-government rhetoric, these forces continue to undermine stability, acting with impunity and contempt for the government and its international backers. Many areas are simply not safe enough for Afghan and international officials to carry out their duties. These setbacks are also expensive, creating "insecurity inflation" for reconstruction projects. At the same time, Afghan citizens are unable to organize or freely participate in activities required to recreate a functioning, representative political system. Confidence in government and the rule of law requires that discrete daily interactions between citizen and state are secure. Until key areas throughout the country are made secure, the state-building project in Afghanistan will continue to founder.

The State of the State

There is dramatic difference between the legal structure of the government and de facto authority throughout the country. The current legal structure of the government is derived from the new constitution ratified in January 2004. Under this arrangement, Afghanistan is a highly centralized state. The government in Kabul consists of an executive, a legislature, a judiciary and several quasi-independent national commissions, including the Civil Service Commission and the Human Rights Commission. The executive comprises the offices of the president and at least 26 ministries. The military and police forces of the country are under the command of the Ministries of Defense and Interior, respectively. The judiciary is an independent branch controlled by the Supreme Court, and the legislature is comprised of two houses, the Wolesi Jirga, or house of the people, and the Meshrano Jirga, or house of elders. The 34 provinces that make up the country are administrative subdivisions of the central state, with no independent political or legislative authority. Provincial governors are appointed by the president, and most government staff in the provinces are directly subject to the line authority of the central government ministry for whom they work. Each province is subdivided into districts, which are governed under the same basic set up.

In reality, political, military and administrative control of the existing government apparatus is highly atomized. Thirty years of upheaval and war has fractured control of the remaining government infrastructure. Significant strides in institution-building were made in the mid-twentieth century, but the government in Kabul was never able to fully penetrate the rural areas. Central government and provincial institutions were slowly built and a trained civil service implemented programs and maintained order in major towns. Traditional leadership structures often controlled decision making in more isolated regions and tribal areas. Following the 1979 Soviet invasion, central government control quickly receded to Kabul and key regional centers. Throughout the countryside, resistance groups destabilized the central government and governed their most secure areas.

Following the collapse of the Soviet-backed government in 1992, the mujahideen parties and renegade government militias took over, dividing the country into a series of autonomously-governed warring fiefdoms. During this period, the state apparatus was divided among the regions. During the Taliban period, the role of remaining government offices and international assistance diminished. Taliban authority was largely focused on imposing order, and did little otherwise to govern.

When Taliban authority receded throughout the country in late 2001, an array of factions and local leadership structures reassumed control of the countryside. Several of these factions, notably Jamiat-i-Islami (Rabbani/Ismael Khan), the Shura-i-Nizar (Masood/Fahim), Hezb-i-Wahadat (Khalili/Akbari), and Jumbish-i-Milli (Dostum) relied on long-standing organizational structures and foreign support to retake their previous domains. Some areas, especially in the south and east, were controlled by local ruling councils, a combination of tribal leaders and militia commanders. In most cases, authority relies upon a loose confederation of military commanders whose allegiance to higher authority is proportional to the strength of the regional power broker. The factional leadership once again assumed control of existing administrative, financial and military resources in their areas of operation. Military and police, the civil service, customs and taxation, and relations with foreign powers are the primary tools of state control. So long as these tools remain outside of the definitive control of a unified government, the government will lack legitimacy and remain at risk.

The Security Situation

Afghanistan is facing three interrelated security problems: 1) the Taliban, Al Qaeda and their supporters; 2) factional militias; and 3) drug traffickers and other criminal elements. Each presents pernicious security and governance problems, hindering state formation and extending the need for international military forces for years. Each relies on support from external state and non-state actors. Without the continued presence of international military forces, these elements of insecurity could destabilize the fragile balance that prevents an increase in warfare. The status quo, however, also presents hurdles to progress. Confidence in government and rule of law are based on discrete, daily interactions between citizens and the state. So long as impunity goes unchecked, citizens, civil servants and politicians will continue to serve military, rather than legal authority.

Most critically, all three elements creating insecurity have a longer-term view of their involvement in Afghanistan than the international community. Afghanistan has been through five significant regime changes in the last 30 years, all supported to some extent by external forces. Based on past experience, Afghan factions and civilians have little reason to believe that the current government or its international backers will be around forever. It is critical for the US and its partners to realize that the role of foreign actors in the last 30 years of conflict has created enormous distrust of the stated intentions of those foreign actors. The Soviet invasion, the US abandonment of Afghanistan following the collapse of the Soviet Union, the civil war supported by countries in the region, the Pakistani backed Taliban, and Al Qaeda have all demonstrated that foreign intervention serves the interests of foreign backers, not of the vast majority of Afghans. There is already a strong belief among Afghans that the US presence serves some broader US interest to control the region, oil and Islam. Furthermore, having experienced 30 years of deliberate disinformation campaigns, the Afghans have little cause to believe information provided by any party. Thus, the only valid means of convincing Afghans of the intentions of the government and its foreign backers is to physically demonstrate those intentions—through the provision of security, aid and successful representative politics.

The Judicial System

Afghanistan has a mixed civil law and sharia-based formal legal system. This system has emerged and evolved in the last 120 years, since the creation of the bureaucratic state. The state legal system interacts with a deeply-rooted system of customary law and practices. This non-state system is comprised of tribal custom and "folk sharia"—local conceptions of Islamic law. These three bodies of law—state law, sharia law and customary law—overlap in subject matter, and each provides challenges of implementation for the other two.[3] Due to the significance of the sharia in both the state and non-state systems, the clergy straddles both.

Historical Overview

From the 1880s until the 1960s, Afghanistan essentially had a dual judicial system. A system of sharia courts headed by clergy handled areas of law such as criminal law, family and personal law laid down in the sharia. A separate system of government courts handled state law issues, such as those relating to commerce, taxation and civil servants. As the body of state law grew, so did the writ of the state courts, until competition emerged as the courts battled over substantive jurisdiction.

In 1963, the long-serving King Zahir began a process of reform intended to democratize Afghanistan by increasing the power of the elected government, establishing separation of powers between the branches of government, and reducing the role of the monarch and royal family in the affairs of state. In 1964, a new constitution that had been drafted and debated over a year was ratified by a Loya Jirga.

The new constitution made three significant changes to the judicial system. First, Article 97 declared the judiciary an "independent organ of the State" which "discharges its duties side by side with the Legislative and Executive Organs." Second, the constitution created a unified judicial system, assembling the disparate parts of the old system into one hierarchical structure with a Supreme Court at its apex. Third, the constitution created a unified system of laws. For the first time, the constitution and statutes created under the constitution were legally dominant. The basic principles of the sharia were to serve as a guide to the legislature, but the judiciary was proscribed from applying the sharia except when "no provision exists in the Constitution or the laws for a case under consideration."[4] Even then, judges were only required to follow the basic principles of Hanafi jurisprudence.[5]

These reforms created a model for a secular court system. However, several things stood in the way. Most judges in the legal system were trained in the sharia, not in Afghan law and procedure. There was also a dearth of attorneys. In order to rectify this problem, the law faculty at Kabul University was improved, and competitive exams introduced for entrance into the judicial civil service. In 1968, a judicial training program was initiated which required new judges to take an additional year of practical coursework and training in the judicial system. In a few years, the ranks of the judiciary, even at the highest levels, had shifted in favor of those with formal training in state laws and the legal system. In the late 1960s, the Afghan legal community consisted of about 1,200 people, of which 715 were judges, 170 prosecutors and 100 lawyers.[6]

The legal system also required significant codification in order to occupy the field of applicable law with state law. From the mid-1960s to the mid-1970s a codification drive bore fruit. New comprehensive codes of criminal law, criminal procedure and civil law were passed, as well as laws pertaining to civil servants, taxation and investment. Unfortunately, these laws were passed almost exclusively by decree. In 1973, the cousin of King Zahir, Daoud, overthrew the king and declared Afghanistan a republic. Afghanistan's fledgling democracy was nipped in the bud, with the newly established parliament dismissed, and executive control over the judiciary restored. During Daoud's reign, the project of secularization was pushed forward, and the penetration of the courts into the countryside was strengthened by the backing of the autocratic executive. The role of the court as a check against state authority, however, was eliminated.

The structure of the court system was determined by the 1967 Law of the Jurisdiction and Organization of the Courts. This law lays out a four-tiered system of courts: a Supreme Court, a Central High Court of Appeals, Provincial Courts, and Primary Courts at the district level. Within these courts, there are specialized benches to handle different areas of law such as criminal law, civil law, personal law and commercial law. The 1967 law has largely remained in force until 2005, when a new law on the Organization of the Courts was passed by decree. The 2005 law eliminated the national Court of Appeals, vesting all appellate authority into the Provincial Courts and the Supreme Court.

The Supreme Court of Afghanistan has had an unusual structure. The highest court, composed of nine constitutionally mandated justices, is the managerial body for the court system, also known as the Supreme Council of the Judiciary. This body has very few judicial responsibilities, for example deciding questions of jurisdiction, venue, extradition, impeachment and the constitutionality of laws.[7] Actual appellate review of most cases before the court is conducted by the relevant diwan, or bench, on the Supreme Court. These benches, also referred to as the courts of cassation, are each headed by one of the Supreme Court justices and peopled with at least four other judges. The diwans of the Supreme Court can only review the law, and not the facts, with which the case is concerned.

The Current Judicial System

The Bonn Agreement reinstated those provisions of the 1964 constitution pertaining to the judiciary. By law, Afghanistan's judicial system during the two-year transitional period to a new constitution was largely the system created in the New Democracy period between 1964 and 1973. In fact, the judicial system was not reestablished as a system during this period. Lacking infrastructure, trained personnel and a clear body of applicable law, the semi-functioning courts remained quasi-independent, subject to local authority. Following the passage of the 2004 constitution, little has changed in theory or practice.

The court system was led by Fazl Hady Shinwari, the former head of a madrassa in Peshawar, and an ally of the Saudi-backed fundamentalist militia leader Abdur Rassool Sayyaf. Under his guidance the court appointed scores of non-university trained Muslim clerics to all levels of the court system. Shinwari has failed to follow both the 1964 constitution and the 2004 constitution as well as applicable laws, exceeding the constitutionally-allowed number of judges on the Supreme Court and creating a fatwa council to issue extra-judicial religious proclamations.[8] Shinwari attempted to interfere with the first-ever presidential elections in 2004 by declaring a speech by one candidate on divorce and inheritance laws "blasphemy."

In 2006, the new parliament rejected President Karzai's attempt to re-appoint Shinwari as the Chief Justice of the Supreme Court under the new constitution. Instead, Professor Adbulsalam Azimi was appointed and approved. Azimi, a former rector of Kabul University and professor on the Shari'a faculty, served as deputy chair of the Constitutional Commission from 2002–2003, and was the primary drafter of the document. Along with Azimi, appointments included the highly regarded Bahauddin Baha, former chairman of the Judicial Reform Commission and a judge for many years, and Omar Babrakzai, a scholar on customary law issues and the former deputy minister of Tribal Affairs. The top tier of the court was replaced, overall, by professional and moderate justices, who inherited a deeply dysfunctional court, with a backlog of thousands of cases, and a national system in shambles.

The court has limited administrative authority in the provinces, and has even less "legal" authority in the sense that it does not cast a legalistic or intellectual shadow over the judiciary as a whole. Most judges have not received training or legal materials to help them in their work. Interviews with judges throughout the country show that they do not have books indicating the applicable law, nor do they apply those laws even where they do have access.

The other institutions of the legal system include the Ministry of Justice, the Office of the Prosecutor General, and the short-lived Judicial Reform Commission that had been mandated by the Bonn process. Relations between these institutions have been quixotic at best and hostile at worst. The Ministry of Justice—the preeminent legal institution under past regimes—has lost its authority and prestige. The power of prosecution was removed from the ministry under communist rule and placed into the hands of the prosecutor general. This change was made permanent under the 2004 constitution. Relations between the offices were acrimonious and ideological and factions divisions also pervaded the relationship between the ministry and the Supreme Court. However, the Minister of Justice was replaced following Karzai's inauguration in 2004. The new minister, Sarwar Danish, is a Shia scholar who had served on the Constitutional Commission. In 2006, a new attorney general was appointed as well. Abdul Jabbar Sabit, a conservative former Hezb-i-Islami (Gulbuddin) supporter who had been living in Canada, returned to serve first as legal advisor to the minister of the interior where he worked on the reestablishment of the vice and virtue squads that had made the Taliban infamous. His appointment, initially met with skepticism, was welcomed when he launched an ambitious anticorruption platform that seemed willing to take on powerful figures. However, strong-arm tactics, such as a raid on the independent Tolo Television in early 2007 for allegedly misquoting him, has caused some to question his commitment to the rule of law, if not his zeal for the job.

In 2002, the first step towards reconsolidation in the justice sector was for the government to appoint a judicial commission, as required by the Bonn Agreement, "to rebuild the domestic justice system in accordance with Islamic principles, international standards, the rule of law and Afghan legal traditions."[9] A 16-member independent judicial commission was formally established in May 2002. It was, however, dissolved four months later. Political tension among members, the lack of a clear agenda and the impression of undue conservatism among some in the Afghan Transitional Administration seem to be the main reasons for the dissolution of this body. There was reportedly strong competition and recrimination between the Ministry of Justice and the Supreme Court, as both wanted to control the appointment of judges, and the Ministry of Justice wanted to control the attorney general's office. As a result of the heavy involvement of these two entities, the commission was reportedly not sufficiently independent of the government to be effective.[10]

In November 2002, a second commission was appointed by decree.[11] This commission, renamed the Judicial Reform Commission, included a diverse and well-credentialed membership—professional rather than partisan. The commissioners included three former Supreme Court justices, one former minister of justice, two former attorneys general, and four law professors. They were drawn from each of the key institutions in the justice sector in an attempt to balance interests. Despite the high quality and relative non-partisanship of the commission, it was born into a rancorous environment. The commission was accused of being too fundamentalist, too liberal, of being composed only of Afghans living abroad, of being controlled by one ethnic group or another. In truth, the members spanned the spectrum from conservative to liberal, and while several had been outside the country for some years, most had served in various Afghan government regimes over the past 40 years. The most accurate criticisms of the commission membership (and its senior staff) are that they lacked modern management skills, and that they possessed a typical Kabul-centric view of Afghanistan.

The new constitution has largely left the 1964 constitutional structure of the judiciary in tact, with one significant additional power: the explicit grant of the power of judicial review to the Supreme Court. Article 121 states that the "Supreme Court on the request of the Government or the Courts shall review the laws, legislative decrees, international treaties and international covenants for their compliance with the Constitution and provide their interpretation in accordance with the law." When read together with Article 3 of the constitution which requires that "no law can be contrary to the beliefs and provisions of the sacred religion of Islam," the court has the power to strike down laws and treaties on the basis that they are contrary to the "provisions" of Islam.[12] While it is important that there are clear constitutional means to resolve questions of Islamic interpretation that impact the legal system, in the wrong hands such authority can create a grave danger in that an unelected body of clerics can overturn laws produced through the democratic process, as with the infamous Council of Guardians in Iran.

Significant aspects of the structure and jurisdiction of the judiciary under the new constitution are in flux. Under the new court organization law, the Supreme Court should wield greater judicial powers. The Central High Court of Appeals has been eliminated altogether, placing a greater review burden on the Supreme Court. The system has been streamlined into three tiers, and an expanded primary court will be placed in every provincial center so that all claims are first heard at the district primary court level, and that the provincial courts will only function as courts of appeals.

The Question of Applicable Law

Applicable law in Afghanistan is difficult to determine due to the numerous regime changes since 1964. A new constitution in 1964 was superseded by new constitutions or basic laws in 1977, 1980, 1987, 1990 and 1992 (proposed). Each of these regimes passed laws. The Bonn Agreement also recognized all existing law and regulations, "to the extent that they are not inconsistent with this agreement or with international legal obligations[.]" Some laws, especially from the Taliban era, were clearly inconsistent with these requirements. However, many of the laws passed over the years of upheaval are inconsistent with each other, but not with the constitution, international law or the Bonn Agreement. Between 2002 and 2006 when the parliament was seated, the Karzai Administration passed dozens of decrees, some making major adjustments to the legal system. This spate of law making did not have a comprehensive approach, and gaps and uncertainties remain. Thus far, the new parliament has undertaken little actual legislating, and the system of formulating laws is beset by legal confusion as well as competition between the executive and the legislature.

In addition to the lack of clarity about the controlling law, many judges do not have access to legal texts and/or simply apply their version of sharia law to many disputes. Under Afghan law, the application of sharia has been allowed only in a very narrow segment of cases when no Afghan law exists. The current application of sharia, however, extends to many areas covered by Afghan law. Uncertainty about what constitutes applicable law may explain part of this, but also seems to stem from training and orientation rather than from confusion about applicable law. In effect, the judiciary does not have access to laws at present due to a lack of education and materials.

The Non-State Legal System[13]

Afghanistan has a rich and layered legal history. Its closely-knit, autonomous social cultures have produced a variegated system of customary law administered by village elders and tribal councils. This system functions not only to decide specific claims, but to resolve disputes and maintain harmony within the community. For decades, the state and non-state systems co-existed, gradually converging over time. Although the state system began to crowd out the informal system in certain sectors, limited penetration by the Afghan central government into the daily life of rural Afghans meant that both systems functioned robustly. However, beginning in the late 1970s, armed conflict and frequent regime change sent both systems off their rails. The formal system, illegitimate and bankrupt, ceased to serve most of the population, and ceased to satisfy those it served. The informal system expanded to fill the void, but spun out of control as social and power relations mutated with the conflict.

The new government in Kabul, with significant international assistance, is attempting to rebuild Afghanistan's formal justice system as a critical pillar in the effort to establish the rule of law there. In the countryside, however, non-state dispute resolution mechanisms remain dominant. Most Afghans do not have access to state justice institutions. Those who do have access rarely choose to use it. Rather, they rely on a mixture of tradition, Islamic law and current power relations to resolve disputes. The outcomes produced by the informal system are far from ideal, but they remain both more available and more legitimate than what the state system has to offer.

At present, the formal and informal systems coexist in Afghanistan but without official sanction or mutual recognition. At the national level, the state judicial system is attempting to expand its authority and has failed to recognize the dominant position of the informal system. However, at the local level the courts frequently refer litigants to customary forums to resolve disputes from inheritance disputes to murder. This reliance by local officials on the informal system is a result of the incapacity of the state, and recognition that conflicts can only be truly resolved in the rural Afghan context through community based processes. Actors in the informal system similarly deny recognition to the state mechanisms, keeping disputes under the government radar and out of the courts. However, Afghans utilize the existence of the state courts both as a tool of coercion for those reluctant to settle disputes through traditional forums, or as a place to record decisions made through customary processes.

This period of flux creates opportunity as well as danger. The robustness of the informal system could be harnessed to improve dispute resolution and increase the capacity of the state to maintain order and ensure fairness. The formal justice system will take years to build the necessary legitimacy and capacity to function effectively throughout the country. Its areas of comparative advantage are in urban areas, in criminal law, and in protecting citizens' rights. The strength of informal mechanisms is in their low cost, physical proximity to citizens, and ability to achieve consensus. A targeted series of programs including training, legal representation, liaison and monitoring could take advantage of the relative strengths of these systems and improve delivery of justice for all Afghans.

Prospects and Challenges

Reconstructing and reforming Afghanistan's devastated judicial system faces two fundamental challenges: 1) the deep political and socio-cultural impediments to establishing an effective judiciary; and 2) the incapacity or unwillingness of the Afghan government and the international community to implement effective programs. Although the second problem is more easily resolved, it is equally responsible for the failure to achieve any real success in the early years of post-Taliban reconstruction.

Judicial Independence and Judicial Responsibility

In Afghan history, there is neither practical experience with judicial independence in the state system, nor a political ethos to support it. The judiciary has been structurally independent, on paper, for a total of 11 years. In reality, it has never been independent in an institutional sense. Judicial independence is most clearly defined when the judiciary is needed to serve as a check against another government power. However, the judiciary has been seen as an extension of executive authority, not as an entity to challenge the authority. Thus far, the king or executive has held a trump in most cases, especially the important ones. There has been an ongoing struggle between the clergy-dominated judiciary and the executive over the application and codification of sharia. In the brief period between 1964 and 1973, the court system was only beginning to form as an independent entity, and never exercised challenges to executive or legislative authority, such as judicial review of a law. In the one case in the early seventies that might have tested this power—a dispute between the legislature and the executive concerning budgetary authority—the king intervened and the dispute was resolved.

The barriers to judicial independence seem to have political and religious rationales as well. The head of an Islamic state has the duty to administer the sharia, and is therefore the highest judicial authority under Islam. The head of state delegates judicial jurisdiction, *wilaya,* to the *qazi,* who then administers justice. This jurisdiction can be also removed. Therefore, "a consequence of the doctrine of *wilaya* in Islam is total lack of separation between the judicial and executive powers."[14]

Judicial responsibility is an equally critical element of a functioning judiciary. Judges must also be the faithful and neutral arbiters of the law. They must know the law, respect it despite personal misgivings, and apply it fairly. At present, Afghanistan's judiciary enjoys a degree of independence at the central level due to the weakness of the executive authority—but judicial responsibility has been gravely lacking. The judiciary has had a free hand with appointments, and has challenged executive policy through use of extra-judicial pronouncements on the legality of activities it deems un-Islamic. This judicial activism is in line with the long-term struggle by the clergy to dominate the judiciary and the application and interpretation of law. The lack of religious credentials among President Karzai and many in his Transitional Administration left the government open to potentially damning charges that they are not sufficiently Islamic. The fundamentalist groups jockeying for power in the post-Taliban political landscape seized upon the judiciary as an institution they could control and use as a pulpit. However in the countryside, judges complain of constant pressure from local power holders to conform to their will, regardless of the law. For example, the chief judges of the provincial courts of Herat and Nangrahar both complained of convicted criminals being released at the whim of local and regional power brokers in 2002.[15] As discussed above, the chief judge of Herat has been the target of violence. The new chief justice and his associate justices represent a break from these trends. Chief Justice Azimi was legal adviser to Karzai, and has a strong working relationship with the executive. At the same time, he has emphasized professionalism in the judiciary as a critical element of its reform. Finally, the current court has yet to wade into difficult political issues of Islamic interpretation, perhaps a sign of much needed restraint on the court in this area.

Creating an independent and responsible judiciary, as required by Afghanistan's new constitution, is a process likely to take decades. The judiciary must begin a long battle for legitimacy, for only once it is trusted as a non-partisan institution will it have the support to become genuinely independent. This requires creating systems of oversight and transparency. Judicial procedures and decisions must be clear, public and based on law. Fundamentally, this process requires judicial leaders who share this vision. International support to legal education and bureaucratic management now will help pave the way for a better system in the future. Although such contributions will not ensure success, the failure to provide them virtually ensures failure.

Reconstruction

International aid to the justice sector in Afghanistan was largely dysfunctional for the first few years of the post-Taliban era. The dysfunction was not for lack of a strategic plan—significant effort has been made to view the sector as a whole and to establish the coordinating bodies and mechanisms to implement that strategy. Rather, implementation has been piecemeal at best owing to rivalries, limited resources and poor coordination of Afghan actors and donors.

The need for a coordination mechanism for reconstruction of the judicial system was foreseen even in the harried days of the Bonn Agreement. Establishing the rule of law—ultimately the keystone of the agreement's framework—requires a judicial system that can protect rights and correct wrongs. The Judicial Reform Commission (JRC), as described above, was conceived to "rebuild the domestic justice system." In its founding decree, the commission was given an expansive mandate, and the first task of the commission and its partners was to develop a program for implementation. The Government of Italy agreed in April 2002 to take the lead in strengthening the judicial and penal systems and administration of justice. As lead nation, Italy was expected to take a lead in funding activities, raising funds from other donors, and aiding the Afghan authorities to coordinate activities in the sector.

Italy hosted a judicial summit in Rome in December 2002 to discuss overall plans for the sector. At this meeting, the key Afghan actors, including the Supreme Court and the Ministry of Justice, publicly agreed to the leadership of the JRC in the sector, and donors committed approximately $30 million to activities to rebuild the justice sector.[16] These commitments, however, remained vague, and it was up to the JRC to establish specific priorities and programs. With technical expertise from the Asia Foundation, funded by USAID, the JRC conducted consultations with all relevant actors and produced a Master Plan for the sector in January 2003. The Master Plan laid out proposed programs over the life of the commission, in four categories: Law Reform; Surveys, Physical Infrastructure, and Training; Legal Education and Awareness; and the Structure of Judicial Institutions. Within these categories, the Master Plan identified 30 individual projects to achieve objectives over an 18-month period.

Thus, in early 2003, with a clear Afghan authority, a lead donor, some initial pledges, and a strategic framework for initial rehabilitation, work was to begin. Almost immediately, these best laid plans began to go awry. The work on the Master Plan was hurried, and several important actors, especially the Supreme Court and the Government of Italy did not feel that they had sufficient opportunity to give input to the final draft. Particularly galling for the Italian embassy, which was funding the JRC salaries and offices, was that the plan had largely been written by American consultants. The Italian ambassador publicly welcomed the document in a coordination meeting hosted at their embassy, but in private they expressed their displeasure to the JRC leadership. The plan, however, was adopted by the JRC and approved by the Afghan government during the national budget process. Pressure by the embassy was seen as a threat to Afghan leadership in the sector.

These initially minor strains paled in comparison to the deep enmity between the Afghan institutions. Lack of capacity and severe divisions between the permanent Afghan justice sector institutions have made coordination of the sector impossible. The Judicial Reform Commission was mandated by President Karzai to coordinate law reform and reconstruction of the judicial system—a mandate that drew authority and control of foreign assistance away from the permanent institutions. The JRC was meant to set policy and priorities for the sector, and in practice, determine where donor funds would be directed. From the start, the JRC had neither the capacity, the funding, nor the political cover to undertake this significant task, nor to implement critical reforms. Without intervention from the presidency, a turf war between the Supreme Court, the Ministry of Justice, the Office of the Prosecutor General, and the JRC continued unabated. Eventually, the JRC was phased out and disbanded in 2005.

The vast majority of funding for activities in the justice sector has come from Italy, the United States and Germany. Italy has had a Justice Project, tied to the embassy and Cooperazione Italiana. This office is responsible for oversight of the Italian funded projects and for policy. For instance, this office established the Gardez Justice Project a justice sector rehabilitation project integrated with the US military presence in that region. The Italian Justice Project has also drafted a new interim criminal procedure law which it introduced through the Gardez Justice Project and Italian funded training programs. Italian funding has gone to several significant projects: training for judges and prosecutors undertaken primarily by the International Development Law Organization (IDLO); funding for the UN Development Programme (UNDP) to pay salaries and expenses of the Judicial Reform Commission and construct courts; funding to the UN Office on Drugs and Crime (UNODC) for prison construction; funding to rehabilitate the High Court of Appeals in Kabul; and funding to build a national judicial training center in Kabul.

The United States is contributing to the justice sector primarily through projects funded by USAID. These provided technical assistance to the Judicial Reform, Constitutional, and Human Rights Commissions, and then shifted focus to providing advisors to the Ministry of Justice, the Office of the Attorney General, and the Supreme Court and to providing training programs for judges and prosecutors. Most US projects have entailed seconding experts directly to Afghan government institutions. In receptive institutions, this has allowed a large impact, but has also created tension in those institutions less receptive to foreign experts. USAID has also engaged in a large building project, constructing or refurbishing over 30 provincial and district courthouses by 2006.

The UN Assistance Mission to Afghanistan (UNAMA) also supports the justice sector in an advisory capacity to the government, but has no implementation responsibilities. UNAMA has supplied corrections and civilian police experts to assist the prisons and police projects. UNAMA also has a growing rule of law section, but failed to fill key senior posts for the first several years. With increased staff, UNAMA has begun to fill the key coordinating role it was designed for, bringing together working groups under the various coordination structures of the Afghan government and the international community.

Individual foreign assistance projects have yielded results, but overall coordination and cooperation in the justice sector has been lacking. The disjointed Afghan leadership in the sector was exacerbated by weak coordination on the international side. The Italian government, the lead country, had maintained distance from the Afghan institutions. Rather than support Afghan-led decision making, the Italian effort often implemented its projects with limited consultation. JRC efforts to coordinate the sector without Italian support were unsuccessful, and the relationship between the JRC and the Government of Italy soured, leading to an Italian effort to have the commission disbanded altogether. With a new minister of justice and a new Italian ambassador for the justice sector, the coordination improved, but the sector has continued to suffer from the poor foundation of its early trials.

Similarly, USAID has been more interested in delivery of concrete assets, like buildings and numbers of individuals trained, than in establishing an institutional basis for the justice sector. US government funding has also been heavily focused on counter-narcotics, the agenda for which is driven far more by the US and UK than the Afghans. Factional tensions and competition for limited resources are an unvarying element of state-building work in post-conflict situations. Progress in difficult environments is essential to make use of the "easy" projects, such as new buildings—yet the fundamental work of institution-building often takes a backseat to concrete deliverables when funding decisions are made. Ultimately, the US and the UN, occupied with other issues such as the constitution, creation of a national army, road-building and disarmament, placed a low priority on reestablishing the judiciary, and no political capital was spent to put the sector on track.

Conclusion

Rebuilding Afghanistan's judiciary presents a conundrum found in many post-conflict situations. A functioning judicial system is crucial to creating a legitimate, stable government. Yet creating a competent judiciary takes many years, and therefore, tends not to get priority treatment in the immediate post-conflict period. True judicial reform has been delayed in Afghanistan. The work of the international community thus far has focused on providing band-aids to a thoroughly destroyed system.

The Afghan government and the international community must refocus their efforts to resurrect an integrated and effective justice system for Afghanistan. As time has passed and forces have become entrenched, this work has only become more difficult. At present, the real judicial system of Afghanistan is not the formal court system, but rather an informal system of tribal or village councils. These councils, a venerable Afghan tradition, have risen to fill the void, handling every sort of issue from property disputes to murders. Local traditional institutions provide a valuable service, and should be harnessed to improve the delivery of justice for Afghans throughout the country. But the work of establishing local and national institutions under legal government authority must also press ahead.

The work of rebuilding the judicial system must take place simultaneously at the national and local levels. At the national level, the permanent justice institutions are in serious need of both reform and resources. Programs must be introduced to systematize the courts, ensure merit-based advancement, and provide oversight. At the local level, assistance should focus on establishing "pockets of competence"—judicial institutions in key provincial and district centers that function properly. This limited number of locations should be resourced with proven staff, buildings and communications resources. Once functioning, these pockets would establish their legitimacy and draw in citizens from other districts. They could also liaise with traditional mechanisms to ensure that disputes resolved in those forums protect individual rights. Eventually, the number of pockets should increase as both demand and resources increase.

Afghanistan's devastated justice system has to be rebuilt brick by brick, judge by judge, prosecutor by prosecutor, cop by cop. Any plan which attempts to tackle everything at once is bound to fail, with limited resources dissipated rather than concentrated. Instead, long-term thinking must be coupled with short-term objectives to set the process in the right direction. This effort, however, will require a far more cooperative effort than the Afghans and the donors have yet been able to muster.

Notes

1. "Woman Singer Angers Afghan Judges," BBC News, 14 January 2004.

2. By the end of 2006, the US had spent an estimated $110 billion on military intervention, and more than $7 billion on humanitarian and development aid, the majority of which was spent on standing up Afghanistan's security forces in Afghanistan. The international community has spent an additional $7 billion on aid. For more information on aid commitments and disbursements, see "Analysis of Aid Flows to Afghanistan," available at http://www.af, and reports of the Congressional Research Service.

3. A book written in 1900 states: "The law of Afghanistan in the present day [1900] may be easily placed under three headings; (1) those of Islam; (2) those of the Amir, which are based upon Islamic laws, the opinions of the people, and the Amir's own personal views and ideas; (3) Customary laws of the various tribes. In all criminal and political cases, practically the chief part of the law has been made by the Amir, and so in cases as to the Government revenue. But the rest, Islamic law is the general rule. Thus very little is left to custom." Sultan Muhammad Khan, *The Constitution and Laws of Afghanistan,* 1900, cited in Amin Tarzi, "The Judicial State: Evolution and Centralization of the Courts in Afghanistan, 1883–1896" (Ph.D. diss., New York University, 2003), 173.

4. Constitution of Afghanistan, 1964, Art. 102.

5. See Mohammad Hashim Kamali, *Law in Afghanistan* (Leiden: E. J. Brill, 1985). Kamali argues that the primary purpose of this reform was not to deviate from the sharia, but rather to improve the "legality" of the system. Kamali believes that the changes in the system were made to ensure that people could not be deprived of fundamental rights due to the indeterminacy of the sharia. Such indeterminacy violates the notion, first articulated in the 1789 French Rights of Man, that no act can be a crime unless a law exists at the time criminalizing the act—a principle also known by the Latin *nullen crimen sine lege.* See Kamali, 21.

6. Kamali, *Law in Afghanistan,* 207.

7. Research thus far has failed to unearth a single case since 1967 in which the Supreme Court has exercised the powers of "judicial" or constitutional review—"abstaining from the application of laws repugnant to the provisions of the Constitution"—granted in the 1967 law.

8. Shinwari's Supreme Court has attempted to ban cable television, coeducation and women singing on television, not by ruling on a case before the court, by rather by simply declaring them "un-Islamic."

9. Bonn Agreement, Art. II (2).

10. Chris Johnson, William Maley, J Alexander Thier, and Ali Wardak, "Afghanistan's Political and Constitutional Development" (London: Overseas Development Institute, 2003), 25. http://www.odi.org.uk/hpg/papers/evaluations/afghandfid.pdf.

11. The decree appointed ten members, including only one woman. Shortly thereafter, two additional members were added to improve the commission's ethnic and gender diversity.

12. "Beliefs and provisions of the sacred religion of Islam" replaced the far more general "basic principles of the sacred religion of Islam" which was the formulation in Article 64 of the 1964 constitution, and which was in the draft 2004 constitution until last-minute changes at the Loya Jirga. The use of "provisions" suggests an interpretative capacity based more on sharia and less on a shared and evolving notion of Islam's basic principles.

13. For an in-depth examination of the informal system in Afghanistan, and its relation to the formal sector, see Thomas Barfield, Neamat Nojumi, and J Alexander Thier, "The Clash of Two Goods: State and Non-State Dispute Resolution in Afghanistan" (Washington, DC: United States Institute of Peace, 2006). http://www.usip.org/ruleoflaw/projects/clash_two_goods.pdf.

14. Kamali, *Law in Afghanistan,* 209. This structural issue continues to limit Afghan perceptions of judicial independence. For example, a prominent member of the Afghan judicial establishment argues that non-Muslims cannot be judges in Afghanistan. The primary reason is not due to the need to apply sharia, but rather because the judge is an extension of the head of state, and the head of state has to be a Muslim according to the constitution, then the judge must also be a Muslim.

15. Interviews conducted by the author, September 2002.

16. Press Briefing by Manoel de Almeida e Silva, Spokesman for the Special Representative of the Secretary-General on Afghanistan, 26 January 2003.

Part II

Centralization Versus Decentralization

5

Centralization Versus Decentralization: The Importance of Sequencing and Timing

Rani D. Mullen

THE LONGER-TERM CENTER-PERIPHERY relationship in Afghanistan has still not been fully resolved. The Afghan people have made a decision in favor of a centralized or unitary state. But the advice, financial support and rhetoric of international actors—who are so crucial to democratic Afghanistan's functioning and survival—have tended to treat Afghanistan as if it were a decentralized state. In addition, the general debate on which system of government would better serve the unity and longevity of the country continues. The discussion on a decentralized versus centralized state is often conducted without reference to the complex historical and structural realities in Afghanistan and tends to disregard the lessons learned from similar attempts in the region and in other post-conflict countries. In the rush to implement development projects and show quick results on the ground, international donor agencies and governments (as well as the Afghan government) often resort to dogmatic statements on the pros and cons of a centralized or decentralized system. Declarations on the need to build a strong central government or the necessity of decentralization of some government functions to provincial governments are made based on the immediate issue at hand, rather than a holistic understanding of the overall needs of the country and what types of state structures have worked in other similar settings.

This chapter draws upon Afghanistan's complex history, emerging lessons from the centralization versus decentralization debate in other post-conflict countries, and decentralization experiments in other South Asian countries to argue that the issue of centralization versus decentralization in Afghanistan is not a zero sum game. Rather, it is an issue of sequencing and timing. In particular, given the recent resurgence of the Taliban and other forces trying to undermine the Afghan government, the priority should be on strengthening the central government so it has the ability and resources to successfully administer the state. Building up this capacity will help decrease the power of the local provincial administrators, who often still function in lieu of the central government. It will also help increase the badly needed legitimacy of the central government. However, this chapter does not advocate a sole focus on the strengthening of the central government, but rather a change in emphasis and timing.

While central government capacity and power grows, local government structures (as discussed in the chapter by Wilder and Lister) should not be neglected. Some resources need to be funneled toward building up existing structures of local and then provincial government, particularly over the medium- to longer-term. The issue here is also one of sequencing, with greater initial emphasis on the local rather than provincial level. Enhancing local capacity will facilitate the reach of the central government to the local level as well as communicate local needs and priorities—where service delivery matters most—to the central authorities. Building up democratically functioning local government systems in the Afghan provinces is essential, but without a functioning central government the flow of state government resources and programs to the local level will not be effective or efficient. In Afghanistan, centralization will need to occur before official decentralization can be attempted, but responsible local and provincial administrative structures should nevertheless be built up and professionalized to ensure overall functioning of the system. As capacity grows at the provincial and local levels, greater political and, eventually, fiscal decentralization should be discussed. In the longer term, Afghans might indeed decide to move towards a more decentralized state model. But for now Afghans have decided on a centralized system and the international community should support this decision.

Afghanistan has made great progress in building a path towards a more stable and democratically functioning country. However, as late as the summer of 2007, the central government in Kabul still lacked the power and capacity generally associated with strong and capable states. At the current, crucial juncture in the Afghan state-building process, it is essential to recognize that without such a state, there is no power to redistribute.

Afghanistan's History of Centralized Powers: In Name Only

Before delving into how the Afghan state has been organized historically, it is worth reflecting on what one means when referring to the "state." In 1918, Max Weber famously defined a state as one which has the monopoly on the legitimate use of force over a given territory.[1] Since then, scholars have intensely debated this definition and sought, among others, to expand this definition to differentiate between strong versus weaker states. Most scholars of the state, however, go back to Weber's analysis and find that in order to be considered a state this entity must at least have coercive power over a defined territory. Keeping this general definition of a state is mind gives us a greater appreciation for the enormity of the task Afghanistan faces today as it tries to rebuild a democratically functioning state after nearly three decades of civil war. It also helps us understand that Afghanistan as a state is a fairly recent phenomenon and that historically a centralized, unitary entity was seen as the means of achieving this state status.

The form of Afghanistan's state over the past two and a half centuries has been that of a centralized country with political and administrative powers based in Kabul. This legacy of highly centralized government is reflected in Afghanistan's various constitutions. And yet in contrast to the state structure and the state's legal basis, the reality on the ground has always been quite different. In 1747, when the Pashtun Ahmad Shah through tribal alliances and conquest founded what we know today as Afghanistan, the structure that was set up was a tribal military apparatus. The state structure enabled the king, Ahmad Shah, and the Pashtun tribes allied under Shah to conquer and control other territories. But this alliance was also a burden. Ahmad Shah and his successors constantly had to battle the various Pashtun tribes to gain power and legitimacy over them and over greater Afghanistan, and did so by building an army which was dependent on the king and often recruited from non-Pashtun groups.[2] The process of centralization as a means for building a state was thus already in use during the founding decades of Afghanistan. Subsequent leaders, notably Amir 'Abd al-Rahman Khan, who reigned from 1880 to 1901 with large financial support from the British Empire, further centralized the state by setting up a centralized administrative system, including a national military structure and judicial system. Khan effectively used his external funding to decrease the power of the tribes and increase the power of the center by setting up a Kabul-based patronage system. This centralized system continued under Khan's successors and was formalized when Afghanistan received its first constitution in 1923. The constitution mentioned decentralization of power as a standard of administration. However, it was not a decentralization of political power to local governments but rather power given to subnational administrators to govern regions for the centralized power based in Kabul.[3] A change of regime to the dynasty of Nadir Shah in 1928 changed the relationship with some Pashtun tribes by giving them preferences and exemptions from taxes, but maintained the same general system of a centralizing state. This system continued until the 1950s when the superpower rivalry of the Cold War once again increased the flow of external resources to the Afghan state. Access to increased resources allowed Nadir Shah's son, Zahir Shah, to expand and further centralize administration. Zahir Shah thus presided over what among many Afghans is viewed as the golden age of the centralizing Afghan state.

It was only with the 1973 coup by Daoud Khan, and the subsequent 1978 communist coup with the ensuing revolts and ultimate civil war, that the pattern of state control established during the previous centuries started to break down. During these years of civil war the state and its capacity to rule over regions disintegrated to the point of anarchy. Into this anarchy stepped the Taliban, providing rule and order and eventually reestablishing a centralized system.

When the US-led Coalition forces defeated the Taliban in November 2001, the question of which type of state structure would be best suited to Afghanistan's, history reemerged. The issue of a centralized versus decentralized state was debated particularly among international scholars. Afghan policy-makers and scholars were largely wary of the decentralized, federal systems suggested by international advisors. And indeed the constitution that was adopted in January 2004 states in Article 1 that "Afghanistan is an Islamic Republic, independent, unitary and indivisible state."[4]

Yet a centralized state cannot be easily resurrected after 25 years of civil war. The experience of war, with its many factions and leaders, meant that Afghanistan became a de facto decentralized country with local and provincial power holders managing economic, political, as well as administrative affairs in their regions. The power vacuum at the center enabled power-grabbing by provincial and local strongmen, resulting in a de facto decentralization of power. The end of the war, the new government in Kabul, and the passage of a new constitution and subsequent elections which set out a centralized government (albeit with the option to decentralize some tasks in order to further development and participation) is only slowly changing this reality. Despite a central government in Kabul that is legally and structurally a centralized government, the reach of this centralized government does not extend to many areas of the country. The reality on the ground belies the constitutionally mandated centralized structure of the state.

Despite the fact that Afghanistan has a history of centralized governments, it would be misleading to assert that the authority of these governments reached effectively out to the village level. During much of its two and a half centuries of existence, Afghanistan has been ruled by a centrally structured state whose reach often did not extend beyond the district level. The state's inability to penetrate the countryside through taxation or other revenue-raising activities and, from the local perspective, the lack of local services provided by the central state meant that there was little interaction between these two levels. The inability of the state to raise taxes in the amounts needed to run the state and the subsequent dependence on foreign aid meant that the state was a weak one, while the inability to provide services to much of its citizenry living beyond urban centers meant that the state was unable to function as a developmental state. The state that existed prior to the civil war should therefore be thought of more as a centrally administered, weak and minimal state which conducted foreign policy, addressed security concerns and dealt with other matters that individual provinces or districts could not deal with on their own. The Afghan state was historically not what we would associate with a strong, centralized and developmental state, capable of improving the wellbeing of its citizenry.

Current Status of Centralization in Afghanistan

With the end of the civil war in 2001 and the subsequent roadmap agreed upon in Bonn for moving Afghanistan toward a democratic state, the issue of what type of state would be best suited to Afghanistan's needs arose again. Most international experts on state-building and rebuilding advocated a federal model in order to better address ethnic cleavages within Afghanistan. However, at international conferences and during consultations with the transitional government many Afghans spoke strongly against a federal or decentralized system, since they associated this type of system with the years of communist rule and disintegration of their country.[5] Instead, popular support in Afghanistan was for a strong, unitary government, a central state with the power to rein in the local and provincial actors who were responsible for perpetuating the long civil war. Without much debate on this issue the Constitutional Loya Jirga passed the 2004 Afghan constitution which stated that Afghanistan is a "centralized unitary state."

It has thus been clear for some time that Afghans wanted to build a centralized state structure. However, there are two factors which undermine this centripetal wish. The first centrifugal factor is the channels of resource distribution used by multilateral and bilateral donor agencies for reconstruction and development programs. None of the top ten bilateral donors to Afghanistan currently channels a majority of their resources directly to and through the Afghan government. It is not only coordination between donor nations which is a problem, but it is also the policies of individual donor nations that matters. The US government is the largest financial supporter of the Afghan state but channels and implements its foreign aid primarily through its own government agencies. The second largest implementing agency for US aid to Afghanistan is private sector contractors, followed by UN agencies, while in fourth place comes the Government of Afghanistan. The money given to the Afghan government is only one-twentieth of the overall US aid budget.

Japan is the second largest bilateral donor and the third largest donor to Afghanistan. However, the Government of Afghanistan is only the fifth largest implementing partner of Japanese aid and only approximately one-seventh of total Japanese aid to Afghanistan is channeled through the Afghan government. Similarly India, Germany, the United Kingdom and Iran, the other large bilateral donors of aid to Afghanistan, channel their support largely through their own respective government organizations, the private sector, NGOs and the United Nations. Even the World Bank and the Asian Development Bank, which are the two largest multilateral donors to Afghanistan and are mandated to lend only directly to governments, are increasingly using NGOs for project implementation. These policies of bilateral and multilateral institutions can explain the need to urgently implement projects in the face of severe government capacity limitations in the short term. However, these policies also undermine the power of an already fragile central government.

The second factor working against centralization is the political and security situation in rural Afghanistan. The Afghan government's lack of presence in many areas is due to its lack of financial resources, which is linked to the issue mentioned above, but also due to lack of security. It is impossible to discuss the issue of centralization and decentralization without taking into account the reality of the tenuous nature of security in many parts of the country. The continued threat to Afghanistan's stability posed by the Taliban, Al Qaeda and regional and local warlords and the factional fighting amongst various militia forces, threaten the workings of government in many parts of the country. In addition, crime has become a part of daily life in Afghanistan, even in heavily patrolled Kabul. In such an environment of personal insecurity, it is difficult to talk about a functioning central government as defined by Max Weber. The security problem is the main issue hindering the development of a strong central Afghan government and security is in turn linked to other issues discussed in this volume, such as the drug economy and corruption. At the same time, the Afghan government's cautious approach in dealing with local and regional strongmen and the international community's inability to provide international security forces to effectively cover all of Afghanistan enables the continued reign of many warlords and militia groups, thereby undermining the formation of a strong and centralized government in Kabul.

Afghanistan is thus in the situation of being a country that has used democratic means to determine that it wants to build a centralized state structure, but this is being undermined by the international community's method of aid distribution as well as the tenuous security situation in the country. Despite having a constitution that states that Afghanistan is a centralized state and having conducted presidential and parliamentary elections to buttress its legitimacy in making that determination, international and domestic factors are undermining the centralization process. The reality on the ground is that Afghanistan today has not even achieved the level of weak centralization of its past. With a lack of resources to extend state power beyond urban centers and a security situation that further hampers this reach while cementing the power of regional strongmen (some of whom now have the added legitimacy of being elected members of parliament), Afghanistan is a de facto decentralized state today. This involves a state structure that has neither the advantages of a truly decentralized system, such as greater accountability of program implementation at the local level, nor the advantages of a strong, centralized and democratic system, including the ability to maintain control and deliver services through its territory.

This weak Afghan state, essentially a decentralized one with power in many areas of the country still resting in the hands of local strongmen, does not have the power or state structure needed to consolidate its democratic basis and improve the wellbeing of its citizens. De facto decentralization has led to political power resting at the district or province level rather than at the local government level. And, the lack of coordination among international actors supporting local governments has led to a haphazard mid-level state structure, which often varies even among districts within the same province, particularly with regard to their access to donor-distributed financial resources. As detailed in another chapter in this volume, there is also a general lack of coordination and consultation among the international community on how to work together with and support local governance structures.[6] These factors have resulted in an undermining of the decision of a sovereign country to build a centralized state structure. If Afghanistan is going to move beyond its history of civil war toward a democratic and centralized future, it will have to first consolidate power so that there is a strong state capable of making and implementing the decisions needed to improve the wellbeing of its citizens. International and multilateral support of this process will be the key to its success or failure.

What Can Be Learned from Post-Conflict Countries and Neighboring Countries about the Sequencing of State Structure

While Afghanistan's political history is unique, it can nevertheless learn from state-building efforts in other countries emerging from civil strife. The majority of consolidated democracies today, from Germany to India, are strong states with some degree of decentralization. However, not all of them started with decentralized state structures. Understanding some of the different types of state structure formation undertaken in other post-conflict countries and among some of Afghanistan's neighboring countries will help us to understand the range of state re-formation paths. Not only have post-conflict countries opted for differing state structures, the success of these structures in helping to promote state formation has also varied. These examples will help illustrate that state formation is a process that evolves. Different types of systems are suited to different countries' needs and these needs can vary at different times.

The paths undertaken by countries emerging from long internal conflict are far from uniform. In the case of Serbia and Montenegro, Bosnia and Herzegovina, and Macedonia, countries created as a result of the disintegration of Yugoslavia, the institutional frameworks which arose from the respective peace settlements included various types of decentralized, federal arrangements. The purpose behind the newly instituted, federal power-sharing arrangements in these three cases was to accommodate different national groups within the countries.[7] However, the effectiveness of the institutional frameworks in enabling country management and promoting accommodation between the respective national groups has varied. On the one hand there is the relatively successful example of Macedonia, where decentralization—but not ethno-national based federalism—to 85 municipalities continues to bridge cleavages between different groups. On the other hand there is the example of the recent vote in Montenegro for independence from the federation with Serbia. In between these two outcomes is the case of heavily decentralized and paralyzed Bosnia, where central government competence is weak and ethno-national based federal and regional governments exert stronger power. One lesson from these cases is that ethno-national based federal systems in post-conflict countries can only work to accommodate different national group agendas when there is a clear will to stay together in a united state and where the political incentives do not encourage groups to set up local "fiefdoms." When a post-conflict country is ethnically divided and the will to stay united is weak, federal systems, particularly ethno-national based federal systems, might be less successful. Decentralization in these types of countries can actually lead to the indirect encouragement of regional parties and agendas, thereby further exacerbating ethnic cleavages and separatist aspirations.[8]

In another part of the world another set of countries which arose from the same state structure also bear witness to the range of state-building options and prospects for success. For over 30 years, Eritrea was part of Ethiopia, but after a long war, Eritrea gained its independence in 1993. In response, Ethiopia drew up a new constitution in 1994 which set up a federal republic composed of ethnically-based states. This new ethno-national based decentralized system was not without controversy in the country. Opposition parties have contended that the more decentralized system will lead to disintegration of the country, as witnessed by the independence of Eritrea. The government parties contend that unless some measure of autonomy is given to ethnic groups within a federal entity, these groups will seek to attain this autonomy outside of the federation. Ethiopia is thus an example of a more decentralized power structure being implemented with the ostensible purpose of preventing the country's disintegration. And yet here again, decentralization of power is to units organized along ethnic group lines thereby solidifying them. Whether decentralization in Ethiopia will therefore succeed depends not only on the course of politics in the country, but also on the strength of the ethnic cleavages that are being reinforced through their ethno-national decentralized system.

Eritrea on the other hand opted for a unitary government in line with their goal of building a strong and unified state, as stated in its draft constitution. At the same time, Eritrea recognized that some degree of decentralization in the future will be essential to building up its democracy. The exact division of power between center and the periphery is therefore left up to future legislation. Though Eritrea has yet to hold presidential and parliamentary elections to move beyond the transitional government framework, it is clear that in this case a unitary government structure was chosen with the specific goal of building a central nation-state.

Sudan has also recently emerged from decades of civil war to form a transitional power-sharing Government of National Unity. Under the terms of the peace agreement, southern Sudan has received a large measure of autonomy and a referendum on possible independence is to be held at the end of a six-year transitional period. The decentralized federal arrangement in this case is a temporary one and its inclusion a condition without which the southern Sudanese rebels would not have signed the peace agreement. Decentralization in Sudan was meant to install peace and illustrate the feasibility of federal arrangements, with the intention of demonstrating to the southerners that secession is not necessary. But this decentralized arrangement might work so well, or at least better than the previous centralized government, that it might lead to calls for greater separation and perhaps even independence of southern Sudan from the north. Or it might not work well in terms of being a federation of equal partners and that might also lead to secession of southern Sudan. The Sudanese case of decentralization illustrates that understanding the motives of parties agreeing to a decentralized state structure is important. Unless the idea of politically equal subnational governments is fully respected and national structures are legitimately able to bridge the subnational divide, the outcome in Sudan is likely to be a move towards secession.

Afghanistan's South Asian neighbors have also attempted decentralization to varying degrees and with varying results. Pakistan, Afghanistan's immediate neighbor, had until recently a decentralized system only on paper. Until 2001, decentralization in Pakistan denoted administrative management of districts by the provinces, with little real input by the local governments. However, in 2001, under a strong military dictatorship, the country embarked on the devolution of political power through the Local Government Ordinances. Currently, a uniform three-tiered local government structure is being implemented throughout Pakistan, ostensibly in order to bring greater accountability and democracy to the local level. The fact that decentralization can also help quell demands for local autonomy was surely part of the rationale behind this restructuring of center-periphery relations.

The rise in the local voice and autonomy associated with decentralization, however, has also led to an undermining of central government authority. Pakistan's decentralization experience is thus an example of how decentralization which is not accepted as legitimate by some sections of a population can lead to questioning the authority of the state. A state such as Pakistan will likely be able to weather such challenges to its authority and legitimacy through changes in its regime. A weaker state such as Afghanistan, however, might face difficulties surviving significant challenges to its authority.

Pakistan's 2001 structure of decentralization is similar to that implemented in India in 2000, with the same three-tiered structure mandated throughout the country with similarly stated goals. The main difference between these two countries is that India is a consolidated democracy which passed decentralization legislation through democratic channels and implemented decentralization as a means of deepening democracy. Decentralization in India is built on a rich history of democracy at the national level. Pakistan, however, is not a democracy and the attempts at decentralization therefore need to be seen not as an attempt to deepen democracy, but rather as a means for preempting criticism of the regime in power. These different motivations for implementing decentralization have also led to a different degree of support for local democratic governance, which will ultimately affect the quality of local governance in both countries. The lesson from comparing the decentralization processes in Pakistan and India for Afghanistan is that decentralization is not likely to be real or successful in a country that is not a functioning democracy at the national level. And there is another lesson, too. Despite having very different types of central governments, India and Pakistan do have one thing in common: they are both strong states, which despite the guise of federal systems did not attempt to give away power to local governments until recently. Countries can thus look on paper as if they are decentralizing, but meaningful decentralization that leads to real strengthening of local governance and deepening of democracy is best done in an environment where the central government is democratic and committed and capable of transferring political power to regional and local governments.

Nepal is another South Asian neighbor whose structuring of center-periphery relations holds lessons for Afghanistan. Nepal has traditionally been a highly centralized state with little democratic representation in the constitutional monarchy. Despite reforms in 1990 which established a multiparty democracy within the framework of a constitutional monarchy, there was a lack of voice and accountability at the local level and the monarchy remained very influential with many ill-defined powers. This lack of democratic participation was one of the reasons behind the Maoist insurgency which was launched in 1996 and resulted in a civil war. The civil war ended with the 2006 democracy movement. The new House of Representatives in Nepal then declared Nepal a secular state and severely curtailed the powers of the king. The lesson to be learned on center-periphery relations in Nepal is that a centralized system that does not try to take steps towards devolution might, if the state structure is not democratic and does not improve the wellbeing of its average citizen, eventually implode, bringing change by force. The history of Nepal is a reminder of the importance of timing in changing state structures and the dangers of not deepening democracy once a centralized government does exist.

Conclusions

As seen in the cases from post-conflict and South Asian countries, the issue of how to structure political power between the center and the periphery in a country like Afghanistan is not a zero sum game. A power structure that has worked in one post-conflict country might not necessarily work in another, even if both countries were born out of the same state. And deciding on a centralized political structure in order to build peace and unity in a country does not have to preclude future decentralization once a strong and legitimate state capable of coordinating development within the country exists. Moreover, given that Afghanistan has only recently emerged from decades of civil war with a weak central government, and that Afghans used democratic methods to choose a unitary, centralized state in order to bring the various factions in the country together and solidify peace, the international community should support this democratic process of self-determination as much as possible. Greater support should be lent to the central government, both politically and financially, in order to help them build up their capacity and effectiveness. When the central government is seen as the only legitimate and effective power and has the capacity and wherewithal to reach out to citizens in all rural areas, then it will also have the power to deepen democratic institutions through decentralization. But a state needs to first have power to give away power, particularly in post-conflict settings.

If Afghanistan continues to have a de facto decentralized state, it will only reinforce illegitimate power structures rather than the constitutionally mandated and democratically elected central government in Kabul. The dangers of these current arrangements are clear—one only needs to look at the Balkan example of Serbia and Montenegro. As studies of these cases have shown, decentralization in a post-conflict environment decreases separatist leanings directly by giving the groups that fought against each other control over their political, economic and social affairs. In the medium to longer term, however, it can increase conflict and secessionism by encouraging the growth of regionalism.[9] On the other hand, once a legitimate and capable central government has been established, meaningful decentralization needs to be undertaken to help root democracy down to the village level. The dangers of not eventually devolving political and financial power to subnational governments are clear when looking at Nepal and the Maoist insurgency's demand for greater power at the local level. In Afghanistan, international support for the democratic central government is the immediate and urgent task. While donors should continue to support the building of democratic subnational administrative structures, official decentralization of political powers should wait until there is an effective central state with the legitimacy to decentralize.

Notes

1. Max Weber, "Politics as a Vocation," in H. H. Gerth and C. Wright Mills, eds., Max Weber, *Essays in Sociology* (New York: Oxford University Press, 1946), 77–128.

2. Barnett Rubin and Helena Malikyar, "The Politics of Center-Periphery Relations in Afghanistan" (Unpublished Paper, New York University Center on International Cooperation, March 2003), 3.

3. Ibid., 5.

4. Islamic Republic of Afghanistan, "The Constitution of Afghanistan" (Unofficial Translation), 2004. http://www.af/resources/aaca/constitution/FinalDraftConstitution English.pdf.

5. Liechtenstein Institute on Self-Determination, "Stability and Viability in Afghanistan: Building a Viable and Effective Afghan State" (Policy Brief, April 2003). http://www.princeton.edu/lisd/publications/Afghanistan_April_2003.pdf.

6. See Chapter 6 by Andrew Wilder and Sarah Lister, "State-Building at the Subnational Level in Afghanistan: A Missed Opportunity."

7. Florian Bieber, "Power Sharing after Yugoslavia: Functionality and Dysfunctionality of Power-Sharing Institutions in Post-War Bosnia, Macedonia, and Kosovo," in Sid Noel, ed., *From Power Sharing to Democracy: Post-Conflict Institutions in Ethnically Divided Societies* (Montreal and Kingston: McGill-Queen's University Press, 2006).

8. Dawn Brancati, "Decentralization: Fueling the Fire or Dampening the Flames of Ethnic Conflict and Secessionism," *International Organization,* vol. 60, no. 3 (2006): 651–685.

9. Ibid.

6

State-Building at the Subnational Level in Afghanistan: A Missed Opportunity

Andrew Wilder and Sarah Lister

STATE-BUILDING EFFORTS IN COUNTRIES emerging from conflict often fail because there are not coherent overarching strategies guiding state-building activities. Strategies that do exist frequently shy away from understanding and engaging with the complex political contexts in which reconstruction and state-building activities take place. Complex issues are simplified down to a manageable level for which technocratic "solutions" can then be found. In the rush to implement "quick impact projects," policy making is often removed from its political context as understanding and interacting with these political dynamics would require skill sets few agencies prioritize, and would take time which is viewed as a luxury in the rush to show visible results. International agreements such as the Bonn Agreement can further contribute to policy reductionism by imposing unrealistically short timeframes for putting conflict-devastated countries back on track.

This chapter looks at one important consequence of the lack of a coherent state-building strategy in Afghanistan during the period of the Bonn Agreement. It examines how the state-building agenda in Afghanistan was seriously undermined due to the lack of understanding and engagement with subnational governance institutions, and the failure to develop a subnational state-building strategy to strengthen these institutions and to bring them back under the authority of the central government. The vast majority of Afghans interact with state institutions at the provincial and district levels, yet the near exclusive focus of state-building efforts from 2002 to 2005 was on strengthening central government institutions in Kabul. The few efforts that were made addressed subnational governance as a reconstruction issue with "bricks and mortar" solutions, or as a public administration problem with technocratic solutions, rather than as a critically important component of a state-building strategy requiring political approaches and solutions.

The analysis in this chapter is based on field research initially conducted in six provinces of Afghanistan (Badakshan, Bamiyan, Faryab, Herat, Kandahar and Wardak) between November 2002 and July 2003,[1] and ongoing governance research in these same provinces by the Afghanistan Research and Evaluation Unit between November 2004 and October 2005.[2] The chapter begins by outlining the political context during the 2002–2005 period of the Bonn Agreement, and describes the misalignment between the de jure state with authority primarily in Kabul City, and the de facto states controlled by regional powerholders in the rest of the country. It then identifies some of the major missed opportunities to align the de jure and de facto states in order to strengthen subnational governance as well as the authority of the central government. These included the need to prioritize addressing the security concerns of Afghans through disarmament and police reform, to understand and address the political economy of subnational power, to assert central government authority over the appointment of key provincial and district officials, and to take advantage of the initially strong (but now weakening) sentiment for central government authority. The chapter concludes that the Afghanistan Compact agreed between the Government of Afghanistan and the international community in January 2006 represents the first time since the fall of the Taliban that there is a widespread consensus on the importance of subnational governance for state-building efforts in Afghanistan. As such, the compact provides hope that policies and programs to strengthen governance at the subnational level will now be given much higher priority than they were during the Bonn period. The chapter argues, however, that reform of subnational governance must be viewed as part of an overarching political strategy, the absence of which has been one of the major impediments to successful state-building efforts in Afghanistan.

The Political Context

The September 2005 parliamentary elections, followed by the convening of Afghanistan's newly elected National Assembly in December 2005, marked the end of the four-year political process outlined in the Bonn Agreement. The agreement signed in Bonn by most of the major Afghan political factions in December 2001, following the defeat of the Taliban by US-led Coalition forces, outlined the roadmap for an internationally supported political process. The major components of this process included the holding of an Emergency Loya Jirga (grand council) in June 2002 to elect an interim president to lead a transitional government, a Constitutional Loya Jirga in December 2003 to ratify a new constitution, a presidential election in October 2004, and the legislative elections in September 2005.

The defeat of the Taliban and the signing of the Bonn Agreement were widely seen by Afghans and the international community as a moment of great opportunity to end 23 years of conflict in Afghanistan and to build a modern, democratic and peaceful state. However, despite the apparently successful progression through the steps laid out in the agreement, by the end of the four-year process the Bonn objective "to end the tragic conflict in Afghanistan and promote national reconciliation, lasting peace, stability and respect for human rights in the country" seemed more distant than at any time since the signing of the agreement. The security situation, in particular, had deteriorated significantly, with the director of the Defense Intelligence Agency testifying before the US Senate Armed Services Committee hearing in March 2006 that 2005 had seen a 20% increase in attacks over 2004, and that the Taliban-led insurgency was still growing and posed a greater threat to Afghanistan's central government "than at any point since late 2001."[3] Another major setback was the dramatic increase in poppy cultivation and opium production since 2001, which is now estimated to account for approximately one-half of Afghanistan's overall economy. The role of the illicit narcotics economy in corrupting already weak state institutions and fueling insecurity is increasing fears that instead of achieving the state envisioned in the Bonn Agreement, Afghanistan is perilously close to becoming a narco-state.

The Nature of the State(s) in Afghanistan

The Afghan state is formally one of the most highly centralized states in the world, especially in political and fiscal terms.[4] In practice, however, centralized state institutions in Afghanistan have historically co-existed uneasily with a fragmented, decentralized and traditional society. This coexistence broke down during the war years as power became highly decentralized and factional leaders, operating in relatively distinct geographic areas, organized loose alliances to gain control of, or resist, the center. More than two decades of conflict had a profound impact on the nature of politics at the local level and between the local and national levels. One of the most significant changes during this period was that decentralized power, which historically rested largely in the structures of customary institutions (primarily tribal and religious) with considerable legitimacy, shifted to those who through participation in the conflict and war economy controlled military and financial resources. The increasing gap between traditional customary institutions and power at the local level, and the bad experience local communities had with the decentralization of power to militia commanders, especially during the civil war years of the 1990s, seriously eroded the legitimacy of decentralized power.

The lack of public support for decentralized power holders created an important opportunity for the Karzai Administration to reassert the authority of the central government at the subnational level. During the 2002–2005 period of the Bonn Agreement, significant changes did take place that appeared to represent a centralization of politics. First, as some centralized administrative structures were restored and strengthened, Kabul's authority did grow. This was particularly true of the Ministry of Finance, where strong leadership and a commitment to reform did result in a significant increase in the fiscal authority of the central government. Second, many of the factional leaders (or their representatives) with regional powerbases were given positions in the cabinet or other senior government positions and they moved to Kabul. Additionally, the new constitution, presidential and legislative elections, and the convening of the National Assembly are serving to further centralize politics. However, this apparent shift of politics towards the center has not yet been matched by a corresponding increase in the power and authority of the central government in the provinces.

To better understand the shift of politics, but not power, to the center it is useful to distinguish between de jure and de facto states. De jure states exist by fiat of the international community, which recognizes them as sovereign entities whether or not they have a government that can effectively control or administer the territory. De facto states actually administer a territory.[5] States that enjoy international recognition and exercise control through strong institutions are both de jure and de facto.

In Afghanistan, the de jure state, currently led by President Karzai and his government, has very weak institutions and a lack of both military and administrative control in large parts of the country. The de facto states that exist in many areas outside Kabul are controlled by local and regional strongmen whose power is based on financial and military strength, as well as personal, factional and historical loyalties supported by the current political economy of Afghanistan. In southern Afghanistan the growing Taliban-led insurgency is presenting an even more direct and serious threat to the authority of the de jure state.

During the war years, where power was derived primarily from military power, the term *jangsalar,* or "warlord," was commonly used to describe the factional leaders and militia commanders. However, the presence of international Coalition forces and the International Security Assistance Force (ISAF), the creation of the Afghan National Army (ANA), and disarmament efforts have all made it more difficult for de facto power holders at the subnational level to assert their power solely through the overt use of military force. While illegal armed militia groups still play an important role in the power equation, and increasingly Taliban insurgents in some areas, three other factors are playing an increasingly important role in strengthening the position of de facto power holders at the subnational level. The first is growing economic power, based primarily on illicit narcotics trafficking, which is transforming many "warlords" into "druglords." The second is the use of official positions in the de jure state to legitimize the roles of de facto power holders. This has been particularly important given the favored tactic of the Karzai Administration of avoiding confrontation with de facto power holders and instead accommodating them with important positions in central and provincial government institutions. The third is the growing disillusionment with the central government and the delegitimizing effect of corrupt and ineffective local administration and judicial institutions, a police force that is often regarded as promoting insecurity rather than security, and the failure to meet public expectations for the delivery of social services. These factors, in turn, are encouraging the public to turn to the de facto power holders rather than the central government to solve their problems.

Aligning the De Jure and De Facto States

> There is currently a paradoxical situation where the international community and Government of Afghanistan want to bring security to Afghanistan through those people who don't want security and have been the greatest cause of insecurity. How can the government be successful with this strategy? (District Governor)

The state-building agenda in Afghanistan has been seriously undermined by the absence of a clearly discernible political strategy to rebuild the Afghan state so that it enjoys both de jure and de facto power at the national and subnational levels. After signing the Bonn Agreement one of the major policy objectives of the Afghan government and its supporters should have been to align the de facto states operating in Afghanistan under the authority of the de jure state. Instead it was decided to accommodate rather than confront de facto power holders, and to adopt a "big tent" approach to government. Rather than leave powerful warlords and militia commanders outside where they could oppose the government, they were brought inside the government where in theory they could be controlled. This, however, created a situation where those with a vested interest in keeping central government institutions weak and ineffective, and their own personal power and regional fiefdoms strong, were placed in positions of authority over the very institutions that needed to be strengthened. As one provincial governor warned in 2003, the end result of this strategy would be that those controlling de facto states at the subnational level would take control over the de jure state rather than vice versa.

> The most negative point of the government is keeping warlords strong in the regions. Most cabinet members are warlords and leaders of previous parties that are responsible for all the problems of this country. . . . If the government is going to be successful, ministers shouldn't be commanders and shouldn't have the right to do whatever they want. . . . If the government moves against a warlord there won't be a vacuum of power. The central government will step into power when they remove local warlords. Keeping warlords in power is weakening the government. The more the government pays them off, the stronger they will become and the weaker the government will be. (District Governor, Bamiyan)

The origins of the "big tent" strategy can be traced back to the Bonn Agreement itself, which established a government that rested on a power base of warlords, which subsequent political developments have served to consolidate rather than challenge.[6] A major contributing factor to this strategy was that the objective of the US-led Coalition in Afghanistan was not to engage in nation-building, or to align the de jure and de facto states, but to fight a narrowly defined war on terror, defeat the Taliban and Al Qaeda, and capture or kill Mullah Omar and Osama Bin Laden. As a result, the policy was not only not to confront those who controlled de facto states, but to rearm and strengthen them in order to use them in the war on terror.[7] Despite the calls of the Afghan government, the UN and NGOs during 2002 and 2003, the US actively opposed the expansion of ISAF outside Kabul City to curb the powers of the warlords, fearing that this might alienate potential militia allies and distract attention and resources away from the war on terror. For similar reasons Coalition forces turned a blind eye to drug production and trafficking as this was perceived to be a distraction from the war on terror. However, once the warlords had been rearmed and legitimized by being given official positions, and enriched through drug trafficking, it became much more difficult and potentially destabilizing to move against them. Even when US policy-makers belatedly recognized that the war on terror had to be more broadly defined to include a stronger state-building component, this fear of destabilization became the new grounds for continuing the policy of accommodating rather than confronting former warlords and drug lords who were now deeply entrenched within the de jure institutions of the state.[8]

In the absence of a coherent state-building strategy, policy-makers relied heavily on reconstruction strategies and activities to strengthen the authority and legitimacy of the central government at the subnational level. In addition to addressing Afghanistan's very real humanitarian and development needs, there was a strong belief that the popularity and legitimacy of the new Karzai Administration would be increased if people benefited from tangible assistance programs that they had not experienced under previous governments.[9] However, due in part to the shortsighted public relations strategies of donors, UN agencies and NGOs, which highlighted all the money being given and projects being implemented, the expectations of Afghans for reconstruction assistance were raised to unrealistic levels.[10] The failure of assistance activities to meet expectations, combined with the perception of most Afghans that corrupt government officials and highly paid aid agency staff are the main beneficiaries of external assistance, have resulted in a situation where reconstruction activities have arguably done more to decrease rather than increase the popularity of the central government.[11]

Subnational State-Building Priorities

A successful overarching political strategy to align the de jure and de facto states and to strengthen subnational governance institutions needed to integrate security and rule of law, governance and reconstruction components. The lack of a strategy, however, meant that there was no mechanism to prioritize and sequence needs, and therefore no rational means to allocate scarce human and financial resources to achieve overall strategic objectives.[12] The resulting ad hoc approach to state-building resulted in deeply flawed outcomes, such as a relatively effective (although unaffordable) Afghan National Army, but a deeply corrupt and ineffective Afghan National Police. Similarly, lots of attention and resources were devoted to developing the executive branch of government, some to the legislative branch, and very little to reforming and strengthening the critically important judiciary. The following section examines three subnational state-building priorities that were not sufficiently prioritized during the Bonn period, perhaps fatally undermining the ability of the de jure state to assert its power and authority at the subnational level in Afghanistan. These are as follows:

1. Disarming warlords and commanders, and reforming the police;
2. Understanding and addressing the political economy of subnational power; and
3. Appointing competent, qualified officials to key subnational positions.

Disarming Warlords and Commanders, and Reforming the Police

> Disarmament is the top priority—the administrative system can't function as long as people are armed because you have to do what the armed people tell you to do, not what the rules tell you to do. (Deputy Governor)

During the field research on subnational administration the strongest and most consistently articulated issue raised in interviews in all provinces was that if the effectiveness and authority of the de jure state was to be restored, disarmament of commanders and their armed groups was the top priority. Many provincial- and district-level government staff emphasized that until disarmament puts an end to the "rule of the Kalashnikov," the rule of law and authority of the central government could not be restored. In one district, where two feuding commanders had been disarmed, the difference between the quality of local administration in comparison with those still dominated by local factional commanders was striking. According to the district's governor:

> Before I came to [this district] there was no district administration. All NGO assistance and humanitarian assistance—about where to build schools, clinics—used to go through the commanders. Land disputes went to the commanders to be solved. Since I've been here and the commanders were disarmed, people now come to the administration to resolve their problems. When I came, no one thought the administration could make a difference. People really want a powerful administration system and a reduced role for the commanders.

While the security sector reform strategy for Afghanistan did have a disarmament, demobilization and reintegration (DDR) component—the Afghan New Beginnings Program (ANBP)—it was very slow to get up and running and to achieve significant levels of disarmament. The original ANBP plan announced in early 2003 was to disarm and reintegrate an estimated 100,000 members of the Afghan Militia Forces (AMF) prior to the elections scheduled for June 2004. By June 2004 however, resistance from the unreformed Ministry of Defense (MOD) meant that the number of disarmed had just exceeded 10,000, and the target figure of disarming 100,000 was subsequently reduced to 40,000. Another problem was that the DDR program only sought to disarm AMF members who came under the authority of the MOD.[13] At the end of the original DDR program in July 2005 there were still an estimated 1,800 armed bands consisting of more than 80,000 individuals in Afghanistan. In 2005, a subsequent process—the Disbandment of Illegal Armed Groups (DIAG)—was launched to disarm these groups, but by this time the task was much more difficult as they were much more deeply entrenched within the new economic and political power structures of Afghanistan than in 2002. Clearly, if the authority of the de jure state was to be strengthened at the subnational level, much more thought, effort and resources should have been devoted towards achieving a successful DDR program during the first couple years after the signing of the Bonn Agreement.

Closely linked to the issue of disarmament was the need to prioritize strengthening and professionalizing the police force to reinforce the control of the de jure state at local levels. Although security is one of the top priority concerns of Afghans,[14] civilian administrators are unable to rely on competent and loyal police forces to maintain security within their provinces. In addition to being poorly paid and ill-equipped, in several cases provincial police chiefs are the former warlords themselves. They have appointed their local commanders as district police chiefs who, in turn, have accommodated large numbers of their militia members into the police force. As a result, the police are widely perceived to be part of the security problem rather than the solution.[15]

Many interviewees expressed their concern about the impact that this practice was having on the image and professionalism of the police force. One of the only district police chiefs interviewed without a background in the mujahideen, who had just two weeks previously replaced a police chief who was still a commander for one of the jihadi parties, expressed his concerns and frustrations as follows:

> I have 28 officers in my *tashkeel* [staffing quota], of which 18 are in post who have been approved temporarily by the Ministry of Interior. All are former jihadis and totally unqualified. There is not a single trained police officer in the district other than myself. . . . I'm trying to change the office from a mujahid commander's office into a proper government office. . . . But I have no communications systems, no transportation, no trained police, and most of my officers and soldiers are illiterate and are still loyal to the factional commanders. It's difficult for me to have no authority and to work with officers with no qualifications. . . . If you're not going to change the character of the police then we should forget about the police.

The security sector reform effort of the government and the international community to train the Afghan National Police (ANP) failed to adequately address this important issue of "the character of the police," and illustrated the negative consequences of failing to understand and address the political context within which programs are implemented. The practice of demobilized factional commanders and their armed men being incorporated into local police forces, and then being selected for training without adequate vetting to determine where their loyalties lie, worked to strengthen not weaken commanders.[16] Rather than de-legitimizing their power and authority in the regions, giving militia commanders official positions in their areas of influence has legitimized their power.

By the end of the Bonn process the international community had recognized the importance of reforming the police, and the US made major financial contributions to energize the previously inadequate programs to strengthen the capacity of the ANP. By this time three valuable years had passed, however, and the job was much more difficult than if reforming and developing the capacity of the ANP had been prioritized at the beginning of the Bonn process.

Understanding and Addressing the Political Economy of Subnational Power

> We warned people we would punish them if they grew poppy, but in some areas local commanders encouraged farmers to grow, saying central government is weak and won't do anything. They have their own interests in mind as they tax the poppy. There's now no war on so commanders are looking for alternative livelihoods. (Provincial Governor)

The financial resources that underpin the control exerted by regional and local commanders come from a variety of sources, including the narcotics trade, customs revenues, smuggling, unofficial taxation levied by local commanders and revenues from mineral and natural resources such as mines, oil and gas fields, land and water. Not only do the financial resources provide the commanders with the opportunity to arm themselves and resist the authority of the de jure state, they enable them to engage in more "legitimate" activities designed to win support, such as providing salary supplements to government employees. Their growing economic power is also enabling local commanders and warlords to become increasingly important players in the "licit" economy, in sectors such as the booming urban real estate market.

One of the most serious threats to the de jure state in Afghanistan, and one of the biggest challenges it faces in increasing its authority at the subnational level, is the dramatic spread of the opium economy. In 2004, poppy cultivation expanded to nearly all 34 provinces of Afghanistan (up from 18 provinces in 1999), and reached its highest recorded level ever in Afghanistan. According to the UN Office on Drugs and Crime (UNODC), Afghanistan produced approximately 87% of illicit opium worldwide in 2005. At approximately $2.7 billion, the total value of opium exported by traffickers that year equaled more than half of Afghanistan's GDP.[17] In 2006, poppy cultivation reached a new record level, and early projections suggest that this level is likely to be exceeded in 2007.

Provincial administrators speak of the alleged involvement in the narcotics trade by elites at all levels, including government ministers, commanders, police and provincial and district governors:

> Poppy cultivation and processing is strongly supported by commanders and police. They are very involved and take their share. No one could produce poppy if they did not allow it . . . opium and heroin is transported in vehicles with official plates. (District Governor)

The narcotics trade not only provides financial resources to warlords and commanders to support their de facto power,[18] but the failure of central government to control both the growth of poppy and the processing and transportation of opium is a visible sign of the weakness of the central administration and its inability to enforce its edicts. To quote one district governor:

> We received a letter from Kabul about not growing poppy which we announced to the people, but we can't stop farmers from growing poppy with 40 soldiers. . . . If smuggling continues the prestige of the administration will be reduced—both at the national and international levels, as well as the local level. Smugglers always try to hurt and weaken the administration system.

The dramatic increase in poppy cultivation and drug trafficking has been a well-documented development that has given rise to many dire warnings. In 2004, for example, the World Bank warned that the drug economy would contribute to a "self-reinforcing 'vicious circle' that would keep Afghanistan insecure, fragmented politically, weakly governed, poor, dominated by the informal/illicit economy, and a hostage to the drug industry."[19] Despite this knowledge, policy-makers turned a blind-eye and resisted suggestions to deal with significant individuals involved in the trade (although there has been more appetite to crack down on farmers cultivating poppies). The failure to move decisively against traffickers in the early years of the Bonn Agreement when they were less well-resourced and entrenched in the corridors of power is one of the greatest strategic mistakes of the Bonn period.

It is not just the illicit economy, however, that is supporting the de facto decentralized states in Afghanistan. Revenues from customs duties are considerable, especially in Herat and Kandahar. At the time of the original field research in 2002 and 2003, the process of revenue remittance to Kabul was regarded as one of "negotiation." The study teams were told that revenues from the Daulatabad salt mines in Faryab and the lapis lazuli mines in Badakhshan were all captured by commanders and not remitted to the government. While the situation with regards to customs revenue remittance has improved since the original field research was conducted, there are still many other sources of unofficial taxation by commanders at all levels, including taxes on productive and transport activities. Furthermore, some de facto power holders in the provinces are reportedly still funded by neighboring and regional states seeking to increase their influence in the country.

De facto power holders often manipulate the structures of subnational government to ensure the continued access to resources that underpin their control. For example, there is evidence that as municipalities became more lucrative sources of financial resources, a "commanderization of municipalities" took place. Provincial and rural municipalities are the only structures of subnational administration that are legally permitted to retain and spend revenues from taxes and fees that are raised. The dramatic increase in land prices in urban areas has created tremendous rent-seeking opportunities in provincial municipalities (and even more so in Kabul). Urban land mafias, often under the control of the factional leaders of de facto states, are reportedly muscling their way into the municipalities of the major cities of Afghanistan to gain control of the lucrative revenues raised through the illegal development, rental and/or sale of state-owned properties.

An important contributing factor to the weakness of state institutions at the subnational level is that provinces and districts have received virtually no financial support from Kabul, and have, by necessity, become financially autonomous. Currently, provincial and district administrators have no option but to look for sources of revenue elsewhere and the legitimacy of the de jure state is called into question when it has no resources to do anything. In the absence of budgeted government resources, the role of local administrators has become that of intermediaries, able to refer difficulties to NGOs or commanders, but without the resources to tackle problems themselves. Receiving financial resources from the center could prove to be an effective way of linking these provinces back to the center, especially in resource-poor provinces, and enhancing the legitimacy of state institutions at the subnational level.

Since the signing of the Bonn Agreement there has been a tendency for the government, donors and international financial institutions to focus on the quantity of economic growth with less attention given to the quality and political effects of growth.[20] More attention needs to be devoted to understanding who benefits from growth, not only to ensure that the benefits are widely distributed, but to ensure that growth is not further consolidating the power and influence of druglords and warlords who have a vested interest in seeing the state remain weak and ineffective. An effective political strategy to increase the authority of the de jure state at the provincial and district levels must therefore be based on a sound understanding of, and engagement with, the political economy that underlies subnational power.

Appointing Competent and Qualified Officials to Key Subnational Positions

> Commanders still try to influence appointments and transfers. If Kabul appoints someone they should insist that that person get appointed—not give in to commanders who are resisting these appointments. We need support from our departments to resist the influence of commanders. (District Governor)

For perhaps the first time in modern Afghan history the provinces welcomed rather than resisted the authority of central government during the Bonn period. Interviewees in all six provinces during 2002 and 2003 were virtually unanimous in their support for the restoration of central political authority over provincial and district administration. The central government, although weak and ineffective, was viewed as more legitimate than warlords and factional commanders who derived their power from guns and illicit economic activities. This strong sentiment for central government authority, however, was not capitalized on and is now weakening as disillusionment with the central government increases. The absence of a state-building strategy at the subnational level meant that relatively straightforward activities to increase the effectiveness and prestige of subnational governance were only belatedly prioritized if at all. These could have included repairing provincial and district government offices and equipping them with the basic necessities for a functioning office, providing communications equipment to link district and provincial offices to Kabul, and providing some minimal discretionary budgets to provincial governors and district governors to respond to emergencies or to address priority community needs. More difficult but much more important, however, was the need to staff provincial and district governments with trained administrators who were appointed according to their competence and loyalty to the central government. This would have had the dual effect of weakening local power holders and increasing the legitimacy of local government structures.

In theory, all appointments to mid- and senior-level government positions at the subnational level are made in Kabul. In reality, especially in areas controlled by powerful militia commanders, appointments made by the central government are often rejected and favorites of the commanders appointed instead. Government employees, therefore, often owe their employment, and therefore their loyalties, to these militia commanders rather than the central government. In Herat for example, when the former commander Ismael Khan was governor, all district governors were reported to be in their positions because they had fought in the jihad with Ismael Khan. Even since his removal as governor, many figures in the Herat provincial administration remain in position because of Ismael Khan's continued power base in the region. In other areas where overall command is less clear, there is either conflict or those in authority try to maintain stability by keeping a balance between opposing factions, splitting the major appointments between rival factions. Some political factions provide subsidies to their representatives in local government, which further reinforces loyalty to regional and local power holders.

The control of civilian appointments by local militia commanders has two particularly detrimental effects in terms of the administration. In particular, it limits the influence of civilian administrators who may not wish to be tied to any particular faction, but nonetheless feel forced to abide by the decisions of local and regional commanders. In the words of one district governor:

> If I don't have a commander around, immediately I become strong and get respect. If there are armed people around I can't say anything.

Additionally, it prevents the appointment of qualified and competent bureaucrats and technical staff, which further weakens the administration, both in practice and in legitimacy. As was the case with the police force, the lack of qualified professional staff and the presence of large numbers of untrained former combatants in government positions was a frequently heard complaint:

> All these people with jihad backgrounds don't have professional skills. They know their authority but not responsibilities. I'm not saying that they all get thrown out but that they should be given some training. . . . Decision-making on hiring heads of departments should be done in Kabul, but because our governor is someone who does everything through arms it doesn't work like this. For example, the head of the Agriculture Department is an illiterate mullah. Kabul appointed another qualified head but because the current head is supported by the governor, they refused to accept Kabul's appointee. (Deputy Provincial Governor)

Attempts have been made to transfer some government employees away from their home areas, thus cutting their ties to their networks and supporters. Historically this policy was used to ensure that government employees did not build up their own power bases, and the reintroduction of such a policy had widespread acceptance among interviewees in this study. However, the attempts made so far have only been partially successful, and have not managed to break the power of commanders who often simply refuse to obey orders to move. In Badakshan, for example, when a policy was announced in 2003 to transfer all district governors to different districts, only 10 of the 27 district governors—those without strong jihadi backgrounds or commander connections—were transferred. Low salaries are also a factor in the failure to transfer administrators away from their home areas. Government staff simply cannot afford to live away from home without the added income provided by land or other sources of livelihoods (e.g., shops), as well as free housing. Indeed, it seems likely that in some areas the only reasons there are government employees at all is because government jobs require relatively few hours, and are therefore perceived as a bonus on top of other income sources.

A frequent criticism heard about President Karzai's administration is the appointment of so many unqualified and unpopular individuals to fill key provincial positions, especially those of provincial and district governors and chiefs of police. The central government's reputation and influence at the subnational level, which to a considerable extent is determined by the quality of its personnel, has been seriously damaged by the extremely poor quality of provincial appointments.[21] While the international community often tried to pressure the Karzai Administration into appointing qualified candidates into key ministerial positions, little pressure was applied to appoint strong candidates into key subnational positions.[22] If the authority of the de jure state is to be enhanced, and the power of the de facto states diminished, the Karzai Administration will have to pay much greater attention to appointing qualified individuals to fill key subnational positions.[23] To address this need, one of the benchmarks of the Afghanistan Compact was the establishment of "a clear and transparent national appointments mechanism" for all senior level appointments at the central, provincial and district levels. In September 2006, President Karzai issued a decree to create a five-member Special Consultative Board for senior-level appointments,[24] but by the summer of 2007 little had been done to make the board operational.

Conclusion

The absence of a coherent overarching strategy guiding state-building interventions is the major cause of the ad hoc and often contradictory approaches that have characterized state-building efforts in Afghanistan since the signing of the Bonn Agreement. This chapter has examined one important example of this failure to develop an effective state-building strategy by looking at the consequences of Kabul-centric policy making and state-building efforts. Virtually ignored during the Bonn years were the considerable opportunities, as well as the political importance, of strengthening subnational governance and the authority of the de jure state based in Kabul over the de facto states operating at the subnational level.

The chapter has highlighted that strengthening subnational governance is not only a technical issue, but must be understood as part of a broader political struggle between the de jure state and fragmented de facto states in Afghanistan. Afghanistan's current political context is very different from the history of tension between a centralizing state and a decentralized society based on the power of traditional institutions with substantial legitimacy. Following the signing of the Bonn Agreement there was a widespread desire for the authority of the central government to be extended to the provinces, replacing the illegitimate de facto states controlled by warlords and druglords. While these wishes were often expressed in terms of a desire for a centralized state, this does not necessarily imply a centralization of the rules of operation with all activities based in Kabul. Instead, a balance must be achieved between the need to centralize the current reality of too much decentralization of power to illegitimate de facto states with the need to decentralize the theory of an overly centralized state. This task, however, will become increasingly difficult as the perceived corruption and ineffectiveness of the central government undermines its legitimacy, and people instead look for local solutions to their problems.

The integrated nature of the current political, security, fiscal and administrative problems facing Afghanistan means that strategies to legitimize and strengthen the de jure state at the subnational level that rely solely on reconstruction strategies will be inadequate. Instead, there is a need for a political strategy that guides, integrates and coordinates programs designed to rebuild the Afghan state. Strengthening subnational governance institutions will both result from and contribute to a political strategy to align the de jure and de facto states in Afghanistan.

The Bonn years represent a major missed opportunity to engage strategically at the subnational level in Afghanistan to bring about positive political change. It was not until 2005 that subnational governance belatedly began to get the serious attention of policy-makers.[25] This initially generated some confused thinking, and ad hoc and contradictory initiatives to create new subnational governance institutions.[26] Through the development of the Afghanistan National Development Strategy and the Afghanistan Compact,[27] progress was made during late 2005 and 2006 in clarifying this thinking and getting the government more engaged in identifying ways to address subnational governance problems.[28] The Afghanistan Compact, agreed upon at the London Conference in January 2006 by the Government of Afghanistan, 50 participating countries and 15 international organizations, marked the first time since the fall of the Taliban that the government and its major donors explicitly acknowledged the importance of subnational governance for achieving development and political goals. More importantly, they stated their commitment to address the issue. During the four years that it took to collectively recognize the importance of addressing the problems of subnational governance, the problems have become much more complicated and difficult to resolve. If more opportunities are not to be missed, there is an urgent need to move beyond recognizing the problem to developing and implementing a strategy that includes the subnational level as an integral part of state-building efforts in Afghanistan.

Notes

1. The research was carried out jointly by the Afghanistan Research and Evaluation Unit (AREU) and the World Bank. Major findings have been published in two volumes: Anne Evans, Nick Manning, Yasin Osmani, Anne Tully, and Andrew Wilder, *A Guide to Government in Afghanistan* (Kabul and Washington, DC: AREU and World Bank, 2004); and Anne Evans, Nick Manning, and Anne Tully with Yasin Osmani and Andrew Wilder, *Subnational Administration in Afghanistan: Assessment and Recommendations for Action* (Kabul and Washington, DC: AREU and World Bank, 2004). The views expressed in this paper are those of the authors alone.

2. For a specific study on progress in public administration reform see Anne Evans and Yasin Osmani, *Assessing Progress: Update Report on Subnational Administration in Afghanistan* (Kabul: AREU, 2005). The lack of a strategy for strengthening subnational governance institutions is highlighted in Sarah Lister, "Caught in Confusion: Local Governance Structures in Afghanistan" (Kabul: AREU, 2005).

3. Tom Raum, "Analysis: Osama Haunts Bush in Afghanistan," Associated Press, 2 March 2006. See also Michael Bhatia, Kevin Lanigan, and Philip Wilkinson, "Minimal Investments, Minimal Results: The Failure of Security Policy in Afghanistan" (AREU Briefing Paper, June 2004).

4. The new constitution reaffirms that Afghanistan is a unitary country but states that "the government, while preserving the principle of centralism, shall—in accordance

with the law—delegate certain authorities to local administration units for the purpose of expediting and promoting economic, social, and cultural affairs, and increasing the participation of people in the development of the nation" (chapter 8, article 2). This therefore allows for a measure of de-concentration within the constitution, but it is not, in practice, likely to lead to significant shifts in the structures of subnational administration.

5. See M. Ottaway, "Rebuilding State Institutions in Collapsed States," *Development and Change,* vol. 33, no. 5 (November 2002): 1001–1023; and R. Jackson, *Quasi-States: Sovereignty, International Relations and the Third World* (Cambridge: Cambridge University Press, 1990).

6. See Barnett Rubin, "(Re)Building Afghanistan: The Folly of Stateless Democracy," *Current History,* April (2004): 165–170.

7. The initial support for the Taliban when they first came to power was primarily due to the fact that they disarmed and got rid of the very warlords that the US-led Coalition then rearmed and brought back into the center of Afghan politics. Many Afghans believe that these warlords have been much more effective at using the Coalition than vice versa.

8. For a discussion of how fears of destabilization resulted in so many candidates affiliated with illegal armed groups making it through the parliamentary election candidate vetting process, see the section entitled "Law Makers or Law Breakers?," in Andrew Wilder, *A House Divided* (Kabul: AREU, 2006), 14–15.

9. The highest profile and most political project designed to boost the popularity of the Karzai Administration and its US government backers was the Kabul to Kandahar highway rebuilt by USAID at a cost of over $300 million. President George Bush took such a personal interest in seeing the road completed that he was given a clump of gravel and tar dug up from the newly paved highway. According to the deliverer of the unusual gift, the US State Department's Afghanistan Coordinator, "I couldn't imagine that senior levels of government would be so interested in a chunk of asphalt." See Andrew Higgins, "U.S. Ambitions Run Into Reality on an Afghan Road," *Wall Street Journal,* 6 February 2004.

10. See Nicholas Stockton, "Strategic Coordination in Afghanistan" (Kabul: AREU, 2002).

11. Evidence of anti-aid sentiment was provided by the parliamentary election campaign of the former minister of planning, Ramazan Bashardost, who ran the most issues-based campaign in the October 2006 parliamentary elections. His populist campaign, which focused on the issues of corruption and misuse of aid money by the government and non-government organizations, clearly resonated with voters. Despite having no traditional power base, Bashardost ended up winning the third highest number of votes in an election contested by 2,775 candidates.

12. For a discussion questioning the levels of human and financial resources devoted to holding five elections during the Bonn period, relative to other state-building priorities, see Wilder, *A House Divided* 46–47.

13. See Bhatia et al., "Minimal Investments, Minimal Results," 17.

14. The security concerns that Afghans identified focused primarily on personal security concerns related to the absence of the rule of law and the culture of impunity within which warlords and militia commanders operated, and not the Taliban and Al Qaeda which remained the preoccupation of international security forces in Afghanistan. For a study on Afghan public opinion see Dawn Stallard, *Speaking Out: Afghan Opinions on Rights and Responsibilities* (Kabul: Human Rights Research and Advocacy Consortium, 2003).

15. One article quotes a colonel in the ANA as saying the ANP spends the daytime acting as policemen and the nighttime committing crimes. "One hundred percent of the police are thieves." According to a US military officer quoted in the same article, "In

many of the districts, the ANP is as much a representative of the local bad-ass as it is the population that they're there to ostensibly serve and protect." Sean Naylor, "The Waiting Game: A Stronger Taliban Lies Low, Hoping the U.S. Will Leave Afghanistan," 31 March 2006. http://72.14.203.104/search?q=cache:wZGqk8JCp7IJ:www.armedforcesjournal.com/story.php%3FF%3D1404902_0206+Sean+Naylor+Securing+the+Future+Afghanistan&hl=en&ct=clnk&cd=1&client=safari (accessed 2 April 2006).

16. See Bhatia et al., "Minimal Investments, Minimal Results," 15–19.

17. Cited in Government of Afghanistan, *Interim Afghanistan National Development Strategy* (Kabul: Islamic Republic of Afghanistan, 2006), 95.

18. Adam Pain, *Opium Trading Systems in Helmand and Ghor* (Kabul: AREU, Issues Paper Series, 2006).

19. W. Byrd and C. Ward, *Drugs and Development in Afghanistan* (Washington, DC: World Bank, Social Development Papers, no. 18, 2004).

20. See Sarah Lister and Adam Pain, "Trading in Power: The Politics of 'Free' Markets in Afghanistan" (AREU Briefing Paper, June 2004), and Mark Sedra, *Challenging the Warlord Culture: Security Sector Reform in Post-Taliban Afghanistan* (Bonn: Bonn International Center for Conversion, 2002).

21. A graphic illustration of the seriousness of the problem was President Karzai's appointment in 2005 of an individual who had served time in a US federal penitentiary for heroin trafficking to be the governor of a province that was an important trafficking route for opium and heroin.

22. There were a few notable exceptions, including the US government's assistance in removing Ismael Khan as governor of Herat. The flourishing poppy production in Kandahar and Helmand led to pressures to remove Gul Agha Sherzai and Mullah Sher Mohammad as the respective governors of these two provinces. In all three of the cases however, the officials were not removed from office but transferred or promoted to other important government positions. Ismael Khan was brought into the cabinet as minister for energy, Gul Agha Sherzai was appointed governor of Nangahar, and Mullah Sher Mohammad was given a seat in the Meshrano Jirga, the upper house of parliament.

23. One hopeful sign that this problem is now recognized is that the "Afghanistan Compact," signed in London by the Government of Afghanistan and all the major donor governments in January 2006, included benchmarks requiring progress in the area of merit-based appointment of qualified personnel.

24. Government of Afghanistan and UNAMA, "Implementation of the Afghanistan Compact" (Biannual JCMB Report, November 2006), 15.

25. This was primarily driven by the recognition that stronger subnational governance institutions were needed to fight the dramatic increase in poppy cultivation, as well as the need to clarify the functions of the constitutionally mandated provincial and district councils prior to the October 2005 elections.

26. One example of this was the investment of a tremendous amount of human and financial resources in conducting provincial council elections, without any clear sense of what the role of these councils would be. For a more in-depth discussion of the confused thinking and initiatives on subnational governance see Lister, "Caught in Confusion."

27. For a more detailed discussion of the Afghanistan Compact see P. J. Middlebrook and S. M. Miller, "Lessons in Post Conflict Reconstruction from the New Afghanistan Compact" (Foreign Policy in Focus Policy Report, 27 January 2006). http://www.fpif.org.

28. See Sarah Lister and Hamish Nixon, "Provincial Government Structure in Afghanistan: From Confusion to Vision" (Kabul: AREU, 2006).

7

Civil Society and State-Building in Afghanistan[1]

Susanne Schmeidl

> Afghans are good at lying. It starts from the president and comes all the way down to me. In Afghanistan there has been little success to date in implementing what was promised in the Bonn Agreement and the most crucial issues have not been addressed. People need civil society, people need a constitution but the situation isn't right for it. It's not that the people aren't ready mentally, socially and politically. It's not that the people don't understand or that they are not ready. In our districts we are hanging, like carcasses on a butcher's hook. Even in Kabul with the presence of ISAF and others the DDR process has been delayed. We cannot fool foreigners about our country. They understand what is going on but somehow we act as if we can hoodwink the foreigners. We should have had more time. Afghanistan is not ready for a constitution. The police, the rule of law, a proper judicial system—these things have not been developed yet. On the one hand, we talk about democracy and civil society, but can we achieve those things? We have started collective action but we also need to work on an individual basis and the process must be continued. We have learned a great deal from this process. The people are like fingers of the hand and we must come together as a fist if we can fix the broken bones of the hand.
>
> —Civil Society Representative, Kabul Province[2]

The concept of state-building has become increasingly important in the post-Cold War era with the rise of the phenomenon of fragile and failed states. In response, international assistance has made state-building—especially at an institutional level that tries to reform security, justice, administrative and fiscal sectors—a main intervention method. The focus on civil society development was also considered important as the building of a strong democratic state also necessitates support from the grass-roots level. "[T]he existence of a vibrant civil society is considered as a precondition to go beyond 'formal' democracies, to achieve long lasting attitude changes and to overcome resistance by former, undemocratic leaders."[3]

In spite of this linkage, the processes of state-building and civil society promotion are too often utterly disconnected. State-building tends to be performed top-down by outside actors, in what Hippler calls "imperial" state-building whereby "external players first crushed an existing power or government system . . . by force in order to begin a process of material and political reconstruction."[4] The focus tends to be on a centralized process that builds entirely new institutions with few like-minded local elites that are modeled after what the interveners—mostly western democratic states—tend to perceive as fitting for "an effective, central state that operates under the rule of positive law and in accordance with contemporary standards of transparency and accountability."[5] Civil society development, on the other hand, is a rather uncoordinated and decentralized process that is usually left to international and local NGOs. This is often based on the assumption that civil society as such is best left to grow organically on its own.

This lack of coordination, however, can lead to the perception of civil society as a threat or competition to the state rather than its very foundation. It also ignores that the state "must be considered as more than the 'government.' It is the continuous administrative, legal bureaucratic and coercive system that attempts not only to structure relationships between civil society and public authority in a polity but also to structure many crucial relationships within civil society as well."[6]

Thus, building strong state institutions and functioning administrative structures are only part of a successful state-building process. After all, states are supposed to govern and serve their citizens. For that, they need to be perceived as useful for and legitimate by the people. A state "fulfils certain functions for the society affected[,] something which has to be assessed on the basis of the needs of the population and its socio-economic and political groups."[7] This is often why security and justice play a tremendous role in state-building, as in addition to having enough to eat and drink, wanting to not have rights violated and not be killed tend to rank highest among human priorities.[8] Furthermore, society needs to agree on its future path—rarely can this be indoctrinated from the outside and above. Traditionally, societies that have formed into states have undergone processes where conflicts over ideologies were fought until an agreement was found. Such processes of "ideological integration"[9] clearly can be violent, as European state-building history only too obviously shows. Yet, they are necessary if we want a sustainable state with people having the feeling that they belong, and especially, belong together.

In light of the above, for state-building to be successful, it needs to be an integrative and participatory process that involves a broader spectrum of actors, not just elites. A clear and possibly central role for civil society in state-building should be found, especially as it is the people who are directly affected by the outcome of such a process. External actors can always leave. As such, civil society development should be coordinated with the state-building exercise and vice versa. But what can civil society realistically contribute to state-building and security? This chapter tries to explore this question for the specific case of Afghanistan, taking into consideration the experience of the first four years since the Bonn Agreement (2002–2005).[10]

The Concept of Civil Society and Its Application in Afghanistan[11]

It is possible that the reason for a lack of concerted effort to integrate civil society into the post-conflict state-building process is the fact that the concept of civil society is not yet widely understood. Unfortunately, the term "civil society" is often used either too broadly or too narrowly, presenting two contradictory trends. While uncritically considering civil society as everything outside the state, essentially making it into an all-encompassing "conceptual rag bag,"[12] can be quite counterproductive, doing the reverse is equally damaging. This overall "fuzziness" of civil society, meaning that "it can be all things to all people,"[13] too often leads in many post-conflict environments to the narrow support for NGOs as the only means for civil society promotion. This civil society cum NGO funding behavior ignores the many other forms of civil society actors in non-western settings.[14] Thus, before venturing into a deeper discussion of civil society in Afghanistan, it is worthwhile clarifying the notion of "civil society."

Essentially, civil society is intertwined with modern state-building. Initial discussions led by philosophers and great thinkers tried to define civil society as a sector, among others, that existed independently of an all-encompassing state. Thus civil society might best be analyzed in its relation vis-à-vis other sectors, especially the state.[15]

What we generally understand as civil society clearly entails some type of private, non-clientelistic organization and identity that exists beyond the confines of a state apparatus. For many anthropologists, such as Gellner, "civil society . . . is a result of the historical appearance of 'modern man' who is engaged in free economic and political activities."[16]

It is generally agreed that civil society seems to emerge when people come together on a common platform to pursue common goals and to create an awareness that goes beyond the direct result of their collective action. In the words of the Centre for Civil Society at the London School of Economics, "Civil society refers to the arena of uncoerced collective action around shared interests, purposes and values. In theory, its institutional forms are distinct from those of the state, family and market, though in practice, the boundaries between state, civil society, family and market are often complex, blurred and negotiated."[17]

The Afghan context shows how difficult it is to sort out the concept of civil society in traditional societies in transition. A historical review of Afghan society to the present day may lead us to conclude that there is a lack of several of the requirements for a strong civil society—at least in the western sense.

First of all, even prior to the war, Afghan society was and still is strongly based on clientelistic networks. This means that groups form less along interests but more along family and kinship networks. These networks tend to be more oriented around extended family ties than ethnicity. The latter, however, changed somewhat during the wars, when warlords began to mobilize support around regional, ethnic or religious groups.

Second, collective action, with the one exception of the mujahideen resistance (jihad) that emerged within the Islamic brotherhood against the communist regime and Soviet invasion, seemed to be short-lived without long-term orientation. It has largely been needs-based, and reactive to problems such as the creation of irrigation groups in rural areas, or groups that formed around building common public goods such as a well or mosque. Personal influence of individuals was limited to small communities, even as small as a single extended family. This is not necessarily unique to Afghanistan, as Oxhorn argues for Latin America, that "if you are poor, have darker skin or live in an indigenous rural community, you may not see yourself as 'rational individual' maximizing your personal interests, but rather as a member of a community trying to cope with a variety of pressing social needs."[18]

Third, an attempt to analyze civil society vis-à-vis the state in Afghanistan is also difficult, as "[n]either the empires of the Safavids and Mughals of the sixteenth and seventeenth centuries nor the Durrani rulers of the eighteenth and nineteenth centuries managed to preserve their rule permanently or extend state structures beyond the few urban centers.[19] Thus, Afghanistan never knew a situation where the state was able to reach into all parts of society or was strong enough to undermine other local (power) structures. Furthermore, Afghanistan's most recent experience is that of state failure after the communist government was toppled and non-state actors had to pick up state functions by default. Therefore, the lines between state and civil society in Afghanistan are extremely blurred.[20]

Fourth, to make civil society a purely urban and intellectual phenomenon may also lead to the wrong conclusions such as a 1999 report of Amnesty International that argued that civil society in Afghanistan was destroyed during the Tablian, simply because the urban intelligentsia had moved away. Many Afghan intellectuals would agree with this as they see civil society in Afghanistan or *jamea-e-madani,* the Afghan term, often linked to an intellectual "urban society" as the word *madani* can be either seen as originating from *medina* (city) or *madaniat* (civilization). Afghans from a more traditional and rural background, however, tend to see the word more as signifying "civilized society" which they generally contrast with the armed militia.[21]

Thus, "the claim that Afghanistan has a civil society, even [a] potentially strong one, rests on the assumption that civil society is composed of much more than intelligentsia."[22] In a basic way one could argue that many Afghans might simply view civil society as an alternative from their warmongering past, and also to set them apart from the warlords, those holding power through guns. Maley and Saikal even argue that "in some circumstances, it may be useful to add 'uncivil society' as an operational category"[23] in Afghanistan in order to avoid seeing all segments of civil society as universally good.

Indeed, the wars in Afghanistan had a great impact on societal development and hence civil society in Afghanistan. The heightened insecurity emphasized the need to stick together in small communities which can best be described as "survival networks." Clearly it was easier to trust a small set of known people than larger society in general, especially with the general experience that state institutions did not provide for the people, and with inter-communal feuds. The necessity for "survival networks" grew stronger as the war began to polarize Afghans due to ethnicity-driven recruitment by warlords. Distrust grew to an extent that clientelism spread into almost every sphere of Afghan society: politics, economy, education and even the formation of so-called civil society organizations such as NGOs, social and cultural associations and interest groups. These survival networks seem to function even outside Afghanistan in the diaspora community, a reason why many returning Afghans slot smoothly into the present political and economic environment despite years of exile.

This experience, however, is not unique to Afghanistan, and can be found in other non-western contexts and traditionally oriented societies with war experience. In Latin America, for example, Oxhorn notes that for a member of a poor rural community "the idea of trusting people outside your community, much less often corrupt state institutions, seems naïve at best, and dangerous at worst."[24] The existence of clientelistic networks is also quite widespread in Africa. Orivs, for example, argues that "patron-client networks are so pervasive in Africa largely because they provide crucial resources to all involved," and because "in an extremely insecure situation, these networks provide the best available means of social and economic security."[25] The same is true for Afghanistan, where the society would have been unlikely to survive the many years of war if it had not been for these extant clientelistic networks. Thus, their formation can be seen "as a rational response to a situation in which being too trusting can prove exceedingly dangerous."[26]

Clientelistic networks in their pure form, as they predominate in Afghan and African society, "are seen to be far too hierarchical and unequal to be part of civil society, [as] the very limited autonomy of clients vis-à-vis patrons denies them equal citizenship."[27] Such networks can be related to Max Weber's non-modern forms of authority (patriarchal and neo-patrimonial, etc.) where there is no real "public sphere."[28]

However, with the lacking state history in Afghanistan, where no real forms of institutional authority, other than the patriarchal household and tribal/clan leadership, existed, there was never really a strong incentive to act collectively in political terms, aside from the initial jihad against the communist government. But what may have started out as a genuine movement against the Soviet occupation was later on hijacked by individual warlords who used the resistance to increase their own power base. This is illustrated by the fact that once the communist regime was toppled, a fierce in-fighting over power began among the warlord factions, with many Afghans opting out of further struggle as the communists had been defeated.

Discarding patron-client relationships as part of civil society may very well be an interpretation based on neo-liberal democratic norms rather than realities in countries such as Afghanistan. In certain contexts, patron-client networks may actually form quite legitimate elements of civil society as "informal groups that pursue their collective interests vis-à-vis the state, often retaining some autonomy from the state, and providing a means (however imperfect) of both political participation and accountability."[29]

In light of the above, we have to be careful not to use a western lens and only look for the civil society with which we are familiar and possibly also comfortable in our own contexts. If we exclude traditional groups, we are possibly left with not much at all, or run the risk of supporting rather unviable structures that lack legitimacy and may cease to exist with western funding taken away. "Because they are relatively new, disorganized, and poor, associations such as trade unions, professional bodies, and independent media have few if any roots in rural society where the bulk of the population resides, . . . [and they usually depend] on the state or western donors."[30]

Based on a distinction put forth by Kamali[31] for civil society in contemporary Muslim countries that also resonates with Orvis'[32] discussion on Africa, civil society in Afghanistan can be divided into two basic groups:

1. An indigenous civil society based on a core of quasi-traditional and quasi-modern influential groups. This can and should include patron-client and tribal structures, as well as groups that function along similar lines such as neighborhood shuras and community councils in urban areas. It is important not to forget religious networks here.
2. A modern civil society constructed on a core of westernized intellectuals and modern social groups. This certainly includes NGOs; social, cultural and professional organizations; interest groups; and women's and youth groups, as well as newer shuras set up along the thinking of modern civil society organizations. Modern business associations should also be included here as a form of collective action of the private sector.

Such a distinction is largely based on the overall rural (traditional) and urban (modern) divide which has blurred over time and will continue to do so. The displacement and exile experience of many Afghans has especially exposed traditional rural groups to modern settings. The figure on the following page is an attempt to depict how civil society looks in Afghanistan and relates to sectors.

The role of family is particularly interesting in Afghanistan. As in many traditional societies, it influences other sectors, especially traditional civil society such as tribes. For example, the hiring of family members in NGOs is a common practice in Afghanistan, the brother of the famous Panjshiri commander Ahmad Shah Masood was made a vice-president, and trade networks are often organized along traditional tribal and family lines (e.g., the Hazarboz among the Pashtun tribes). But other sectors (e.g., state and market) overlap as well. For example, prominent businessmen sit in political decision making bodies and have been made into politicians (e.g., the current minister of agriculture is a prominent businessman), former academics and NGO leaders are now ministers (Foreign Affairs, Education, Rural Development) and, during communist

Civil Society in Afghanistan

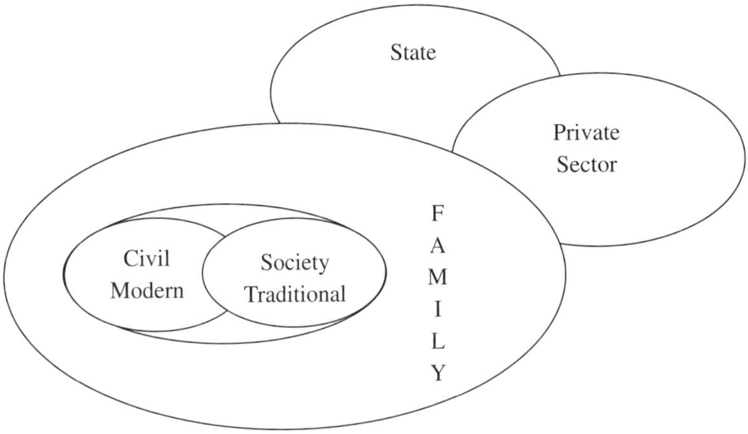

times, modern civil society organizations were set up by a regime and by no means independent of the state, but essentially co-opted and used.[33]

Traditional Community Institutions

Afghanistan is a very heterogeneous country where traditional communities tend to differ among different regions and groups. The smallest common denominator for a form of solidarity group, or what was earlier referred to as survival network in Afghanistan, is the *qaum*.[34] "A qaum may, for example, be based on family, tribe, geographic location or profession."[35] The differentiation is fuzzy and linked to the context and situation.[36] These qaums can be considered as the most important framework for rural Afghanistan. They provide for its people in terms of food, shelter and also security. The leadership among traditional communities comes from what is called *spin giri*—the white bearded elders who either function in the role of higher level (e.g., *khan, mir, beg, wakil*) or more local decision makers at the village level (e.g., *mirbak, malik*). Furthermore, religious leaders (e.g., *mullahs, syyeds, pirs*) and religious networks (e.g., Sufi orders) also play a big role in traditional civil society.[37] All of them have a rather high form of legitimacy among Afghan society that should not be underestimated.[38]

In order to solve the problem of decision making at a higher level, the institution of a *jirga* was created "where all influential elites can be brought together to agree on actions and solutions."[39] Jirgas primarily aim at the resolution of conflicts between individuals, families, clans, sub-tribes and tribes, but also between government and tribes. The Loya Jirga (grand council) has been used by many Afghan rulers—just as during the Bonn process—to bring together people's representatives from all over Afghanistan for consultation.

A more modern decision making structure—the *shura*—emerged through the mujahideen years, when the military commanders saw a need for more frequent meetings and exchanges. These shuras are now quite common in Afghanistan, and, on a local level, function similar to jirgas as a main forum for conflict resolution and problem solving. Both bodies are very reactive to problems at hand and are not used for long-term planning. In addition to more traditional shuras that communities form themselves, NGOs have also set up shuras or community councils in order to help with their project implementation. The most novel form are the Community Development Councils (CDCs) of the National Solidarity Program (NSP) of the Afghan government that assist communities in basic reconstruction needs. The basic difference between more traditional shuras and their modern reincarnation is membership, representation and legitimacy. In traditional decision making bodies, only influential men of a certain age, family background and economic power (land holding is especially important), with negotiation skills and good linkages to the government, were included. Modern community councils, especially if set up from the outside, are often required to be more representative, including women and younger community members. Often traditional shuras have an influence over who attends the more modern community councils (even if in principle they are supposed to be elected locally) and favor educated members within their communities to participate.[40] Thus traditional shuras, while not as representative as more modern forms, tend to have greater legitimacy.

Modern Civil Institutions and NGOs

Modern civil society institutions in Afghanistan are a largely urban phenomenon and for many Afghans reflect what they call *jamea-e madani.* As such it parallels somewhat the thinking of the great western intellectuals, especially as these organizations are often linked to political interests. More or less active since the 1920s, modern urban associations (e.g., professional, media) emerged often with a modernizing agenda in mind. The political association ranged from communist to nationalist to Islamic. During the communist regime in Afghanistan, the government managed to co-opt or even set up social and cultural associations, using them as a forum to reach out to the people and transmit their values. This is the reason why most of these associations vanished during the war, especially the Taliban period, and only have begun to reemerge in recent years. As a fairly uniquely urban and intellectual element, they are still trying to find their role and place in Afghan society.[41] A mix between these kinds of associations and more traditional thinking is visible, when they call themselves shuras, such as the professional shura in Herat or a handicap shura in Kandahar. In the post-Taliban period, there was an upsurge in these organizations. For example, youth groups emerged all over Afghanistan, with a 2004 survey identifying 144.[42]

The political affiliation of many urban associations has made a transition to parties very fluid. Traditionally, of course, there are the old communist parties and the ones associated with the mujahideen resistance (jihadi parties). Especially since 2001, numerous new political parties have emerged in Afghanistan that mimic their counterparts in western nations, claiming to be multiethnic, democratic and non-religious (especially as jihadi parties are associated with Islamic principles). Many parties were set up by individuals who returned from exile and tend to draw a great portion of their support from urban centers.[43] Thus, it is very difficult to differentiate between them and to ascertain what their actual representation in society is.

NGOs, as in many non-western countries, are a rather secular phenomenon that did not grow out of the grass-roots level, but out of a donor need for implementing programs inside Afghanistan. Their births are more or less set in the early 1980s during the struggle against communist rule. Similar to urban associations, their founders and staff tend to be educated with many being set up from exile (Pakistan, Iran, Europe, North America, etc.). The basic problems of these NGOs—albeit, it is important to note that there are a few very solid ones with genuine goals—are that they are uniquely service providers and have little reference and responsibility to the general public they serve. In addition, some funds to the mujahideen movement were also channeled through NGOs, blurring the lines between humanitarian and reconstruction work and political goals.[44] During the times of state collapse in Afghanistan, many of these NGOs began to perform state functions in the areas of reconstruction, education and health care which made them rather influential.

Even though essentially more modern in nature, especially in the ability to adapt a modern discourse such as human and women rights, these NGOs often do not function much differently than traditional groups by being based on clientelistic networks. There are even talks of "mafia-like" behavior among certain big NGOs that function as gate keepers to resources rather than as channels to local communities. Therefore, trust in NGOs has slowly vanished in Afghanistan, with many Afghans considering them to not be a part of civil society. The question of how sustainable many of these NGOs are is also valid. Most of them exist because of outside resources rather than internal drive. It is very likely that they will vanish as donor funds die off, although there will likely be a few exceptions. Others will, and already have, transform themselves into private businesses, as many have functioned along such lines for quite some time already.

Active Civil Society Contribution to State-Building in Afghanistan

Until now we have reviewed the forms of civil society that exist in Afghanistan. The remainder of the chapter explores the role that civil society has played in the state-building process and could continue to play. This is best done by looking at the Bonn process and the steps that were identified in the "Agreement on Provisional Arrangements in Afghanistan Pending the Re-Establishment of Permanent Government Institutions" (hereinafter: Bonn Agreement) that was signed on December 5, 2001. Essentially, the Bonn Agreement laid a pathway to a new Afghanistan with democratic ideals and participatory political structures. Concrete steps were identified for the building of a new Afghanistan. The Emergency Loya Jirga in June 2002, leading to the transitional government, was the first major step to enhance political participation in Afghanistan, including that of civil society actors. The adaptation of the Afghan constitution at the end of the Constitutional Loya Jirga in January 2004 was the second big step in the process of providing legitimacy to the Afghan government. The last major step that concluded the period outlined in the Bonn Agreement was general elections which were achieved in two parts with the October 2004 presidential elections and the September 2005 parliamentary elections.

Civil Society and the Bonn Process

At the time the United Nations and Germany organized the Bonn process, some felt that there was a missing group among the representatives, that of civil society. In order to change this, the two advisors to Ambassador Ladkhdar Brahimi, Ashraf Ghani Ahmadzai (who later became the head of the Afghanistan Assistance Coordination Agency and then the minister of finance) and Professor Barnett R. Rubin, suggested organizing a parallel meeting of civil society actors. As the UN lacked the capacity and mandate to do so, they approached the *German Stiftung Wissenschaft und Politik* and swisspeace (who had already during Taliban times urged the need to work with civil society) about their willingness to organize such a meeting. Both organizations agreed, with swisspeace taking the lead. The main idea was to facilitate an active exchange between the political groups of the main meeting and civil society actors, but also to provide space for civil society to develop their own vision of a new Afghanistan.

Despite the relative short time (ten days from the UN contact to when the meeting occurred), the two organizations managed to identify, invite and secure travel documents for 76 individual Afghan civil society members that included diaspora representatives. Due to communication problems with Afghanistan, most of the representatives came from organizations that were either based inside Pakistan and Iran but all worked on or even in Afghanistan. Recognizing the importance of the trade community, ten businessmen were also included in the group. Participation of women was 41%.

Despite the fact that the meeting overall was considered useful, especially for the participants themselves who felt they had never been asked to come together collectively as a group to voice their vision of a future Afghanistan, its impact on the resulting Bonn Agreement and ensuing state-building process can be considered close to nil. Even though a joint meeting was arranged with ten representatives from the civil society group being invited to the political meeting, the discussions were non-committing with only lower-level individuals present. Nevertheless, it was one of the first official interactions between a form of organized civil society (even if ad hoc) and political power holders. Thus, the symbolic (and inspiring) value of the meeting can be considered important on its own.

The potential political process that this civil society meeting advanced was even more important. Generally, when people come together and are asked to discuss problems and solutions, a common group identity begins to emerge. This was enhanced by the setting, with civil society in one meeting and the political actors, which were held responsible for the problems of Afghanistan, in another.[45] One can argue that at least for the participants at this meeting, the realization of the possible importance and utility of a civil society for Afghanistan was born. This was evident through active participation, the calling of extraordinary meetings at late hours to continue discussions, and many informal discussions during lunch and dinner times. As such, the impact of the meeting may be long term in that it raised the political consciousness of the individual civil society actors who participated. It should not come as a surprise that in the end the group voiced a desire to form a more formal platform for civil society engagement in Afghanistan. This was the birth of the Afghan Civil Society Forum (ACSF), with the participants of the meeting asking swisspeace to help develop it.

Two facts about the participants need to be highlighted. Unfortunately, due to the time constraints, nobody from traditional communities was invited. Thus, a major group was missing at the meeting. Second, several of the participants later made it into government posts, such as Hanif Atmar (minister for rural economy, now education), Masoom Stanekzai (minister for telecommunications, now special advisor to the president on security), Mahbooba Hoquqmal (deputy of the first Loya Jirga Commission and then state minister for women affairs). This shows already how close the space between government and civil society is in emerging states, but also the potential role individual civil society actors can play in the state-building process by entering into it.

Emergency Loya Jirga Leading to the Transitional Authority

Following the Bonn process, the first step of the Bonn Agreement was the holding of an Emergency Loya Jirga (ELJ) in June 2002 in order to establish a Transitional Authority and ideally officially confirm President Hamid Karzai as its leader. As noted earlier, a Loya Jirga has been used in the past by Afghan rulers to engage its people (or at least the elite representatives) and form consensus. As such, the Loya Jirga in itself can be seen as a form of civil society participation in the state-building process.

In order to also allow the voices of non-traditional elites into the process, the recently founded Afghan Civil Society Forum and swisspeace[46] organized a big civil society gathering in Kabul with the purpose of highlighting possible concerns and recommendations to the ELJ. In an effort to coordinate activities, the meeting was discussed with members of the Loya Jirga Commission and also the United Nations Assistance Mission to Afghanistan (UNAMA). Through this discussion, another purpose for the meeting emerged: a confidence-building process within civil society regarding the upcoming Loya Jirga, and between civil society and an emerging government.

The May 2002 meeting was considered to be the biggest civil society gathering in Afghanistan since the war. A good mix from civil society participants from all over Afghanistan, and also from the diaspora, was present. The meeting was well attended by about 200 members from diverse civil society groups, including traditional representatives, the latter making up for the omission of this group at the Bonn meeting. Participation came strongly from within provinces, and non-NGO affiliation was encouraged. The participation of women and youth was 30% each in order to allow for a more representative group. In addition to internal discussions and interactions with the Loya Jirga Commission, dialogue with government officials was also organized. President Karzai gave the honor of engaging in a rare question and answer session with participants of the conference. The president has not participated in many similar public platforms since.

Despite the fact that recommendations were shared with the Loya Jirga Commission, it is unlikely that there was much impact on the ELJ itself. This, however, may not have mattered much, as the ELJ was disappointing to many given that it was not used much as a public forum. Many important decisions, such as to keep the king from standing against Karzai, were made behind closed doors, and the plenary was used to announce decisions rather than to discuss them. Thus, the civil society meeting had more prospects to function as an exchange forum for an ideological discourse than the Loya Jirga itself.

Despite its limited reach to the ELJ, similarly to the first civil society meeting in Bonn, the symbolic value of this second meeting was extremely high. The fact that the president allowed open questions and even challenges—one youth participant posed a question as to why the president associated himself so closely with warlords—and also the fact that limitations were visible—the same youth participant was later threatened by the bodyguards of the president who belonged to a warlord faction—was important. Similar to the Bonn meeting, a larger number of civil society representatives were exposed to a civil society group consciousness. This is visible with many participants reporting that this meeting had a great impact on their lives and thinking, with an active carrying-home of messages. The meeting also helped to reduce prejudice within a society with an immense level of distrust. Participants saw that they were not the only ones who suffered, but that members from other provinces, districts, ethnic and community groups had similar problems and grievances. Such an experience can be very empowering, but also function as a very basic form of reconciliation. This became evident when groups began to mix more as the conference continued. Many recall a special feeling of unity in the conference they wished could be carried back to their communities.

Following this meeting, ACSF and swisspeace organized other topic and dialogue forums in order to continue the process of consciousness-building among civil society, but also to spark activism. The three follow-up meetings focused on private sector, youth groups and NGO-government dialogue. The last meeting had actually been requested by the government in order to counter the negative rhetoric against NGOs. As a success for the ACSF, one can say that after less than one year it had been accepted as a legitimate platform for dialogue and information exchange. Thus, civil society clearly can play the role of facilitator among civil society actors, but also between civil society and government.

The Constitution-Making Process[47]

Even though Afghanistan succeeded in developing a very good constitution, the process can be described as more than problematic. It took two months longer than required by the Bonn Agreement for the government to announce a constitution drafting commission, and another month for it to be officially inaugurated. There were similar delays during the appointment process of the Constitutional Commission.

It was furthermore decided to hold public consultations without a written text. Public consultations were set up essentially as a brainstorming exercise, as there were no specific plans for a second set on deeper consultations once a text had been drafted. Even though Afghanistan has had constitutions in its history, it could not be assumed that all Afghan people, especially those living in rural areas, would be aware of the new process. Thus, the importance of public outreach for a solid constitution was clearly underestimated or even undervalued. Even though civic education and consultations were seen as part of the process, there was no clear plan or sufficient budget "for a large-scale public outreach campaign that would inform the Afghan people about the constitution-making process, and also explain to them the purpose of a constitution, and above all, the importance of their contribution."[48] "The UN . . . justified the absence of a fuller public process with three concerns—security for the members of the Constitutional Commission and the public; the risk that the process might be hijacked by extremist groups; and the danger of public confusion."[49]

It is here that ACSF-swisspeace felt it had a contribution to make. After initially holding loose meetings among civil society actors and NGOs in Kabul who were interested in working on the constitution, the consensus emerged that there was a lack of knowledge about the constitution and constitution-making process within civil society. In response, ACSF formed a consortium of 13 Afghan NGOs in order to start a public outreach campaign.

The basic idea was to use modern elements of civil society (NGOs) to engage with more traditional and grass-roots elements (community leaders) of civil society in order to develop a decentralized public outreach process. The first step was to work with communities in selecting representatives that would function as civic education providers. The second step was to educate these individuals on the constitution-making process, the purpose of the constitution, possible options for the form of government that could be decided upon, and finally on outreach and consultation techniques. A total of 1,809 (251 women) community representatives from all districts across Afghanistan were educated.

Professional Background of Civic Educators in the Constitution-Making Process

Professional Category	Male	Female	Total
Professional	27	3	30
Government Worker/Official	143	16	159
Media/Culture	1	1	2
Nurse/MD	25	2	27
Teacher/Principal	225	90	315
Religious Leader	57	3	60
Social Worker	171	11	182
Community/Shura Leader	83	—	83
Farmer	26	—	26
Private Sector	9	—	9
Other	791	125	916
TOTAL	1,558	251	1,809

The table above illustrates two things. First, it shows the blurred lines between civil society and other sectors, such as the large number of government workers being sent for training. Second, communities showed a preference to send educated individuals to these training sessions, rather than high level community representatives. Still some traditional leaders (elders and mullahs) also participated. The fact that the "other" category captures a great deal of individuals shows the difficulty of NGOs and individuals themselves to specify professional categories.[50]

Exact figures on how many individuals were reached were difficult to attain. A feed-back form that was supposed to be filled out by all the 1,809 civic education providers[51] resulted in a fairly high figure of 16,000 villages and approximately 4 million individuals (78% men, 22% women) being reached. Sippi Azarbaijani-Moghaddam, the external evaluator of the project, however, doubted the ability of the community leaders to adequately estimate population figures, as some of the individuals she interviewed claimed to have spoken to 200 people in a village mosque where maybe only 50–70 would fit. Her more conservative estimate was that this decentralized process managed to educate a total of about 10–15% (2–2.5 million individuals) of the Afghan population about the constitution-making process.[52] This is an excellent outcome for a two-month process.

As ACSF considered its role as a linkage between civil society and the government, it was in touch with the UN Constitutional Support Unit and also the Secretariat of the Constitution Commission early on. However, not all individuals at these institutions were as perceptive to the positive advantage of civil society involvement in constitution making. There was an overall fear of opening a can of worms that would spill out uncontrolled. A somewhat elitist belief seemed to exist that possibly it was best, given the short timespan to complete the constitution, to write the document behind closed doors with a few experts.After all, what did regular Afghans, especially the uneducated masses, know about a constitution to begin with? This ignored the fact that Afghans in general did more or less have a clear idea about what they wanted, even if they would not be able to express it in a constitutional language. This "translation task" was after all up to the Constitution Commission.

In the end, the commission was quite glad when ACSF offered to help out in the public outreach process, as clearly it was filling a deep void.[53] However, no public information material was ready from the Constitution Commission (or UNAMA) at the time civic education was supposed to begin. ACSF and its partner NGOs had to struggle themselves to draw up such material, with the Constitution Commission secretariat producing their own material much later. At the end of the process, "the director of the secretariat [of the Constitution Commission] in Kabul praised the positive cooperation and achievements of civil society actors. He was especially mindful of the outreach to people in remote communities and to women. He felt that the inclusion of civil society added credibility and legitimacy to the process. He also acknowledged civil society involvement in developing the public education strategy and materials."[54]

However, when ACSF offered to assist in a broad-based consultation process through its network of partners, the offer was rejected with the argument that NGOs could possibly alter what the people had to say. The fact that civil society consultations could have helped to diffuse the fear of fundamentalists hijacking the process was obviously less appealing than the basic fear of public confusion, or an overall fear of the unknown outcome of larger public consultations. "Repeatedly, staff of the UNAMA Constitutional Support Unit . . . stressed that the constitution-making exercise is 'not a referendum,' that the goal of consultations is 'quality,' not quantity."[55] Clearly, however, there was little trust placed in civil society.

It is interesting to note that the reservation did not initially come from the Afghan staff but from one western advisor to the Constitution Commission and an Afghan-American working for UNAMA, both having grown up in western democracies. One would think that they were able to grasp the importance and need for a greater public consultation and be quite happy for civil society support. But their apparent fear of losing control of the process was obviously greater, and this greatly influenced the Afghan decision makers. In an evaluation later on, the fears were described as losing "the perceived ownership of a politically sensitive process."[56] The Constitution Commission felt in the end that civil society was more visible, and it looked as if people were charged with making the constitution and not government.[57] That this is essentially a positive assessment seemed not to have sunk in, with government agencies perceiving civil society still as competitors in a political process that should have been seen as inclusive.

Even though ACSF and its partner networks in the end were not allowed to consult directly with the people, it developed an alternative approach. It simply designed a series of regional "feed-back" workshops where selected representatives from the public outreach process were invited back to share their views with constitution commissioners. In the end the Constitution Commission quite appreciated these alternative platforms, as often their own consultations were hampered by local government officials or power holders who impaired freedom of speech.[58] The largest of these regional workshops was held in Kabul during July 29–31, 2003 jointly with the Constitution Commission, as now it saw a chance to have a platform where some contested issues could be consulted prior to the Constitutional Loya Jirga (CLJ).[59] Thus, despite the feelings of civil society as competition, it can be said that the civil society contribution helped to enhance an initially flawed constitution-making process and allowed a wider reach and discourse with the greater public.

It is important to note that the hopes and faith of the people in the process were much stronger at the beginning of the civic education outreach. People then were almost unanimously grateful to the government for engaging them by educating them on the constitution-making process and soliciting their opinion. Unfortunately the imperfect consultation that followed the wider public outreach reversed some of those views. Many people believed that in the end the government was not interested in their views after all, and that the process was more or less a charade. This does show the power of participatory processes in post-conflict settings where trust is a general problem.

After the consultations, the Constitution Commission drew up a draft constitution that was sent to the regional centers for viewing. ACSF-swisspeace also organized a set of 22 consultation workshops and provided feedback on the draft constitution that was distributed at the CLJ that was held in Kabul in December 2003/January 2004. A specialized workshop to harness the voices of women and their recommendations for the CLJ was also organized shortly before the CLJ in Kabul (December 8–9, 2003).

Similar to the ELJ in 2002, the CLJ in 2004 was not used as a platform for consensus building, but proved rather divisive. In addition to the fact that several important decisions were made behind closed doors, ethnic politics were used to push certain articles through.[60]

In light of the above, "even though the Afghan constitution resulted in a very solid document oriented along democratic ideals that gave also considerable rights for women, the process was tremendously flawed."[61] An ideal opportunity to work on an "ideological integration" in a divided Afghanistan was missed with divisions deeper in the end. Existing discourse and the reaching of compromises was held among a few elites and did not include the greater set of representatives. A prominent Pashtun NGO leader furiously recalled that many Pashtuns felt used by Karzai and then sold out immediately by the end of the Loya Jirga. He said that the Pashtuns would never forgive him for this.[62]

The 2004 Presidential and 2005 Parliamentary Elections

Despite the fact that both election processes were slightly different, civil society involvement in both was essentially a follow-up on the public outreach during the constitution-making process. The main goal was to keep people informed about what was going on and engaged in the state-building process. The success with which the ACSF consortium had managed the public outreach during the constitution-making process prompted UN electoral officials to approach them early on to team up for the presidential civic education outreach. This resulted in the fact that during 2003–2005, the ACSF and the International Foundation for Election Systems (IFES) were the two official partners of the Afghan government—Joint Electoral Management Body (JEMB) which included government and UN employees—in providing civic education on voter registration and elections.[63] While still considered a partner during the presidential election, the UN outsourced the entire civic outreach for the parliamentary elections to the ACSF consortium and IFES. This can be seen as a success of the civil society approach—and also a commitment of civil society to contribute to a difficult state-building process.

Until ACSF was engaged in both elections, there was much debate if it was a wise idea to participate in another flawed process. After all, security was not favorable prior to the elections and deteriorated further during the outreach. Second, there were reservations among civil society actors with the rush for elections while other requirements of the Bonn Agreement were lagging behind—mainly reforms in the security and justice sector and the DDR process—but also other visible reconstruction. Furthermore, there was still too much emphasis on strengthening the authority of the central government, and too little on the development of a political discourse. "The country's long-term stability, however, rests on the ability of its institutions to accommodate the latter process and to provide channels through which the various components of Afghan society can find expression and accommodate competing interests."[64]

In the end ACSF decided that despite the problematic natures of the elections, civil society had little ability to stop a process that was already agreed upon and relentlessly pushed by the international community at all costs. Furthermore, as funds for engaging civil society tended to be linked to political processes, the ACSF consortium had to link future civic education to upcoming elections if it was to continue. Most importantly, however, ACSF sees knowledge as a basic human right and a form of empowerment. By continuing with its civic education engagement, ACSF provided civil society with the tools to understand what was being imposed upon them and to slowly emerge into rational actors that could make their own decisions. Possibly ASCF was able to make a contribution in this regard.

During the civic education outreach, the ACSF consortium continued to engage with traditional elements within Afghan society and utilize their functions as community representatives. Prior to setting up face-to-face civic education sessions, consultations were held with influential elders and mullahs, and community mobilization sessions were organized. Mullahs were especially important in helping to legitimize the election process, but also in gaining access to women. The *ulema shura* in Kandahar, for example, issued an edict in 2004 that stated that the participation of women in elections did not contradict the Koran. Mullahs in Herat, Jalalabad and elsewhere helped with public outreach for women, such as educating women themselves, opening up their mosques for education sessions for women, or convincing men to allow their female family members to be educated.

Traditional elders were also instrumental in allowing access to women and thus enhancing women's participation in elections. The Tribal Liaison Office, another civil society organization set up by swisspeace that aimed specifically at engaging traditional elements within Afghan civil society,[65] utilized a very pragmatic cost-benefit perspective to explain how local elites would benefit from women voting in terms of supporting their own political base.[66] This resulted in extremely high voter turn-outs of women in the southeast (40%)—unprecedented in Pashtun areas, especially as compared to the south of the country (20% participation of women). Thus, "the approach to work through powerful, but change-oriented, local elders proved successful in negotiating political space for the participation of women by recruiting women into the civic education process and allowing women to vote in both presidential and parliamentary elections."[67]

The ability to hold civic education sessions for women can also be considered as having a long-term impact on the advancement of women. Most women civic educators explained that elections were only one of the many topics that were discussed during the sessions. Often the sessions functioned as exchange forums for women about their own rights but also aspirations. One female lead trainer from Paktia fittingly said, "Now women have the information that other kinds of human rights exists. They can make a comparison between what they are used to from their traditional settings and make a choice what they believe will be better for them in the future."[68] Thus, civic education sessions, in addition to providing information, can be considered as a rudimentary form of empowerment and obviously a consciousness-building process with long-term impact.

Overall, ACSF and its network of 15 partner organizations was able to educate 1.7 million Afghan voters during the presidential elections and nearly 8 million during the parliamentary elections. In both bases, women's participation was about 30%. The civic education force expanded from 412 in the presidential to 1,591 individuals in parliamentary elections, covering nearly all districts outside the central area of Kabul, which was covered by the IFES.

Despite the fact that ACSF and its network had to function in a deteriorating security environment, their ability to embed themselves deeply into traditional elements of civil society helped enhance their security. During the presidential civic education outreach, ACSF mourned no losses among their civic education force, while attacks on the UN staff were numerous. Even though three civic educators were killed during the 2005 parliamentary public outreach and numerous threats and attacks occurred, they were considerably low in comparison to the overall rising level of violence in the country. According to most civic educators, traditional communities, once in agreement with the civic education outreach, did their utmost to protect them from harm. Overall rural communities thirsted for information about what was going on and appreciated the education they received. Many times the educators came from within the communities to begin with.

Through this civic education effort, civil society performed an important role in the Afghan state-building process. It assisted the government not only to spread information about the election process through the country, but it also contributed to the legitimacy (or at least a certain acceptance) of the elections within civil society.

Similarly, as during the constitution-making process, the legitimacy for public processes decreased further between the presidential and parliamentary elections. A complaint from civil society that began during the constitution process and continued on was the fact that warlords and criminal elements continued to be in power, even within government. Civil society had the expectation from President Karzai, legitimized by them during the presidential elections, to stand against the warlords. They were disappointed when this did not occur. On top of this, warlords were able to run in the parliamentary elections.[69] One could say some voted with their feet, by simply not going to the polling stations during parliamentary elections. Of course, critiques of the elections (especially within government) often like to point their fingers to poor civic educations for a low voter turn-out, forgetting the fact that civic education merely provides information and does not tell people what to do.

It is important to emphasize that in addition to the large-scale public civic education outreach, other NGOs and media organizations contributed to the process through radio and television programs, mobile theater and cinema, and other forms of outreach. Thus, the entire process was well supported by civil society, as the emerging Afghan state did not even have the capacity to organize such an extensive outreach itself.

Involvement of Civil Society in Security Arrangements

As a last element for civil society engagement in state-building, a more controversial contribution—that of security—should be mentioned. It has been noted in the beginning that states tend to gain legitimacy when they provide basic services to the people. In a post-conflict context security tends to be among the top priorities. Still, security has been an area where the Afghan government consistently has failed to deliver. Despite benchmarks in the Bonn Agreement, the disarmament, demobilization and reintegration process (DDR) remains problematic and incomplete, and only about half of the desired Afghan National Army has been established.[70] The national police force is in similar bad shape. At the same time, insurgency and violence is on the rise in Afghanistan. A recent informal poll among civil society by ACSF showed that merely 10% of all Afghans feel protected by international security forces (as of course their mandate has nothing to do with fighting crime) and only about 30% by the Afghan government. The majority, however, feel that they still have to fend for themselves.[71] Similarly, as was described above, civil society tended to rely on traditional structures when it came to protection during their large-scale public outreaches.

As security is also associated with development programs, the frustration among Pashtun communities in the southeast, east and south is understandably high.[72] Due to high levels of violence in their areas, reconstruction efforts have been slow. This can lead to a deadly vicious circle, where frustrated and disenchanted individuals are easily recruited into non-governmental opposition (such as the Taliban in the south of Afghanistan) which leads to more violence which leads to no development and so on.

In response, traditional civil society (spearheaded by the Mangal tribe) in the southeast, fed up with a lack of security and an associated lack of development, reinstated their tribal police, the *Arbakee.* "The notion of an Arbakee is an old concept in rural Pashtun Afghanistan which can be best compared to what we consider as community policing. . . . Due to the association of the Arbakee with traditional structures, *jirgas* or *shuras,* Arbakee can only function in areas with strong and cohesive tribal structures. This at present is only true for the Southeast of Afghanistan, and Arbakee are essentially unique to this area."[73]

Only in certain exceptional cases (and more recently) does the government pay for the Arbakee to assist them in government tasks, such as providing security during the presidential and parliamentary elections, where they clearly outnumbered the Afghan National Police by providing three to four times as many men. "Currently, in Paktia there are Arbakee in existence in every single district, except for the provincial center. Their engagement ranges from contributing to district security, protecting national forests against illegal logging, to road, and in rare cases border, security."[74]

Through awareness raising of the Tribal Liaison Office and swisspeace with the Afghan government and international actors, a certain acceptance for engagement with the Arbakee has been achieved for the southeast of Afghanistan. Despite a criticism that security should exclusively remain a government task and that it is dangerous to outsource it to non-state actors, temporary arrangements with the tribes of the southeast for their Arbakee were brokered.

Unfortunately, rather than continuing an exploration of the role that traditional (and also modern) civil society can play in contributing security, the Afghan government, and also some international actors, have recently begun to embrace the idea of tribal militia in the fight against the Taliban. That tribal militia, however, are not the same as Arbakee has been conveniently overlooked.

> It is important to draw a clear line between the Arbakee and militias of any sort that are associated with warlords for the following reasons: The Arbakee are a very temporary body that is only established for solving specific problems, and only for the length of time required to do so. The size of the Arbakee depends on the kind of operation, in many cases it is simply for the purpose of dispute resolution or executing the decision of a jirga or shura. Despite the

> fact that each Arbakee has a clear leader (mir), the accountability goes back to the tribal council (jirga or shura) that called upon the Arbakee, which in turn is accountable back to its own community. Furthermore, Arbakee only function in the very limited realm of the tribe they represent. Their fighters are volunteers from within the community and are paid for by the community. This emphasizes again that their loyalty is with their communities, and not an individual leader.[75]

Conclusion: Possible Areas of Engagement for Civil Society

The above discussion, even if only a short glimpse tied to the experience of the author, sheds some light on what civil society in Afghanistan is, and also what functions it could fulfill in state-building exercises. The examples put forth make a strong argument for the necessity of involving civil society, especially traditional civil society, and the advantages for doing so. While there is clearly a need for an enabling environment for civil society activities,[76] such as security and rule of law, the examples suggest that sometimes civil society is able to function even under difficult conditions and sometimes can make its own contributions to working in insecure environments. The following initial lessons can be observed that might be able to enhance our knowledge of how to better engage civil society in state-building processes in the future.

First, a state-building process needs "ideological integration." This is usually an organic process that is based on an intensive discourse among the different actors in a country. The examples presented in this chapter have shown that civil society is able to contribute to such a discourse by organizing meetings, dialogue forums and public outreach campaigns. Of course, such a discourse also occurs over the media through radio, television programs and written publications. In addition to the overall work described here, the Afghan Civil Society Forum also publishes a bimonthly magazine called *Jamea-e Madani* (*Civil Society*) that has engaged the intellectual community into a critical discourse about events going on in their country. During the presidential elections a joint edition with the Joint Electoral Management Body had to be dropped as the government body wanted to censor articles that were critical about the holding of elections in an insecure environment. The magazine was published later on with different donor funds and without JEMB contribution.

Second, in post-conflict environments, justice is a very important issue. While the formal justice system clearly rests with the government, civil society can make a contribution to a more informal process of transitional justice or reconciliation. It may be somewhat bold to claim that civil society had been engaged in a reconciliation process in Afghanistan. Nevertheless, the activities of the Afghan Civil Society Forum had some aspects of reconciliation built into it. Continuously bringing people from different backgrounds and regions together in large gatherings has an impact on how different groups perceive each other, and also how they interact with one another. As it was noted, in many conferences it was important for the participants to find out that they were not the only ones who had suffered, but that in the war everybody had to make sacrifices at one point in time. In the opinion of the International Crisis Group, "democratic institutions can only develop in an environment that allows open discussion about governance, something that continues to elude Afghanistan more than two years after the signing of the Bonn Agreement."[77]

Especially in Afghanistan, there are no clear victims or perpetrators, with groups shifting between these positions throughout the war. Another concrete, even if small, example might be a youth meeting that ACSF organized with the Afghan Youth Coordination Agency and swisspeace in Bamyan in 2004 where some prejudices and fears could be diminished. Many participants from Pashtun areas that were invited declined to come out of fear of revenge for the Taliban genocide of the Hazara people. The few Pashtuns who overcame their fear and did come, however, were quite surprised at the warm reception and of course the fact that they were able to live and report on the meeting. Thus, meetings that exchanged participants from different regions, even without a clear reconciliation agenda, were able to contribute to the process of dealing with the past, or at minimum, to a confidence-building process. Civil society is an ideal facilitator here.

Third, the many civic education outreaches with which ACSF was engaged served the purpose of building capacity within civil society by providing citizens with the knowledge of what was happening in their country. With such knowledge it is easier to become an informed actor, and possibly, activist. Adult education and information distribution is an element for which civil society networks are ideal. All capacity building processes tend to be elements of consciousness-raising and empowerment. As discussed, the meetings organized by ACSF, as well as the public outreach, helped people to understand more about their own role in the state-building process. This can be a building-block for people joining into a more organized civil society movement if they see a utility in doing so.

Such outreaches allow for a better exchange between modern and traditional elements of civil society, with a mutual learning process occurring. Throughout the three civic education outreaches discussed here, NGO staff became more and more aware about the functioning of traditional structures, and learned from each other about how best to engage them.

Fourth, the entire outreach work of civil society, public education and also consultation sends the indirect message that people matter for state-building. The great appreciation among Afghans for being included showed that sending this message is very important for keeping people engaged with a process rather than turning against it. Sometimes even small gestures such as civic education or consultations can demonstrate inclusiveness.

While civil society can assist in this process, states and the international community need to decide to engage in it. The drawback of an inclusive approach is that once civil society is engaged, expectations are raised, and if the state cannot follow up, disappointment and frustration can be high. Therefore, engagement needs to be planned long-term and, as it was done in Afghanistan, not simply for short processes only. That a feeling of inclusion may lead to an increased legitimacy of processes should be a good incentive for emerging states to engage with their population. Civil society-state partnerships in post-conflict peace-building can increase the legitimacy of political processes or the entire state-building exercise.

Fifth, the capacity-building element should not be limited to civil society. As described, civil society can function as an important partner of fragile states in terms of adding to their capacity, especially the capacity to reach out to the people. Civil society can be the space that links sectors together or a facilitator of interactions.

Last but not least is the importance of civil society to assist in the provision of services. While this is often a much contested domain as states are quick to see civil society as competitors rather than collaborators, it may be simply a task of finding the appropriate ways to foster successful synergies. The National Solidarity Program of the Afghan government that works with NGOs to implement a large-scale community funding scheme is a good example of how effective collaboration may work. A second suggestion was put forth in the area of security, where tribal police (Arbakee) could work under government leadership to enhance security in the southeast. When carefully planned and designed, civil society-government contribution can go a long way in peace processes.

Despite all these possible areas of engagement of civil society in a state-building process, it is important to emphasize that civil society in Afghanistan is still growing, especially the modern elements. While traditional civil society is much stronger, it still needs a strengthening of its capacities and also in finding ways of how to fit into the peace and reconstruction process. When working with local civil society, we need to find ways of fostering good partnerships with international civil society in order to bring in the capacity that is lacking. The experience of swisspeace in this process has been very positive, as programs worked well due to the merging of inside and outside knowledge and capacity. Nevertheless, the swisspeace experience also shows that there is much more need for capacity-building for the future if this process is to continue.

Another problem is the approach of the international community, especially as it relates to funding. As noted before, the tendency to look toward NGOs as civil society is still too prevalent. There is a shying away of working with traditional civil society as it is perceived as undemocratic, and also due to not wanting to strengthen parallel structures. The need to adapt our engagement methods to the society in question, and not get stuck in a modernization agenda that may backfire is very important here. We may need to be more creative and find new ways of how to work with traditional civil society elements, such as tribal elders and religious leaders. Swisspeace has tried to demonstrate some innovative ways through its work with ACSF and the Tribal Liaison Office that both strongly integrated traditional elements into their work. This should be evaluated and built upon.

Notes

1. This chapter greatly benefitted from comments by Professor Howard Adelman.

2. ACSF-swisspeace, "People Make the Constitution: Civil Society and Civic Education on the Constitution-Making Process," *Final Narrative Donor Report (*Kabul: ACSF-swisspeace, 2004).

3. Thania Paffenholz and Christopf Spurk, "Civil Society/Civic Engagement and Peacebuilding," Research Paper Commissioned by the Social Development Department of the World Bank, 2006, 2.

4. Jochen Hippler, "Nation-States for Export?: Nation-Building Between Military Intervention, Crisis Prevention and Development Policy," in Jochen Hippler, ed., *Nation-Building: A Key Concept for Peaceful Conflict Transformation* (London: Pluto Press, 2005), 3.

5. Astri Suhrke, "The Limits of State-Building: The Role of International Assistance in Afghanistan," Paper Presented at the Annual Meeting of the International Studies Association, San Diego, 21–24 March 2006.

6. Alfred C. Stephan, *The State and Society: Peru in Comparative Perspective* (Princeton: Princeton University Press, 1978), xii, as cited in Theda Skocpol, "Bringing the State Back In: Current Research," in Peter Evans, Dietrich Rueschemeyer, and Theda Skocpol, eds., *Bringing the State Back In* (New York: Cambridge University Press, 1985), 7.

7. Hippler, "Nation-States for Export?," 9.

8. During the work of swisspeace in Afghanistan in various civic education outreach programs, the message that came back was clear: "When will there be justice and peace and we will be rid of the warlords?" A good example might be a widow whose sole purpose for voting was to prevent the warlord from continuing to beat up her sons.

9. Hippler, "Nation-States for Export?."

10. Much of what is presented in this chapter rests upon the experiences and observations of the author during her work in integrating civil society in the peace and reconstruction process in Afghanistan during the initial four years of the Bonn Agreement (2002–2005).

11. Much of this discussion builds upon a concept note written in late 2003 that tried to secure funding for more research on civil society. Susanne Schmeidl, "Understanding Civil Society in Non-Western Countries: Some Initial Thoughts on Afghanistan" (Kabul: ACSF-swisspeace, 2003). This was extended into the following papers: Sippi Azarbaijani-Moghaddam, Conrad Schetter, and Susanne Schmeidl, "The Transition from Relief to Development from a Human Security Perspective: Afghanistan" (New York: Commission on Human Security, 2002); Conrad Schetter and Susanne Schmeidl, "Afghanistan: Aktuelle Situation und Möglichkeiten der Befriedung," in Erich Reiter, ed., *Jahrbuch für internationale Sicherheitspolitik 2004* (Hamburg: Mittler, 2004).

12. N. Chandhoke, *State and Civil Society: Explanations in Political Theory* (New Delhi: Sage Publications, 1995), 38, as cited in Shirin Akiner, "Prospects for Civil Society in Tajikistan," in Amyn B. Sajoo, ed., *Civil Society in the Muslim World: Comparative Perspectives* (London: I. B. Tauris Publishers, 2002), 149.

13. Marlies Glasius, "Civil Society," (2002), Fathom Knowledge Network. http://www.fathom.com/feature/122536/index.html.

14. UNDP, Civil Society Development and Governance Division, *Civil Society Sourcebook: Participatory Organizational Evaluation Tool* (CSOPP Resource Center: Toolbox, 2000).

15. See here also G. Mohan, "Good Governance at the Grassroots: The Role of Social Capital in Participator Development," Paper presented at the 2000 Annual Meeting

of the Association of American Geographers, Pittsburgh, as discussed in Kristian Berg Harpviken, Arne Strand, and Karin Ask, *Afghanistan and Civil Society,* Report Commissioned by the Norwegian Ministry of Foreign Affairs (Peshawar/Bergen: Chr. Michelson Institute, 2002).

16. Masoud Kamali, "Civil Society and Islam: A Sociological Perspective," *Archives Europeenes De Sociologie,* vol. 42, no. 3 (2001): 465, who cites Ernest Gellner, *Conditions of Liberty, Civil Society and its Rivals* (London: Hamish Hamilton, 1994).

17. http:/www.lse.ac.uk/collections/CCS/what_is_civil_society.htm (accessed 13 June 2007).

18. Philip Oxhorn, "Making Civil Society Relevant (Again)," *Focal Point: Spotlight on the Americas,* vol. 2, no. 3 (2003): 1.

19. Andreas Wimmer and Conrad Schetter, "State-Formation First: Recommendations for Reconstruction and Peace-Making in Afghanistan," ZEF Discussion Paper, no. 45, 2002. http://www.zef.de/publications.htm, 8.

20. I found evidence of this during my work in Afghanistan as many government officials considered themselves as civil society and wanted to participate in civil society discussions that also criticized government, not understanding the clear distinction.

21. This comes from multiple discussions with traditional leaders in Afghanistan during my work on civil society promotion there.

22. Harpviken et al., *Afghanistan and Civil Society,* 1.

23. William Maley and Amin Saikal, "Civil Society and Reconstruction: Some Reflections," *Afghanistan Info,* vol. 52, nos. 7–8 (2002): 7.

24. Oxhorn, "Making Civil Society Relevant (Again)," 1.

25. Stephen Orvis, "Civil Society in Africa or African Civil Society?," *Journal of Asian and African Studies,* vol. 36, no. 1 (2001): 27.

26. William Maley, *Rescuing Afghanistan* (Sydney: University of New South Wales Press, 2006), 18.

27. "Patron-client networks are also rather nebulous and informal, making them poor candidates for inclusion in civil society according to the conventional view," in Orvis, "Civil Society in Africa or African Civil Society?," 27.

28. Max Weber, *Wirtschaft und Gesellschaft* (reprint 1980; Tübingen, 1921).

29. Orvis, "Civil Society in Africa or African Civil Society?," 27.

30. Ibid., 23.

31. Kamali, "Civil Society and Islam," 478–479.

32. Orvis, "Civil Society in Africa or African Civil Society?."

33. Jawed Ludin, "Civil Society in Afghanistan," Background Paper for the Second Afghan Civil Society Conference, 15–19 May 2002, in Kabul, Afghanistan.

34. Azarbaijani-Moghaddam et al., "The Transition from Relief to Development."

35. Harpviken et al., *Afghanistan and Civil Society,* second sentence of footnote 11.

36. Azarbaijani-Moghaddam et al., "The Transition from Relief to Development."

37. Conrad Schetter, "Wiederaufbau zwischen allen Stühlen: Die Internationale Intervention zwischen Staat, Zivilgesellschaft und traditionellen Eliten," in *Schriften zur Demokratieförderung uner Bedingungen fragiler Staatlichkeit,* Issue 1: Afghanistan (Berlin: Heinrich Böll Foundation, 2006), 9–25. See also Sébastien Trives, "Afghanistan: Tackling the Insurgency—The Case of the Southeast," *politique étrangère,* vol. 1 (2006).

38. Counterpart International, *Afghanistan Civil Society Assessment* (Washington, DC: CPI, 2005).

39. Masood Karokhail and Susanne Schmeidl, "Integration of Traditional Structures into the State-Building Process: Lessons from the Tribal Liaison Office in Loya Paktia," in *Publication Series on Promoting Democracy under Conditions of State Fragility,* Issue 1: Afghanistan (Berlin: Heinrich Böll Foundation, 2006). http://www.boell.de/downloads/asien/afghanistan_en.pdf.

40. Compare here also Harpviken et al., *Afghanistan and Civil Society.*

41. Discussion with representatives from the Journalist Association and other social and cultural associations in Kabul during October and November 2002.

42. Afghan Civil Society Forum and Afghan Youth Coordination Agency, *Mapping Youth Organizations in Afghanistan* (Kabul: ACSF, 2005).

43. Compare here also Schetter, "Wiederaufbau zwischen allen Stühlen."

44. Susanne Schmeidl, "(Human) Security Dilemmas: Long-Term Implications of the Afghan Refugee Crisis," *Third World Quarterly,* vol. 23, no. 1 (2007): 7–29.

45. The youngest delegate expressed this with the following words: "We are told to respect our elders, since they are said to be wise and to guide us the way, yet you have not taught us anything but that you are only able to use weapons and to rule by might. How are we supposed to be the future of Afghanistan if you are not able to give us better role models?"

46. In the first years, the Afghan Civil Society Forum was managed by swisspeace upon the explicit wish of civil society members.

47. Most of this draws on my own observations and International Crisis Group, *Afghanistan's Flawed Constitutional Process* (Kabul and Brussels: ICG Asia Report no. 56, 2003). Selected points of this discussion were already presented in Susanne Schmeidl, "The Emperor's New Cloth: The Unravelling of Peacebuilding in Afghanistan," *Friedens-Warte—Journal of International Peace and Organizations,* 1–2 (2007): 69–86.

48. Schmeidl, "The Emperor's New Cloth," 78. Compare here ICG, *Afghanistan's Flawed Constitutional Process.* "Compounding the problem of factional domination of the process is the absence of a real public education and consultation. The UN-drafted plan contains minimal public education and consultation elements to which scant funds are allocated."

49. ICG, *Afghanistan's Flawed Constitutional Process,* i.

50. In a complementary special women-outreach program, 11 women's NGOs educated an additional 1,074 women in 15 provinces where outreach to women was considered to be difficult (Farah, Ghor, Helmand, Kandahar, Khost, Kunar, Laghman, Logar, Paktia, Paktika, Parwan, Samangan, Uruzgan, Wardak, Zabul). This mainly occurred in the provincial capitals. In contrast to the global outreach, the women were not tasked to spread the message further, except to their own extended families.

51. The response rate was about 39%, with 702 individuals from 26 provinces completing forms.

52. Sippi Azarbaijani-Moghaddam, *Technical Lessons Learned from the Afghan Civil Society Forum (ACSF/swisspeace); Civic Education for the Constitution Project* (Kabul: ACSF-swisspeace, 2003).

53. Of course there was other public outreach being conducted through media, mobile cinema, theater and other forms of civic education than the face-to-face approach ACSF-swisspeace was engaged in.

54. Azarbaijani-Moghaddam, *Technical Lessons Learned,* 71–72.

55. ICG, *Afghanistan's Flawed Constitutional Process,* 19.

56. Sippi Azarbaijani-Moghaddam, *Technical Lessons Learned,* 72.

57. Apparently the comment was an indirect criticism to a widely distributed poster that ACSF and its partners had drawn up for the civil society public outreach which was indeed entitled with the logo, "People Making the Constitution."

58. Compare here ICG, *Afghanistan's Flawed Constitutional Process,* i. "Civil Society across Afghanistan consistently identifies provincial governments as an important source of insecurity. Yet, the consultation process is organized mostly in provincial centers with the cooperation of those governments." The following quote from a Kunduz civic education provider compiled by Sippi Azarbaijani-Moghaddam illustrates this problem as well: "I was finishing off a session in a school. The commander had been

present throughout and people did not say very much. Eventually I finished off the session and made preparations to leave. The commander left the school ahead of me. As he was concentrating on walking down the stairs I felt someone put their hand in my pocket. I was alarmed and thought I was being robbed. Then I felt a hand in my other pocket. I walked down a few steps with their hands in my pockets. After a while they removed their hands and I sped down the stairs. I went to a corner and examined my pockets. There were many crumpled pieces of paper in there with comments. The first one said, "There can be no constitution process without disarmament and demobilization."

59. Participation of women in this workshop was at 36%.

60. This played out mainly in President Karzai playing the Pashtun card to push the presidential system which backfired in discussions over official languages and criteria for selecting ministers. See ICG, *Elections and Security in Afghanistan,* ICG Asia Briefing, 30 March 2004, 8–9; and Schmeidl, "The Emperor's New Cloth," 78–79.

61. Schmeidl, "The Emperor's New Cloth," 78.

62. Personal discussions in early 2004.

63. IFES covered the six provinces around Kabul (Kabul, Parwan, Logar, Wardak, Panjshir and Kapisa) and ACSF-swisspeace with its network covered the other 28 provinces.

64. ICG, *Elections and Security in Afghanistan,* 10.

65. See Karokhail and Schmeidl, "Integration of Traditional Structures into the State-Building Process," for a critical assessment of TLO.

66. Clearly at this point elders had already swallowed the fact that their new government had decided on a voting system that gave men and women equal rights—something they clearly did not agree with, but were willing to live with.

67. Karokhail and Schmeidl, "Integration of Traditional Structures into the State-Building Process," 74.

68. Interview with lead trainer during the filming of a documentary about TLO, *Spin Giri: The White Beards* (Berlin: Heinrich Böll Foundation).

69. For many Afghans, the idea of due process was difficult to grasp. The fact that even though by law warlords were not allowed to run for office, this only was legitimate if they had been accused, tried and convicted. But until then, they remained innocent until proven guilty. This clearly shows the difficulty to push elections ahead when developments in the reform of the justice sector lag behind.

70. See Maley, *Rescuing Afghanistan.*

71. This was done in preparation for the 2006 London conference.

72. ICG, *Afghanistan: The Problem of Pashtun Alienation* (Kabul and Brussels: ICG Asia Report no. 62, 2003).

73. Karokhail and Schmeidl, "Integration of Traditional Structures into the State-Building Process," 63.

74. Ibid.

75. Ibid.

76. A recent Agha Khan conference in Kabul in June 2007 dealt with this topic.

77. ICG, *Elections and Security in Afghanistan,* 10.

8
The Afghan Economy

Wolfgang Danspeckgruber and Robert P. Finn

WITH THE FALL OF THE TALIBAN, Afghanistan emerged in the winter of 2002 ravaged from decades of civil war and occupation. A country that had descended into chaos from an already unenviable position as one of the poorest nations on earth suffered famine, genocide, widespread placement of explosive mines and the deliberate destruction of its infrastructure. By almost every indicator, Afghanistan was at or near the bottom of the list. Millions of Afghans were resident as refugees in Pakistan and Iran where they lived in poverty and suffered social and political discrimination, and where they created significant security problems for their hosts. Many things have changed for the better in Afghanistan and dramatic increases in income, investment and the development of infrastructure have taken place, but the overall rate of progress has failed to satisfy Afghans and endemic and structural problems threaten to sideline what progress has been made.

In order for Afghanistan to lift itself from the cycle of destruction and civil war, it needs certain things. Simply, they are security, governance and a working economy. The first two have received much attention from Afghans and the international community and remain problematic, but the third has lagged even further behind. The world is well aware of the security problems in Afghanistan, which since 2005, seemed to be increasing rather than decreasing. The resurgence of the Taliban, the problems with Pakistan, and other security problems including those of governance are not the direct subject of this chapter, although they necessarily appear on its pages. The question of the Afghan economy, however, is very much of concern.

Until and unless Afghanistan develops a self-sustaining economy, it will remain, as it has for over a century, a state dependent on the largesse of others for its governmental functions. Worse, an impoverished Afghanistan can become a hotbed for radicalism and such a failed state may harbor terrorists. Now, after decades of war, Afghanistan depends on others to feed and support its population as well, with results that indicate the need for serious consideration and efforts to fundamentally change attitudes and practices. The Afghans are known, rightly, as a nation of traders, but only a small city-state can build its economy solely on trading. Afghans have to develop the skills and attitudes necessary for value-added economic structures, to create saleable objects and the networks of distribution and information to compete in the rapidly growing world economy. Assistance is, in the end, not a viable answer for a stable Afghanistan, both intrinsically and also pragmatically, in that it simply is not going to be available. Assistance levels and enthusiasm are already beginning to slow as an array of problems ranging from lack of progress to decreased security and the negative impact of the universally unpopular war in Iraq take their toll on the effort for Afghanistan. A careful analysis of Afghanistan's overall economic potential seems to demonstrate major capabilities from agriculture to infrastructure to trade, mining and energy which could very well offer a hopeful and relatively prosperous future, certainly one independent from the overarching poppy problem.

Post-2001

The Afghan government is well aware of this and has launched a major international effort to bring investment funds to Kabul. It has also modernized many of its laws that apply to business, including tax laws and those governing corporate entities. One of the earliest achievements of the government on the macroeconomic level was the replacement of several currencies with a unified national currency, the Afghani (AFN). That took place in 2002 in just six months with little difficulty. "Old Afghani" notes were exchanged with "New Afghani" notes at a ratio of 100 to 1. In 2006, its value was 60.58 AFN to 1 Euro. This was a truly amazing feat for a nation just beginning to emerge from decades of civil war. The Japanese estimated that they would have needed two years to complete the same process in their country. The stability of Afghanistan's currency since then has been another positive factor. Several international banks have now opened offices in Afghanistan.

The development of extensive cell phone systems in Afghanistan with more than a million subscribers marks a radical change in internal communication. USAID announced in 2006 that 26 out of 33 provincial communications network facilities are operational. This is the first step in a provincial/district telecommunications network which enhances private sector growth and assists local government. As late as 2002, the minister of roads said that he had no ability whatsoever to communicate by telephone with any of his provincial offices. Young Afghans trained in western universities will bring expertise and methodologies to help in the creation of a new economy that is integrated internationally. One US government (USG) program is sending large numbers of Afghan government officials abroad for occupational training to help them bring their skills in line with the demands of a new Afghan economy. However, one has to be realistic about the levels of resistance and ignorance that continue to plague the system. Afghanistan's goal is to bring itself up to the level of a self-sustaining, albeit poor nation, rather than remaining at the very bottom of the world's income levels.

Many of the problems of Afghanistan stem from the economic attitudes of its ruling class: tribal, feudal and militaristic. The meager wealth and economic assets accrued during the monarchy and the Soviet occupation became the subject of partisan feuds and squabbling that led, for example, to the destruction of Kabul. Regional military commanders, the famous warlords, seated themselves at the interstices of trade and commerce to take advantage of the income they provided. Petty rivalries, such as in the Mazar-i Sharif area, prevented the redevelopment of the oil and gas reserves which had produced $200 million per annum by Soviet accounting methods in the 1980s. Instead, General Dostum and Commander Atta's forces engaged in endless skirmishes, literally fighting over cows. The result was numerous deaths and the suspension for several years of US assistance to the area. Monies that could and should go to development are still being spent on local military forces because of security concerns. In the spring of 2006, several warlords rearmed their militias at the request of President Karzai, to the dismay of the international community and particularly the Japanese who have spent some $100 million to disarm militias. Clashes reoccurred in May 2007 in northern Sheberghan.

Whereas parts of the country are now arguably living centuries in the past, Afghanistan is undergoing a fast-forward development that will, if it succeeds, bring Afghanistan into the twenty-first century. The change will be rapid, uneven and sometimes harsh. The history of the modernization of Europe contains many difficult chapters where economic forces led to wholesale changes and the elimination of many ways of life. The clearing of Scotland for sheep farming in the eighteenth century is one example. One main reason for emigration to the New World was to find a way to survive in the face of these changes, and it is interesting to note from the Afghanistan perspective that many of the American founding fathers came from Scottish and Scots-Irish families that were closely linked to their tribal roots and had been the victims of those very economic policies.

The resistance of the Taliban and their acceptance in the Pashtun tribal communities, although couched in religious terms, in fact contains a large element of the prescient awareness that their ancient way of life is threatened by the forces of modernity as represented by the Kabul government and the international Coalition. The creation of a modern economy, with its concomitant benefits to health, education and living standards, is the obvious sweetener for the process of eliciting cooperation for changes that now appear mainly frightening and negative.

Some in Afghanistan have already got the message to a degree. Ismail Khan, the self-styled Emir of Herat, used—extra-legally—the revenues that he obtained there to renovate and restore Herat, bringing a certain level of security and prosperity along with his medieval analysis of the social nature of society. Now that he is a minister in Kabul, he is expertly channeling government funds for the continued development of Herat. His colleagues in the Northern Alliance could do better than to solely indulge in private consumption. However, what Afghanistan needs is a national program and not an emir inspired by Harun ar Rashid.

Ex-Minister Ghani labored for several years to use the meager assets of Afghanistan for the people rather than personal advantage, as did former Minister of Village Affairs Atmar, the current minister of education. There are many others as well, but there are also numerous government officials, and their relatives, who have continued traditional practices of using the resources of the state for private advantage. They undermine the efforts of the Afghanistan National Compact presented to the international community in London in February 2006.

Many of the military commanders who had plunged Afghanistan into a miasma of civil war allied themselves with the international Coalition and became important members of the transitional government set up by the international community. They retained control of access to Afghanistan's energy and mineral resources in the north, and to the customs taxes at the international access points of Herat, Mazar-i Sharif, Jalalabad and Kandahar that were the country's main sources of income. They also retained their military forces, including within the city of Kabul, in violation of the Bonn Agreement. The transitional government set up by the Bonn Agreement resulted in the distribution of government ministries to various commanders on the basis of a spectrum of political representation that resulted in the establishment of ethnic fiefdoms in the ministries that quickly set up networks of nepotism, bribery and corruption. This was superimposed on a dysfunctional and virtually unpaid bureaucracy that had been trained and politicized by the Soviet occupation and the follow-on socialist regime. Other members of the government who came from the Afghan diaspora were often met with resentment and socio-cultural problems when they approached Afghan problems with foreign solutions, as for instance the excellent former Afghan Interior Minister Ali Jalali.

The Bonn Agreement set up a transitional government that included representatives of most of the factions of Afghanistan, excluding activist Taliban. The program of two Loya Jirgas, one to elect a president, one to establish a new constitution and then the holding of national elections was followed successfully, if tardily. As of 2006, President Karzai, the elected leader, was beginning to deal with a parliament that predictably contained many truculent leaders with ties to fundamentalist groups and even the Taliban, and which promptly ran into trouble with the minister of finance when he sought to raise teachers salaries in the face of insufficient revenues. This was a harbinger of serious problems to come. Minister of Finance Ahadi told the international community in London in early 2006 that the Afghan government would need its support at least until the end of the decade to cover ordinary government costs. However, the level of government is clearly not acceptable in many parts of Afghanistan where little or no government presence has resulted. In the spring of 2006, the Taliban reappeared in force. This coincided with a return of sympathies for them among portions of the population as Afghans saw figures and policies that had previously enabled the Taliban to reemerge in the new regime. "Where the road ends," US Lieutenant General Karl Eikenberry recently observed, "the Taliban begins."[1]

One main factor in Afghan development has been the consistent failure of the international community to underwrite the cost of bringing Afghanistan up to a healthy level. In 2004, Karzai requested $27.6 billion over seven years in international aid, but donor promises fell far short. By 2005, the United Nations Development Programme (UNDP) ranked Afghanistan 173 out of 178 of the Human Development Index, with 70% of Afghans living below the poverty line, 77% without access to safe water, and only 12% of the population with access to adequate sanitation.[2] Still the per capita expenditure for Afghanistan (about $25 per capita) has not only predictably been far lower than that of Bosnia (about $135 per capita), but also of East Timor and Rwanda which are both countries with a much shorter-term problem, more congenial climate and higher levels of infrastructure and social development. Funding levels stand at about half of its requests and actual disbursements total only about one-quarter of total requests. In addition, much of the funds originally earmarked for Afghanistan got diverted after the tsunami struck.

The exhausted patience of the Afghan people towards the subsequent lack of development, as well as their perception of the directed use of funds, was a factor in the riot that took place in Kabul in late spring 2006 in response to a traffic accident caused by US troops. Financial support in absolute terms has significantly increased for Afghanistan, and governmental revenues actually met some 20% of the need by early 2006. Between 2002 and 2006 the EU, for example, gave some $4.9 billion in addition to deploying 15,800 troops and promising a further $2.4 billion.[3] But expenses have been increasing geometrically, and financing the new national army and police that are designated to eventually take over security in the country will provide a serious economic challenge to the Afghan government. UNDP estimates that over $650 million will be necessary to fund a four-phase initiative, the Law and Order Trust Fund Project, to establish a police force, a counter-narcotics commission, and to reform justice infrastructures.[4]

Afghanistan has experienced the largest refugee return in history. Roughly six million Afghans left their country between 1979 and 2001. In October 2001, UNHCR estimates placed the number of Afghans who fled to Pakistan since September 11 alone conservatively at 80,000, with an additional 8,000 in a refugee camp on the Iranian border.[5] But within four years, some 19% of the total Afghan population returned. Even so, refugees are faced with the problems of dislocation, rehabilitation, mines and health. Predictably, many of the refugees have not gone back to their places of origin for whatever reasons, and Kabul and other large cities have become swollen with refugees for whom there is little available assistance. Refugees in the countryside complain that conditions there are even worse, and that they have received little more than some plastic sheets and food. Anecdotal evidence in the press notes that some refugees in the south have lost faith in the new government in the face of perceived abandonment by Kabul. The booming markets of Kabul and Kandahar have yet to be reflected in the towns and villages remote from communication, transportation and, in many cases, observation. Infrastructure development, and especially secondary roads, are necessary to change this situation.

Infrastructure

The ring network of roads that was the pride of Afghanistan in the 1960s is being re-created by the international community. The lead project was the refurbishing of the Kabul to Kandahar road, done in 2003 in nine months by the United States with the cooperation of Japan. The project was the equivalent of building a two-lane highway from New York City to Washington, DC, through much more difficult terrain. Since then, the road north from Kabul to Herat through the Salang tunnel has also been completed. The Indians and Iranians have made substantial progress on a link from the Iranian port of Chahbahar to the ring road in Afghanistan, and work is ongoing on connections to all of Afghanistan's neighbors. The United States and the international community are also building several thousand miles of farm-to-market roads.[6]

With the return of the refugees, a spectacular increase in school enrollment has taken place in Afghanistan, with about five million children attending nationwide, some 40% of them girls. With this increase, tens of thousands of teachers have been able to find work, many of them women. Teaching standards are low, but enthusiasm is high. USG problems in fulfilling its nationwide program of school building were detailed in the *Washington Post* in the spring of 2006. A multimillion dollar program subcontracted several times over resulted in a scandalous failure to produce acceptable schools. Nevertheless, the social and economic impact of schools has resulted in their becoming a particular target of the Taliban, who have destroyed several hundred schools in the southeast provinces. Higher education is slowly beginning to recover from the years of destruction and intimidation, with Kabul University Rector and former Finance Minister Ashraf Ghani spearheading a modernization project that intends to bring his university up to accreditable standards within a few years. There are also programs for occupational training for government officials and a new American University of Kabul. Several of the traditionally prestigious high schools of Kabul have been refurbished by the EU and member states that initially sponsored them, and the US has printed millions of new textbooks. Still, the impact of new training and new methodologies free of ideological and political extremism is still down the road. Basic literacy levels are still appallingly low, estimated at 30% overall, roughly 43% for men and only 14% for women.

The road-building project has been a particular target of the Taliban and Al Qaeda. Roads offer access to the government and its security forces, and also enable local residents to travel and trade and establish wider linkages outside their communities and thus mitigate the influence of local power figures. The more roads and infrastructure, the less the influence of the Taliban. Roads are economically and psychologically critical for the creation of a new Afghanistan. Trade with Iran and Pakistan has now increased to the $2 billion level, and it is mostly done by road at this point.

Former Finance Minister Ghani estimated in the spring of 2005 that income from roads could bring the Government of Afghanistan $200 million a year. Afghanistan's northern neighbors stand to be primary beneficiaries of a road system that could enable shippers in Tashkent to bring their goods to the sea in less than two days, whereas now they have to ship them through Russia and can only get them to a port in a week. In the economy of the twenty-first century, Afghan access could be of essential importance for landlocked Central Asian countries as they confront China's determination to become the greatest world power and a resurgent Russia intent on maintaining its sphere of influence. China is already refurbishing the Karakorum Highway through Pakistan to provide its own outlet from Central Asia, and has helped with port and road construction establishing a link between the port of Gwador in Pakistan and Karachi.

The Railroad in Afghanistan

At the dedication of a bridge across the Pyanj River with Tajikistan in the spring of 2006, Tajik President Rahmanov expressed the hope that a rail link would soon follow the road link. A rail line already comes to the border of Afghanistan at Termez in Uzbekistan and there is discussion of another link extending the Pakistan railroad line to Kandahar as the first step of a network that would link Afghanistan to Central Asia on the route Kandahar-Herat-Kushka (Turkmenistan).

At the end of the nineteenth century Amir Abdur Rahman opposed any railroad construction for fear that this could be used by Britain and other great powers to occupy Afghanistan. His major concern was hence the security and national survival of Afghanistan in the Great Game.[7] Today however, it has become clear that experts and the Afghan leadership realized the major cross-access the country provides for the entire subcontinent. Like Switzerland, Afghanistan enjoys a setting at the center of a significant east-west and north-south axis. In terms of rail network connection, this would offer a link to the EU network via Iran, a connection to the Central Asian rail network via Termez–Mazar-i Sharif and via Tajikistan, and to the South Asian rail networks from Queta and Peshawar in Pakistan via Spin Buldak and Jalabad, respectively, in Afghanistan.[8] Experience in other mountainous countries like Austria and Switzerland has shown that railways can run parallel to road projects. In climactic adverse conditions, in difference to roads, rail offers a more reliable transport even in high snow or heavy rains. The construction of a railroad system both following the ring road and even crossing through the country and connecting to the outside networks as described above could offer four major advantages:

1. Increase of economic interaction and contribution to stability and cohesion;
2. Enormous new source of income for the region and the nation;
3. Significant job creation and contribution to local pride;
4. Enormous potential for transport under any climactic condition of bulk and heavy loads such as petroleum, coal, stone and other mining products.

However the railroad project has to anticipate significant reluctance and hindrance by conservative tribal leaders who may need to be convinced to accept "intrusion" and enhanced control from both the central authorities and possibly foreign powers. Security concerns will play a critical role, but the prime factors determining the railway should be economic and strategic considerations.

On the larger regional scale is the creation of a north-south transport route, besides the east-west energy and transport routes. In 2000, Russia, India and Iran signed an agreement on such a route in St. Petersburg. This corridor would stretch from a port in India across the Arabian Sea to the Iranian port of Bandar Abbas in the Persian Gulf. From there goods would transit Iran via Tehran and arrive at the Caspian Sea. It has been predicted that such a north-south transport corridor would reduce the shipment time from the Indian Ocean to Russian Baltic ports by ten to twenty days and be a significant cost decrease.[9] This would tremendously enhance the relevance of an Afghan rail and road transit and increase its commercial importance for the country. Iran has also built a 150 kilometer railway to connect its Khorassan Province with the Herat Province in Afghanistan, which will permit it to eventually connect easier to Uzbekistan and Tajikstan. Iran has engaged in a major railroad construction effort and the new Bafq-Mashhad line will significantly reduce the distance connecting Turkmenistan, and all of Central Asia to the Persian Gulf via the Tajan-Mashhad-Bandar Abbas line which ends at the Iranian port of Bandar Addas.[10]

Security problems have meant that the road from Spin Boldak on the Pakistani border to Kandahar is both less complete and less used. Traffic for Kandahar still travels the roundabout but more secure route from Peshawar to Jalalabad, thus adding to the time and cost overhead. Police, army and Coalition forces are regularly attacked along the new roads built since 2001, with the level of violence increasing to its highest levels in 2006. In 2006, along with military and security forces, foreign workers laboring on road projects became particular targets. Turkish press on June 22, 2006 noted that a Turkish driver working for a US road-building firm was killed near Herat, the third Turk thus killed that year. Foreign volunteer workers from such organizations as Médecins sans Frontières have long since been driven out of significant areas of Afghanistan, mostly in the south and east, but, as Ahmed Rashid noted in an article in

July 2006, attacks now occur nationwide. Economic development is increasingly hindered by security problems, which have the double effect of deterring or destroying economic progress while providing incentives for protectionism and warlordism that further sap the limited economic resources available for development. Additionally, sparring among local power brokers with dubious backgrounds inhibits growth on both the macro and micro levels. Lacking security, an entrepreneur is not likely to either open a market or build an oil refinery.

Energy

Afghanistan is an energy deficient country. Five years after the overthrow of the Taliban, even Kabul does not have sufficient electricity supply. Obviously Afghanistan cannot develop a self-sufficient economy without an energy supply. During the Soviet period, Afghanistan exported some $200 million worth of gas (mainly) and oil to the Soviet power grid. The resources are located in the northwest part of the country, for the most part. When the Russians left, they took the plans with them. The United States Geological Survey finally produced an overall survey of the energy resources in the area in the spring of 2006. President Karzai announced that the energy resources of the area were in fact several times greater than had been expected. Efforts are underway to bring this energy to Kabul. Among the difficulties in the project are, once again, security concerns. An American firm which has been attempting to establish a refinery in the area of Mazar-i Sharif has had to overcome both the security problems and apprehensions on the part of the international community that work in the area is impracticable.

Afghan energy resources can make a serious contribution to the economy both within the country and as a trading tool in the region. The resources which were already in production in the communist period alone would be a significant factor. In the 1960s until the 1980s the Soviets had identified some fifteen sites for potential oil and gas exploration, all of them located in northern Afghanistan with proven, probable and possible natural gas reserves of about five trillion cubic feet. But there is the potential to "hold a sizable undiscovered gas resource base, especially in deeper sedimentary layers."[11] The most important, Khwaha gogerdak, Djarquduk, Yatimtaq, near Sheberghan, and west of Mazar-i Sharif were developed. The gas production in the late 1970s reached 385 million cubic feet per day. The development of new resources in the area is contingent upon more detailed work on ascertaining the dimensions of the deposits, and in this, as in so many other areas, lack of security even more than lack of infrastructure is a hindrance. Afghanistan's difficult geography is also a factor that cannot be overlooked, but it may turn out that local production, even taking into account the costs of production and shipping in Afghanistan's difficult terrain, is a cheaper alternative than importing energy, especially given the potential for volatility in the region.

Another energy source which potentially could help Afghanistan is that of alternative means, such as solar and wind energy. Afghanistan's topography could be suitable for either of these. Solar energy, in particular, could provide modular power for villages and individual dwellings. The technology is readily available for solar-powered stoves, radios, water heaters, electricity and other uses. Subventions could support a local manufacturing capacity, and eliminating the cost of fuel transportation would contribute towards cost effectiveness. Some work is underway in this field.

Afghanistan has not properly utilized its water resources in the mountainous north. Its share of the Amu Derya, which forms the border with Tajikistan and Uzbekistan, could be tapped for hydroelectric power, as well as the streams in Afghanistan which feed into the Amu Derya. Local generating facilities could supply power for the towns and villages of the region, if not for the country as a whole. Tree cutting in the region necessarily has a negative effect on the water supply. Water supply in the area fluctuates seasonally, and the ongoing irrigation problems of Central Asia that have resulted in the drying of the Aral Sea also impact on Afghanistan's usage capabilities. But the fact remains that water in the north is an underused economic capability for Afghanistan.

The United States Assistant Secretary of State for South and Central Asia, Richard Boucher, testified before Congress in the late spring of 2006 concerning a new energy grid which the USG is helping to sponsor that would connect Central Asia with South Asia. The concept would transfer power from the Central Asian countries through Afghanistan to Pakistan and India to help meet the power needs of the new century. Afghanistan would of course be able to draw on the power resources passing through its territory. One can look at the suggestion as another aspect of the race for energy resources that will help to determine economic progress in the new century, with China, India and Pakistan as the main players in this particular conjecture. Afghanistan's benefit is as transit facilitator and potential user. The commercial and physical feasibility of the project, like many others in the area, is apparent.

However, the political aspects of a series of bilateral relationships will play a determining role in the project. President Karzai has made a series of public remarks asking that Afghanistan's development not be held hostage to the vagaries of either bilateral relations in the neighborhood, or of international politics. He specifically meant the ongoing delicate relations between Pakistan and India, which have ramifications for Afghanistan in many different areas. He also meant the relations between the United States and Iran, which at this writing continue to be very problematic over the nuclear issue. Iran is financing the completion of a major dam complex in Tajikistan, and there is intent to bring the electricity thus generated across Afghanistan into Iran. Afghanistan would then again benefit both by transit fees and by the ability to aggrandize its own power system. In this context, President Bush's remarks during his 2006 visit to India that the US embargo of Iran would not apply to a pipeline across Afghanistan came as welcome news to the Afghan government. Another discussed pipeline that would bring gas from Turkmenistan comes within a similar context, although in this case the problems stem from the troublesome nature of the Turkmen government as well as the question of whether Turkmenistan can actually supply gas in sufficient quantities to make the pipeline commercially viable. One must also mention yet again the security concerns of all parties to such discussions. In this case, the concerns are not only Afghanistan specifically, as Pakistan faces an ongoing insurgency in Baluchistan which has negatively affected its development of energy resources in the area.

Mining

A further source of significant income for the Afghanistan economy is mineral wealth. Interestingly, Afghanistan is the place where the earliest records exist of mining anywhere in the world—some 6,000 years back. The website of the Ministry of Mines, the Afghanistan Geological Survey, is managed by the British Geological Survey. Afghanistan has significant resources in copper, gold, chromium, iron oxide and other ferrous metals, and in semi-precious stones. Of special interest could be uranium, mercury and tin-tungsten, all special metals of significant value and to be found in many locations. The most interesting uranium prospect can be found in the Khanneshin carbonatite volcanic complex in the so-embattled Helmand Province. There especially, British forces try to deny the reoccurring Taliban reemergence, perhaps precisely for the uranium deposits. Gold, silver, platinum and some 93 precious metals can also be found in numerous sites. They are especially located in Zabul and Ghazni which are "the most prospective for skarn-type, porphyry-related and possibly epithermal-style gold mineralisation, due to the subduction-related geological environment during the Cretaceous-Tertiary. . . . More than fifty sites have been recorded to date, including the largest resource currently known in Afghanistan the Zarkashan skarn deposit. . . . The provinces of Badakhshan and Takhar are also prospective for gold mineralisation with a number of deposits identified to date, including the Vekadur Au-Ag deposit."[12]

A contract with a Polish firm for the production of emeralds from the Panjshir Valley brought in an unspecified amount of income to members of the Northern Alliance estimated at between $50 million and $100 million a year. Lapis lazuli and other semi-precious stones are also found in abundance in Afghanistan. A serious inventory and exploitation of Afghanistan's mineral resources is necessary for this neglected sector to become a contributor to Afghanistan's economy. The road currently being built across the central highlands will make the resources of the area more accessible to economic development, including water and mineral resources. Similar access development is necessary in the northeast of Afghanistan as well.

Coal mining in Afghanistan has experienced a renaissance with estimated production in excess of 200,000 tons annually. Demands exceed supply and new, below standard mines are opened daily. Coal has been traditionally used in Afghanistan for heating in homes and for small industry.[13] Today, it is the highly active brick ovens for which coal is used. But in the absence of reliable transport infrastructure, i.e., road and railways, this is mostly in the northern areas where the coal fields are. The south has some less valuable fields.

Health and the Role of Women in Society

Afghanistan's health sector has vastly improved since 2001, but conditions are still near the bottom of world levels. One out of four instead of one out of five children dies in the first year and more than a third of women are likely eventually to die in childbirth. Life expectancy overall remains in the mid-forties, thus effectively reducing the work life of an average person by several decades, even assuming that they are not afflicted with malaria, malnutrition or a host of other endemic illnesses. The economic impact of poor nutrition and health standards is a major challenge the international community must meet to create a self-sustaining Afghanistan. Health education on the personal level as well as the education of health professionals is essential to reduce the economic and social drain of poor health standards on Afghanistan. Security enters into this aspect as well. Health workers have been driven out of some sectors in the south, and in 2006, workers in the north and west were killed.

The expulsion of the Taliban and Al Qaeda gave women in much of Afghanistan a chance to return to the public sphere. Female teachers and doctors returned to work in many places, and some women stopped wearing the burqa, seen by many as a symbol of gender oppression. The new constitution contained a quota for women in the parliament, and women enthusiastically supported the election process which they saw as enabling for them. In a number of contests, women's votes determined the outcome. Severe problems remain, however. The new parliament's refusal to confirm a woman minister, and its similar refusal to renew the mandate of the liberal minister of culture, who brought women back to Afghan television, were indicative of widespread conservatism in Afghanistan. Murders of women, including a television personality, continue to send a chilling message. Women have a difficult time participating in any public fora, including the marketplace, and women working for NGOs have been killed. The economic situation of women, particularly of widows, is of particular concern, in spite of many programs for women sponsored by the international community. Afghanistan's leadership needs to work seriously on societal attitudes towards women to further their complete participation at every level of society.

Agriculture

Agriculture has traditionally been the main occupation in Afghanistan. At one time self-sustaining, Afghan agriculture has suffered from the same neglect and destruction as the rest of society. The fertile areas north of Kabul were systematically mined, fruit and nut trees cut down, and the villages destroyed during the years of war and the Soviet occupation. Afghanistan remains one of the most intensively mined countries in the world, with figures for killed and wounded as a result of encounters with landmines only obscured by the overall destitution and insecurity in the country. From 2003–2005 the International Campaign to Ban Landmines recorded 3,102 landmine casualties in Afghanistan, with 1,076 deaths and 2,026 injuries.[14] Demining programs are expensive and difficult to implement except in very limited areas. In Afghanistan millions of mines were delivered by plane and helicopter and spread across the countryside, in addition to those buried in the ground. Children and livestock are particular victims of the mines scattered from the air.

The lack of farm-to-market roads has hampered the revival of agriculture and encouraged the spread of easily transportable opium as a market crop. For the first time, a road is being built across Afghanistan through the mountainous Hazarajat, one of the poorest and most remote areas of Afghanistan. Lack of funding, local rivalries and ongoing security problems—often based on local rivalries over road routes—have all served to hamper the road-building process. Security problems also add to the market cost of agricultural products that do make it to urban centers.

The revival of Afghanistan's traditional export crops, raisins and other dried fruits and nuts, suffers from the twin difficulties of destruction of infrastructure and difficulty of export. Trees and vines that were destroyed over twenty years take several years at least to bear fruit, even when they are replaced. The market for Afghan products still exists, particularly in India. Ongoing discussions among Afghanistan, Pakistan and India, and particularly between India and Pakistan, have not yet resolved the problem of transshipping, offloading and reloading that significantly add to the cost of export. If bilateral relations continue to improve and a direct rail link from Afghanistan to India is built, sealed rail cargo transit could provide one way to alleviate the problem.

There have been many discussions of new export venues for Afghan crops. Central Asia and western China could provide ample markets for Afghan export goods, especially during the winter season. Luxury agricultural products, such as spices and flowers, could also be grown for the international market in the Middle East and Europe. The climate of Kabul is particularly suitable for roses, with which the city abounds. The development of air cargo capacity, including civilian airports, is critical to the planning of such an industry. So far, major airports are still controlled mainly by military units, either Afghan or foreign, and normal civilian traffic is problematic. When Afghanistan's airports are brought up to standard and open for unabridged commercial traffic, the possibilities of volume production of agricultural luxury goods for export will become more feasible. A flower that sells for a few cents in Kabul can easily demand a price of as many dollars only a short flight away in the Gulf.

Afghanistan's geography is varied, majestic and difficult. In the south, vast flat areas receive much sun and little water. In the north, mountain valleys preclude major crop agriculture and demand labor intensive agriculture on more or less subsistence patches. A further problem in the north and east is rampant deforestation, caused in the north by wood-cutting to provide fuel for drug laboratories, and in the east, in Nuristan and its neighbors, by logging of wood for sale to Pakistan for use in furniture. The deforestation will result in desertification and water management problems within a few years if steps are not taken, as the examples of neighboring regions show. Forest management and tree farming are areas where international funding can help create a viable future for Afghanistan.

In the south, an extremely dry climate predicates the implementation of dry farming techniques, while the relatively flat landscape provides the opportunity for large agribusinesses. One factor in the growth of the poppy industry in this area is that the poppy plant has minimal need for water. Farmers in the Helmand area have complained that the government has not provided irrigation canals which would enable them to profitably grow other crops than opium.

Poppy Industry

The elephant in the room of the Afghan economy is, of course, the opium industry. Fully 87% of the world's opium was produced in Afghanistan in 2006. The UN forecasts that production, which dropped some 20% in 2005, will increase again in 2007. The implications of the opium industry are manifold and well known. Most of the income from the opium goes to the middlemen who refine and market the crop, and not to the Afghan farmers who depend on the crop for sustenance-level income. The income from the crop thus goes to support the Taliban and tribal leaders, as well as other regional leaders in every area where the crop is grown. This includes, either directly or indirectly, senior government officials and their families. The failure of the Kabul government to come to terms with this is one main complaint against it. In addition, the need to borrow money to grow the crop maintains a cycle of poverty and dependency that reinforces the traditional power structure in the countryside.

In the first years of the new government, the anti-drug program got off to a poor start. Coalition forces that had drug eradication on their to-do list were insufficient in numbers to carry out this task along with fighting the Taliban. Senior military officials of the Coalition admitted that they did not have the forces to do both in numerous private conversations. Funds for drug eradication were also not readily available, nor have they been since with the exception of the United Kingdom and the United States. The United Kingdom was given the lead in drug eradication under the division of responsibilities for helping Afghanistan that was devised at the Bonn conference. It expended nearly $90 million in an attempt to purchase and destroy crops that was largely regarded as a failure. Crops were concealed from the government—both with and without the cooperation of local officials—crops were destroyed for show after the opium had been harvested, and many farmers decided to increase their opium acreage in hopes of getting money from the government the next year.

The anti-drug program planned by the US and the UK and implemented in 2005 and 2006 with a budget of some $800 million has been described by Afghanistan expert Barnett Rubin as a disaster. Crop replacement schemes yet to be enacted, the decision to allow physical implementation of the scheme by Afghan officials, has predictably proven to be a recipe for failure and corruption. The inability of the government and international community to create the infrastructure and social services to help farmers make the adjustment to a different economy has largely not taken place, leaving farmers to either fend for themselves or seek succor in another area, i.e., in traditional alliances and/or connections with the Taliban and their Pashtun tribal allies.

There have also been serious disagreements between the Kabul government and foreigners over the plan and its implementation. President Karzai spoke out strongly over aerial spraying of fields and initially favored a plan loosely modeled on that of Thailand, which encompassed significant government economic support for alternative crops and occupational training over a period of years, with strong strictures against crop growers at the end of that. He has since changed his rhetoric to support going after the middle tiers, those who process and transport the drugs. The international community has noted that there has not been significant action against the upper level of dealers, those either in or outside the government who benefit the most from the drug trade.

For the impoverished farmers who grow opium, the moral question is a far second to that of economic survival. In many anecdotal reports, farmers have expressed willingness to stop growing opium if they can be given an economically viable alternative. Turkey and Thailand are two countries that have controlled drug production. Replacing the drug economy, which composes some 60% of Afghan GDP and does not contribute to national reconstruction, with a different economy, will be very difficult and very expensive. In its 2006 world drug report, the UN noted that drug production worldwide had decreased 5% in the previous year, but pointed out that the two weak links in the chain are Afghan production and European consumption. It is remarkable how little the European consumer states have contributed to the elimination of Afghan drug production, with the exception of the UK.

The UN report also commented on the increasingly dangerous levels of use of hard drugs in European countries. Afghanistan is also beginning to experience an increase in the use of drugs, as is typical in producer states. Domestic consumption has been a traditional part of Afghan society but increased availability and the array of economic and social problems in the country contribute to increasing demand. This, too will necessarily impact on Afghanistan's economic productivity.

Cottage Industries and Tourism

For Afghanistan, cottage industries that provide sustenance income, particularly to women, are critical. The quality and design of Afghan textiles are internationally well known. A single person—usually women and/or children, in the actuality—can weave a carpet in a month or so of work. The income, even after deducting for expenses, can feed a family and more. There are numbers of initiatives that are already working on projects in this mode to provide income for families. What is needed is a professional overview of the carpet industry and marketing, with a view to making Afghan carpets and other textiles available to a broad international market. Such goods are already available in the luxury market. They face competition from all of Afghanistan's neighbors, but have proven themselves to be competitive and even preferred over time. In a world increasingly driven by consumerism, Afghanistan can stand to make reasonable income from such work, but there needs to be systematic organization to prevent exploitation of the weavers and to make sure that quality, design and market availability are ensured. The same techniques can be applied to other traditional crafts as well, such as metal work and jewelry making. Quality alone will not be sufficient to guarantee Afghanistan's place in a highly competitive market situation, but quality can ensure that Afghanistan has a place in that market. The development of small-scale niche industries is another area where Afghanistan could establish itself. The example of the handmade volleyball and kitchenware industry in Sialkot in neighboring Pakistan shows the kind of opportunity that exists. Turkey has taken small local production in tiles, glassware, carpets and marble and made itself a successful world competitor. Afghanistan could do the same, and in some of these very fields.

Tourism is now one of the world's major industries, and Afghanistan has enormous potential in this field, along with obvious problems. Endowed with magnificent scenery, numerous historic, cultural and religious sites, Afghanistan had a significant tourist sector in the past. When security is restored, it could have such a sector again. In spite of difficult contemporary conditions, Afghanistan has begun to make plans for the restoration of its magnificent cultural heritage. The tomb of Babur and its garden are being restored in Kabul, as is the Kabul Museum, once home to a world-famous collection thought to have been looted. But large parts of the collection in fact were hidden and preserved, including one portion which heroic museum officials enclosed behind a false wall to prevent destruction by the Taliban. Minister of Culture Raheen has spearheaded the effort to bring the museum back to life. A former royal palace in Kabul is being reconstructed as the national parliament, and the international community is organizing to determine how the famous Buddhas of Bamiyan should be reinterpreted and preserved. Even now, the immanent presence of the Buddhas in their outlines on the cliffs presents the visitor with a moving statement of Buddhist principles about the evanescence of worldly existence. The Great Mosque and other sites of Herat's extremely important cultural heritage are already being restored, and the city of Kandahar has religious and historical sites and a vibrant local culture and architecture that could provide the material for a tourist industry. Afghanistan is an archeological treasure trove whose potential has barely been touched.

Tourism for Afghanistan brings serious questions of safety and infrastructure at this point. A few years from now this hopefully will not be the case. Serbian tourists reappeared—a little nervously—on the Dalmatian coast of Croatia only a few years after their forces tried to destroy the historic city of Dubrovnik. The cultural, archeological and religious sites of Afghanistan will continue to be attractions that have the potential to make a significant economic contribution to Afghanistan, and plans to develop these assets should be worked on now.

Donor Funding and Development

The government of Afghanistan presented an Afghanistan Compact to the international community in London in January 2006. The compact contained a series of targets relating to development which the government believes it can carry out, such as reducing the number of dependent women, increasing health standards, aggrandizing government income so that it can support government services, developing government capability to function efficiently in the different ministries, and increasing the network of government services and presence nationwide. The goals are essentially quite modest, but nevertheless informed observers such as the US ambassador expressed concern that the goals could be met. There are several factors which will impinge on the practicality of the plan.

Since 2001 the Afghan government has sought budgetary control of assistance funds for a number of reasons. One is the important psychological factor of developing the concept that it is the government of Afghanistan that is helping its people, and not just foreign organizations. A second is to develop the capacity of Afghan government officials to in fact do just that. The disintegration of governance imposed by the civil war has left a gap in comprehension of the parameters of power by warlords, tribal leaders and an endless array of international and Afghan organizations that run the range from the largest UN organizations to a host of small Afghan organizations, many of which are seen mainly as vehicles for personal gain. Family and social connections between the latter and persons prominent in the Afghan power structures have led to widespread resentment. The Afghan perception that the overwhelming majority of assistance funds were recycled to the assistance community, foreign and domestic, has fueled this resentment. At the same time, the ability of the organizations and the economic necessity of the individuals involved, to work for the higher salaries these organizations provide has led to a weakening of the very indigenous Afghan structures that need to be strengthened to create an Afghan economy that is self-sustaining and self-governing. Turning university professors and engineers into drivers because they speak a foreign language is not a good use of Afghanistan's human capital.

The other side of the coin, of course, is the fact that the needs of rebuilding and the high costs of doing so in Afghanistan mitigate towards an international presence that is expensive and effectively self-perpetuating. It clearly is more difficult to repair the ravages of war in impoverished and vast Afghanistan than in Bosnia, with a highly educated and capable population and the methods and experience of a European society. Yet it was Bosnia that received a dramatically higher per capita level of assistance from the international community. Work in Afghanistan requires four-wheel drive vehicles, radios, security and many other costly items that both diminish the money available for projects and estrange, to a greater or lesser degree, those implementing the programs from those they wish to help.

More important, however, is the gap between the international assistance community and Afghan government officials. The difficulty of building partnerships between the two has a number of different aspects. One is the sheer inability of some government ministries to function, for a whole range of reasons. Another is the history of Afghanistan, which placed the international assistance community and government officials at loggerheads for a number of years. Now, when it is time for the two to communicate, there is a reluctance to give up independence of action on the part of NGOs with a corresponding problematic relationship on the part of government cadres trained in the ethos of a fragmented control society. Widespread graft, corruption and nepotism in the government only heighten the problem. The practice of doling out government ministries on the basis of ethnic or political affiliation rather than solely on the basis of ability has not stopped and has resulted in a number of individual ministries that are packed with members of the minister's affiliation group.

The result is a slower growth of healthy bipartisan relationships that both get the job done and increase the psychological and professional capabilities of Afghan government officials. Widespread criticism of the lack of government presence and its ability to govern effectively are the pragmatic effects that translate into apathy towards the government. A government cannot build an economy if the people do not believe in it, and they will not believe when they do not see results that they attribute to the government.

A second factor which will make the implementation of the government compact problematic is the cost factor. As mentioned earlier, the funds available for Afghanistan have always been a fraction of the government's target. At three international donor conferences since 2002, $24 billion was pledged. Still the most recent London conference produced pledges that were mostly not new money. Static input will not produce the required results. The new parliament already created a major problem in the spring of 2006 when it voted an across-the-board increase in teachers' salaries that the government had not included in the budget. Further clashes between rationalized government targets and the populist votes of parliamentarians—based on very real needs, perhaps—will no doubt occur. The biggest problem will be funding for the national army and police, which threatens to overwhelm the whole rest of the government. The deteriorating security situation in mid-2006 indicates that these expenses are very much more likely to increase.

The three interrelated problems of Afghanistan are drugs, governance and security. The last of these is a prime factor that will impede and to an extent cripple the Afghan government's plans to provide governance, infrastructure and basic amenities. Physical destruction of schools, health facilities and other government structures coupled with attacks and killings of governmental and non-governmental workers has already resulted in the diminution of government presence and programs. The inability to travel safely effectively stymies the development of the international transport industry, especially that through Pakistan. Investors, however well-intentioned they may be, need to make a profit on their investments. Events such as the June 2006 trashing of Kabul's first new international hotel, which had been financed by the Agha Khan, will deter others from similar investments.

Aside from all of these serious problems, the government's plan may simply prove to be too ambitious for Afghanistan to carry out at this time. Perception of failure on the part of the international community and the Afghan people will cloud economic ambitions. Afghanistan needs more success stories.

Conclusions

Afghanistan has a difficult uphill road to walk before it can create a self-sustaining economy. The problems of poverty, war and low levels of education have made it one of the poorest nations on the planet. In raw terms however, it has the potential to develop an economy that would lift it out of destitution. Afghanistan has significant reserves of natural gas; limited petroleum reserves; significant water resources especially in the mountainous middle region, and the north and northeast; and great potential for mining, especially of copper, gold chromium, iron oxide and other ferrous metals and semi-precious stones. It will continue to need the help of the international community for years to come, hopefully increasingly in the form of private capital. But there is significant growth potential, especially if merged with the old trading and farming tradition and the favorable geopolitical location of Afghanistan on top of a critical east-west, north-south axis from the EU into South Asia, from the Indian Ocean and the Persian Gulf into the Caspian Sea region and Central Asia. The construction of a functioning, reliable and safe road and rail infrastructure seems critical to any endeavor concerning Afghanistan's economy.

Unfortunately, Afghanistan could easily turn into a narco-state and a number of critics argue that it already has. For this reason alone the international community, and particularly the wealthy EU and Asian neighbors which could be the market end of Afghanistan's drug industry, need to cooperate to fundamentally change the economic structures that push Afghanistan in this direction. Afghanistan is also the state where the world community, under the auspices of the United Nations, agreed to intervene to deliver a nation from the rule of terrorism. The world community cannot shirk that responsibility in the face of ongoing difficulties. It must continue to stay the course and put Afghanistan on a healthy track toward development. Afghanistan is not a country that cannot be helped, but it is a country that needs long-lasting, firm and considered assistance. Afghans can and will do most of the work themselves, but they cannot do it alone.

Notes

1. Lt. Gen. Karl Eikenberry, Commander, Combined Forces Command—Afghanistan, in Liechtenstein Institute on Self-Determination, "Creating Security and Stability in Afghanistan and the Region" (Summary Report, October 2006). http://www.princeton.edu/lisd/publications/AfghSummary_2006.pdf.

2. UNDP, "United National Development Programme in Afghanistan." http://www.undp.org.af/home/UNDP_in_Afghanistan_2005.pdf.

3. EU Council Secretariat, "EU Engagement in Afghanistan." November 2006. http://www.operationspaix.net/IMG/pdf/UE_factsheet_Afghanistan_2006–11–13_.pdf.

4. UNDP, Law and Order Trust Fund Project. http://www.undp.org.af/about_us/overview_undp_afg/sbgs/prj_law_order.htm.

5. UNHCR, "Afghanistan Humanitarian Update, no. 27," 29 October 2001. http://www.unhcr.org/cgi-bin/texis/vtx/afghan?page=news&id=3bdd57c24.

6. Through January 2006, USAID has constructed 421 kilometers of farm-to-market roads, 116 kilometers of provincial and district roads, 704 kilometers of national and provincial roads, 389 kilometers of Kabul-Kandahar Highway, and 246 kilometers of Kandahar-Herat Highway.

7. See also C. Raja Mohan, "India and Afghan Railroads," *The Hindu,* 20 February 2003.

8. See Liechtenstein Institute on Self-Determination, "Creating Security and Stability in Afghanistan and the Region."

9. Regine A. Spector, "The North-South Transport Corridor," *Analyst* (Central Asia-Caucasus Institute), 3 July 2002.

10. Mohammed Saeednejad of the Islamic Republic Railways argued that "on average 500 kilometers of railways have been laid in the country annually" since 2000. Then Iran laid 3,300 kilometers of track. But still, it has less than 10,000 kilometers of railway in a country of 1.64 million square kilometers. See Hooman Peimani, "Iran Stakes a Claim to the Silk Road," *Asia Times,* 14 August 2003.

11. "Afghanistan Fact Sheet," June 2004. http://www.eia.doe.gov/emeu/cabs/afghan.html.

12. Afghanistan Geological Survey, Afghanistan Ministry of Mines. http://www.bgs.ac.uk/afghanminerals/Index.htm.

13. Several potentially harmful trace elements exist in relatively high concentrations in some coal deposits, notably HG ranging from approximately 0.17–2.4 ppm for some Jurassic coals, and F ranging from 772–1540 ppm (dry basis) for some Tertiary coals. John R. Sanfilipo et al., "Coal Mining in Afghanistan: Third World Problems and Opportunities," Geological Society of America 2006 Philadelphia Annual Meeting, Paper no. 33–11.

14. International Campaign to Ban Landmines, Landmine Monitor, 2003–2006. http://www.icbl.org/lm.

9

The Failure to Bridge the Security Gap: The PRT Plan, 2002–2004

Barbara J. Stapleton

THE INTERNATIONAL SECURITY ASSISTANCE FORCE (ISAF) was created following the unanimous adoption of UN Security Council Resolution 1386 on December 20, 2001. ISAF's mandate was limited to the stabilization of Kabul and its immediate environs and was established on an initial six month basis. The first peacekeeping force of 5,000 was led by the British. It rapidly won the confidence of the Kabul population and appeared to be an effective first step by the international community to square up to the fundamental, if onerous, requirement of providing security. Afghanistan's recent history underscored the urgency of the need to bridge the security gap at the outset if peace and stability were to be established in the long-term and international efforts to help the Afghans rebuild their war-shattered country were to be expedited.

The Bonn Agreement "constituted a road map for the re-establishment of rudimentary state structures."[1] The agreement had been reached on December 5, 2001 with strong US, European and UN support. The approach that would be taken to the pivotal question of security was spelled out in Annex 1. The establishment of new Afghan security and armed forces was to provide the means by which the central government would assert its control over the means of violence, thereby maintaining security. But these national forces would take considerable time to develop and interim measures were necessary. To this end, the UN Security Council was asked by the participants at the talks to deploy a UN mandated force to "assist in the maintenance of security for Kabul and its surrounding areas." It was envisaged that "such a force, could as appropriate, be progressively expanded to other urban centers and other areas."

Contrary to the expectations of the Afghan people, early moves to expand the British-led ISAF 1 beyond Kabul failed to materialize. It was not until October 2003 that what diplomats refer to as an "adjustment" of ISAF's mandate (via UN Security Council Resolution 1510) was agreed. This allowed the German government to set up the first Provincial Reconstruction Team (PRT) under ISAF/NATO, rather than the Coalition's command. But apart from temporarily increasing forces for the elections, the expansion of the internationally mandated peacekeeping force would be primarily enacted through the deployment of more PRTs, with a timeline for the north and west only, to the consternation of the plan's critics.[2] The slow pace of NATO's PRT build-up also caused frustration in the US government. Though the Bush Administration had opposed the expansion of ISAF 1 in 2002, by 2004 its ability to place "boots on the ground" had been severely constrained by ongoing commitments in Iraq, and increasingly urgent calls were being made for ISAF/NATO expansion throughout Afghanistan.[3]

Following the overthrow of the Taliban regime, regional commanders and other de facto power holders were able to restore and strengthen their positions, effectively unopposed. The Coalition's strategy of employing some commanders of private militias to prosecute the "war on terror" in the south and southeast flew in the face of the aims of the disarmament process[4] and was one of several factors which contributed to the restoration of the status quo ante the Taliban.

The post-Taliban security situation derived from socio-political realities that had developed during the previous 23 years of war. The 1978 Saur revolution not only brought the preceding status quo to a violent end, the political, economic and cultural devastation that it engendered, in terms of the Soviet invasion and response of western nations, also destroyed the mechanisms through which relations between the center and the periphery had been conducted. This weakened community leaders and rendered local communities highly vulnerable.[5] The subsequent collapse of the Afghan central state in 1992 saw military commanders on both sides increasing their power at the expense of both government and opposition. "The age of the warlords had finally begun, after a long preparation."[6]

Following the Bonn Agreement, a number of notorious warlords[7] were placed in official positions of power at all levels of the Afghan Interim Administration. This outcome may have been driven by realpolitik, but it did little to establish public confidence in the Bonn process. From 2002, Afghans watched with growing alarm as the weakness of the Karzai government, increasing corruption fuelled by sharp increases in the trade in narcotics and illicit taxes, combined with the absence of sufficient neutral forces on the ground, resulted in the reestablishment of lesser and greater power blocs throughout the country.

From the beginning of its intervention in Afghanistan, the international community had been involved in attempts to further the aims of two overarching agendas: the so-called "war against terror" and the state-building process. It rapidly became clear that, for the Bush Administration, the interests of the former outweighed those of the latter. The US remained essentially detached from the state-building process until late in the day and valuable time was lost.[8] The immense financial and human resources committed to Coalition efforts to prevent Afghanistan from again becoming a safe haven for international terrorism was one thing,[9] the requirements for building long-term peace and stability, given the magnitude of the challenges, quite another.[10] The difficulties entailed reconciling these key agendas and the shift in focus by the US-led Coalition from Afghanistan to Iraq, militated against meaningful progress in the vital area of security sector reform[11] outlined at the Tokyo meeting on consolidation of Peace in February 2003. This served further to narrow the brief window of opportunity in which conditions for holding "free and fair" elections could be established if the tight timetable laid out in the Bonn Agreement was to be adhered to.

From November 2003, a marked increase in levels of US engagement in state-building processes became apparent. This saw a deepening of US involvement in security sector reform, particularly in the acceleration of Afghan national police and army recruitment and training, as well as a significant expansion of the PRT plan in the hitherto neglected south and southeast of the country. During the course of 2004, the US embassy in Kabul led a determined thrust, supported by European donors, to keep the Bonn process on track and hold national elections on time despite the existence of formidable obstacles to the electoral process.[12] Against a background of almost daily catastrophic incidents in Iraq, speculation that Bush required a foreign policy success in Afghanistan prior to the US elections due in November 2004 was rife in the international media. The nature of the exit strategy from Afghanistan the US was also believed to be seeking was more difficult to determine however, as the massive fortress of the new US embassy in Kabul took shape and investments into the Bagram and Kandahar bases indicated plans for a long-term presence.

The obstacles to holding presidential and parliamentary elections based on a democratic process were epitomized by the successful manipulation of the disarmament, demobilization and reintegration (DDR) process by the powerful. DDR is the cornerstone of what international donors in Kabul referred to as the "reform agenda" and which was viewed as "the de facto peace process" by Afghans.[13] Weeks away from the October 2004 presidential elections, which had been benchmarked to progress in the disarmament process by the Afghan government at the Berlin donors meeting in April, the DDR process had still only delivered superficial results where it counted. Critically, the military divisions, under various factional commands which had been identified by the United Nations Assistance Mission to Afghanistan (UNAMA) as potentially hazardous to the maintenance of peace and stability, remained structurally intact.[14] In this regard, the September presidential decree to "accelerate" disarmament prior to the elections by demobilizing a further 27,000 soldiers amounted to "no more than empty words" according to the Japanese government's former special representative on DDR who visited Afghanistan to assess progress in DDR prior to the October elections. Overall, he concluded that to date, the DDR process, which aimed to defactionalize the Afghan militia forces, had been "an abysmal failure."[15]

Since 2002 insecurity had delayed the reconstruction process believed by UNAMA and donors to be the sina qua non in establishing the legitimacy of the Karzai government. Justice, the rule of law and human rights issues were not made a priority.[16] Indeed, the UN mission itself had struggled to overcome the constraints imposed as a result of the head of mission's (Lakhdar Brahimi's) conviction that a "light footprint" was the correct approach. Other experts believed that precisely the opposite was required, given the limited nature of Afghan capacity and the fact that the security situation discouraged many professionals in the Afghan diaspora from returning.

The repeated calls made in 2002 by President Karzai and by Lakhdar Brahimi to the UN Security Council for additional peacekeeping forces to be deployed regionally were not being heeded. But fears that time was running out for the state-building process did galvanize the development of a compromise plan by the US with UK support.[17] The result, the PRT plan, was publicly launched by officers of the Coalition at the US embassy in Kabul on November 21, 2002.[18] It revolved around the regional deployment of mobile civil-military teams to facilitate reconstruction, thereby shoring up the Bonn process. It immediately raised suspicions that the plan was not only a second-best option to the expansion of ISAF, but that it also amounted to a relatively cheap means of keeping a lid on the situation in Afghanistan while Coalition focus and resources moved to Iraq.[19] A military architect of the PRT plan at the conceptual phase told the author in November 2002, "In the final analysis, [PRTs] represent the outcome of a simple choice between doing something or doing nothing with the available resources, given the fact that nothing else is on offer."[20]

Though it was clear that "something had to be done," the "what" and the "how" continued to elude policy-makers. And as the security vacuum provided the optimum conditions for the narcotics trade to spread its tentacles of corruption from the top to the bottom of Afghanistan's fragile polity, the problem of warlordism became more intractable.

The PRT Plan

The PRTs initially averaged 50 to 100 people and consisted of a mobile civil-affairs team (CAT) and a Civil Military Operations Center (CMOC) to provide a static "storefront" for the mobile CATs. CMOCs were tasked with gathering and disseminating information relating to reconstruction needs. A Coalition quick-reaction force provided protection solely for the team. The PRTs also had the crucial "reach back" facility which connected them to Coalition assets such as air support. By October 2003, the UK, New Zealand and Germany had all stood up PRTs, and development specialists from the development wings of PRT contributing governments, including USAID, the UK's Department for International Development (DFID), and the German Agency for Technical Cooperation (GTZ), were embedded in the PRT structure. Political representatives from the US State Department and the British Foreign and Commonwealth Office (FCO) were also important components. After a slow start, the Afghan Ministry of

Interior (MOI), the focal point for the Afghan government's relationship with the PRTs, had MOI representatives in all Coalition PRTs and some NATO PRTs by mid-2004.

The primary mission of the PRTs has remained unchanged in Coalition, UNAMA and ISAF/NATO statements on the subject: to expand the legitimacy and/or authority of the central government throughout the country. But exactly how this goal was to be achieved by the PRTs has never been officially defined beyond generalized statements, such as "facilitating reconstruction efforts" and "increasing security by virtue of their presence." At a PRT Commanders Conference in Kabul eighteen months after the plan's launch, the commander of Coalition forces, General Barno, summarized the PRT mission as "providing the military component to accelerate success in Afghanistan where security and reconstruction go hand in hand." Yet beyond the rebuilding of sections of the ring road linking Afghanistan's main cities, progress in reconstruction continued to be eroded by insecurity while President Karzai's nickname amongst Afghans, "the Mayor of Kabul," had stuck fast.

Three Provincial Reconstruction Teams tested out the concept between December 2002 and May 2003, in Gardez in the east, Kunduz in the north, and Bamyan in the central Hazarajat. A total of eight PRTs were planned, to include Mazar, Kunduz, Jalalabad, Herat and Kandahar. The arrival of General Barno in November 2003 saw the expansion of the PRT plan as a structure for the delivery of some of the political aims and objectives of the US government's "Accelerate Success" program. The so-called "acceleration program" had also been established in Kabul in November at the US embassy in Kabul and was run by Ambassador Zalmay Khalilzad from December 2003. It sought to speed up reconstruction and, above all else, to ensure that national elections would be held in Afghanistan more or less according to the Bonn timetable.

Development of the PRTs: December 2002—June 2003

The deployment of the early PRTs was officially linked to the Coalitions' simultaneous announcement that it was moving into Phase IV or "reconstruction,"[21] the implication being that success in the counterinsurgency in the south now enabled some military resources to be diverted from the "war against terror" to reconstruction.[22] Coalition spokesmen repeatedly stated that the focus of PRTs was to support the reconstruction process. This was to be achieved by providing an "enabling environment," thereby expediting the reconstruction process. In doing so, the argument ran, the PRTs would contribute to the establishment of security by facilitating the delivery of tangible benefits from the Bonn process to the population at large. Instability was defined at this stage as an outcome of: 1) terrorist activity; 2) tensions between regional leaders and the central authorities; 3) poor economic conditions; 4) dilapidated infrastructure; and 5) limited central government capacity.

Only limited US government funding, estimated to be between $12 million and $18 million, was made available to PRTs in 2003. Further constraints derived from slow moving funding lines such as OHDACA's (Overseas Humanitarian Disaster and Civic Aid).[23] In effect, critics were quick to point out, PRT funding amounted to a mere drop in the ocean given Afghanistan's overall needs.[24] NGO expectations that the military might play a role in the implementation of major infrastructural projects, as they had done in the Balkans, were also disappointed, as in Afghanistan everything had to be flown in and the expense resulted in only essentials being transported.

The activities of PRTs may not have matched official claims made for them, but this undoubted expansion in civil-military affairs was to remain an extremely controversial issue amongst non-governmental and international organizations such as the International Committee of the Red Cross (ICRC). The focus of civil-military teams on quick impact projects (QIPs) meant that they conducted some activities similar to those of the assistance community including carrying out needs assessments. However, these teams were composed of reservists/soldiers with weapons, wearing the same uniform as the Coalition, a belligerent force in the country. Agencies feared that this confused Afghan perceptions regarding their own neutrality and impartiality, which in turn could adversely affect their future operational capacity. Médecins sans Frontières (MSF) cited the involvement of the military in humanitarian assistance as a factor in their decision entirely to withdraw from Afghanistan following the killing of five members of an MSF Holland team in June 2004.

Strict US Department of Defense funding guidelines prevented a shift in PRT focus away from the selection of assistance type projects, such as wells, schools and clinics, to those projects aimed at rebuilding the local government infrastructure. Coalition-led attempts to alter these guidelines, supported by UNAMA, failed. By June 2003, at a meeting with NGO representatives in Kabul, US Coalition Officer General Eikenberry pronounced what many present thought a fitting epitaph for the PRT plan. It was, he said, "an empty vessel."

The Deepening Security Crisis in 2003

The issue of narcotics was by now dominating debate on the causes of insecurity. Economic interests in the trade in opium and heroin, which cut across all groupings, linked those whose interests did not lie in the development of a strong central government capable of establishing law and order. In March 2003, during a speech to the Afghan Development Forum in Kabul, the minister of finance, Ashraf Ghani, issued a bleak warning that should the Bonn process collapse, Afghanistan would continue its drift into becoming a narco-mafia state.

By 2004, contradictory claims on progress in both politics and reconstruction in Afghanistan reached a new peak. In President Bush's January State of the

Union message, he "touted successes in Afghanistan as putting that nation on the path to 'light the way' in transforming a troubled part of the world." In the same report, a statement by Lakhdar Brahimi on December 3 was also cited, "Countries that are committed to supporting Afghanistan cannot kid themselves and cannot go on expecting us to work in unacceptable security conditions."[25]

Brahimi's comments were made in the wake of a series of fatal attacks on the assistance community in the south and southeast between September and November 2003. The earlier killing of an ICRC expatriate in March 2003 in Kandahar province had profoundly shocked the aid community. The gunning down of a female expatriate UNHCR employee, in broad daylight in the center of Ghazni city on November 16, had a traumatizing effect. Only days before on November 11, a carbomb had been detonated outside UNAMA's southern regional office in Kandahar.[26] Only the fact that the bomb was incorrectly packed had prevented a far worse outcome in terms of fatalities and wounded. UNAMA responded to these incidents by withdrawing UN agencies from much of the south and southeast. On the heels of the devastating attack on UN headquarters in Baghdad, these security incidents were a turning point for the UN in Afghanistan in more ways than one, driving, for example, the UN's decision to "Afghanize" the electoral process. The number of international NGO staff in Kandahar City shrank to a handful from over 100 the year before. Few expatriates now operated outside the city limits. Some programs were, however, quietly maintained further afield by local Afghan NGO staff.

Over one-third of the country was now designated "high risk" for UN agency staff and there was an increasing sense of parts of the south being lost, if not to the insurgents who were operating openly in provinces like Zabul and Uruzgan, but to increasing anti-US sentiments among local communities.[27] In the south and southeast, the local population had been antagonized by Coalition operations involving house and body searches, the latter being particularly offensive to cultural norms and consequently deeply resented. The Coalition's apparently partisan alliances with particular subgroups of tribes also produced resentment as well as unreliable intelligence. The latter led to civilian casualties, only some of whom were acknowledged by the Coalition.[28]

Expansion of the PRT Plan

In November 2003, plans to vitalize the PRT plan were referred to by General Barno at press briefings. Two new funding lines were added to existing Overseas Humanitarian Disaster and Civic Aid (OHDCA) support for Coalition PRTs: the US State Department's Economic Support Fund (ESF) and the Department of Defense's Commanders Emergency Response Program (CERP). The ESF alone provided $50 million for projects identified by PRTs in 2004 with an initial $10 million to speed the PRTs on their way. The CERP was the fast-track to funds set at $100,000 a month, which could be allocated virtually at the discretion of the Coalition PRT commander, usually to facilitate the QIPs that were the bedrock of "hearts and minds" strategies in the south. Reportedly, the faster the monthly allocations were spent under this budget line, the faster it was replenished.

The number of PRTs was to be doubled with a focus in the south and east in areas where the insurgents had been operating increasingly confidently, such as Assadabad in Kunar province bordering Pakistan, in Qalat in Zabul Province, in Khost and in Tirin Kot in Uruzgan. At the same time, NATO/ISAF would expand to the north and west of the country, theoretically before the elections.

A Shift in Focus

UNAMA had succeeded in carving out a mediating role between NGOs and the Coalition. UNAMA's position was based on support for the positive contribution PRTs could make, in the absence of other mechanisms capable of addressing the security gap and with the increasingly urgent need to facilitate reconstruction and create jobs to boost confidence in the Bonn process. In reality, the UN did not have much choice in the matter.

In an ongoing effort to shift the PRT plan away from the focus on minor reconstruction projects and towards security, UNAMA, in consultation with the Coalition and some NGOs had, by April 2003, identified priority areas where the PRTs could "maximize their comparative advantage," namely in areas where NGOs would not operate. These included the rehabilitation of key administrative structures at both the provincial and district levels, such as local government buildings, governors offices, customs houses, fire and police stations, law courts and military barracks for Afghan National Army units. Calls were also coming from a number of quarters, including some NGOs, for PRTs to involve themselves in supporting the largely stalled security sector reform process (SSR) and disarmament in particular. The provision of "an enabling environment for SSR" was increasingly referred to in discussions with donors and the UN concerning the evolving PRT plan.

PRT Developments—The North/South Divide

From a security perspective the situation in the north could be contained in the short-term, depending on the validity of the disarmament process and the cantonment of medium to heavy weapons. The situation in the south and southeast, where the insurgency had proved resilient to numerous Coalition operations, was more complex. There, the PRT mission which only got fully underway in early 2004, would not be detached from the conflict.

The different operating conditions between north and south have also influenced the extent to which PRTs succeeded in shifting their focus away from QIPs. Lessons learned by PRTs operating in the very different socio-political context in the north, where people longed to be free from the regular abuse of power by commanders, did not necessarily translate to the south. It is important to bear in mind that the dominant perception of security and insecurity in Afghanistan tended to reflect the experience of development actors assisting the Afghan government in the rebuilding of the country, rather than that of rural Afghans. In this regard, areas deemed high risk by the UN were often experienced as relatively secure by local populations.[29]

The North

The British PRT set up in July 2003 in Mazar-i Sharif led the way in effecting changes in direction. In common with other PRTs, the British approach was primarily directed at enabling an improvement in security and the extension of government authority. How they went about this differed from other PRTs. Promises made to NGOs to avoid any duplication of effort with the assistance community were kept. The Mazar-i Sharif PRT also strictly focused its comparatively limited resources (approximately $5 million in year one) on restoring local government infrastructure and supporting police training in particular. It rapidly expanded to cover the five northern provinces which amounted to an area the size of Scotland with wide-ranging patrols of six-man military teams in contrast to the comparatively risk-averse approach of the German PRT in Kunduz, which focused on development projects. Overall, the Mazar-i Sharif PRT was geared to the facilitation of the diplomatic and developmental-led approach led by the British DFID and FCO representatives embedded in the team. As the New Zealand PRT (including a DFID representative) followed a similar approach in Bamyan, hopes were raised that this would prove to be the model for all PRTs.

NATO's attempts to redefine itself in a changing world saw it take command of ISAF in August 2003. This had ended the six-month search for a lead nation which had become increasingly difficult. NATO expansion, in the form of PRTs fanning out over the northern half of Afghanistan, seemed to make sense. However, some European defense ministers of NATO member states did not share this conviction. The reluctance of NATO member states to commit further resources to the PRT plan received wide coverage in the international media embarrassing the civilian NATO leadership in the run up to the NATO summit at Istanbul in June 2004. At this meeting NATO's future direction was to be decided and the question of commitments to Afghanistan led the Summit's agenda.[30] In late May, NATO Secretary-General Jaap de Hoop Scheffer warned NATO representatives at a closed meeting "that the alliance had failed to commit sufficient resources to underwrite its new Afghan mission and was flirting with failure."[31] The costly business of setting up forward support bases, which included medical and air support, was one factor that delayed the NATO plan to roll out PRTs in the north, but some European leaders may also have been awaiting the outcome of the US elections due that November.

The relatively stable north was the focus of Phase I of ISAF/NATO's expansion beyond Kabul. This began in October 2003 when NATO took over the former Coalition PRT in Kunduz which would now be manned by German troops, civilian development specialists and others. The German government had been keen to restore relations with the US following their fallout over Iraq, but standing up a PRT under Coalition command would not have been a popular move domestically. These considerations informed diplomatic efforts, led by Germany, to alter ISAF's mandate at UN headquarters in New York.

Security considerations forced delays to holding any elections from June to September to early October 2004. The decision to hold the Afghan elections in two stages had been announced by September, with presidential elections scheduled finally for October 9 and parliamentary elections to follow in April 2005.[32] The Istanbul summit produced an increase in NATO forces in Afghanistan from 6,500 to approximately 9,000 to boost security in the run up to and during the elections.[33] A battalion (500) of these additional forces were "over the horizon" troops, based in Germany. In between the two sets of elections these extra forces would be withdrawn. Nevertheless, sufficient resources were committed by NATO member states to allow Phase 1 of the planned PRT expansion, which should have been in place before the NATO summit, to go ahead. By October 2004, multinational PRTs had been stood up in Maimana, Faizabad and Pul-i-Khumri to join Kunduz and Mazar under NATO command. Apart from the move of the Bamyan PRT from Coalition to NATO control, this completed Phase I.

Phase II was planned for completion by the October 2004 elections and related security plans had been predicated on this, but, to the outrage of members of the US government, no takers appeared in time.[34] Political upheaval in the western region of Afghanistan the previous month, which saw Ismael Khan's removal as provincial governor of Herat but still in control of armed forces, could not have encouraged states, such as Italy, who were reportedly considering the possibility. Phases III and IV, in which NATO was to sweep counter-clockwise from the southwest to the southeast of Afghanistan, did not possess a timeline.

The British PRT in Mazar-i Sharif was widely viewed as having been more focused on security challenges. While the British approach to security issues was more robust and involved an imaginative use of limited resources, their location made a critical difference. Warlordism remained the paramount problem in the north and clashes between rival warlords continued periodically. British patrols engaged in dispute resolution and potential flashpoints were rapidly identified and reacted to. Their success in helping push the factions back into their boxes temporarily also had a positive psychological effect.[35] But ultimately the Mazar-i Sharif PRT's efforts amounted to crisis management. Regional power realities remained unchanged. This was clearly demonstrated by the failure to get the terms of the ceasefire agreement implemented, brokered by the UN with PRT assistance in October 2003, between the respective commanders of Junbesh and Jamiat forces in the north, General Dostum and General Atta.[36]

The British PRT also had limited success in the minimal DDR-related activities it undertook. The PRT presence in Mazar-i Sharif was tolerated on the basis of a consensus of the main factional players. Regular security meetings were held between UNAMA, the PRT and the factional leaders in which potential flare-ups were identified and assessed, to be doused with PRT assistance if required. But it was a hard balance to maintain and when it suited them, the factional leaders could overturn the consensus at any time and both the UNAMA and the PRT were powerless to act.

In July 2004, for example, tensions unexpectedly erupted when the provincial chief of police accused General Atta publicly of being involved in drug smuggling. The Jamiat response was to send troops to surround the police headquarters. The police chief, General Akram, was a Pashtun. Reportedly, he had been carrying out his duties reasonably professionally, closing down illegal checkpoints and impounding narcotics. As a result, he had received increasing PRT support, ranging from the provision of uniforms and the refurbishment of police stations to back up (if needed) for the dismantlement of illegal checkpoints. When General Atta demanded the police chief's replacement on television, and in a tit-for-tat, accused Akram of being involved in drugs smuggling, the Ministry of Interior immediately gave way. The promotion of law and order, which was being supported by the PRT, lost out to bigger politics being played out in Kabul at the time.[37]

The South

> As we were leaving, a guy came up to me and pointed to the watch on my wrist. "Americans have all the watches," he said. "The Taliban has all the time."
>
> —*A US official close to the aid process recalling a visit to Qalat, Zabul Province in early 2004*[38]

Sequential UN security maps have illustrated a division between the "Pashtun belt" which is demarcated in a widening band of "high risk" red and the rest of the country. In effect, this divided the country into areas where the reconstruction process under the Bonn Agreement could progress, from those where it could not. The split between north and south was also emphasized in that only Coalition forces operated in the south.

The realization that the south was there to be won or lost at the community level had come very late in the day. Until December 2003, the PRTs had mainly deployed to relatively stable areas. An early exception had been Gardez, in the province of Paktia in the southeast, where the PRT had been involved in a number of steps to stabilize the city in early 2003. These had included replacing the corrupt and ineffective chief of police and moving in a unit of Afghan National Army forces directly to handle security issues such as illegal roadblocks and other forms of intimidation, with PRT support if necessary.

The so-called "Gardez effect" saw the revival of the local economy in which a number of PRT projects from school buildings to a police training compound were also initiated. This approach was heavily promoted as validating the

PRT concept. However, the "Gardez effect" only reached twenty kilometers from the town, while aid agencies based in Gardez reported it was as little as ten. Beyond that, power remained under the control of tribal structures. On a second visit to Gardez in August 2004, to check reports that the PRT effect there had evaporated, a more complex picture emerged.

Coalition resources had been stretched ever thinner by demands in Iraq and Afghanistan. In addition, US military reservists, many of whom faced a third tour of duty, reportedly had had enough.[39] Those who could were getting out of the military. A senior reservist, interviewed by the author in Gardez, cited declining numbers in US civil affairs reservists to eight or nine per PRT as one factor lessening the PRT's impact given the size and difficulty of the terrain to be covered.[40] He also reported that, rather than bringing appropriate skills with them, the civil affairs team during his nine-month tour of duty had picked up relevant skills "on the job."[41]

In line with the Coalition's stated objective that PRT assets were to be focused on keeping the Bonn process on track in regard to holding elections in 2004,[42] the efforts and resources of the Gardez PRT had, in the first half of 2004, been directed out of Paktia into the neighboring province of Paktika bordering Pakistan. In what the UN considered a highly insecure region, wells, clinics and schools were built or rebuilt in as many villages as possible. This paved the way for a more successful electoral registration process in Paktika than had been anticipated, and contributed to the overall balance in registration figures between the north and Pashtun south, without which it had been feared, holding elections might have triggered renewed civil war on ethnic lines.

The Gardez PRT's diversion to Paktika, where insecurity prevented setting up a permanent PRT base until August 2004 in Sharan, may have helped keep political objectives under Bonn on track but, in the meantime, an entire building season had been lost in Paktia where hopes raised on the back of earlier Gardez PRT needs assessments were to be disappointed. Moreover, the pressure to get quantifiable results on the ground fast had resulted in shoddy and very poor quality work by the local contractors hired to implement the PRT-selected projects in both provinces.[43] The problem, according to the reservist interviewed in Gardez in August, was that if more qualified contractors were brought in from Kabul, "security problems would erupt immediately."

The PRT focus in the south remained on the provision of schools, clinics and wells, in contradistinction to the north. This had the advantage of providing fast, visible "results" which could be promoted both to the Afghans and to policymakers in Kabul and Washington. But it was beyond the PRT's remit to provide the trained human resources in terms of midwives, nurses and teachers which Afghan communities did not possess. Moreover, despite PRT discussions since the plan's inception on the need for a computerized tracking system to allow checks on the upkeep of completed projects, by October 2004 there was still nothing in place.[44] Both in the north and the south, the provision of key utilities such as electricity, water or asphalted roads, remained a very slow moving process.

The Provincial Stabilization Fund (PSF), to which DFID had contributed over $30 million, was part of the Afghanistan Stabilization Program. This in turn was a component in the Ministry of Finance's national development coordination strategy, the National Priority Program (NPP), which had emerged by mid-2004. The NPPs were an attempt by Kabul to assert its control over development and came on the back of the former and largely moribund government coordination strategy, the "consultative group" mechanism, in which the UN had played a leading role.

The PSF was "to enhance the capacity of provinces, and particularly of Governors' offices, to plan, manage and implement development projects." The Provincial Reconstruction Office (PRO), which had been set up prior to the NPP plan by the Gardez PRT as a means of overcoming the PRT's limited manpower by tapping into and building Afghan capacity, had anticipated the increased focus on attempts to build local capacity. The PRO's provision of computers also strengthened coordination between the center and the province, while a DFID development expert advised on good governance. However, reports elsewhere that the PSF was being squandered on four wheel drive vehicles and other "necessities" prioritized by provincial governors, were less encouraging.

The PRT objective remained an overwhelmingly political one: to channel funds to maximum effect at the district level to win support for the government. But notwithstanding the increase in comparatively well-funded PRT budget lines, getting results on the ground was still subject to delays. Funding cycles did not always tie in with local conditions, such as the building season in Afghanistan which ended abruptly with the arrival of winter. The limited availability of Coalition maneuver units, needed to support and protect the civilian elements in PRTs, constrained PRTs' ability to access high-risk areas. By mid-2004, according to one UNAMA analyst in the southeast, this problem had been overcome. "But" he added, "sufficient resources were not available to achieve the needed effect and those that were, were not the right type, meanwhile we are up against the clock."[45]

The objective of winning back the south through the delivery of significant reconstruction within an overall political concept was also central to a plan which had been presented the previous year by the UN's deputy SRSG, Jean Arnault, following the killing of the UNHCR employee in Ghazni and the car-bomb detonated outside UNAMA's regional office in Kandahar. At this meeting, which took place on November 20, 2003 in Kandahar, attended by IO and NGO representatives, Jean Arnault announced a new priority for PRTs. They were to access "dangerous areas where NGOs and UN agencies cannot go and where urgent reconstruction in the form of roads and water is to be given by the civilian component of PRTs."

The accompanying security package was to be led by trained Afghan police appointed by the Ministry of Interior, augmented by local authorities loyal to the central government. Finally a PRT, with its ability to "reach-back" to Coalition airpower, provided support. An emphasis on "good governance" was added to the existing PRT reference points of "security" and "reconstruction." This reflected deepening international concern regarding the decreasing legitimacy of Karzai's government, largely as a result of the continuing inclusion of what the Afghans refer to as "mafia" at all government levels.

This new blueprint, which attempted to reverse trends in the south which amounted to a loss of control by the central government, was to be tested out in two pilot projects: in Shawali Kot in the north of Kandahar province; and Shurabak near the border with Pakistan. At first the plan was referred to as the "Provincial Stabilization Strategy," before being relabeled the "Regional Development Zone" (RDZ) plan. Ten months later there was still little to show for the initiative. It had failed mainly because it lacked a viable security plan and an apparent inability to commit sufficient resources to make a strong enough impact quickly enough.[46]

The three hundred MOI police promised "within weeks" by the UN in November did not arrive in Kandahar until late January. Half of their weapons were unusable. The local security situation in Kandahar was complicated by different tribal commands over the five police structures in the city itself. Governor Yousuf Pashtun, the technocrat who had replaced the former provincial governor of Kandahar, Gul Agha Sherzai, in August 2003, lacked the authority to deploy the MOI police which could have led to further instability in the city.[47] Moreover, all the pillars of Gul Agha's power structure, despite his removal, remained in place. His brother, for example, remained in command of the militia forces that provided security for the Coalition in the immediate environs to Kandahar airbase. Gul Agha's poster, over a year following his dismissal, was still seen all over Kandahar City.

The Regional Development Zone plan sounded impressive from a distance, but in reality the PRTs were sidelined. As in the north, a "joined up" approach to the implementation of security sector reform processes was mandatory if local power realities were to be changed. This needed to include the dissolution of Afghan Militia Forces divisions and private militias, the development of an ethnically representative and professional national army and police force—where promotion through the ranks was earned and not bought—and the establishment of the rule of law, capable of protecting the powerless and providing a counterpart to the police. Instead, progress in these crucial and interlinked areas was eroded from the start by the power brokers included in, and those left out of, the Afghan Transitional Authority. In the vicious cycle thus created, the central government was unable to extend its authority. Coalition support to government forces in September 2004, which led to the removal of Ismael Khan as governor of Herat Province, represented a new development however.

By October 2004, the impression that the Coalition and UNAMA were going in circles became stronger. Ever more plans on paper had still not resulted in an effective mechanism to coordinate reconstruction efforts or to ensure a centrally institutionalized procedure, through which valuable lessons learned could be transferred to incoming PRTs under ISAF or the Coalition. Meanwhile in many parts of the south, information on the Taliban proved even more difficult to win from local communities trapped between an elusive and increasingly ruthless insurgency[48] and the opposing forces of "Operation Enduring Freedom."[49] The Coalition's counterinsurgency strategy, which mixed friendship and force, met more local resistance than was reported. Since 2003 Afghan NGOs working in the south informed the author about a number of incidents that indicated a rejection, in some communities, of civil affairs projects implemented in the aftermath of Coalition operations in the area.[50] This offered worrying parallels between the US-led intervention and the Soviet past when resources were also poured into the country to no avail.

Short-termism was a problem that affected many actors in Afghanistan and the PRTs were no exception. Throughout Afghanistan the turnover of personnel on six to twelve-month long maximum rotations undermined PRT efforts. This meant that the highly complex forces and factors at play in varying localized contexts were only just being understood as PRT personnel rotated out, "to be replaced by more wide eyed innocents full of plans and enthusiasm" as a jaded development specialist in one PRT put it. In his opinion, there had been no coherent attempt by policy-makers to understand the varying local problems as they really were and to plan accordingly. This would have required time, which had been a commodity in singularly short supply in relation to policy formulation for Afghanistan.

Opposing Narratives

The PRT plan was surrounded by conflicting narratives from the start. The name itself, chosen by President Karzai, was a misnomer. Efforts by the assistance community to re-label PRTs as "provincial stabilization teams" came to nothing.

The fanfare which surrounded the plan's official launch (to which representatives from the diplomatic, donor and assistance communities in Kabul were invited) proved with hindsight to have been a major error. Long lists of civil affairs skills were presented as being virtually on tap from an apparently endless supply of US military reservists, which included economists, doctors, lawyers, engineers, telecommunications experts and civil aviation professionals.[51] The failure to deliver at these levels created lasting mistrust amongst many NGOs and Afghans, particularly in the south, regarding the "true" purpose of PRTs.

At the only joint evaluation of the PRT plan in which UNAMA, UN agencies and NGOs, as well as the Coalition, participated in Kabul in May 2003, the Coalition acknowledged that the plan had been oversold and that "confusing or conflicting messages" on the PRT's scope and role had been delivered by Coalition representatives. It should be recalled that the oversell occurred as the US was closing the door on the expansion of ISAF in late 2002 and shifting military resources and focus away from Afghanistan towards Iraq.

In the first few months of 2003, debate on PRTs was fuelled internationally by the possibility that they might be a model for the provision of humanitarian relief as a political tool in the management of future interventions. At one point, as the likelihood of a war in Iraq grew, the PRT concept was discussed as intensively in Washington as it was in Kabul. This produced more confusion in the field. The heightened international focus over a plan which had been largely developed in Bagram resulted in policy-makers in Washington making claims for PRT objectives which were subsequently not endorsed by policy-makers based in Afghanistan.

Policy-makers supporting the plan in Kabul, Washington and London continued to boost the PRT's "evolutionary" assets. NGOs and other critics reiterated that PRTs were neither mandated nor resourced to address a security crisis which continued to worsen. By July 2003 the Agency Coordinating Body for Afghan Relief (ACBAR), an umbrella organization for national and international NGOs working in Afghanistan, issued a policy brief that concluded that PRTs had been recognized by all actors, including the Coalition and UNAMA, to be "a minor component" in the complex and challenging security situation which had developed since the Coalition's intervention.[52] The increase in both PRT numbers and funding of Coalition PRTs in 2004 rendered the PRT plan less dismissable by its critics, but a significant and lasting impact by PRTs on the interdependent areas of security and reconstruction remained hard to discern.

Despite repeated claims by the Coalition to the contrary, PRTs did not signify any revolutionary development in military thinking.[53] At a PRT Commanders Conference held in Kabul in 2004, General Barno informed a batch of incoming PRT commanders that "PRTs were the great experiment" and they were "the great experimenters." Rhetoric aside, the provision of quick impact projects to local communities to establish "force protection" and garner intelligence in return was viewed throughout by most military representatives as standard military practice.[54] The Soviets had seeded military-political units throughout Afghanistan. Prior to the inception of the PRT plan, the Coalition's CATs had focused on the south, implementing QIPs to "put a smile on the face of the military" as one reservist put it. Similar "hearts and minds" strategies were utilized by the US military in the Vietnam War and were also a component in counterinsurgency strategies used by the British army dating back to Malaya and Borneo in the 1950s and 1960s. But important differences did exist between the US and other military forces. The US rank and file did not possess the policing and peacekeeping skills common to British, New Zealand and Canadian military training and experience. Contrastingly, the US military was trained for combat only. In the view of some analysts it was therefore singularly ill-suited to postwar peace-building despite "soaring rhetoric" to the contrary.[55]

Future Directions

By October 2004, the PRT concept was considered to have validated itself by leading donor nations, by the Coalition and by NATO. But on what grounds? If evaluations of PRT endeavors were conducted, the non-military world had not had access to them—beyond the one exercise conducted under UN auspices in May 2003. The overt rationale for PRTs—the facilitation of reconstruction and the improvement of security—had not made significant headway against a security situation which continued to deteriorate. In the view of many developmental NGOs, a PRT presence actually militated against long-term development processes. But the PRTs had always been linked to the provision of information and it is in this regard that their added value was more apparent.

By Autumn 2004, PRTs were established in half of Afghanistan's 32 provinces and more were planned. This countrywide structure provided donor governments, and the development and political experts belonging to them, with a unique means of both directly accessing areas of the country that otherwise would be impossible and for the PRTs to act as their eyes and ears, allowing checks for example, to be made on the ground against claims made by provincial governors or by government ministers. Given that USAID contributed in the region of $1 billion to reconstruction in 2004 and that the US government was increasingly anxious to stop treading water in Afghanistan where provincial and district government was effectively non-existent, the PRTs were a uniquely useful device. The definition of the PRT concept stated in the 108th Congress Report to the House of Representatives (2004) referred to this: "the PRT concept is based on expansion of security throughout Afghanistan, but each is also prepared to assist local oversight of assistance managed by the USAID Mission in Kabul, complement DoD humanitarian assistance, and support expansion of central Government of Afghanistan services."

An unstated appreciation of these oversight capabilities underpinned the PRT discussions that had included donors, Coalition, NATO/ISAF and Ministry of Finance as well as Ministry of Interior representatives in the second half of 2004. These discussions directly linked PRTs to a longer-term involvement in "reconstruction" and "development." This was then due to plans to merge the overall direction of PRT efforts under the government's latest coordination strategy for development, encapsulated in the "National Priority Programs" (NPPs).

To be successful, these centrally developed plans had to ensure effective delivery of services and projects through the provincial and district levels of government. To this end, it was envisaged that PRTs would build local capacities and pull the relevant actors together, from provincial and district governors down to the community shuras. PRTs would also, by virtue of the development and political expertise embedded within them, be in a position to prioritize projects as well as match them to donors.

The extent to which PRTs could deliver on an increasingly ambitious agenda which included the accurate reflection of needs on the ground, the development of a civil-military framework to promote good governance at district and provincial levels, and the projection of sufficient security to facilitate the reform agenda and disarmament in particular, would, however, not only depend on the ways in which PRTs were resourced or its staff were rotated but far more crucially on factors that were outside the PRTs' remit. These included political reform of key ministries such as the Ministry of Interior, effective measures to reduce the narcotics trade and the expansion of organized criminal networks, the establishment of an equitable tribal policy where none existed and so forth.

Two key challenges to the PRT agenda in the north had to be overcome if progress in the above mentioned areas was to be made. First, the promotion of "good governance" was often interpreted as code for boosting a Pashtun political agenda. Widely-held fears of the reassertion of Pashtun dominance provided a rich seam for Tajik actors to exploit. Any attempts by PRTs to promote good governance would, therefore, need to be broadly based and multiethnic. Second, ISAF/NATO needed to demonstrate the political will to insist that the price for inclusion in the political sphere was a genuine disarmament process. A number of factors militated against real progress in decommissioning hazardous military units however. Among these, Karzai's failure to establish himself as a truly national leader predominated.

In the south the insurgency continued to be fed by recruits from the Gulf Arab financed Deobandi madrassas, located in Pakistan's Northwest Frontier province and Baluchistan. But the Taliban had also maintained cultural and social networks in many parts of southern Afghanistan. In Taliban strongholds like Zabul, where one NGO representative interviewed in 2002 recalled people saying, "we are so desperate we would take help from the Devil," nothing much had changed. Clearly there were no quick-fix solutions but the delivery of improvements to the grinding nature of daily existence via the provision of water, electricity and roads would have helped delegitimize extremist propaganda.

The attainment of the short-term political objectives that punctuated the Bonn Agreement determined international priorities but reaching these objectives also dangerously diverted attention from security facts on the ground, which with regard to the south were also subjected to consistent spin. Following the presidential elections, the UN and the military finalized plans to transfer "ownership" of development and reconstruction to the new government. But this politically correct terminology could not disguise the reality to those who worked outside Kabul: a government which, despite some remarkable achievements, remained hamstrung by capacity constraints at all levels, a political inheritance which challenged hopes for the fragile democratic process, and increasing corruption fed by growing uncertainty about the future which had led to a "grab what you can while you can" mentality developing amongst the Afghans. PRTs may have contributed momentum to processes leading up to the elections, but this was overshadowed by the increasingly profound nature of the challenges to reform and the building of a sustainable stability. In this regard, the view of UNAMA political analysts based in different regions that forward momentum gained in 2003 in the replacement of corrupt provincial officials with more competent ones had been lost by the following year, was of great concern.[56]

Conclusion: An Imperfect World

> Your enemies will make you laugh and your friends will make you cry.
> — *Dari and Pashto saying*

The US-led Coalition's reliance on the use of proxy forces on the ground in the overthrow of the Taliban and the decision not to expand ISAF forces following the stabilization of Kabul had fundamentally set the course.[57] The security gap could only widen into a vacuum and as a result, crisis management and damage limitation characterized an increasingly reactive international response, epitomized by the PRT plan.

The extent to which western capitals failed either to grasp or effectively respond to the magnitude of the challenges to stabilization in Afghanistan was reflected in national approaches towards standing up PRTs. These tended to be predicated on the ISAF/NATO peacekeeping mission and its UN mandate and an overriding political vision informed by the concept of Afghan "ownership" whereby PRTs would "assist" the authorities in the provision of reconstruction and security. The fact that the emperor, in the form of "the authorities," had few, if any clothes and that a shadow state was increasingly able successfully to manipulate official state-building and reform efforts where they counted, formed the background against which PRTs moved ever more center-stage during the period under discussion. PRTs offered both a distraction from this publicly unacknowledged state of affairs as well as a mechanism through which international efforts could be directed to address official shortcomings. Whether this amounted to a strategic engagement in Afghanistan on the part of the international community was another matter.

At the end of 2004, Afghanistan was already at the crossroads so widely referred to by 2006/2007. Then, the Afghan people had delivered a strong mandate for change via the presidential elections. They had withstood numerous atrocities in the run up to the elections and braved sustained intimidation in turning out to vote in overwhelming numbers. In so doing and in rejecting the claims of those who opposed the legitimacy of the electoral process itself, the Afghan people delivered a number of important messages to the powerful in Afghanistan and to the international community. Above all else, people wanted stability underpinned by law and order in order to bring about development. In voting for Karzai, people had voted for a political process to bring this about. Afghans hoped that with the support of the international community, the Karzai government would be able to deliver on its promises. However, from the vantage point of 2007, international and Afghan perceptions that Afghanistan risked being lost by default had become, if anything, more acute.

Notes

1. See William Maley, *The Afghan Wars* (New York: Palgrave Macmillan, 2002).
2. See AFP, "Afghan Peacekeeping Expansion 'Too Little, Too Late': Aid Agencies Warn," 7 October 2003.
3. Democratic representatives lambasted "some of our European allies" for the "pitifully" small NATO contingent in Afghanistan; see Deutsche Welle, "US Blames Europe for Failures in Afghanistan," 30 September 2004.
4. As did the use of armed militias for security by private contractors like Louis Berger in the south.
5. See for example, Antonio Giustozzi, *Respectable Warlords?: The Politics of Statebuilding in Post-Taleban Afghanistan* (London: LSE, Crisis States Programme, September 2003), and N. Nojumi, *The Rise of the Taliban in Afghanistan* (New York: Palgrave, 2002).
6. Giustozzi, *Respectable Warlords?*
7. The author is using Giustozzi's definition of a warlord "as a particular type of ruler, whose basic characteristics are his independence from any higher authority and his control of a 'private army' which responds to him personally."
8. This was the commonly-held view among diplomats and senior members of UNAMA during 2003. Also see Anne Barnard, "Afghan Projects Slow to Reach Villages," *Boston Globe,* 17 October 2004.
9. By September 2004 the cost of Coalition forces in Afghanistan was estimated at $900 million a day.
10. See for example, R. S. Jennings, *The Road Ahead, Lessons in Nation Building from Japan, Germany and Afghanistan for Postwar Iraq* (Washington, DC: United States Institute of Peace, April 2003).
11. SSR included reform of the police and the judicial system as well as disarmament, demobilization and reintegration of the Afghan Militia Forces, the building of a new Afghan National Army and counter-narcotics.
12. "Afghan Elections: The Great Gamble" (Afghanistan Research and Evaluation Unit Briefing Paper, November 2003).
13. Forty representatives of civil society organizations from all over Afghanistan met in Berlin 29–30 March at the invitation of the German government, facilitated by swisspeace and the Freidrich-Ebert-Stiftung Foundation. Their joint statement was formally presented by two of the civil society participants at the donors Berlin conference which followed 31 March–2 April.
14. See *Elections and Security in Afghanistan* (Kabul and Brussels: ICG Asia Briefing, 30 March 2004).
15. Author's interview with Professor Kenji Isezaki, Kabul, 11 September 2004.
16. See for example, *Afghanistan's Bonn Agreement One Year Later: A Catalog of Missed Opportunities* (Human Rights Watch, December 2002).
17. C. Watkins, "Provincial Reconstruction Teams (PRTs): An Analysis of Their Contribution to Security in Afghanistan" (M.Sc. Thesis, Oxford Brookes University, 2003).
18. For an overview of the launch of the PRT plan, then-referred to as Joint Regional Teams, see B. J. Stapleton, "A British Agencies Afghanistan Group Briefing Paper

on the Development of Joint Regional Teams in Afghanistan," British Agencies Afghanistan Group (London), January 2003.

19. R. A. Clarke, *Against All Enemies* (New York: Free Press, 2004), 241.

20. Stapleton, BAAG, 2003.

21. Phase III was the military term applied to the stabilization of Afghanistan.

22. This move was not formally confirmed until Donald Rumsfeld visited Afghanistan in April 2003 and publicly alluded to the Coalition having moved into a reconstruction phase.

23. When the author first visited the Gardez PRT in June 2003 the PRT Commander complained of waiting months for funds to drill a single well.

24. Advocacy coordinator for CARE quoted by Reuters, 11 May 2003.

25. "Aid Workers: Afghanistan in Jeopardy," *USA Today,* 22 January 2004.

26. UN investigations into the carbomb incident pointed to non-Taliban elements being responsible, according to UN and NGO sources the author spoke to.

27. For example, see Xinhua Net, "Anti-US Resentment on Rise in Southeast Afghanistan," Kabul, 15 March 2004.

28. At a meeting with the Afghan government's National Security Council in September 2004, it was reported that Coalition mistakes in this regard had greatly reduced in number. In the same month however, Afghan staff of DACAAR, a Danish NGO, were directly targeted by coalition special forces in Waradesh village in Kunar Province. Six civilians were killed in the aerial bombardment. The coalition later took full responsibility for the incident.

29. "See Human Security and Livelihoods of Rural Afghans, 2002–2003," Feinstein International Famine Centre, Tufts University.

30. See for example, "NATO's Incredibility: Its Real Challenge Lies in Afghanistan, not Iraq," *Financial Times,* 26 June 2004.

31. See "NATO Flirts With Failure In Afghanistan," *International Herald Tribune,* 21 May 2004.

32. BBC News, 28 June 2004.

33. BBC News, "NATO Seals Afghanistan Expansion Plan," 1 October 2004.

34. See Deutsche Welle, "US Blames Europe for Failures in Afghanistan," 30 September 2004.

35. For example in contributing to the ceasefire brokered by the UNAMA between General Atta (Jamiat) and General Dostum (Junbesh) in 2003.

36. This involved merging the 7th and 8th Divisions into a greatly reduced 15th Division under a new commander loyal to the central government.

37. At around this time Marshall Fahim was dropped as Karzai's running-mate for the October elections and a sop to Tajik sensibilities may have been required.

38. Report by Jon Sawyer, *St. Louis Dispatch,* June 2004.

39. The author met many civil affairs reservists through her work in Afghanistan and this was a commonly held view toward the end of 2003.

40. From a highpoint of civil affairs teams numbering 50 in 2001, averages had declined to eight or nine.

41. Interview with senior reservist at Gardez PRT headquarters, August 2004.

42. Stated by Lt. General Barno at the PRT Commanders Conference in Kabul, 8 May 2004.

43. According to the reservist interviewed, "you could put your foot through the sidewalk."

44. The question of the sustainability of PRT projects remained at the forefront of the NGO critique of PRT achievements.

45. Interview with UNAMA political analyst, Gardez, August 2004.

46. Author's interview with well placed source, Kabul, October 2004.

47. Complete loss of face was avoided by the UN appointing many of the MOI police contingent as security guards outside UN offices.

48. See *Kabul Weekly* report on the beheading of ten elders from Uruzgan for supporting the elections, 13 October 2004.

49. Declan Walsh, "Frustrated US Forces Fail to Win Hearts and Minds," *The Guardian,* 23 September 2004.

50. These have included wells filled in, a restored mosque damaged during OEF operations left unused, and schools burnt down.

51. See Stapleton, BAAG, 2003

52. See "Provincial Reconstruction Teams and the Security Situation in Afghanistan," Agency Coordinating Body for Afghan Relief, Kabul, July 2003.

53. The PRT commander of the first New Zealand-led PRT described PRTs as "standard military practice" to the author.

54. Author's interview with the PRT commander of the New Zealand PRT in Bamyan, May 2004.

55. See Jennings, *The Road Ahead.*

56. Author's interview with UNAMA political analyst, September 2004.

57. See Maley, *The Afghan Wars,* 276, where opposition to the expansion of ISAF 1 is identified as being led by the US and France. European objections may have been driven by fears that expansion of ISAF would provide an exit strategy for Coalition forces with the Europeans left "holding the baby."

10

Keeping the Peace Without Peacekeepers*

Eckart Schiewek

FOLLOWING THE FALL OF THE Taliban, it was widely felt that Afghanistan required a massive transfer of socio-political technology for it to overcome its legacy of thirty years of war, general underdevelopment and poverty.[1] The Bonn Agreement, an agreement among Afghan military leaders victorious on the ground and the pre-war elite in exile around the former king, attempted to "end the tragic conflict in Afghanistan and promote national reconciliation, lasting peace, stability and respect for human rights in the country" through a transition from an essentially self-appointed group to an elected government. The holding of universal and free elections was for the first time agreed upon by leaders who fought each other bitterly for the last thirty years.[2] The United Nations Mission's mandate was geared towards maximizing national ownership of the transition as requested by the Afghans who met at Bonn.[3] Not only the UN but also major international donors were maintaining a "light footprint." The absence of "blue helmet" UN troops or any significant UN police presence meant that the UN's efforts of peace-building and peacekeeping were diplomatic in nature. The mission paired "classic diplomacy" with new activities, such as monitoring, verification and assistance in rebuilding institutions. This chapter looks at the subnational dynamics and the role of international actors attempting to avoid a recurrence of violent conflict in north Afghanistan.

Traditional Principles of Afghanistan's Statehood

Explanations of the Afghan war have frequently mentioned but neglected the internal dynamics and localized internal conflicts, which only recently received

*The views expressed herein are those of the author and do not necessarily reflect the views of the United Nations.

some scholarly coverage.[4] When ambitious colonial officers integrated segments of previously competing empires into the new buffer state, the provinces of north Afghanistan were the last to be attached and resisted fiercely until 1892.[5] Integration through modernization ended in failure several times.[6] When the US-led international Coalition (hereafter referred to as "the Coalition") allied itself with the United Front,[7] the Afghan opposition to the Taliban, a window of opportunity opened again for modernization and integration.[8] The heat of battle, and Coalition money, produced only limited military cohesion, and did not translate into joint political action.[9] The United Front was a political oxymoron.[10] The sole political perspective had been formulated by the exiled former king of Afghanistan, H.M. Zahir Shah, and elaborated with increasing sophistication during the 1990s through the "Rome process." Lack of political cohesion within the United Front forced its components into accepting H.M.'s plan for holding the Emergency Loya Jirga.[11] The immediate outcome was expressed in the Bonn Agreement concluded on December 5, 2001, and put forth a tight timeline for an Emergency Loya Jirga, constitution and elections. In the agreement, the UN was asked to assist this process through ensuring a politically neutral environment through the United Nations Assistance Mission to Afghanistan (UNAMA).[12] While the Bonn Agreement left most decisions completely open and to the discretion of the Afghans, many actors imagined a return to the pre-revolutionary Afghan state—as it existed under the presidency of Daoud (1973–1978)—and immediately conceptualized their activities as "reconstruction" (*bâzsâzi*) rather than "construction" (*âbâdi*). Many of the underlying assumptions for "reconstruction" severely challenged the forces that had just overthrown the Taliban. While the Bonn process was meant to bring about new elements such as democracy, constitutional checks and balances, a government monopoly of violence, and the notion of equality, "reconstruction" meant for many Afghan actors a return to Islamic statehood,[13] Pashtun hegemony and centralism. Universal values and a return to the old order of the "fifty years before April 1978" was formulated as complementary[14] or mutually conditional upon each other.[15] Both collided with the realities on the ground.

One of the defining features of the Afghan state established by the "Iron Amir" Abd ar-Rahman in the late nineteenth century was the extreme application of the principle of centralism, moderated by incompetence and corruption.[16] Challenged for its survival, in the 1980s the communist regime resorted to military decentralization through the creation of local militias.[17] The inability to control the militias of north Afghanistan led to the overthrow of the Najibullah government.[18] A countrywide centralism reemerged with the Taliban from 1994 onwards, but was not any more centered in the traditional hub of Kabul, but clustered in Kandahar around the seat of *amir al-mu'minin* (Commander of the Faithful) Mulla Omar.[19] After the fall of the Taliban, regional command structures, both military and civil, reestablished themselves.[20] The success of the United Front against the Taliban and Al Qaeda had proven the power of decentralized regional bases, and challenged the notion of a centralized Afghanistan. Also, the fall of the Pashtun Taliban[21] at the hands of non-Pashtun forces,[22] sometimes influenced by irredentist subnationalisms[23] challenged the old ethnic pecking-order, which in public perception was nearly equal to centralism and an Islamicate state.[24]

The Struggle for Power in North Afghanistan

North Afghanistan was an area never fully controlled by the Taliban and maintained pockets of United Front presence.[25] From 2000 onwards, offensives from these pockets and similar resistance centers in the provinces of Bamyan, Ghor, Nimroz, Nangarhar and Laghman disrupted major Taliban offensives at the main frontlines north of Kabul and west of Taluqan. In early 2001 Ahmed Shah Massoud decided to increase the role of the pockets by reactivating previous regional leaders Ismail Khan and Rashid Dostum.[26] Dostum attempted in May 2001 to push towards Mazar-i Sharif from his base in Balkhab with a small cavalry attack.[27] The Taliban carried out a little-known massacre of local civilians in the area as a reprisal.[28] After the US intervention started on October 5, 2001, Dostum became the driving force of an offensive via Sholgara district to Mazar-i Sharif.[29] Both Dostum's and Ata's forces had a team of US Special Forces with them in October 2001, which proved instrumental to their advance.[30] Mazar-i Sharif fell on November 9 to Dostum, Muhaqqiq and Ata. Kabul fell on November 13 to Fahim. Military victory was achieved without any political plan agreed upon by all partners.[31] While the convening of an Emergency Loya Jirga was greeted with popular approval across the country, key actors in the fight against the Taliban such as the commanders of Balkhab, upper Faryab and Samangan were sidelined in the Interim Administration.[32] Jamiat's monopolization antagonized all other parts of the United Front and threatened to create spoiler effects.[33] To counter centrifugal tendencies, Karzai granted regional leaders the power to appoint civilian officials in their regions, reminiscent of the regionalism prevailing after 1992.[34]

The Bonn Agreement had not included the Taliban as a defeated party. Most of the Taliban militias of the north belonged in the past to the Hezb-i-Islami of Gulbuddin Hikmatyar, which was on the very fringe of the agreement and had to realign themselves.[35] The reintegration of these commanders "protected" the Pashtun communities of the north.[36]

The new military and political framework became the Ministry of Defense's order of battle, the so-called Afghan Militia Forces (AMF) through which the subsidies paid by the US were channeled to individual commanders and supposedly also to the soldiers.[37] While during the years of 2000–2001 the total military strength of the United Front was estimated somewhere near 35,000 and the Taliban at between 50,000 and 70,000, the new Ministry of Defense now aimed at an army of 200,000 fighters.[38] Even if allowing for large scale reintegration of ex-Taliban fighters, a lot of fresh recruiting would have been required. Most commanders, however, transformed the recruitment into a taxing tool. These local violence providers were levying *askar puli* (soldier money) from the population under their control for assumed recruitments to units existing only on paper.[39]

Junbish secured in the AMF a regional post of the Operational Command North, and Army Corps VIII with four divisions. Ustad Ata also received command over Army Corps VII with four divisions.[40] Junbish engaged in creating a parallel power structure, which politically reached out to commanders within "officially" Jamiat formations like Army Corps VII or VI (Qunduz).[41] This policy succeeded immediately in early 2002 to "convert" two of the four divisions of the Army Corps VII to Junbish (Division 19 and 95).[42] The Hazara parties received only one division in the north within Army Corps VII (Division 38).[43]

The strategic center of gravity across the north became Mazar-i Sharif and the nearby Sholgara district. The main prize was of course the city.[44] The Taliban had looted most UN and NGO offices following the withdrawal of international UN and NGO staff after September 11, 2001. Much of the loot and buildings had been taken over by the United Front.[45] Through a process of individual negotiation, all compounds were returned to the international organizations whose staff returned to Mazar-i Sharif from December 2001 onward. The property and security of Afghan citizens however, was much harder to secure. Empty offices, schools and private houses converted to military bases added up to a list of roughly 60 locations within city limits, and troops quartered in these locations lived off the land. Local groceries, restaurants and bakeries had to provide the troops with food, at least in part for free. In addition every military post assumed quasi-executive and judicial authority over their neighborhood, sometimes resorting to forced recruitment.

In early January 2002, the Ministry of Defense moved "central" (Panjsheri Jamiat) troops to Mazar-i Sharif in a move to secure control over the airport, 5 kilometers to the east of the city, for Jamiat alone. In a parallel development, Jamiat and Junbish-aligned commanders clashed in Sar-i Pul, Balkh and Qunduz Provinces. Around January 6–8, this round of fighting claimed 40 lives. Throughout January 2002, tensions increased in the power struggle over Mazar-i Sharif. On January 25, major troop movements took place by all parties towards the city. Five hundred Panjsheri fighters accompanied by ten tanks and 2,300 local Jamiat troops entered the city from the east and south. Junbish moved close to 2,000 troops in the city from the west and north. During the next week, negotiations between the parties facilitated by Hizb-i Wahdat were accompanied by small clashes around the city. This violent struggle became a threat to the peace process started by the Bonn Agreement and even was brought to the attention of the UN Security Council.[46] It is not surprising that given such coverage, frequently "north Afghanistan" and "warlordism" were seen as synonymous.[47]

UNAMA's Good Offices and the Creation of the First Security Commission

Besides threatening the holding of the Emergency Loya Jirga, the mere presence of nearly 5,000 battle-ready troops on high alert—some equipped with heavy weapons—in a major city of Afghanistan, constituted a danger in itself for the security of the Afghan citizens. It had become evident that none of the parties trusted each other or the Kabul authorities enough to engage in serious agreements.[48] After consultations of the Special Representative of the Secretary-General (SRSG), Ambassador Lakhdar Brahimi, with Chairman of the Interim Administration Hamid Karzai, a joint delegation of UNAMA and Afghan government officials was dispatched to Mazar-i Sharif on February 3, 2002 to follow up on negotiations previously carried out by telephone and proxies. The International Assistance Force (ISAF) and Coalition forces facilitated transport and protection of the delegation. Headed by UNAMA Chief of Staff Dr. Karl Fischer, the mission managed to draft a consensus document:

> (1) Establishment of an authorized military commission with the forces involved in guaranteeing the security of Balkh province. (2) Withdrawal of all irresponsible armed persons and groups from the city of Mazar-i Sharif and their deployment to the places identified by the commission. (3) Formation of a disciplinary police force of six hundred persons from all involved military forces, equally and jointly in all police districts (*hawza*) in the city in the frame of the police headquarters of Balkh province. The inducted persons sever all connections with their former organizational structures. (4) Preparation as soon as possible of a security map by the security commission that gives clear and complete information. (5) Military forces deployed to the police districts and will act under the order and administration of the Chief of Police of Balkh province. (6) Distribution of license cards to carry weapons to bodyguards shall be authorized by the security commission. (7) Evacuation under the super vision of police forces of all premises and governmental institutions and offices by occupying military forces. (8) In case of outbreaks of internal differences and military clashes between the existing military forces in the northern region an authorized security commission will be assigned from the northern leadership. Further decisions will be made after the commission reports on the implementation of the agreement. (9) Captives and prisoners should be handed over as soon as possible to the security commission. From now on no force has the right to arrest. The ICRC in agreement with the northern leadership can visit the prisoners any time deemed necessary. (10) Provisions of this arrangement shall be implemented within ten days. (11) Implementation of this agreement will be supervised by a joint delegation of the Interim Administration and the United Nations.

The document was signed by Sayyid Nurullah (Junbish), Ustad Ata (Jamiat), Sardar Sa'idi (Hizb-i Wahdat), and Dr. Karl Fischer (UNAMA).[49]

The Security Commission[50] was composed of the representatives of the major armed factions of the north and the law enforcement organs.[51] UNAMA accepted an observer role, which was filled through Political Affairs Officers Patterson and Urazbaev. General Rozi of Junbish acted as "head" of the commission and moderated the discussions, a professional non-aligned officer from Balkh provincial police acted as a secretary. The Security Commission soon also became charged with events beyond the city of Mazar-i Sharif. When fighting erupted in Tashqurghan (also called Khulm) district to the east of Mazar-i Sharif in mid-February over resource exploitation, the Security Commission deployed to the locality. It negotiated a local cease-fire, the cantonment of some heavy and light weapons with the local police headquarters, and an exchange of hostages taken.[52] On February 28, 2002 all members of the Security Commission met with the factional leaders of the north and reported on achievements and shortcomings as requested by the agreement's provision number eight. The new multi-factional police force had not come into existence. While some elements of non-Jamiat forces were integrated, this was far-off the original idea of a neutral force, or any police force.[53] Most houses and properties were not totally vacated but now only occupied by fewer and less visible armed men. Initiatives to verify complaints regarding behavior of the military were only undertaken at the behest of the parties represented in the Security Commission, which excluded the population at large. As an observer, UNAMA brought a number of complaints and its own observations to the attention of the Security Commission, but could not influence the agenda, which was in the hands of General Rozi. A planned joint verification by the Interim Administration and UNAMA headquarters never took place due to the lack of interest of the security ministries in Kabul. UNAMA's mandate of good offices and assistance to the Interim Administration could not warrant a more active role at that point.[54] At that point too, Coalition forces in the north had resolutely declined to get involved in "green-on-green" fighting, and ISAF was limited to an embryonic presence in Kabul.

One event pulled together the factions again: the traditional New Year (*Nawroz*) ceremony—the raising of Imam Ali's standard (*janda*) at his shrine in central Mazar-i Sharif on March 21. Observance of this ritual was said to guarantee fertility and peace, but it had been forbidden under the Taliban.[55] Given the previous four years of drought, it was natural that the factions attempted to gain political legitimacy by organizing the ceremony and hosting notables from outside of the region, and turned to the Security Commission. The event became a success with thousands of visitors from Kabul and was graced with the presence of ex-President Rabbani, Chairman Karzai, and US Special Envoy Khalilzad.[56] The rain started the next day.

Renewed Conflict and the Creation of the Second Security Commission

Throughout April, as reform of the security sector faltered and elections to the Emergency Loya Jirga were held, both sides increased recruitment and readiness of their forces.[57] The plans for disarming the AMF were also seen to be dominated by Minister of Defense Fahim, who would engineer the process to keep most of Shura-yi Nazar's troops in the army, whereas Dostum's and the Hazara troops would be helped to return to civilian life. While the discussion over how to disarm the AMF continued, the Ministry of Defense expanded Jamiat formations.[58] Jamiat felt threatened by Junbish's political expansion. In the run-up to the Emergency Loya Jirga elections, a Junbish delegation headed by Ahmad Khan of Samangan toured areas which previously had been Jamiat strongholds and mobilized local Uzbeks.[59] Lawlessness increased rapidly in the city of Mazar-i Sharif, as police officers were turning a blind eye to crimes committed by criminals close to their respective factions and ethnic groups.[60] During a visit of SRSG Brahimi on April 14–15, UNAMA negotiated with the heads of all parties in the north to put an end to the increasing tensions. At that time, it was estimated that 8,000–10,000 troops were positioned in the city. Jamiat under Ustad Ata disposed of 4,000–5,000, Hizb-i Wahdat under Sardar Sa'idi of 2,000, and General Dostum's forces were estimated at 3,000. This represented roughly a 100% increase of the troops active in the January-February crisis. Jamiat also had now acquired additional tanks which matched Junbish's armor of approximately 30 tanks.[61] Ustad Ata set a deadline of National Revolution Day, April 28,[62] for all troops not belonging to Army Corps VII (e.g., non-Jamiat troops) to leave the city. The increase in tension threatened the elections to the Emergency Loya Jirga in the provincial centers, where a second stage was to be held from May 21 to June 5. In Sar i Pul, Jamiat had reinforced its headquarters in the old fortress (*bâlâ hisâr*) above the city center where the elections were to take place.[63]

On April 30, heavy fighting broke out between Jamiat and Junbish forces in Sholgara, and in the evening also in Sar-i Pul which involved there the use of heavy artillery. In Sar-i Pul, Junbish managed to overrun Jamiat positions in the city, storm the headquarters in the old fortress above the city, and also take over the Jamiat-dominated district of Sayyad to the northwest of the provincial capital. Kamal Khan's success relied on successful mobilization of the ethnic group of Sar-i Pul Arabs in addition to the Uzbeks, which had been marginalized for at least a century. In Sholgara, a gridlock developed with Junbish forces hanging on to the old district center of Boyni Qara and Jamiat dominating a third of the district and the new district center (Sholgara Bazaar).

With tension in the rural areas, delegations of elders mediated between the two sets of leaders entreating them not to resort to violence, a process which UNAMA encouraged and reinforced behind the scenes. The UNAMA Political Affairs Officers in charge of the north shuttled between Ata and Dostum over the period April 28 to May 1, expressing concern and requesting the leaders to meet face to face and to take steps to deescalate the situation lest it, deliberately or accidentally, start to spin out of control. A high-level meeting was finally organized for May1 with the additional participation of Ishaq Rahguzar, the governor of Balkh Province.[64] Both leaders, Ata and Dostum, accepted that both the presence of tanks and their high number were detrimental to the security of the area and the holding of the elections to the Loya Jirga. An agreement was reached to reestablish the Mazar Security Commission originally created on February 3, but with a broader mandate encompassing all five provinces of the north.[65] In the case of Mazar-i Sharif the Security Commission was to review the levels and deployment of military forces within the city, redeploy those troops not based permanently in Mazar, and limit and control numbers; redeploy forces from and remove unofficial military bases; remove unofficial posts; and establish the 600-person police force in Mazar-i Sharif City and ensure its operation. The agreement failed to balance distribution of key offices in the security sector with both the chief of police and the governor of Balkh staying Jamiat.[66] Membership included the governor and was set as the military deputy and political advisor of both Dostum and Ustad Ata plus the leaderships of the Hazara parties.[67] The fundamental change, proposed by Dostum with which Ata agreed, was that the commission should be chaired by the UN on the grounds of its neutrality.

The key outcome of the May 1 meeting—a redeployment of armor away from Mazar—was subsequently followed up on May 5 in a meeting presided by Deputy Special Representative of the Secretary-General (DSRSG) Jean Arnault. The new set up of the Security Commission now included both the major military and political deputies of all factions: General Majid Rozi, Sayyid Nurullah (Junbish), General Sabur, Zalmay Yunusi (Jamiat), Sardar Sa'idi, General Murtaza (Wahdat-Khalili/Muhaqqiq), Shaykh Baqir Sultani (Wahdat-Akbari), Sayyid Hassan Safa'i (Wahdat-Kazimi), Commander Najib (Harakat-Mohseni), Haji Zaher Wahdat (Harakat-Anwari), and both heads of police (provincial and urban). General Ra'uf, the non-factional deputy of the National Security Department acted as secretary to the Commission. UNAMA was represented by Mervyn Patterson, the political affairs officer in charge, as a full member with the explicit mandate to guide discussions and preside over meetings, and to report directly to the DSRSG. The political affairs officer started to chair the meetings representing UNAMA, and also managed to include in the meetings representatives of the British and US forces in the city. While the US forces maintained a positive distance at the beginning, the UK team enthusiastically backed the creation of this local peace-building mechanism. Both Coalition teams were strengthened over time only through the deployment of political advisors.[68] The location of the meetings changed as well. At the beginning, meetings were held in governmental offices, which in all cases were attributed to one faction. In order to present a neutral space, UNAMA offered its meeting room.

The Interim Administration had this time also invested itself, in marked contrast to its representatives' refusal in February to even sign as a witness. This time Kabul was presented through Deputy Minister of Defense Atiqullah Bariyalay, who also signed the agreement on May 1.[69] After the Emergency Loya Jirga, where Karzai had been requested by delegates that his government start providing security, the office of the national security advisor was created which would oversee the work of a council of all security agencies and ministries.

Lacking proper resources, the newly appointed national security advisor, Dr. Zalmay Rasul, could not draw on professional staff at that time and had to confer important tasks to various politicians thronging Karzai's court in Kabul. A mission headed by presidential advisor Sulayman Yari was dispatched to Mazar-i Sharif and the four other northern provinces in July 2002 and discussed with elders, intellectuals and others how the Security Commission could be improved through the inclusion of civil society. The dispatch of the mission showed that while Kabul did approve of the Security Commission, it had no capacity to help. Mr. Yari stated to his interlocutors in Mazar-i Sharif that problems in Kabul were even worse than in Mazar-i Sharif and therefore people should not expect any assistance from the central government. Another mission member, Advisory Minister Mulla Muhay ad-Din Baluch, promptly fell asleep in the meeting with elders in Sholgara, yet another member—Qari Alam Rasekh (Jamiat)—drew virulent criticism for having surrendered north Afghanistan to the Taliban when he was governor of Faryab in 1997. Sending representatives which were themselves factional to "support mediation" of the Security Commission did not help.

Junbish—clearly the dominant military force of the region—chose to step back and seek a dialogue with Jamiat for political, military and economic reasons. Junbish's leader had an ingrained desire to be included in the political process, where he had been at a disadvantage from the beginning.[70] The threat of exclusion from the Loya Jirga elections could be used by UNAMA effectively to obtain cooperation from Dostum. During the Emergency Loya Jirga, elections were cancelled in several districts upon recommendation by UNAMA in the wake of the fighting of April 30.[71] This penalty hit all factions and diminished by sixteen the total of 166 elected delegates in the five northern provinces, but made sure that the elections could go ahead.[72] Ustad Ata also explored independent strategies from Kabul with the aim to satisfy personal needs. The Shia parties, given their military irrelevance—together they controlled two T-62 tanks and a handful of APCs—espoused a disarmament and stabilization policy. This allowed them to cut their military expenses and focus on the political process at the same time. On the economic side of the 2002 consensus was an agreement among the leadership of north Afghanistan to share the revenue of Balkh province—between $700,000 and $1.8 million monthly from customs and the fertilizer factory—55% for Junbish, 33% for Jamiat, 18% for Wahdat, with Junbish covering also Wahdat-Kazemi and Harakat.[73]

On the political level this consensus led to the formulation of a joint political program for the constitution by Jamiat, Junbish and the Shia parties. Key intellectuals such as Zalmay Yunusi (Jamiat) and Fayzullah Zaki (Junbish) lobbied for a federal system, bicameral parliament, statute law above sharia to dissolve the Shia-Sunni split, and a prime minister at the head of the executive. These proposals were entertained in public appearances throughout the second half of 2002 and the first months of 2003 by all senior members of the regional leadership (Dostum, Ata and Muhaqqiq).[74] The consensus in favor of a federal parliamentary system played an important role in pacifying the north, but was at odds with the vision of re-establishment of the traditional features of Afghanistan's statehood which were vigorously backed by many international players and Chairman Karzai.

This consensus of May 2002 stopped being articulated in the New Year celebration on March 21, 2003, when the minister of defense, in his speech in Mazar, vigorously backed a central state model. Neither Ata nor Governor Rahguzar touched the issue and left Dostum lobbying in his speech for a federal model.[75] Ata appeared on his local radio channel on the evening of that day and announced that "a federal system would be good in the long term, but for the short term a centralized state would be the best solution for Afghanistan's problems." Only a minority within Jamiat led by the intellectual Hafiz Mansur in Kabul continued to lobby for an alliance.[76] This political disengagement signaled a return of the Junbish–Jamiat rivalry, which erupted in April[77] and October 2003 in bloody clashes. Still, the Security Commission as a regional conflict management institution continued to meet regularly until December 2004.

Achievements of the Security Commission: Mazar-i Sharif and Sholgara

The Security Commission met at least once per week, but in most cases was active on a daily basis, with delegations deployed to outlying areas and special meetings to receive complaints.[78] Its first task was the urban police of Mazar-i Sharif. In the absence of any trained police personnel, the Security Commission returned to the previous decision to form a 600-strong multi-factional unit. This posed clear limitations to the efficiency of the force as at best they were disciplined soldiers, and all their weapons came from the factions.[79] Elders and notables proposed as an alternative to create a "neighborhood police force" vetted through neighborhood headmen (*kalantar* or *wakil-i guzar*), elders and clerics. This solution was advocated by the representatives of the Shia parties of the Security Commission, who were conscious of their support-base within the urban population and by Junbish, which was speculating that this would weaken the current strong Jamiat control. The Jamiat-dominated Ministry of Interior refused the plan, invoking the principle of centralism.[80] The Ministry of Interior also ignored repeated attempts by the Security Commission to have at least the payment of salaries out of LOTFA monitored by UNAMA.[81] Meanwhile, the new force of 600 men assembled on May 8 in the Mazar sports stadium and started its duties. Resources were a major problem and had to be produced by every participant of the Security Commission.[82]

Still, Jamiat's domination of the police leadership impeded smooth functioning, as the non-Jamiat patrolmen did not obey the Jamiat officers. Jamiat officers continued to extort local businesses and their new subordinates could not do more than report these cases to the Security Commission. As soon as the commission got involved, the situation was redressed immediately on the spot (e.g., payments were made, stolen goods given back), but it proved impossible to permanently fire the miscreants from the police force. It can be seen as a success that through this process many problems were recorded and raised for the first time, for example a totally criminalized law enforcement structure. In May–September 2002, a combined survey of all intelligence agencies (Junbish, Jamiat and non-factional officers) and UNAMA revealed 103 armed posts within the city. This was a significant increase over the approximately 60 locations occupied by the factions in November 2001.[83]

The task of "cleaning" the city was undertaken in earnest throughout August 2002, after orders by the leaders to their subordinate commanders had not proven effective. The whole Security Commission, followed by 60–100 police officers of the new force, started to patrol the locations of the posts, verifying their complete evacuation. Eventually, the Security Commission found weapons caches, which were promptly confiscated. Acting on complaints brought forward by the population, the political affairs officer led the group to occupied houses not previously recorded by the survey. Any armed men found were immediately arrested and their weapons confiscated by the newly raised police force. Some central government agencies such as the National Directorate for Security resisted.[84] The Security Commission decided to populate the vacated premises immediately with new occupants wherever possible. For example, the previous Balkh television station had served as a position for Hizb-i Wahdat (Akbari) commander Shaykh Baqir Sultani. In his presence, the post was not only vacated but the Security Commission immediately moved a nearby UNICEF-sponsored tent school into the premises. In order to reoccupy the place in the future, Wahdat would have been required to displace a school, which would obviously have hurt their standing among the urban population. Some instances produced standoffs which called for diplomatic involvement of the Coalition forces.[85]

By mid-September, 90% of the previously listed posts and "garrisons" were vacated from their armed occupiers, the remainder being "official" locations dedicated to an official Ministry of Defense unit or the NDS. In about 60% of the cases though, no new use could be found for the building in question due to the resistance from the governor, Ishaq Rahguzar (Jamiat), who cited formal legal arguments against the Security Commission taking such actions. This in turn allowed the reoccupation of the bases through factional forces at a later stage in May–June 2003. The partisan exploitation of the NDS was also weakening the commitment of other factions to the agreement of May 1, 2002. The unclear property issues of many buildings in the city, rapidly increasing prices, and constant disputes among citizens, invited the return of armed men. Where arbitration was attempted, the Security Commission found itself quickly under criticism by the governor and the courts (all Jamiat) who were now empowered and immediately sided with their faction.[86]

It became clear that demilitarization would have required a proper police force. The senior leadership of the police was clearly responsible for abetting the highly irregular conduct of the force. By mid-summer, even the Jamiat representatives in the Security Commission acknowledged that Ustad Ata's brother Hajji Fida had become unbearable as chief of the city police (*amir-i amniyat*). He was replaced by Ustad Zarif (also Jamiat) in September 2002 after months of lobbying by UNAMA.[87]

In the rural areas, conflicts continued due to local rivalries over resources. An increasing availability of resources at the lowest level of capability to fight small wars proved to be the major obstacle.[88] On September 4, Ata and Dostum strongly condemned factional fighting, publicly disowning any military activity. Both declared that they would not accept commanders deserting the other faction. In a follow-up declaration on September 30, Ata and Dostum together with the Shia parties' leaders declared that any commander breaking the peace would be disarmed by both of them acting together:

> In the name of God, the merciful and benevolent. Decision dated Saturday 9.6.81 [30 September 2002] of the Leadership Commission of North Afghanistan for ensuring security in the Northern Parts. Under the leadership of the honorable Major General Abdul Rashid Dostum, general operational commander of the North, special representative of the President of the Transitional Islamic State of Afghanistan and Deputy Minister of Defense, the Leadership of the North unanimously has come to the decision: Wherever from this day onwards armed men—be they official units or not—engage in armed maneuvers and disrupt the security of cities and villages, shall they be disarmed without hesitation or further discussion. Neither the Leadership nor our people will have any more patience to endure such immoral acts any longer. The Leadership of the North, the national and international community cannot tolerate such incidents. With regard to the implementation of this decision orders are given to the areas and commanders of Sholgara, Gusfandi, Kohistanat, Darra-yi Suf, Sar-i Pul and other areas: This decision has to be observed and implemented. Otherwise anyone not obeying will be heavily punished and judged in a court of law. With peace. Signed by Dostum (Junbish), Ata (Jamiat), Sa'idi (Wahdat), Safa'i (Wahdat), Sayyid Azim (Harakat) and Sayyid Hasan (Wahdat).

Spurred on by UNAMA and a positive recognition of the UN Security Council[89] the regional leaders decided to act on October 26. Under the personal leadership of General Dostum, the Security Commission conducted several disarmament missions to lower Darra-yi Suf, Kishindeh, Sholgara, Andkhoy, and Khulm districts from October to December 2002, reaching Faryab province in early 2003.[90] Local commanders delivered their weapons to depots of AMF units, where they were made available to control through Coalition forces and UN representatives. General Dostum and representatives of the other parties went to great pains to persuade their local commanders of surrendering their guns to the depots of the AMF units under their control, employing a set of tools ranging from outright coercion and direct threats to bribery. The main constraint in the process was the relative small size of both the UN and the Coalition, which did not allow sustaining the AMF depot monitoring process, and the fact that the AMF units could potentially release the weapons at will.[91] One important lesson learned from the October 2002 exercise was that all AMF units had to be decommissioned in their totality and not gradually as the Ministry of Defense proposed, a lesson which became key to the countrywide disarmament, demobilization and reintegration (DDR) program during 2004.[92] A second lesson was the need to focus disarmament on strategic areas.

Sholgara: Regional Center of Gravity

The district of Sholgara or Boyni Qara sat in the center of the strategic struggle for control over the north, as it controlled the water supply for lower Balkh Province and offered access to three out of five provinces of north Afghanistan. The valley witnessed fierce competition for land and water throughout the last century.[93] Even the Taliban government had been unable to settle these conflicts.[94] Desertification had drastically diminished total water resources available over the last 30 years.[95] In the overpopulated district, internal conflict already broke out in February 2002.[96] The main perpetrators were six major and a dozen minor commanders.[97] The problem was accentuated by the local district commissioner Damullah Umar (Jamiat commander), locked in a heritage dispute with his nephew, the local main Junbish commander Hajji Habib (Division 95). The only positive factor was the neutral district police commissioner, Akbari, belonging to the Shia Hazaras. The second stage of elections to the Loya Jirga in May 2002 was cancelled by UNAMA following the fighting of April 30 and the refusal of local commanders to observe a truce.

The first disarmament activity occurred in July 2002 after three days of deployment by members of the Security Commission and UNAMA.[98] Time, pressure and an increasing and publicly assertive stance by the Security Commission (essentially Majid Rozi from Junbish and UNAMA) eventually produced significant results, with the local Junbish division commander, Hajji Habib, emptying one ammunition dump and handing-over most of his medium and heavy weapons in August 2002.[99] The tempo of Jamiat weapon surrenders, principally of light weapons, also increased. In total, two truckloads of assorted munitions and nearly 300 weapons of varying calibers were recovered in August 2002. Six Jamiat and Junbish commanders were instructed by the Security Commission to relocate to Mazar-i Sharif. This resulted in a period of tranquillity in Sholgara through August and September 2002. The Security Commission team in the area noted then the first night when small-arms fire was not heard in the area and when inter-commander radio traffic was zero. Factions continued activities to expand their influence, but their ability to do so was now circumscribed.[100]

Responsibility for security had been conferred upon the local police—they, although emboldened by the events, still had limited power vis-à-vis local commanders and their sphere of control was largely restricted to the market of Boyni Qara, which the Security Commission had declared a weapons-free zone. The inability of external agencies to support them at this juncture critically inhibited their further development while the Ministry of Interior showed no interest at all.[101] The Security Commission, in consultation with local district commissioner Damullah Umar, loyal to Jamiat, allocated revenue from the market to be given directly to the police to cover salaries and food costs. Junbish agreed to provide fuel from the taxation of the Turkmenistan border crossing at Aqina.

For the rest of 2002, only localized incidents occurred in the district and were swiftly dealt with by the Security Commission and the police.[102] Factional conflict refocused on the area of Kishindeh, the Uzbek-dominated district to the south.[103] Interest in the area was now being displayed by Commander Ahmad Khan (Division 19 in Samangan) who was blocked from accessing Mazar via the main road since Jamiat gained exclusive control over the gorge at Tashqurghan. An alliance had developed between him and Hajji Habib (Division 95 in Sholgara and Dehdadi). Also, the leadership of Army Corps VII attempted to intervene in the area, arming and recruiting some local commanders.[104] Although Jamiat was informed by UNAMA that its maneuvers had been noticed, it nevertheless opted to attack Uzbek Kishindeh from Tajik Aq Kupruq.[105] Most local Uzbek Jamiat commanders stayed neutral, resenting the fact that Jamiat had deployed Tajiks. This led to a total defeat of the Jamiat offensive with many Jamiat combatants taken prisoner and released subsequently through the Security Commission. After the fighting and through mediation of the network of the previous Sufi leader and commander Abd al-Rahman Haqqani, the local commanders of both sides engaged in a series of non-aggression pacts in front of the Security Commission, that included the promise of later disarmament. This pact allowed for elections to the Emergency Loya Jirga to proceed in Aq Kuproq, lower and upper Kishindeh in late May 2002.

Both Sholgara and Kishindeh became the scene of the weapons collection exercise led by Dostum, Ata and Sa'idi through the Security Commission in November 2002, which produced a total of 3,500 weapons from Sholgara and Kishindeh. This weapons collection program particularly targeted heavy weapons like mortars, grenade launchers, recoilless rifles and anti-aircraft guns. As a result, the situation calmed further over the winter months. During UNAMA's weekly monitoring visits no armed men were seen in the bazaar.[106] The peace of Sholgara lasted for about seven months until March 2003, when the underpinning consensus between Junbish and Jamiat faltered and led to a resurge of violence in Sholgara but not in Kishindeh.

With the advent of the British Provisional Reconstruction Team (PRT) from May 2003 onwards, a decision was made to refocus energies on Sholgara, and at the same time to strengthen the police force of Sholgara proper and renew disarmament efforts. This action relied in particular on the close monitoring of the district through an international police advisor, regular visits by UNAMA and the PRT which reacted robustly to trespassers, and a successful political reconciliation. In June 2003, a renewed disarmament drive was undertaken in Sholgara, which this time yielded mostly light weapons.[107] Violence persisted and again several commanders were banned from the valley on August 24.[108] In a systematic tour the Security Commission approached all villages where elders and landowners nominated guarantors and pledged in writing that no weapons were left in the village and that no one would dispute the sole control of the Sholgara police force over the village's security.[109] At the same time, a significant amount of resources went into strengthening the police in Sholgara, bypassing the Balkh police headquarters. This was possible through the secondment of senior police general Fazli by the Ministry of Interior to the PRT. Through the UK's Department for International Development, vehicles were provided to the force, UNAMA helped in repairing the detention facility, and the PRT's police advisor visited the police on a regular basis and became a reliable partner of district police commissioner Akbari who now started to arrest criminals. This fulfilled an important precondition to holding elections for the convening Constitutional Loya Jirga in Sholgara. The elections were held on September 6, 2003 and produced an equal repartition of delegates for all three factions present in Sholgara, further stabilizing the district.

Constraints of the Security Commission

The Security Commission had no sanctions available except the "voluntary" collection of a commander's weapons or a temporary removal of the commander from his native district to the court of one of the leaders of north Afghanistan. Without an independent monitoring capacity, rearmament could only be ascertained through observing the arms market. Except for the joint Junbish-Jamiat patrols deployed on rare occasions, UNAMA could field at most three patrols, the Coalition four.[110] Special Forces patrols accompanied Security Commission missions to various hotspots, and through their presence encouraged mediation to take place and secured the missions against attack. In early 2003, US forces presented a new concept through the insertion of a Civil Affairs Team which was to be known later as Provincial Reconstruction Team. When factional fighting broke out in Faryab in April 2003 and UNAMA requested an escort, the US PRT however answered that their request to go had been denied by the command for security reasons. UNAMA had to deploy only civilians together with the Security Commission.[111]

With the arrival of the UK PRT in May 2003, a strengthening in UNAMA's staffing—including a military advisor and an additional political affairs officer posted to Mazar-i Sharif—the situation improved. Still, the PRT had very limited effect.[112] In August 2003, the Ministry of Interior deployed a liaison officer to the PRT who was tasked to ensure the flow of resources from the center (salaries, rations, uniforms) to the police headquarters in Balkh Province, but was overwhelmed and finally became a party to their diversion. The diversion of resources through corruption in the Afghan government was a major constraint.[113] The Security Commission through the added resources from the PRT and a strengthened UNAMA field office managed to again restore calm and order in these places, and even managed through April and May 2003 to demilitarize the Faryab capital of Maymana, where a functioning police force existed. Despite the confrontation between the leadership, factional representatives in the commission worked closely together and even started searching for new job opportunities beyond their factions.[114]

A Last Clash of the Armies of the North

Throughout the late summer of 2003, both factions were again preparing for a major clash in the run-up to the Constitutional Loya Jirga. Both major factions saw the elections to the Constitutional Loya Jirga as an important step to formalize and legitimize their power. In order to dominate the elections each faction obviously required gaining control over territory and inhabitants. Also, control over mass media became increasingly an issue. Jamiat had managed to successfully monopolize the state-run radio and television of Balkh province, Junbish dominated Jawzjan. In this highly charged political atmosphere the international members of the Security Commission decided to push weapons collection operations to far away regions such as Balkhab—four days by car from Mazar-i Sharif—which was a capital lack of judgment. The absence of the major part of the PRT and UNAMA meant that the traditional watch over Mazar-i Sharif and Sholgara had to be neglected. Worse, no international member of the Security Commission was alerted by the Junbish and Jamiat representatives abandoning the mission to Balkhab and returning to their bases.

In a couple of days in late September and early October 2003, the biggest military clash between Junbish and Jamiat occurred in Balkh and Faryab simultaneously. Over the summer of 2003 Jamiat had prepared the defection of several Junbish commanders in the Chimtal area close to the exit of the Sholgara gorge, where Junbish planned to build a transmitter for the newly established Junbish television. From this area the transmitter would have covered the whole city of Mazar-i Sharif. When the defection of Habib, the local commander and an ethnic Arab, was thwarted, he and a bodyguard disappeared in a Jamiat-dominated area of Mazar-i Sharif City. Jamiat denied all responsibility, but Junbish started to threaten with a military operation if the two men would not be released. Reports emerged that the two men were killed in Mazar-i Sharif while in police custody. Following a military build-up by Junbish in the districts to the west of Mazar-i Sharif, a huge military force threatened Jamiat by early October 2003. More than 1,500 men had come from Sar-i Pul under Kamal Khan (also an ethnic Arab), commander of Division 82, and positioned themselves near Chimtal district. A central task force of 1,500 men mainly of Jawzjani Uzbeks operated in Aqcha under Faqir (also an ethnic Arab), the deputy commander of Division 53, and a further 1,000 troops were raised by the Charbolak Pashtuns around the core of Division 70. On October 7, Junbish took to the offensive and managed to capture significant territory up to the bridge of Imam Bukri at the exit of the Sholgara gorge, and close to the center of Balkh district. Jamiat counterattacks faltered in the face of massive artillery barrages. Jamiat also was largely unsuccessful in cracking isolated Junbish positions to the east of the main confrontation line, such as the fertilizer factory living quarters, or Junbish positions in the Balkh district capital. In a parallel operation, Junbish's Division 200 overran within 36 hours all bases and installations of Jamiat's Division 024 jihadi in Faryab including Almar district. Most of the Jamiati division surrendered and joined Junbish. Similar clashes took place between Junbish and Jamiat in Sar-i Pul and led to a strategic victory for Junbish, except in one district: Sholgara. The Sholgara police force, backed by the support of the PRT's police advisor, maintained calm in the valley. The force prevented a further clash to the south of the bridge of Imam Bukri by continuously manning the police checkpoint at the Sholgara gorge and thereby blocking the advance of a strong Junbish task-force of more than 500 men, including tanks and artillery from Sar-i Pul. A sustained, non-factional and well-mentored unit of Afghan district police had demonstrated that they could stop a factional fight from spreading in their area.[115]

The situation in Mazar-i Sharif, however, was critical. In late September 2003, a total of 131 military factional positions existed in the city with a total of over 1,300 armed men observed in these positions on a regular basis. This again showed an increase from the 103 positions surveyed in September 2002. With Balkh district falling to Junbish, Ata started to mobilize for a battle for the city itself, which would have been very difficult given that all parties had their bastions inside. UNAMA led by DSRSG Jean Arnault immediately deployed together with Minister of Interior Ali Ahmad Jalali to Mazar-i Sharif. Both met with the factional leaders in the PRT and demanded an immediate ceasefire. Two mobile observation teams of the UK PRT were immediately dispatched from Balkhab and arrived after 48 hours of continuous driving. The remaining PRT's mobile observation team in Mazar-i Sharif teamed up with a UNAMA political affairs officer (the author) airlifted from Kabul and visited all frontline positions. Assisted by frequent Coalition overflights and loitering gunships, this small group persuaded individual units to observe a cessation of hostilities. Within two days the bulk of the PRT had redeployed from Sar-i Pul and was able to build on the momentum achieved by the first small group.

The clash served as a late wake-up call on the eve of the Constitutional Loya Jirga to Ata and Dostum that military confrontation could result in mutual destruction. In an agreement framed later with the assistance of the Coalition, Junbish and Jamiat agreed to the complete cantonment of all heavy weapons of both army corps. This cantonment idea later became one of the central elements in the DDR program.[116]

The Security Commission's work from mid-2003 onwards was based on the international community holding the factions accountable to their earlier commitments, including a visit by the UN Security Council ambassadors on November 5, 2003. In a meeting with the Security Commission which included all heads of faction such as Ata and Dostum, Ambassador Pleuger of Germany, then presiding over the council, stressed that the current ceasefire had to hold. Military conflict was not only a detriment to the authority of the central government,

Pleuger said, but was also hampering the implementation of the Bonn Agreement and therefore also implicitly threatening the recognition of Ata and Dostum as political players. The government deployed a senior delegation to Mazar-i Sharif headed by Vice-President Amin Arsala and attempted to address the issue of factional control over the Balkh police force through appointing a new provincial chief of police, but refrained from changing Jamiat's hold over the governor position.[117] In December 2003, the clash contributed to Dostum's election to the Constitutional Loya Jirga being cancelled by the Executive Committee Constitutional Commission.[118] The Security Commission became the main vehicle for the DDR program throughout 2004 and in December 2004 dissolved itself as all AMF units had by then undergone demobilization under the DDR program.

Conflict Management and Institutional Development

The Security Commission resulted from the conclusion that conflict management had to be carried out by a neutral third party. Control over access to resources proved to be a major reason for violent conflict, which then assumed a factional character. The Security Commission's success was rooted primarily in diplomatic conflict resolution and mediation, but as seen in the Sholgara example, the commission also managed to produce success through a decentralized approach to police reform together with a political stabilization. However, issues related to the building of institutions and the nationwide reform of the security sector were outside of the mandate of the Security Commission.

The focus of the international community's security-sector reform was throughout 2002 and 2003 primarily on the military rather than the police and valued quantity over quality.[119] The centralized reform process was held up by corruption.[120] The required focus on the existing personnel in charge of the police only came through the pay and rank reform initiated by Minister Jalali in August 2005. Only new integer and professional police leaders would have brought forward support from the communities which were extremely reluctant to send recruits to serve under the paramilitary and factional police officers, who were frequently criminals themselves. However, the centralized process took, although hampered by countless interventions, until January 2007 to install for the first time competent and encouraging provincial police leaders.

Centralism made a comeback after the disappointing results of "warlordism" in the sphere of governance.[121] Warlords were seen as the direct result of the loss of centralism, and a lot of the prevailing insecurity and small warfare in the countryside was blamed on them.[122] Disappointing experiences with the regionalized forces of the United Front led to the creation of a centralized Afghan security force, the Afghan National Army.[123] Two standard responses to conflict by the international community—constitution-making and elections—led to legitimacy and control being concentrated at the top in the hands of a directly elected president, who was both head of state and government, and further strengthened by fiscal centralism. Since then, central government witnessed the revival of a "Pashtun elite."[124] While the constitution postulates the equality of all citizens and recognizes several national and official languages, it also enshrines the national anthem in Pashto.[125] Similarly, from the Emergency Loya Jirga onwards, prominent Islamists had been accommodated through the gradual Islamization of Afghanistan's state and constitution.[126]

However, the reconstructed centralism in 2007 still lacks self-control and is eaten up by corruption, endangering its legitimacy in the eyes of the population. The "reconstruction" of the Afghan state under the old paradigms seems to have failed. Resulting frustrations are frequently voiced by advocates of "the mujahideen" across all regions of the country.[127] In London on January 30, 2006, the Government of Afghanistan reaffirmed its commitment to centralism and promised to deliver what had not been delivered with the same system in the previous years.[128] Since then, the reform of the corrupt police and Ministry of Interior has dragged on into 2007 and is unlikely to be completed until 2008. Tax revenue generation has failed to reach its planned objectives. Other reform programs have mostly lost impetus and legitimacy through the over-centralization and the ensuing corruption. As central institutions continue to fail, the creation of ad hoc "security commissions," "auxiliary police," "unofficial highway patrol," and private security companies is largely uncoordinated despite the slow reemergence of regional structures in the army and police out of pure necessity. While the Security Commission was seen by many as directed against their efforts to rebuild a central state, regional solutions must complement any central structures in order to safeguard their continued relevance.

Notes

1. The unease with conventional methods of pure diplomacy in reaching a lasting peace agreement was, for example, voiced in Matthew Fielden and Johnathan Goodhand, "Beyond the Taliban: The Afghan Conflict and United Nations Peacemaking," *Conflict, Security and Development*, vol. 1, no. 3 (December 2001): 5–32. These new concepts were developed from good practice elsewhere and frequently had no precedent in Afghanistan (e.g., elections, the demobilization exercise after World War II in Japan and Germany). The need to adapt these concepts to the realities in Afghanistan can be briefly demonstrated with the example of the Disarmament, Demobilization and Reintegration (DDR) program, which was based on the Bonn Agreement and subsequent security-sector reform donor conference in Geneva. The long time span of the conflict and extremely weak, mostly person-centered military structures in place meant that the "classic" DDR package of assembly, disarmament, demobilization and re-integration into civilian life would not be applicable. Assembly of troops for DDR was frequently the only occasion for these troops to assemble since their official inception. Disarming troops which had multiple weapons per person hidden in caches controlled by their village commanders was psychologically important and clearly removed the war-fighting ability on a national scale but challenged the traditional understanding of "disarmament" through the application of a weapons-collection policy. Combatants had come to regard

their lives as warriors as the only job prospects available to them, even a generation before the youngest warrior generation could not return to a job. Here, clearly, the concept of reintegration would not suffice. It was required to build an economy into which they could integrate.

2. The issue whether the Bonn Agreement qualified as a peace agreement is hotly debated. A narrow interpretation defined the conflict as between the Islamic State of Afghanistan, supported by the international community, versus the Taliban. It certainly was not a peace agreement to end this conflict dating back to late 1994. By December 2001 however, the Taliban had very much ceased to exist with no areas under their control, no discernible chain of command, and its leadership on the run (therefore differing from Nazi Germany at the end of World War II where a rump government continued to exist). A less narrow definition of the conflict shared by most observers traces the Afghanistan conflict back to the breakdown of Afghan elite consensus in the 1970s and has the civil war start in between 1975, 1978 and 1979. Most Afghans seem to put the agreement in such a larger perspective and perceive it indeed to be a peace agreement between the Afghan factions which had fought for nearly thirty years amongst themselves since the coup d'état of Prince Daoud in 1973. Given that the Taliban leaders and many rank-and-file members of the movement had earlier belonged to Afghan factions such as Harakat (Muhammadi) or Hezb-i-Islami, such a view seemed warranted by the past of the individuals involved.

3. These principles were frequently articulated by SRSG Lakhdar Brahimi. See for example his extensive interview in *Great Negotiator 2002: Lakhdar Brahimi* (DVD) (Cambridge: Harvard Law School Program on Negotiation, 2004). The central question remained what "national ownership" meant in practice as one was dealing at the beginning of the Bonn process with either military leaders or self-appointed emigré figures. The mission's most problematic task was to determine *which* "national owners" were to be strengthened.

4. The conflict has been explained as a proxy war of the superpowers, regional power struggle for domination of a strategic crossroad, internal ethnic and social conflicts brought to the fore by a breakdown of political processes and the state, or an unresolved center-periphery conflict due to a deeply flawed process of nation- and state-formation. Barnett Rubin, *The Search for Peace in Afghanistan: From Buffer State to Failed State* (New Haven: Yale University Press, 1995), emphasizes the international political dimension. M. Nazif Shahrani, "State Building and Social Fragmentation in Afghanistan: A Historical Perspective," in Ali Banuazizi and Myron Weiner, eds., *The State, Religion and Ethnic Politics: Afghanistan, Iran and Pakistan* (Syracuse: Syracuse University Press, 1986), 23–74, has stressed internal and anthropological causes. Gilles Dorronsoro, *La révolution Afghane* (Paris: Karthala, 2000), points to the social dimension of the conflict. Larry Goodson, *Afghanistan's Endless War* (Seattle: University of Washington Press, 2001), and William Maley, *The Afghanistan Wars* (London: Palgrave Macmillan, 2002), attempt to combine several approaches in tracing and explaining the military developments. Inside Afghanistan, the discussion frequently devolves to attributing the root causes of the war to external factors or reductionism and a blame-game between national and international researchers. Interestingly, some Afghans have recently argued that while the external factor has been important, the main essence of the Afghan conflict has been a struggle for control over resources between various Afghan ethnic, social and political groups, such as Abdul Hafîz Mansûr, *Nuhzat-i Islamî-yi Afghânistân: barrasî-yi intiqadî-yi guzashta, hâl-u âyanda* [Islamic Revival in Afghanistan: A Critical Appraisal of the Past, Present and Future], (s.l. 2001), 124ff. The recent studies sponsored by the London School of Economics (LSE) tracing local dynamics in the west and in the south are Antonio Giustozzi, *The Missing Ingredient: Nonideological Insurgency and State Collapse in Western Afghanistan 1979–1992* (London: Crisis

State Research Centre Working Paper no. 11, LSE, 2007); Antonio Giustozzi and Noor Ullah, *"Tribes" and Warlords in Southern Afghanistan, 1980–2005* (London: Crisis State Research Centre Working Paper no. 7, LSE, 2006); Niamatullah Ibrahimi, *The Failure of a Clerical Proto-State: Hazarajat, 1979–1984* (London: Crisis State Research Centre Working Paper no. 6, LSE, 2006); Antonio Giustozzi, *Genesis of a "Prince": The Rise of Ismail Khan in Western Afghanistan, 1979–1992* (London: Crisis State Research Centre Working Paper no. 4, LSE, 2006); Antonio Giustozzi, "War and Peace Economies of Afghanistan's Strongmen," *International Peacekeeping,* vol. 14 (2007): 75–89.

5. While in 1860 Herat became part of Amir Abd al-Rahman's domain, Balkh in the same year received a visit from Amir Nasrullah of Bukhara who replaced its governor Eshan Uraq. The inclusion of "Afghan" Turkistan was a result of the consensus between Russia and Great Britain around 1880 to designate the Amu Darya as a border between their spheres of influence, thereby directing Pashtun expansionism away from India. See Robert D. McChesney, *Waqf in Central Asia: Four Hundred Years in the History of a Muslim Shrine, 1480–1889* (Princeton: Princeton University Press, 1991); and Jonathan L. Lee, *The "Ancient Supremacy": Bukhara, Afghanistan and the Battle for Balkh, 1731–1901* (Leiden: E. J. Brill, 1996).

6. One of these examples was the reign of the "reformer king" Amanullah (1919–1929), which ended in the overthrow of the modernizing regime through an indigenous revolt abetted by a lack of will by the principal sponsor, Great Britain, to sustain the Afghan state. An immediate return to tribal and ethnic civil war was the result. Jan-Heeren Grevemeyer, *Afghanistan: Sozialer Wandel und Staat im 20. Jh.* [Afghanistan: Social Change and State in the 20th Century] (Berlin: Express Edition, 1987). This book delivers a much more detailed analysis of the period than the English standard of Leon Poullada, *Reform and Rebellion in Afghanistan, 1919–1929: King Amanullah's Failure to Modernize a Tribal Society* (Ithaca: Cornell University Press, 1973). Original Afghan accounts remain rare. A recent edition contains an account written by the son of the last ruler of Maymana. See *Râh dar sanglâkh: khâtirât-i safar-i Maymana, 1299–1300* [Road through the Rocks: Memoirs of Travel to Maymana, 1920–21]; and Fayz Muhammad's account of the 1929 uprising, Fayz Muhammad Katib (translated by R. D. McChesney), *Kabul Under Siege* (Princeton: Markus Wiener Publishers, 1999).

7. In Dari, *Jabha-yi Muttahid-i Islâmî-yi Millî barâ-yi Nijât-i Afghânistân*—United Islamic Front for the Salvation of Afghanistan—further referred to as the United Front, created as an alliance of convenience against the Taliban. The United Front resulted from the earlier alliance dating back to October 1996, and was announced as such on 15 June 1997. The United Front was also called Northern Alliance by the Pakistani and western press.

8. The notion of an "invasion" misses out the fact that the war was already internationalized. Pakistani elements had assisted in the creation and expansion of the Taliban. Al Qaeda, Chechens and Uzbek Islamic militants had become an important force on the Afghan battlefield already in the late 1990s (as evident for example in the fighting around Taluqan from 1998–2001). United Front troops had held out for a number of years in pockets surrounded by Taliban through Russian and Iranian aid. Strengthened significantly through Coalition air power they managed to topple the Taliban in November–December 2001. The first major arrival of US ground troops dates early 2002. This success was mitigated through the escape of Osama Bin Laden, senior Al Qaeda and Taliban, and the incapacity of the United Front to settle internal disputes. But it resulted in the successful denial of control over Afghanistan by Al Qaeda. It was further mitigated through the loss of Ahmed Shah Massoud, the charismatic military leader of the United Front through a suicide attack by two Al Qaeda operatives on 9 September 2001.

9. Rather to the contrary, each component of the United Front assumed the informal and decentralized set up of the resistance period would continue. As they occupied

territory liberated from Taliban control, local arrangements for governance were the rule. When Kabul fell in November to the Shura-yi Nazar troops, Fahim immediately appointed trusted commanders of his own community (Panjsheris) to all vacant positions of government. More than 1,200 positions were filled in the last week of November and the first week of December 2001.

10. In the analysis of one of its leaders, Yunus Qanuni, "While we went as the members of the United Front delegation to Bonn, only the name of the United Front existed. The work of the United Front was not united, and everyone in the delegation represented one member." Quoted by Muhammad Akram Andeshmand, *Amrika dar Afghanistan* [The US in Afghanistan] (Kabul, 2005), 250ff.

11. While contacts to the Rome process existed before, the decision of a militarily successful coalition to agree to a political process run by civilian emigré figures which had left Afghanistan in the 1970s was not easy for many in the United Front. The UN Secretary General's Personal Representative, Francesc Vendrell, was crucial in securing this agreement and had to draw on the trust built up with the United Front leaders throughout the previous two years when he headed the UN political mission, United Nations Special Mission to Afghanistan (UNSMA). The Bonn Agreement is sometimes described not as a comprehensive peace agreement because it did not include a representative of the Taliban. This valid observation must be qualified considering that most Taliban prior to the emergence of the movement had belonged to one or the other Afghan political-military parties which were represented in the Bonn talks through either the United Front, the Peshawar or Cyprus Loya Jirga processes. The main objective was to start a process with those Afghans willing to re-establish a government in Afghanistan. The title of the Bonn Agreement clarifies this as the primary objective, "Agreement for Interim Arrangements Pending the Reestablishment of Permanent Government Institutions in Afghanistan."

12. Annex II of the Bonn Agreement details the tasks requested from the United Nations by the participants of the Petersberg (Bonn) meeting. "(2) . . . shall monitor and assist in the implementation of all aspects of this agreement. (3) The United Nations shall advise the Interim Authority in establishing a politically neutral environment conducive to the holding of the Emergency Loya Jirga in free and fair conditions. The United Nations shall pay special attention to the conduct of those bodies and administrative departments which could directly influence the convening and outcome of the Emergency Loya Jirga." The United Nations Security Council endorsed the Bonn Agreement and the UN's role through resolution 1383 on 6 December 2001.

13. The foundation of the Afghan buffer state in the nineteenth century had relied heavily on the concept of the Islamic "emirate" legitimizing the ruler appointed by the colonial powers as opposed to the neighboring "infidel" regimes ruled directly: Russian colonies in Central Asia, British India and Shia Iran. From the beginning, the Afghan state communicated to its citizens that the primary role of the state would be to ensure religious orthodoxy of the Sunni sect and an Islamic lifestyle. Muhammad Hasan Kakar, *Government and Society in Afghanistan: The Reign of Amir 'Abd al-Rahman Khan* (Austin: University of Texas Press, 1979), 231. The Taliban had pushed the principle of Islamization to an extreme, but until 2001 it was generally accepted wisdom that an "Islamic" nature of the Afghan state was required for the success of any state-building exercise. The government of President Rabbani felt it necessary in 2001 to reintroduce a "religious police" under the same name as the Taliban's. Also for Rabbani the aim of the state was to "ensure a Muslim way of life." This "Department for the Promotion of Virtue and the Abolishment of Vice" [*amr bi'l-ma'rûf wa nahî 'in al-munkar*] had however nothing close of the mandate, powers and resources of the Taliban equivalent. An indicative sign was his lack of insistence to baptize the Interim Administration "Islamic" or insert any "Islamic" elements into the early formation of the state. After the Bonn conference,

President Rabbani agreed to the request communicated to him through the UN envoy, Francesc Vendrell, and transferred power from the Islamic State to the Interim Administration without raising any questions regarding the "Islamic" nature of the new set up. His only condition was that he would be given a leading role in the parliament envisaged by the Bonn Agreement, reflecting a personal rather than ideological interest.

14. Zalmay Khalilzad, "How to Nation-Build: Ten Lessons from Afghanistan," *The National Interest,* Summer (2005): 19–27, presents the pre-war order as "legitimate . . . and based on . . . traditions and history" but is realist enough to recognize the need to accommodate changes effected by the war. See especially 20, 22.

15. See Astri Suhrke, Kristian Berg Harpviken, Are Knudsen, Arve Ofstad, and Arne Strand, *Peacebuilding: Lessons for Afghanistan* (Bergen: Chr. Michelsen Institute, 2002).

16. Earlier attempts at state formation on Afghanistan's territory always divided the country in "appanage" regions, each ruled by a princely governor in near autonomy. In contrast the "Iron Amir" ensured that no single region could develop as a functioning sub-fiefdom. Also the central state apparatus was strictly centralized with all directions flowing from the Amir himself and minimal delegation of powers to other court officials. Muhammad Hasan Kakar, *Afghanistan: A Study in International Political Developments, 1880–1896* (Lahore: Panjab Educational Press, 1971). Also see Ashraf Ghani, "Afghanistan—XI. Administration," in *Encyclopedia Iranica,* vol. I (New York: Columbia University Center for Iranian Studies), 558–564.

17. Antonio Giustozzi, *War, Politics and Society in Afghanistan, 1978–1992* (Georgetown: Georgetown University Press, 2000). The militias were regionally recruited, employed and commanded but paid centrally. The center was riddled by corruption and refused to empower its regular agents in the regions to control the militias.

18. Two excellent eyewitness accounts are Asadullah Wulwaljî, *Khurûj-i Jinrâl Dôstum wa suqût-i Daktar Najîbullah* [The Emergence of General Dostum and the Fall of Dr. Najibullah] (Kabul: 2003); Abd al-Raûf Bêgî, *Afghânistân ba'd az pîrûzî-yi inqilâb-i islâmî tâ suqût-i shamâl ba dast-i Tâlibân 1991–1998* [Afghanistan from the Victory of the Islamic Revolution until the Fall of the North to the Taliban, 1991–1998] (Peshawar: 2000).

19. Mulla Dadullah, Akhtar Usmani, Mulla Baradar or Qari Ahmadullah operated under Mulla Omar wherever they were sent, and overruled local institutions at will. International support elements (Chechens, Uzbeks, Arabs and Pakistanis) to the Taliban were also responsible only to Mulla Omar.

20. The prime legitimacy for the regional structures resided in their roots during the resistance against central state action after 1978, and later in defending the local population against the Taliban. Regional leaders took credit for ending Taliban rule in their own region, and for providing some sort of security and governance in the absence of any functioning authority in Kabul. Kabul, dominated by one faction of Jamiat, attempted in late 2001 to appoint at will the many thousand freed posts throughout the country and resorted quickly to an understanding with the regional power holders. For example neither in the north, west or east, any appointment by Kabul authorities was considered binding, but always required the approval of the regional strongman. With Kabul incapable of providing even basic directions well into 2002, services and governance organized themselves under an interim regional umbrella which was agreed upon by Karzai and Jamiat for the moment. This was neither ethnic irredentism nor conscious attempts at decentralization. In many cases actions were dictated by need and, of course, the greed of local office-holders to lay their hands on the revenue generated under their protection.

21. While originally exclusively Pashtun, the Taliban leadership also eventually included some non-Pashtuns: Tajik clerics from Badakhshan, Takhar and Panjsher, which were formed in Pakistani madrassas rose to prominence such as the minister for planning,

Qari Din Muhammad Hanif, also commanders such as Hashim Habibi (Uzbek) and Ustad Akbari (Hazara) joined the Taliban, but had to endure continuous suspicion and lacked access to power.

22. The allies of the Coalition against the Taliban and Al Qaeda in October 2001 however mostly to the "minorities" of the Tajiks, Uzbeks and Hazaras which managed to remain a majority in north Afghanistan and developed there various sub-nationalisms. The identification of "minorities" with the United Front and Pashtuns with the Taliban has limited roots in reality. There were numerous Pashtuns initially siding with the United Front confronting the Taliban. Pashtun members of the United Front joined the Taliban relatively quickly, quicker than Uzbeks or Hazaras. At a point where sticking it out with the United Front meant hazard and little pay, it was not surprising that many Pashtuns discovered an easy exit route, remembering their joint ethnicity. Most of these opportunistic elements from the Pashtun belt were back in the United Front fold by December 2001 and had quickly forgotten their embarrassing stint with the Taliban. Uzbeks, Tajiks and Hazaras also joined the Taliban for the same opportunistic reasons, but with a different grade of integration into the movement. The perception of an ethnicization of Afghanistan's conflict gained ground from the clashes between Jamiat and Hezb-i-Islami, and reached its peak through the clearly ethnic cleansing carried out by the Taliban against Hazaras and Uzbeks—and to a lesser extent against Tajiks from 1997 onwards—reviving memories of earlier ethnic clashes a century before. M. Nazif Shahrani, "Resisting the Taliban and Talibanism in Afghanistan," *Perceptions: Journal of International Affairs,* vol. 5, no. 4 (December 2000–February 2001): 121–140. I use the term "subnationalism" to describe the ethnically defined expressions of community where also micro-nationalism, ethnic nationalism, ethnism, ethnicism, ethno-regionalism, parochialism, regionalism or linguistic nativism could be used.

23. These urban-based organizations attempted in vain to challenge the government throughout the 1970s in a rural setting and met the full might of the communist counterinsurgency. A detailed case study of northeastern Afghanistan is provided by Asadullah Wulwaljî, *Âyâ quwâ-yi nizâmî-yi ittihâd-i shûrâwî az Afghânistân khârij sâkhta shud?* [Was the Military Force of the Soviet Union Pushed Out of Afghanistan?] (Peshawar: 2001). Some of the subnationalist movements remained intact under a jihadi party such as the al-Hadid group within Shura-yi Nazar of Jamiat. For a description of the "Maoist" integration within Jamiat, see Asadullah Wulwaljî, *"Junbish-i millî-yi Islâmî-yi Afghânistân mêtawânist dar ittihâd bâ sâzmân-i shûrâ-yi Nazâr bâqî bamânad?"* [Could the National Islamic Movement of Afghanistan Continue in an Alliance with the Supervisory Council?] in *Andesha* (Private Journal Published in Mazar-i Sharif 1992–1998 and collected by Patterson & Schiewek), nos. 4, 6, 7, 8 (1374/1995–1996). An altered English version is Asadallah Wulwalajî, "Can Jumbish-i Milli-i Islami Afghanistan Survive in Alliance with Shura-i Nazar?," *Central Asia,* Special Issue (2001). The Najibullah government from 1986 onwards also reached out to the "Maoists." In 1990, even a public commemoration ceremony was held for Tâhir Badakhshî, the founder of the Sitam-i Milli killed by the communist regime, in Kabul and published as Muhammad Hasan Sitafi, *Yâdnâma-yi Muhammad Tâhir Badakhshî* [Memorial of Muhammad Tahir Badakhshi] (Kabul: 1991).

24. Still the new leaders were all, with the exception of the Uzbek Dostum, products of the Islamist movements: Fahim, Qanuni, Dr. Abdullah (the so called, Tajik, "Panjsheri Troika"), Ismail Khan (a Tajik from Herat), Khalili, Muhaqqiq, Anwari (all three from the Shia/Hazara community), and Hazrat Ali (a Pashai from the east).

25. During the domination of the Taliban in northern Afghanistan, resistance forces held out in Kohistan district of Faryab, Sang Charak, Gusfandi and Balkhab in Sar-i Pul, and Darra-yi Suf of Samangan. Local Uzbek and Hazara communities resisted Taliban penetration after the fall of Mazar-i Sharif and the lower hill country in August 1998.

This resistance was led by the ex-Pasdaran branch of Hizb-i Wahdat under Commander Safa'i in Balkhab and the Harakat commanders Sayyid Najib and Sayyid Daud in Darra-yi Suf. Tajik communities in southern Faryab province resisted under Dr. Sadat in the districts of Lawlash and Bandar, strengthened by the cavalry forces of the Uzbek commander Fatihullah originally from Qaysar. From the senior leadership of the United Front, commander Khalili returned first in late 1998, followed by Muhaqqiq and Ata in 1999.

26. Both were inserted in the pockets in March–April 2001. They did not take over management, but were "grafted" on top of the local administration for offensive operations. Their presence increased the strength of the fighting force in each given pocket, as they brought money and contacts beyond the immediate neighborhood of the pockets. While recruitment for the Balkhab fighting force until 2001 had remained strictly local and among internally displaced persons (IDPs) within the pockets, from April 2001 onwards Junbish fighters and officers were recruited from the Afghan emigré community as far as Turkey and inserted via Massoud's helicopters.

27. His force of about 250 cavalrymen overran Taliban positions and for a short time took the district center of Zari in upper Balkh Province. This attack failed strategically due to the lack of support from the local Jamiat leader Ustad Ata, who refused to launch a simultaneous offensive from his stronghold of Darra-yi Suf. The Taliban's air supremacy allowed the Taliban to regroup and kept the Uzbek force in Zari. This attack nearly led to the death of Dostum himself when two horses were shot from under him.

28. This, the hill district of Zari is mostly Uzbek, actually played into the hands of Dostum and the United Front, as it antagonized the population further against the Taliban. Besides the 1998 massacre of civilians in Mazar-i Sharif, the Taliban had since 1997 carried out a series of other massacres, which were not documented. See also Human Rights Watch, "Massacres of Hazaras in Afghanistan," February 2001.

29. He had little choice. At an altitude of more than 2,500 meters, winter would have led almost certainly to the dispersal of his force. See the military historian's account, Richard W. Stewart, *The United States Army in Afghanistan: Operation Enduring Freedom, October 2001–March 2002* (Washington, DC: Defense Department, Army Center of Military History, 2004). This official account of the campaign stresses the importance to strike before winter and admits to the need to impress upon Fahim to get into motion. Other sources (see next note) attribute Fahim's reluctance to the lack of airpower in his front are north of Kabul.

30. A third team was with the Ismaili leader Sayyid Ja'far Naderi who directed his thrust to his native Kayan Valley. An account of this sideshow is published only in a warped version in Robin Moore, *The Hunt for Bin Laden: Task Force Dagger* (New York: Random House, 2003). Sayyid Ja'far later ran into a confrontation with the Andarabi commanders Hajji Leqa and Mustafa of Shura-yi Nazar/Jamiat when expanding into Baghlan and became the target of US air strikes (interview of the author with Sayyid Ja'far). It was the support of the first SF team (Jawbreaker Alpha if one were to believe Moore) combined with a reckless charge of the Uzbek cavalry over the Safed Kotal range between Darra-yi Suf and Kishindeh of upper Balkh Province, which led to the first breakthrough of the war. In quick succession Dostum's force, which included Shia militias of Harakat and Wahdat under Safai, Muhaqqiq and Najib reached the wide valley of Sholgara, also known under its old Uzbek name "Boyni Qara" less than an hour drive to the southwest of Mazar-i Sharif. The wide and fertile Sholgara Valley narrows into a gorge at its northern end, which had become the last Taliban position before Mazar-i Sharif. Here again a lucky combination between precise bombardment and a well-timed cavalry charge won the battle (interview and site visits of the author with Dostum). The published accounts of the fall of Mazar-i Sharif by ex-CIA operatives rely on information passed on by one officer in the northern Special Forces Team who had a

less than perfect command of geography. Gary Berntsen, *Jawbreaker: The Attack on Bin Laden and Al-Qaeda: A Personal Account by the CIA's Key Field Commander* (New York: Three Rivers Press, 2005), 137–140; and Gary Schroen, *First In: An Insider's Account of How the CIA Spearheaded the War on Terror in Afghanistan* (New York: Presidio Press, 2005), 245–255, 315f, 335–337. These accounts also lack clear dates and do contain gaps and contradictions. For example, no explanation is given regarding the surrender/conquest of the key town of Aq Kupruq by Ustad Ata. The reason for these shortcomings might be found in the Panjsher-centric approach of the CIA and a general lack of language skills. A better account is from Robert Young Pelton, "Heavy D and the Boys: In the Field with an Afghan Warlord," *National Geographic,* March 2002. In a recent book, Pelton radically questions—with some justification judging from Afghan accounts—the story given by Moore and alleges that the book had been rewritten by a ghostwriter. Robert Young Pelton, *Licensed to Kill: Hired Guns in the War on Terror* (New York: Three Rivers Press, 2007).

31. The absence of an agreed master plan did not mean that the Afghan factions would not have a vision, which in this case went back to the post-1992 period of a regionalized country ruled by armed faction leaders. Then, a triumvirate of Junbish, Jamiat and Wahdat had proven to be the main force behind the Union Council of the North (1992–1997/1998), integrating all other factions in part through concessions, in part through coercion under the eventual leadership of General Dostum in a "proto-state." Through a financial commission (*kamîsiyûn-yi mâlî*) and an office for cadre staffing (*sawq-i idâra*) control was maintained over revenue and administration in the five northern provinces, offering each political party a share in the executive set up based on its relative military weight. A good overview of this period can be found in *Hidayatullah Hidayat, Dalâ'il-i suqût-i shamâl* [Reasons for the Fall of the North] (Mazar-i Sharif: 2003).

32. This pattern applied across the political landscape, where Jamiat and some other mujahideen actors mainly from the miniscule factions of Ittihad, Mahaz and Nijat that had not been involved in the resistance against the Taliban were rewarded with powerful ministries over non-Jamiat resistance figures. Dostum managed to have his candidates appointed only in the largely civilian Ministries of Water and Power, and Mines and Heavy Industries. The Hazaras fared better by receiving the powerless but profitable Ministries of Agriculture, Trade and Planning, though the first two were filled by politically pro-Jamiat and ethnically Sayyid Hazaras, which are not regarded as "true" Hazaras by the nationalists. The pattern reproduced itself within Jamiat itself, where the most powerful and best posts went to the small group of Panjsheris and their clients rather than to Jamiat leaders of the north. For example many mujahideen resented the elevation of Ata over the more senior Alam Khan Azadi for the position of regional military commander. Most bitterly resented was the lack of an interim parliament or permanent council, which could have accommodated many of these war-weary commanders.

33. North Afghanistan was represented only through three ministers among thirty cabinet members as announced on 22 December 2001: Planning (Muhammmad Muhaqqiq, Hazara, Wahdat), Water and Electricity (Shakir Kargar, Uzbek, Junbish), Mines and Industries (Muhammad Alem Razm, Uzbek, Gurûh-i Kâr). In a conciliatory move, Karzai appointed Dostum as Deputy Minister of Defense on 24 December 2001 and included Dostum and Muhaqqiq in the National Defense Commission, which was supposed to formulate plans for a new national army and disarmament of the existing militias.

34. In the period between September 2002 and January 2003, 21 senior appointments occurred in north Afghanistan, of which one came from the Supreme Court, two came from the Ministry of Interior, three from Chairman Karzai's office, and fifteen from Dostum. Similar ratios were observed in the western region under Ismail Khan. However, the old base for Dostum's power—the "Army of the North" was not rebuilt.

See Antonio Giustozzi, "The Demodernization of an Army, 1992–2001," *Small Wars and Insurgencies,* vol. 15, no. 1: 1–18.

35. This was particularly acute after Hikmatyar in March 2002 declared holy war (jihad) against the US and publicly sided with the defeated Taliban. Hezb-i-Islami did not survive as a political force but continues to exist as a social network spread over the whole country. Not until mid-2004 could Hezb-i-Islami regroup at the central level. The realignments of the major commanders can be seen in the table below (Note: Uz = Uzbek, Ar = Arab and Pn = Pashtun).

Ex-Hezb-i-Islami/Taliban Commanders and Their 2002 Affiliations

District	Name (Ethnicity)	Party affiliation 2002
Balkh	Amir Jan (Pn)	Jamiat
Balkh	Alam Khan (Ar)	Jamiat
Charbolak	Akhtar Ibrahimkhel(Pn)	Junbish
Charbolak	Juma Khan Hamdard (Pn)	Junbish
Chimtal	Nur Muhammad (Pn)	Jamiat
Gusfandi	Karim Khan (Pn)	Jamiat
Darzab	Nasim Mahdi (Uz)	Shura-yi Adalat (Pahlawan)
Gurziwan	Hashim Habibi (Uz)	Junbish

36. Through the mediation of the re-integrated ex-Taliban Pashtun leaders, many intra-ethnic conflicts were mitigated in the months after the fall of the Taliban. The abuses committed against Pashtuns were documented in Human Rights Watch, "Paying for the Taliban's Crimes: Abuses Against Ethnic Pashtuns in Northern Afghanistan," June 2002. While thoroughly documented, the report leaves out the history before the fall of the Taliban and the numerous abuses carried out by local Pashtuns against local communities. The abuses never assumed the scale of the previous massacres of civilians committed by the Taliban. While the Bonn Agreement assured that no single ethnic group would again dominate government, proponents of the subnationalist movements such as Guruh-i Kar portrayed this movement as a first step towards reestablishing the rule of Pashtuns over the peoples of north Afghanistan. Such ethnicized accounts tend to gloss over the oppression suffered by the Pashtun communities mainly at the hands of their own commanders.

37. The total amount of money disbursed through the AMF is difficult to quantify. The yearly recorded budget of 1383 (2003–2004) might be useful to grasp the financial dimensions: 5.1 billion Afghani (equivalent to $110 million) were spent for the AMF with a monthly contribution from the US of $1.67 million primarily but not exclusively for the new Afghan National Army—equivalent to a further $20.04 million. Total state revenue in comparison throughout the same period was less than $220 million.

38. Fahim in December 2001. Fahim at that stage mainly referred to payment figures, not actual soldiers. Being mujahideen in the Panjsher or in another Shura-yi Nazar area did not entail permanent readiness, but rather the receipt of a small stipend and the eventual readiness to come if called upon. At the core of the discussion were "two papers produced respectively by the International Security Assistance Force, which proposed a force of 50,000, and the Ministry of Defense, which suggested a force of 200,000, training of the first battalion of the new Afghan National Guard by International Security Assistance Force started on 17 February." UN, *Report of the Secretary-General on the Situation in Afghanistan and its Implications for International Peace and Security,* S/2002/278, 18 March 2002, 10.

39. For example, Ismail Khan claimed to have entered Herat with 2,000 in December 2001. By January 2002 he was already claiming to have 25,000 soldiers and officers. Dostum in quick succession increased the number of troops from 1,200 (November 2001) to over 20,000 (January 2002). He even boasted of being able to raise 40,000 fighting men in January 2002. The newly "raised" figures obviously were on paper only, but demonstrated the political and financial appetite of their patrons. One faction profiting greatly from the re-creation of divisions outside of the north was the Ittihad party of Sayyaf, which managed to control two major divisions in Kabul and Jalalabad (Division 10 under Dr. Abdullah and Division 11 under Malangyar).

40. Among the divisions of Army Corps VIII, only two (Divisions 53 and 82) were considered fully loyal by Dostum himself. The other two (Division 200 and 70) were commanded by reintegrated ex-Taliban. Ata had a similar problem with all division commanders being senior to him and therefore unwilling to obey.

41. Instrumental to this policy was the travel of Junbish delegations to the *buzkashi* matches of the north and northeast, led by Ahmad Khan, which did not fail to beat the ethno-nationalist Uzbek drum. While Uzbek had achieved the status of a de facto official language in Faryab, Jawzjan and Sar-i Pul during the 1980s already, its position was significantly weaker in Samangan, Baghlan, Qunduz and Takhar, where only throughout the late 1990s Uzbek nationalism was kindled as a reaction to the Taliban's ethnicized warfare. The role of the 1998 massacre of Hazaras and Uzbeks in Mazar-i Sharif, the repeated burning of Uzbek villages and individual homes in the area of Khwaja Ghar 1999–2001 must have played a role in the mobilization, which reached beyond simple alliances with commanders.

42. Both commanders were Uzbek mujahideen with a Jamiat/Ittihad background, and split for personal reasons and due to the lack of perspectives in the largely Tajik Jamiat. Ahmad Khan had for example been sidelined completely by Ata from supplies 1999–2001. It was natural for him to turn away as soon as the option of a viable alternative (Junbish) appeared.

43. Five "divisions" were granted by Fahim upon request by Hazara leaders (of which only two were organized in the "Hazara" Army Corps IX) Division 14, located in Ghazni within the Gardez-based Army Corps II, Division 31 located in Kabul within Army Corps Central, Divisions 34 and 35 based in Bamyan and Panjab. Both were first part of Army Corps Central, then were reorganized both in Army Corps IX of Bamyan, Division 38 located in Mazar-i Sharif within Army Corps VII. Hazara units outside the area of responsibility of these divisions could not officialize themselves (e.g., the sizeable Hazara populations and their militias in Herat, Ghor and Uruzgan). Within each of the Hazara divisions, competition set in among the different parties for leadership positions. Jamiat, which controlled nearly all Army Corps and therefore payment of salaries, was supremely placed to exploit this rivalry and used it at will. UNAMA in Mazar-i Sharif regularly received complaints of the 38 Division against AC VII commander Ata withholding salaries completely or refusing to pay certain officers. For example on 23 October 2003 a number of officers complained in writing to the Ministry of Defense, including the commander and the financial officer.

44. Home to roughly 400,000 inhabitants, and a number of IDP camps around the city, the greater Mazar-i Sharif region might have contained nearly one million people at the end of 2001. Besides the population, a nearby factory produced chemical fertilizer and electricity.

45. Though some of the vehicles allowed Taliban senior officials to escape to Pakistan, as was the case of the Taliban Ministry of Foreign Affairs representative, Mawlawi Halimi, who was caught in March 2002 in Kabul, when he returned from Pakistan in a looted NGO vehicle. The restitution of movable property, in particular cars, would prove to be much harder to achieve. Several cars stayed in the property of prominent commanders of

the United Front, which regarded them as legitimate war booty from the Taliban, such as a UNOCHA Land Cruiser which was captured from the Taliban by Dostum's deputy Majid Rozi, repainted and reregistered in Uzbekistan.

46. "In the north, fighting in late January and early February between Jamiat (Tajik) and Jumbesh (Uzbek) forces left about 20 dead and injured. A team from the Interim Administration and the United Nations traveled to Mazar-e-Sharif, and after mediation the parties promised to abide by an agreement to demilitarize the city and to establish a security commission. . . . Nonetheless, a few weeks after the troops withdrew, fighting erupted between two garrison commanders, resulting in two dead and several wounded, and serving as a reminder that the situation remains unpredictable." UN, S/2002/278, 8. "A long-standing rivalry between the Jumbesh and Jamiat factions negatively affects the general security situation. This rivalry has prevented the establishment of effective security in Mazar City, despite the efforts of the Interim Administration and UNAMA to establish a separation of forces and a neutral, multi-ethnic police force." UN, *Report of the Secretary-General on the Situation in Afghanistan and Its Implications for International Peace and Security,* S/2002/737, 11 July 2002, 4. "A general feeling of fear and instability pervades the region. The rivalry between the two commanders [Dostum and Fahim] has not been resolved, despite several high-level visits by delegations from the Interim Authority and Transitional Government. Outbreaks of fighting recur frequently even though several security commissions have attempted to negotiate settlements or mediate between the opposing parties. These troubles have been a consistent feature of the Northern region for many months, and it is hard to see how a showdown between the two commanders is not inevitable. Tensions in the region are very high, and it is feared that any single incident could become the spark that starts a conflagration." United Nation Field Security Coordination (UNSECOORD), Briefing Email, 15 September 2002.

47. Rivalries to occupy the power vacuum left after the fall of the Taliban were not confined to north Afghanistan, but assumed here a special importance as relatively rich local resources meant that factions could sustain themselves once they managed to control a comparatively small territory. The absence of deep-rooted Taliban strongholds limited Coalition forces' interest and involvement in local power dynamics, maximizing Afghan ownership of the political and military process. Power dynamics in neighboring and similar regions (west, northeast, central highlands, Shamali plains) were in early 2002 dominated by one single regional hegemon (Ismail Khan, Shura-yi Nazar, Wahdat, etc.) with central approval and therefore not contested. Mediation by the United Nations and the ultimate threat by Coalition airpower deescalated dynamics which ultimately might have led to a single faction controlling exclusively the whole of north Afghanistan. The UN and the Security Commission therefore could not solve the "dispute" finally, but prevented a major outbreak of hostilities. The "showdown" never happened until October 2003 and was then mitigated in scope through a strategic investment in the stabilization of Sholgara and the presence of the PRT. The focus of the international media on north Afghanistan was started by the relative ease and security with which journalists could access the "warlords" of north Afghanistan. See for example the article by Sophie Shehab, "Physique d'ours, le padishah-général Dostom reçoit dans son palais de Sheberghan," *Le Monde,* 28 December 2001. Experience showed that "warlords" of the south are shielded much more proficiently and brutally from the press' scrutiny. While brutality of the post-Taliban warlords was not limited to the north, it received much less international attention in other parts of Afghanistan. Much less media coverage followed the well-researched report covering the southeast, Human Rights Watch, *Killing You Is a Very Easy Thing for Us,* July 2003.

48. Other than in the comparable case of Paktiya, where a conflict over the governorship was decided by the demonstration of Coalition airpower, the dense settlement

pattern around Mazar, and the sheer size of the Afghan troops involved prevented such an easy solution. It was also out of question for the Coalition to deploy a peacekeeping constabulary force to the north or to increase its small teams of Special Forces.

49. As evidently visible from the signatures, the agreement was not signed by any of the accompanying officials from the central government in Kabul. Among these were engineer Barakzai, deputy to engineer Arif, Director of the National Security Directorate; Dr. Mushahid, soon to be appointed ambassador to Tehran and later Head of the National Civil Service Reform Commission. Both were part of the Jamiat Shura-yi Nazar faction, which also controlled the Ministry of Interior, and backed the expansive policies of the Jamiat-dominated Ministry of Defense. Also the Directorate for National Security (NDS) was Jamiat-dominated. The asymmetric distribution of power that was the root for the factional conflict was always in danger of evolving into a confrontation between center and periphery.

50. The actual terminology used after the first meeting on 3 February 2002 (1380/11/14) was varying. In reference to provision 2 of the agreement, the first name used was "The Commission for the Removal of Irresponsible Posts from the City" [*Kamisiyun-i Takhliya-yi Shahr az Postaha-yi Ghayr-i Mas'ul*]. This commission also did broadcast its first announcement through local media under the title of Commission for the Implementation of the Peace Process in the North [*Kamisiyun-i Tatbiq-i Prosa-yi Solh dar Shamal*].

51. These law enforcement organs were also deeply factional. Chief of Police for Balkh province, Isa Iftikhari, was loyal to Hizb-i Wahdat, the Mazar-i Sharif City police chief, Hajji Fida, was actually Ustad Ata's brother. The NDS had a branch for Balkh province headed by Abdul Halim, a Jamiat man, and another branch for the northern region headed by Sayyid Kamil from Junbish.

52. See also the mention in UN S/2002/278, 18 March 2002, 10. The local Junbish commanders were previous Harakat-i Inqilabi units and the Jamiat commanders were mostly previous ex-Hezb-i-Islami troops. Both camps had been part of the Taliban armies and had already clashed in early 2000 over the same issue—the exploitation of pistachio forests. The three Jamiat commanders had at that time 522 soldiers against 350 of the one Junbish commander, Ustad Kabir. From both factions, only 191 weapons were surrendered. The major Jamiat commander, Taher Ehsan, was also now rewarded by becoming an official army commander within the structure of the Army Corps VII. Hamidullah Sadbashi, the second Jamiat leader, was appointed shortly after to the position of chief of police for the district of Tashqurghan. In the absence of a professional third party police, this amounted to storing the Jamiat weapons with Jamiat police and military units, and marginalizing the Junbish troops officially.

53. The lack of professional competence in the Mazar-i Sharif and Balkh police, the corruption within the ministry, and the lack of a third party willing to undertake training and sustenance of the police, never created an esprit de corps, as resourcing had to be continued by the original factions. Police officers drawing their salaries from their original factionalized units could not be expected to sever their ties, as requested in the 3 February agreement.

54. All activities were carried out without substantial inputs from the United Nations, which only observed and facilitated an Afghan process. The mediation effort required the workforce of two political affairs officers and a couple of local assistants and drivers—never more than a dozen staff in total. The transitory nature of UNAMA meant that sometimes not even these means would be fully available.

55. The Taliban banned customary rites of Islam, which they saw to have originated in pre-Islamic "pagan" ceremonies. In the two years of 1999 and 2000, local Taliban militia commanders had prevailed upon the leadership and presided over a low-key event. These local forces were led by the opportunistic ex-Hezb-i-Islami commanders mentioned earlier such as Akhtar Ibrahimkhel and Amir Jan Naseri. After the local Taliban commander Amir Jan broke into town with armed men, and raised the standard for a couple of hours, armed Taliban guarded the site to prevent a repetition. The governor

warned off the guardians of the shrine that a repetition would entail terminal consequences. The Taliban in 2001 however managed under pain of death to completely ban the ceremony and later (for other reasons) jailed Amir Jan. Also throughout the north, the Taliban destroyed local saints' shrines and fought their adoration. Relics of the Balkh shrine of Ali Yamchi had been stolen and broken, and the observance of the customary "women's day," which earlier allowed female worshippers and their children to gather every Wednesday at shrines and mosques was forbidden. In Mazar-i Sharif, many Shia *takyakhana* (Shia places of worship) had been destroyed, closed or converted to Sunni mosques. There were 63 takyakhanas before August 1998, of which eleven were destroyed, one closed and three situated in the center were renamed and used as Sunni mosques. Renamed were the mosque Khatam al-Anbiya, also used as a takyakhana, situated at Si Dukkan in the center of the city to "Masjid Hazrat Umar Faruq;" the takyakhana-yi Agha-yi Bahr, situated at Nawabad Qala-e Miri, was renamed to "Masjid Hazrat Usman;" and the takyakhana-yi Umumi, situated in a vegetable market in the center of the city was renamed to "Masjid Hazrat Ali." Destroyed were three takyakhana around Sheikhabad in Dehdadi, one takyakhana and three mosques in Qizilabad, the Masjid-i Mahdawiya and one takyakhana in Ziraat, the takyakhana-yi Sham-i Ghariban in Nawshad and the takyakhana-yi Karta Solh. Closed was the takyakhana-yi Mahdawiya in Sayyidabad.

56. After the dignitaries had left, the customary Buzkashi tournament started to the south of the city near the silo. In the afternoon, Samangan (sponsored by Junbish) scored against Balkh team (sponsored by Jamiat) through ripping off of a leg from the carcass (which acts as ball), and scoring with the leg only, the "police" became involved in the brawl on the side of their respective team, brandishing their weapons. The referee was threatened and onlookers fled the scene fearing an armed escalation. This was avoided through timely intervention, but the readiness to use violence along factional lines had become clear to everyone. In the aftermath of the New Year, complaints were raised in the Security Commission on 27 March that the Balkh provincial chief of police, Fida Muhammad (Jamiat, brother of Ustad Ata) had extorted money from vehicles coming to the city. The Hazara Junbish commander Ali Sarwar "gangs" (nicknamed "the confused") was accused of having stolen a vehicle, and both Junbish and Jamiat accused each other of posturing and provoking tensions.

57. The appointment of the Tajik general Ibadi as commander of the first battalion of the emerging Afghan National Army demonstrated Jamiat's continuing supremacy. At that time the new army was called Afghan National Guard. The first battalion (1BANG) graduated in late March 2002 after 6–7 weeks training by ISAF. Its commanding officer General Ebadi was at that time accused of corruption during the resistance years and the Rabbani presidency even by fellow officers. Of the total strength of 550 men, 150 were absent without leave when checked on 26 April by UNAMA, with an additional 60 on authorized leave. Among the personnel on AWOL were six Pashtun, two Hazara and two Tajik officers. In addition five new officers were encountered in positions originally assigned to the officers on AWOL, all Tajiks. Within four weeks of service, ethnic balance endured a 12% decrease of Pashtuns, a 6.5% decrease of Hazaras, and a 20% increase of Tajiks in the battalion. Tajiks now counted for more than 60% of the unit. At the same time the commanding officer also complained about the loss of 160 weapons.

58. Mainly through the creation in Sar-i Pul of the new Division 026 "jihadi" under Hajji Rahim of San Charak, and the strengthening of Division 01 "jihadi" under Alam Khan Azadi in Balkh and Sholgara. Each division was supposed to recruit along ethnic lines: Division 026 was supposed to enlist Tajiks and Pashtuns in Sar-i Pul, and Division 01 Arabs in Balkh, basing their actions on the long defunct universal national service (*mukallafiyat*).

59. Junbish expanded into Badakhshan and Qataghan, comprising the modern provinces of Baghlan, Qunduz, Takhar and Badakhshan, where since the sixteenth century a significant part of the population is Uzbek. Jamiat's Army Corps VI based in Qunduz

under the command of Daud covered all these provinces. Junbish made significant inroads with the population and commanders in Qunduz, Baghlan and Takhar provinces.

60. For example on 10 April 2002, a national UN employee (FAO) was assassinated in his home. It was never clarified whether this had been in the course of a robbery or a targeted assassination. The victim, Shah Sayyid Alimi, had worked in the most difficult times under the Taliban for FAO and might have been targeted for his refusal to enter in corrupt practices surrounding aid distribution at that time. It seemed that the criminals all had patrons within the military establishment of the north, notably Jamiat. In the absence of a criminal investigative capacity, the UN had to limit itself to a formal remonstration to the Afghan Ministry of Foreign Affairs (controlled by Jamiat) and the formal address of the leaders of the north through a visit of SRSG Brahimi.

61. Ustad Ata captured two tanks when Mazar fell in November 2001, had received ten tanks in March, and acquired 12 in April from General Daud's Army Corps VI based primarily in Qunduz and Takhar. The majority of these tanks had come in July and August 2001 from Tajikistan as military assistance to Masud in his fight against the Taliban.

62. National Revolution Day (*jashn*) marks the fall of the Najibullah regime and the victory of the mujahideen on 28 April 1992, the 8 Saur in the Afghan solar calendar.

63. UNAMA actually had to request Jamiat to remove heavy machineguns from its walls during the preparations for the elections ceremony to the Emergency Loya Jirga. Further tension had been created through the establishment of new Jamiat posts on the outskirts of the city and Junbish harassing people from Jamiat areas, in particular potential voters for the ELJ.

64. Rahguzar, an ethnic Tajik, was actually a former sub-commander of Commander Ata. It was Ata who insisted on "involving the legitimate authority" as this would give him an additional ally in the talks. UNAMA endorsed this wish as he was the weaker and therefore more insecure party, and Rahguzar's participation increased Jamiat's readiness to adhere to the deal as a second Jamiat leader would sign off on the deal.

65. With regard to its mandate, the commission was now specifically tasked to respond to insecurity across north Afghanistan. UNAMA limited this definition to the five provinces of Balkh, Samangan, Sar-i Pul, Faryab and Jawzjan, though petitions reached the Security Commission from Baghlan, Qunduz and Badghis Provinces.

66. Ata refused to accept the request articulated by Dostum that he replace at least the chief of police—his brother Hajji Fida Muhammad. Dostum used the example of his having to replace his brother Qadir as commander of the 53rd Division in 1996 after Qadir had proved himself not up to the job and with no control whatsoever over the troops, and urged Ata to appoint a well-respected senior Jamiat commander so that it would not affect Jamiat's overall control. This request had already been made by SRSG Brahimi, but Ata's need to rely upon his brother could not be underestimated given the heterogeneous nature of Jamiat north, which gave him much less choice than Dostum. Fida was anything but a beacon of law and order, but he was reliable in delivering control over the city for Jamiat.

67. Both Dostum and UNAMA insisted that the provincial governor attend as the legitimate authority, though Rahguzar failed to live up to his task on even a single occasion. He was regularly distancing himself from any situation in which Jamiat might be criticized, prompting a discussion of how factional governors could be expected to advance the state's agenda.

68. At that moment both teams had to rely on their experiences gained since their arrival, gained mostly without any language skills. The odd embedded CIA operative with Dari skills regularly missed the fast flowing debates among their Afghan counterparts, in particular if they spoke dialect or switched to Uzbek or Pashto. The first diplomat with language skills (Russian) was deployed by the US in September 2002. Sadly successors were not chosen according to their language capabilities which resulted in the Coalition being dependent on their (mostly young) interpreters.

69. Bariyalay at that time attempted to project himself as becoming gradually distanced from Jamiat and a professional "national figure." It was unclear how far Minister Qasim Fahim covered his actions. Bariyalay was removed by Fahim and Karzai from office in September 2003.

70. As a working-class Uzbek he was lacking membership or relatives in the emigré community of the Rome process that by and large represented the pre-war elites only. Uzbeks and Arabs were most unlikely in pre-war Afghanistan to make a career in government service. He was neither being accepted by the mujahideen nor by the elitist communist circles due to having been a communist paramilitary. His relationship with Fahim was strained and within the United Front had only been mitigated by Masud. Ata by contrast could count on his well-established mujahideen credentials, which opened up alliances even beyond Jamiat circles. His marriage with the daughter of a Pashtun notable from Sholgara saved him from being boxed into a "minority" category and opened a way to the pre-war Pashtun elite. In order to balance Ata's political capital, Dostum was required to make concessions in the political process, which through the Bonn process invariably moved toward a countrywide election.

71. A total of 2,906 voters elected in the first round during April were to elect directly 166 delegates to the Emergency Loya Jirga in the five provinces of north Afghanistan. Based on Article 11 of the Electoral Procedures, "In case conditions for conducting fair and equitable elections are absent in any constituency, a separate procedure for observation of the election of the members of the Emergency Loya Jirga shall be invoked, as laid out in the 'Procedures for the observation of the elections of the members of the Emergency Loya Jirga and the audition of complaints arising from it,' Article 7." The Independent Commission for the Convening of the Emergency Loya Jirga appointed non-factional delegates. These individuals sometimes were even non-residents who originally came from the area. This step was to prevent abusive behavior of commanders who could have penalized any appointed resident after his return to the district.

72. In Balkh Province, a total of eight seats were not filled through elections in Sholgara (Junbish-Jamiat), Charkent (Jamiat-Shia parties), Zari (Junbish) and Amrakh (Jamiat); in Samangan, the three seats of upper Darra-yi Suf (Shia parties), in Faryab two seats for the twin sub-districts of Kohistan—Bandar and Lawlash (Jamiat-Junbish) and in Sar-i Pul three seats for the three sub-districts of Kohistanat—Kachan, Chiras and Pawgan Starab (Jamiat-Junbish).

73. The estimates made by the author when serving as the UNAMA political affairs officer are reproduced below. This factory generated through the sale of chemical fertilizer

Balkh Estimated Non-Agriculture Monthly Revenue (US$)

	Hayratan Border Crossing Services	
Income Source	Low Estimate	High Estimate
ASTRAS Handling Fees	n.a.	$54,000
AFSOTR Handling	n.a.	$5,111
Custom Revenue	$80,000	$94,000
Fuel custom dues	$374,000	$900,000
	Industries	
Fertilizer plant	$203,666	$702,000
Textile Mill	$30,000	$60,000
Total	$687,666	1,815,111

(urea) about $10,000 per 24 hours of uninterrupted operation at full capacity (low estimate 6,700 kilograms, highest estimate 24,000 kilograms urea produced per day). The factory and the adjacent urban housing complex for the workers (Mikro Rayon) were held by Junbish troops locally recruited from the plant's workers and reinforced by troops from Shiberghan in Jawzjan. The surrounding rural territory was dominated by local commander Shafi'i, as sub-commander of Alam Khan Azadi (01 Division jihadi) and long-standing member of Jamiat Balkh. Interestingly his force survived intact through him joining the Taliban in 1998 and then switching back in November 2001. Fighting around the plant and its gas pipeline always risked triggering a massive explosion with the potential to reach even the city of Mazar-i Sharif, more than six kilometers away. In their negotiations, it was agreed that Junbish would receive 50% of the revenue, Jamiat 33%, Wahdat 17%. Junbish then had to pay salaries of workers, upkeep and management of the plant. This private agreement tremendously enhanced stability around the city. In addition to Balkh Province, the salt mines, qaraqul sheep and customs of Faryab, and the gas and oil fields of Jawzjan and Sar-i Pul represented sizeable budgets.

74. Lobbying was carried out in the north through the press of each faction, talk shows on Balkh radio and television under control of Ustad Ata and a separate television channel sponsored by Dostum. Besides the party organs *Junbish* (Junbish) or *Faryad-i Qalam* (Jamiat), a plethora of newspapers sprung into existence such as *Rah-i Abrisham, Umed,* and *Ba su-yi ayanda* which frequently shared the same pool of writers. UNAMA counted more than 20 weekly, biweekly or monthly print publications in Mazar-i Sharif in early 2003, some of which as in the case of Ulus had working distribution networks across ten provinces in north Afghanistan.

75. Allegedly Ata earlier had met with Fahim and was given a rebuke for him going separate ways and selling out to Junbish. Fahim told Ata that he could have access to much greater resources than the local resources of the north. From this time onwards, Ata reportedly acquired investments in the Russian Federation and South Korea and traveled frequently to these countries.

76. This activity led to joint events in Kabul during May 2003 and culminated in the boycott of the Constitutional Loya Jirga on 31 December 2003 when 48% of the delegates refused to go to a vote in protest over the presidential system, privileges for the Pashto language as "national language" and the lack of a prime minister responsible for the government.

77. During April 2003 fighting erupted again in all areas between Jamiat and Junbish. In parallel, the Harakat (Anwari)/Wahdat (Muhaqqiq) dispute was reactivated. Clashes took place in Faryab, Gusfandi, Sholgara, Darra-yi Suf, and Piruz Nakhjir/Tashqurghan with a center of gravity again in Sholgara.

78. In the following only two out of the hundreds of activities will be discussed: Mazar-i Sharif and Sholgara district in Balkh province. The conflicts in the other provinces could not be covered in the limited space available.

79. From the 600 men, 240 would be from Jamiat, 180 from Junbish and 180 from the Shia factions (Wahdat and Harakat). The representatives of the factions in the Security Commission would also appoint in agreement the officers in charge of police wards and crossroads. Still, Jamiat insisted that all crossroad control officers report to the standby unit (*qit'a-yi muntazira*) responding directly to Ustad Ata. At that time, seven of the eleven ward officers came from a professional background. Each recruit would be vetted by the Security Commission and allocated to various police subdistricts. A written oath signed by every party leader was meant to guarantee that personnel introduced by them would not leave their posts.

80. UNAMA's mandate of "assistance" would not have warranted an engagement against the clear will of the Afghan institution in charge. Still more limiting was the fact that independent means to support such a police force (uniforms, rations, salaries, trainers) were not available from Germany, the lead nation in police reform, even if the political will had existed. The Coalition had a limited capacity to support Afghan institutions and was

bound to channel it through the factional military units of the Ministry of Defense. In the absence of this, the Interim Administration, which controlled the UNDP-administered Law and Order Trust Fund (LOTFA) and the political-military parties were the only ones who could have supported the police force. LOTFA salary payments at that period were only handed out in Kabul and required the physical travel of the respective officer to Kabul who frequently failed to bring back the whole amount to the province. Local revenues (passport and ID card issuance, issuance of number plates, etc.) were not transferred to Kabul in return and were frequently used to pay salaries when the person traveling to Kabul to collect the salaries was lost.

81. UNAMA would have been hard pressed to find the manpower to supervise the payment and local revenue collection on a daily basis, but had basic resources in place which would have allowed for a monitoring activity with regular feedback to Kabul. UNAMA continued to lobby for international supervision of the police through mentors/trainers and if possible the training of a new force, and attempted through the Security Commission to manage the problems on a day-to-day basis. One civilian police advisor conducted short missions to Mazar-i Sharif, but no officer could be posted to the region due to the overall lack of staff on the mission.

82. Junbish representative Majid Rozi found old police uniforms from the communist era in a depot in Shiberghan, the UK Special Forces donated $5,000 for immediate needs such as food and basic refurbishing of the police stations and traders came up with food and carpet donations. These resources were clearly not sufficient but showed good will and established the veneer of a joint police force appearance.

83. Many of the "new" positions were "official" positions like police posts, or declared as armed guards of civilian line ministries allocated to a specific faction. For example, Harakat (Anwari) controlled the Ministry of Agriculture in Kabul and therefore also used the provincial Department of Agriculture in Balkh as a tool to project its military power. Jamiat controlled the governor's office, and the departments of finance, health, education, radio and television, water, pious foundations, and the majority of state-owned enterprises. Junbish controlled the department of foreign affairs, municipality, prosecutor's office, electricity, and the fertilizer factory. This move attempted to shield the positions from evacuation as per the agreement of 1 May.

84. Headed in Kabul by Engineer Aref, a Panjsheri member of Shura-yi Nazar and close confident of Fahim, the National Directorate of Security (NDS) was probably the department with the most funds as it profited directly from the CIA's largesse. Since the fall of the Taliban, the Junbish-aligned Sayyid Kamal ran the NDS office for Balkh province. Also on lower levels the heritage of decades of communist/Junbish domination had many operatives leaning towards Junbish. When in mid-2002 the central NDS—headed by engineer Arif (a Panjsheri belonging to Shura-yi Nazar/Jamiat)—appointed a new Jamiat cadre with Abd al-Hamid as NDS head, a parallel institution which also was in charge of the Balkh Province was built up immediately. While Hamid had also been a left-over of the communist period, distrust ran so deep in Kabul of the Balkh office, that such a step was decided. Both structures continued to exist next to each other and were inherently hostile to each other. The Jamiat corps of Ustad Ata seconded a large number of troops to the new NDS, which established themselves in bases throughout the city, which were only nominally NDS offices. All were, however, heavily armed, totally military in behavior and bore little resemblance to traditional intelligence agency offices, whilst claiming that they were the only legitimate NDS office. The issue of legitimacy notwithstanding, the duplication of structures complicated the already complex task of demilitarizing the city as they were understandably viewed as Jamiat units under another name.

85. For example the Faryabi commander, Gul Muhammad Pahlawan, had refused to vacate premises and underlined the argument with two antiaircraft guns and about 150 armed soldiers. It was the presence of the Coalition forces among the Security Commission leadership delegation which dissuaded Gul Muhammad Pahlawan from opening fire. Negotiations lasted for three days, after which Gul Muhammad accepted

surrender of the weapons, and demilitarization of his compound. In return he was allowed to keep up residence. It was clear that Jamiat Kabul upheld his semi-independent status, where his half-brother Malik Pahlawan was residing under the protection of Minister of Defense Fahim.

86. In one instance in September 2002 provincial governor Ishaq Rahguzar, who himself was a Jamiati sub-commander of Ustad Ata, accused the Security Commission on state-run Balkh television of expelling "rightful owners" from their properties. He did not mention the fact that a Jamiat militia group had usurped a market building following the defeat of the Taliban, and had killed the original owner and builder of the property, well-known businessman Haydar Jawzjani. The Security Commission did nothing other than assisting the heirs of Jawzjani to repossess the building.

87. The reason for this shift was not at the initiative of the Ministry of Interior in Kabul, at but Ata's request. After a kidnapping attempt carried out by two of Hajji Fida's men and Ustad Ata's brothers-in-law (who were also affiliated with the police) was uncovered, Ata was shamed by local actors into agreeing to replace his brother and thereby covering the tracks of his own involvement in the case.

88. Revenue from controlling villages before had been secondary to funding obtained from membership in a military unit. A typical village growing wheat yielded annually about $700 through customary taxes to the local petty commander controlling it. Throughout the second half of 2002, drug seeds and advances from traffickers became available to commanders, who instructed their serfs to plant accordingly. Already throughout the late summer 2002 the profits made from drug trafficking eclipsed all other forms of revenue and were available directly to the commanders on the village level.

89. "A more constructive approach has been adopted by the leaderships of the rival parties, Jumbish and Jamiat. Tensions around Mazar-i-Sharif appear to be abating somewhat after patient and persistent local-level diplomacy yielded increased cooperation between General Atta of Jamiat and General Dostum of Jumbish. In particular, an agreement to disarm the city was reached, and most of the city has been cleared of weapons. The two leaders announced that, in the future, there would be no place for commanders who fight for personal benefit. The intervention of the Joint Security Commission, which includes a representative of UNAMA, has also been successful in ending some low-level conflicts before they escalated or spread." UN, *Report of the Secretary-General on the Situation in Afghanistan and its Implications for International Peace and Security,* S/2002/1173, 21 October 2002, 9.

90. Besides UNAMA, the US Special Forces team and the US State Department representative, Richard Norland, accompanied the weapons collection caravan and added their diplomatic weight to the process.

91. The program was in essence a voluntary arms collection without direct benefits, and addressed primarily the commanders. The weapons collection had the effect of strengthening AMF structures. However in the absence of a neutral destruction of storage capacity of the United Nations, and no personnel to guard it, the AMF depots were the only choice. No military advisor was posted to the region until mid-2003, forcing UNAMA to undertake the task of monitoring the effect of the weapons collection exercise entirely through civilian and mostly local staff. Based on DSRSG Arnault's decision, an additional international political affairs officer (the author who had been primarily responsible for Herat) was made available to serve as back-up from August 2002 onwards. From November 2002 onwards, two political affairs officers (Schiewek and Koepke) were permanently deployed to Mazar-i Sharif.

92. During 2002 and 2003 Atiqullah Bariyalay had formulated a new plan to decommission AMF units gradually. Results of pilot projects undertaken in October 2003 in Qunduz and Gardez were disastrous. A rival plan was formulated targeting not the units but their commanders by First Deputy Minister of Defense Rahim Wardak in close

cooperation with a US consultant. Addressing the commanders as members of their factions had the drawback that no control was possible once a commander chose to quit his faction and join another faction or the drug trafficking mafia. Even arrangements such as the September 2002 declaration could not mask the perverse effects of an unregulated violence economy where the different providers (commanders) catered to an ever-increasing demand by the Ministry of Defense, political parties and drug trafficking networks that were able to outbid each other.

93. The "Iron Amir" 'Abd al-Rahman had settled in Boyni Qara Hazara prisoners who had been chased from their land in southern Afghanistan—mostly from Deh Rawud district in today's Uruzgan province. Hazaras were counted part of the population when in 1927 (1306 in the Afghan solar calendar) King Amanullah distributed land titles. The biggest land owners before the 1950s seemed to have been Uzbeks and Tajiks. I noted *qabâla* and *tûman* (land documents for either irrigated or non-irrigated land) in the name of Hâjjî Barât from Tajik village; Mirbâshî, from Elâtân village; Arbâb Rôziqul, from the old Qipchaq village, and Ghulam Rasoul, son of Roziqul and a Jôra Elbêgî from Boyni Qara. Most of these seem to have been Uzbeks—at least their descendants describe themselves as Uzbeks. The Elbêgî family used to be the representatives of the lower valley, intermarried with the upper valley families of notables and dominated the election of the 1960s: Wakîl Mahmûd Khân s/o Jôra Elbêgî. One Hazara family stood out at that time: Ja'far Khân whose son Muhammad 'Alî Khân led the first rising in Kishindeh/ Sholgara against the communist government in 1978 and was killed early on. Throughout the middle of the twentieth century, Pashtun settlers arrived and cultivated the valley floor and specialized in lucrative rice (*shola*) cultivation. As rice required more water than any other crop, conflicts with the inhabitants of the Hazhda Nahr irrigation system below in the fertile Balkh plain were preprogrammed. The rice farmers became vulnerable in turn to the upstream communities of the neighboring districts of Kishindeh and Darra-yi Suf, which largely had been left out of the Pashtun settlement program.

94. For example, could the Hazara and Uzbek commanders above Rahmatabad village continue to block the flow of water throughout the whole year of 2000, as they had joined the Taliban army and were therefore rewarded with impunity.

95. Where the Balkh River leaves the Sholgara gorge it splits up in a network of channels such as the Nahr-i Shahi leading to Mazar-i Sharif in the east, several lead to the districts of Balkh, Dawlatabad and Chahi directly to the north, and the Nahr-i Aqcha leads via Chimtal and Charbolak to Jawzjan in the west. These channels are called the Hazhda Nahr (Eighteen Canals) as up to the nineteenth century 18 were in operation. The total amount of water fed into the system has decreased dramatically over the 30 years. Recent surveys seem to indicate that at the exit of the Sholgara gorge the output has decreased by 70% compared to the 1970s. See Jonathan L. Lee and Mervyn Patterson, *Water Resource Management and Conflict in Northern Afghanistan* (Mazar-i Sharif: Oxfam, March/April 1996); Jonathan L. Lee, *Water Resource Management on the Balkh Ab River and Hazhda Nahr Canal Network: From Crisis to Collapse* (Mazar-i Sharif: UNAMA and Central Asian Free Exchange, December 2003).

96. Sholgara in 2002 had an estimated population of 124,000 inhabitants, which was rapidly growing through the return of refugees and IDPs. Many conflict-related IDPs (a total of 2,700 families—possibly 16,200 individuals) had been displaced out of the district, mostly Hazaras and Uzbeks who had taken refuge in Darra-yi Suf during the Taliban period. Sholgara also hosted a major non-conflict related IDP population of 7,700 families (approximately 45,000 individuals) due to the drought of 1999–2001 from neighboring districts. Numbers reflect survey and estimates carried out by WFP and UNHCR in late summer 2001.

97. Of Junbish, Hajji Habib—Division 95 commander with general rank, who originally had been a Jamiat commander—Hajji Bashir, Khal Boy, Mullah Ghafur, Baba,

Mullah Malang, Mullah Ghani, Azad Khan, Yusuf Boy and Lal Mohammad all commanding subunits within Division 95 but effectively controlling different villages. The Jamiat commanders were organized in two formations: Nazar Gul, Jan Muhammad, Hazrat Muhammad, Mamur, Hajji Agha Mohammad and Abdul Mohammad were all organized in the majority Arab Division 01 jihadi commanded by Alam Khan Azadi from Balkh district. Dr. Rauf, Wahab and Ajab Khan resourced through the more ethnically mixed (Tajiks, Pashtuns) Army Corps VII directly under Ata. On the Shia Hazara side stood commanders Mohseni, Mukhtar and Hajji Ashraf, which were all affiliated with Division 38 which was only nominally within Army Corps VII, and reflected different Shia parties (Harakat and Wahdat). Wahdat also represented a number of Qandahari Shia Kuchi Pashtuns of Western Sholgara who stood in competition with the Arabs aligned with Alam Khan of Jamiat over grazing rights.

98. No party was amenable to handing over weapons, in spite of being pushed to do so by senior party figures in the Security Commission. Jamiat's senior military member of the Security Commission returned to Mazar on a pretext, thus radically limiting his party's involvement. This led to only small numbers of weapons and ammunition to be surrendered in a tokenistic fashion.

99. This had an unfortunate twist in that he commandeered three Kamaz trucks from an NGO to transport the weapons to the divisional headquarters in Dehdadi near Mazar. He subsequently told the understandably incensed NGO that UNAMA had authorized him to do so, prompting a small squabble between the humanitarian and political assistance actors.

100. Jamiat revised its policy of sending weapons into the area and now provided cash to commanders to buy them, prompting the price of AK-47s to increase threefold and weapons to be smuggled into the area from San Charak. It was estimated that Jamiat had spent $110,000 on the Sholgara operation (supporting its own commanders, buying weapons, attempting to buy Junbish commanders) during 2002.

101. Exceptionally, the cabinet of the Interim Administration in Kabul did, however, and without consultation, announce that the six Junbish and Jamiat commanders which the Security Commission had removed from Sholgara were to be sent to Kabul for trial. Of course no action was forthcoming by the local administration, and the agreement between the Security Commission and the commanders of them being "exiled" in Mazar-i Sharif was greatly weakened by this declaration. They could not be blamed for thinking that their "exile" was only the first step to physically eliminate them.

102. For example on 18 November 2002 the elders of Rahmatabad village including the *chakbâshî* of the village (a chakbâshî is the man in charge of distributing a shared harvest among a group of farmers according to the provision of land, water, seed and labor) clashed with elders from Dilbarjin, Ahmadabad, Daraghan and Sabzikar villages of Charbolak district (a downstream district bordering Sholgara) in front of the district governor's office in Boyni Qara and then later at the water dam of Sabzikar village. Near the dam in Charbulak the mentioned elders were seriously beaten by commander Muhammad Tahir of Jamiat and the inhabitants of the surrounding villages. The Rahmatabad *chakbâshî* was seriously injured and sent to the hospital. In the absence of resource management frameworks local conflicts were pre-programmed and there would always be an incentive to involve commanders to the benefit of the community. When the issue was raised in the Security Commission, the Jamiat representative took it upon him to pressurize the lower villages into giving some share of the harvest to the upstream village of Rahmatabad.

103. The district of Kishindeh in the branching valley of the Darra-yi Suf River used to be a sub-district (*alaqadârî*) of Boyni Qara/Sholgara, but was in the mid-1990s elevated to a full district. Within the district, several areas also later achieved district status. In 2002, six administrative units were found in this territory from north to south following the river Balkh: Lower Kishindeh, Aq Kupruk, Zari and Amrakh, plus the

unofficial "district" of Abdulgan. In the Darra-yi Suf Valley branching off at Lower Kishindeh two more districts had evolved: Upper Kishindeh I and Upper Kishindeh II. These units are also referred to as *mantiqas*. See the memorandum of Frédéric Roussel and Marie-Pierre Caley, *The Mantiqas: The Underground Puzzle of Afghanistan* (Kabul and Peshawar: ACTED, 1994).

104. UNAMA intercepted one weapons transport from the Mazar-i Sharif Army Corps VII to Kishindeh, but not being empowered to take possession of the weapons only could send the transport back to Army Corps VII.

105. *Aq Kupruq* means "white bridge" in Uzbek and is an important river crossing over the river Balkh and market center upwards of Sholgara and lower Kishindeh. Aq Kupruq's population is majority Tajik with Baluch and Pashtun settlers. Earlier a Hezb-i-Islami stronghold, the area converted itself into a Jamiat base following the fall of the Taliban under Mir Ahmad Nazari, who became the commanding officer of Brigade 830 within Army Corps VII.

106. Food rations and payments for the Sholgara police were delivered and the factions reported no incidents since the disarmament drive. Some figures, mostly from outside the district like commander Turan from Aq Kupruq, commander Firuz from San Charak, and commander Abd al-Hamid from Sholgara, were brazen and stupid enough to walk the bazaar with weapons. The Security Commission had to content itself with having them reprimanded, and their Jamiat leaders shamed in the regular weekly meetings. Incidents were still reported by locals, such as landmine victims (including one boy killed), in an area that commander Hajji Bashir (Junbish) had only days earlier claimed to be free of landmines. Outside the district center, commanders with armed bodyguards continued to move through the district, continuing to engage in criminal activities (killings, rapes, thefts). Hajji Agha was recalled to Army Corps VII and Hajji Bashir to his headquarters at Division 95, but no accountability could be enforced due to a factional district administration, the embryonic state of the police force, an unwillingness to apply the military justice system through the Ministry of Defense, and a complete absence of an independent civilian judiciary structure.

107. In total, 184 light weapons were collected. Most of the heavy weapons had been collected throughout 2002.

108. Mulla Ghaffur, Damulla Daud, Mohammad Zahir and Commander Daud of Junbish; Nazar Gul, Dr. Ra'uf, Abdul Mohammad and Jan Mohammad from Jamiat.

109. Guarantees were received from numerous villages. The Security Commission was of course aware that the pledge not to have weapons was incorrect, but nevertheless insisted on the pledge as it gave a contractual mandate to the police activities.

110. Besides the two international Political Affairs Officers, only three local UNAMA assistants were available for missions with a maximum of four vehicles which allowed for no more than three field teams. Until mid-2003, Coalition forces numbered less than 100 with about 40 soldiers available for duties outside their camp. As they were moving in groups of at least ten soldiers this meant that at most they also could conduct four missions at the same time. They were not mandated to cooperate with UNAMA but fell under Mission Enduring Freedom with their own objectives. As local commanders of the SAS of SF elements realized that stability was a precondition to avoid the return of Taliban and Al Qaeda, Coalition forces would on a case-by-case basis cooperate with the Security Commission. They would share some observations and could verify here and there some reported developments pertinent to the Security Commission's mandate.

111. It was only the Coalition Special Forces team that secured permission to go to Maymana after a couple of days had elapsed. They assisted in the demilitarization of the city and performed the destruction of more than 200 metric tons of ammunitions.

112. In several instances the PRT was not experienced and civilian enough in outlook to unearth the local dynamics. Soldiers, who are mostly concerned with their own protection, are never good observers of political and social realities. They are also not

competent to spot criminal behavior carried out by people wearing civilian clothes. The PRT also frequently failed to include representatives of the factions and sometimes even of the UN with its monitoring teams, sometimes going to verify reports completely on its own. This diplomatic mistake allowed factions to maintain their version of events, ultimately damaging the PRT's credibility. The posting of political advisors to the PRT while filling an obvious gap sometimes had the perverse effect of creating a cacophony of competing voices as every contributing country sent their own diplomats who frequently had widely varying skills and experience. Many of the diplomats refused to coordinate their activities with the UN.

113. Nearly all resources poured into the security sector in Kabul were misappropriated before they even reached the individual soldier. Army Corps logistical officers sold fuel on the bazaar, unit commanders pocketed the salaries in a systematic way, police stations turned on passing travelers to feed themselves, and police officers "lost" substantial amounts of pay when traveling back from Kabul. UNAMA was never empowered to supervise the resource flow, which could arguably have been done with relative ease, such as by controlling the payment of salaries, checking the collection of fiscal revenue, etc. This meant that in the absence of proper host government resources, the UN would have required much bigger resources. UNAMA did not have the means to directly protect local civilians. When in September 2003 a number of neutral people were intimidated by police officers after they publicly criticized the situation in Mazar City, and specifically the criminal nature of the police and their leadership, no practical measures were available to UNAMA. One of the most endangered individuals fled with UNAMA's assistance from Mazar, but his relatives were obliged to pay a significant sum to elements in the police to atone for his criticism. UNAMA also did not have access to quick impact funds for classic civil affairs work after mediation reached a local settlement, or even to pay for the fuel of a couple of trucks carrying weapons. The Security Commission therefore had to finance its extensive operations entirely through its members' own sources—which meant the UN had to resort to appealing to armed factions of a (closing) civil war for help.

114. For example, the two representatives of Junbish and Jamiat went to great pains to gain junior positions outside the north. Majid Rozi became commander of the Highway Police in Sarobi, and Sabur became district governor in Nijrab (both districts in Kabul Province).

115. In the week before the main battle, a small fight had erupted in Sholgara in Quland village, the site of clashes between some local Junbish- and Jamiat-aligned commanders in May/June. No reports of casualties were received. Clearly the police managed to keep Sholgara out of the main clash. However, some rearming of Sholgara district has been observed and neither side followed through on their agreement of 24 August 2003 to exile the local commanders. When approached on the issue, General Dostum suggested that "UNAMA arrest the commanders in question."

116. The cantonment of heavy weapons decisively reduced the war fighting ability of the factions and together with the disbandment of the official structures was one of the few successes in an otherwise hopelessly underperforming program. See Simonetta Rossi and Antonio Giustozzi, *Disarmamanet, Demobilisation and Reintegration of Ex-Combatants (DDR) in Afghanistan: Constraints and Limited Capabilities* (London: London School of Economics, Crisis States Research Centre Working Paper no. 2, 2006), 4.

117. The appointment was given to General Akram Khakrezwal, a committed and integral veteran mujahid from Kandahar. Obviously the new Pashtun elite around President Karzai could trust a non-Pashtun. By neglecting the local reformist forces and importing talent, the central government lost support and ultimately strengthened the control of the strongest faction in Balkh—Jamiat. By the end of October, Jamiat had strengthened its hold over Mazar-i Sharif. The control over the police was maintained

through lower positions, which the new provincial chief of police proved powerless to purge. Khakrezwal attempted to conduct a screening process to remove unwanted personnel and removed 30 illegal posts in the city. He requested the takeover of two to three districts in the city by Kabul-based units from the standby police (*pûlîs-i wâkinash-i sarî'*). The standby police units of Kabul however were commanded by General Jurat, a Panjsheri Jamiat officer, and also composed to at least 80% of Panjsheris. Jamiat also gained control over the university through the appointment of engineer Habibullah—a close associate of Ustad Ata—as chancellor, and also profited from Kabul replacing the previous deputy governor Abduh who was a member of Wahdat, with the pliable and uneducated Zahir Wahdat, who was the representative of Harakat's Anwari wing in the Security Commission. The previous mayor of Mazar-i Sharif, Darzabi, was also dismissed by the central government and replaced with pro-Jamiat Muqim. Even the last position held by a representative of Junbish—the regional representation of the Ministry of Affairs—was "purged." Chief Khakrezwal's attempts to rein in the drug trafficking brought him in direct conflict with Ustad Ata, which led to a standoff in front of the chief of police's house during June 2004 when he seized drugs reportedly belonging to traffickers loyal to the commander of Army Corps VII. Developments were to culminate in the appointment of Ata as governor of Balkh in July 2004. Some sources even ascribe his assassination in June 2005 in Kandahar to a Jamiat plot.

118. The elections for Jawzjan took place on 2 December, and following a complaint as per the rules prohibiting "senior government officials including governors, deputy governors, district administrators, mayors, army, police and National Security Directorate personnel" to participate in the elections (Presidential Decree, 18 June 2003, for the convening of the Constitonal Loya Jirga, Article 2), Dostum was "reconciled" through him being included in the president's tier of appointed delegates.

119. Interest in police reform was restricted to professional officer training at the Kabul level, and throughout 2004 a very shallow training was administered in the provinces which only put the old criminalized police in new clothes. Michael Bhatia, Kevin Lanigan, and Philip Wilkinson, "Minimal Investments, Minimal Results: The Failure of Security Policy in Afghanistan" (Kabul: Afghanistan Research and Evaluation Unit, June 2004).

120. Eckart Schiewek, "State and Human Security in the Age of Terrorism: Security Sector Reform in Afghanistan," in *State and Human Security* (Geneva: UNOG-DCAF, 2004), 71–92.

121. Examples of this argument include Mark Sedra, *Challenging the Warlord Culture: Security Sector Reform in Post-Taliban Afghanistan* (Bonn: Bonn International Center for Conversion, 2002); and Human Rights Watch, *On the Precipice: Insecurity in Northern Afghanistan,* July 2002. A recent synthesis of the literature can be found in Conrad Schetter, *Kriegsfürstentum und Bürgerkriegsökonomien in Afghanistan* [Warlordism and Civil War Economies in Afghanistan] (Cologne: Lehrstuhl für Internationale Politik, 2004).

122. Antonio Giustozzi, *"Good State" vs. "Bad" Warlords?: A Critique of State-Building Strategies in Afghanistan* (London: Crisis State Programme Working Paper 51, London School of Economics, 2004); and Giustozzi, *Respectable Warlords?: The Transition from War of All Against All to Peaceful Competition in Afghanistan* (London: Crisis State Programme Seminar Paper, London School of Economics, January 2003). A similar argument was made by John Jenning, "Afghanistan: The Gulf Between Report and Reality," *Middle East Intelligence Bulletin,* no. 6 (January 2004).

123. Anja Manuel and P. W. Singer, "A New Model Afghan Army," *Foreign Affairs,* vol. 81, no. 4 (July/August 2002).

124. This analysis was expressed first through the term of "Pashtun disaffection," coined around May 2002 mainly with regard to the Tajik/Panjsheri domination of the

new National Army cadres and the cabinet, and was quickly picked up by many Afghan and international policy-makers wishing to create a counterbalance against the Jamiat/Shura-yi Nazar domination in Kabul. Its most complete explanation can be found in International Crisis Group, "Afghanistan: The Problem of Pashtun Alienation," August 2003. See also the valid critique of a "Karzai-fronted, but Fahim-dominated government" by Larry Goodson, "Afghanistan's Long Road to Reconstruction," *Journal of Democracy,* vol. 14 (January 2003): 82–99, at 94. In a gradual process starting from the Emergency Loya Jirga of mid-2002, the biggest share of the cabinet positions and key ministries was acquired by educated returnees from the pre-war establishment, which happened to be nearly all Pashtuns. By December 2004 most power positions within the cabinet had been occupied by Pashtuns. Also a majority of the governors and the biggest groups of officers in the army and police now are Pashtun.

125. Article 20: The National Anthem of Afghanistan shall be in Pashtu and mention "Allahu Akbar" and the names of the ethnic groups of Afghanistan. See also on other issues, Gait Archambeaud, *Le principe d'égalité et la Constitution de l'Afghanistan de janvier 2004* (Paris: L'Harmattan, 2005).

126. Islamization started with adding the adjective "Islamic" to the designation of the Interim Administration and later adopting the title of "Islamic Republic" at the Constitutional Loya Jirga. In the public sphere, an "Islamic" agenda was pursued through witchhunts of "converts." The feeling of the need to Islamize culminated in early 2006 in the reintroduction of the "religious police" *(amr bi'l-ma'ruf wa nahiy 'an al-munkar),* once a staple of the Taliban.

127. Michael Bhatia, "The Future of the Mujahideen: Legitimacy, Legacy and Demobilization in Post-Bonn Afghanistan," *International Peacekeeping,* vol. 14 (2007): 90–107.

128. The "new" project is to "recruit competent and credible professionals to public service on the basis of merit; establish a more effective, accountable and transparent administration at all levels of Government; and implement measurable improvements in fighting corruption, upholding justice and the rule of law and promoting respect for the human rights of all Afghans." Ministry of Foreign Affairs of the Islamic Republic of Afghanistan, "Building on Success: The London Conference on Afghanistan," 31 January–1 February 2006, "The Afghanistan Compact," 3.

Part III
The International Perspective

11

The Afghanistan-Pakistan Border and Afghanistan's Long-Term Stability[1]

Amin Saikal

BORDER SECURITY IS AN ISSUE of perennial concern for most countries. The sovereignty and social-economic development of states are in many ways conditioned upon and determined by the ability of a state to control its borders. And, there are few political entities in modern history whose destiny and fortunes have been as much affected by border vulnerabilities as Afghanistan. As a landlocked country, with treacherously long borders and extensive cross-border ethnic ties with all its neighbors, Afghanistan's political and territorial existence as a weak state with strong society has been profoundly underlined ever since its foundation in the mid-eighteenth century by the degree to which it has been able to settle its borders and persuade its neighbors not to violate those borders. Yet Afghanistan has experienced many invasions, just as in the first four decades of its foundation it invaded some of its neighbors, and to this day it has not reached a lasting, satisfactory settlement of all its border issues.

One of its borders that has proved to be especially troublesome is that with Pakistan. Determined primarily by the British in the late nineteenth century, this border has served as a major source of dispute with Pakistan ever since the creation of the latter in 1947 out of British India. While successive Afghan governments, until the rise to power of the Pakistan-backed Taliban in 1996, had demanded a resolution of the disputes on the basis of a renegotiated settlement of the border, Pakistan's refusal to do so had resulted in enduring tensions and at times open border clashes between the two sides. Since the advent of the internationally backed post-Taliban government of Hamid Karzai, the issue has once again become a critical source of anxiety for Kabul. This time, at stake is the security, stability and reconstruction of Afghanistan. It is through this border not only that the remnants of the Taliban and their Al Qaeda allies continue to operate against the Karzai government and its supporting NATO forces from sanctuaries in Pakistan, but also where most of the narco-economic activities detrimental to Afghanistan's national unity and viability take place. If the border is not secured, it could seriously imperil Afghanistan's transformation. As a significant non-NATO US ally in the war on terrorism, Pakistan under President Pervez Musharraf has made a demonstrated military effort since early 2005 to hunt Al Qaeda and Taliban fighters on its side of the border and possibly enhance border security. However, this is unlikely to prove effective unless it is accompanied by a number of additional measures. They range from creating a well-resourced, formidable Afghan border guard, to a mutual acceptance of the Durand Line based on a renegotiated settlement, to Islamabad exerting jurisdiction over the "free tribal" border areas that have so far operated autonomously of Pakistan's central governments. Beyond this, what is required is a restructuring of Pakistan's fragile domestic environment, with the aim of institutionalizing democracy and marginalizing pro-Taliban and Al Qaeda Islamic extremism in Pakistani politics.

This chapter has three main objectives. This first is to provide a historical sketch of the nature of the Afghan borders and vulnerabilities to which they have given rise. The second is to focus in some detail on the Afghan-Pakistan border and the complexities associated with it. The third is to outline the possible options and measures required to make the Afghan-Pakistan border secure and mutually acceptable to the advantage of both sides.

Border Settlements

The borders of present Afghanistan were largely fixed in the late nineteenth century. They were substantially determined by the two rival imperial powers of the time—Great Britain and Tsarist Russia—with only nominal contribution by Afghan authorities. An Anglo-Russian commission demarcated the northern border in the 1870–1890s. It was fixed very much along the line of the Oxus or Amu Darya (River) from Pamir to today's Turkmenistan, and the Oxus Line was linked westward to Iran's northern boundary. In the process, Afghanistan ceded the small piece of territory of Panjdeh, which the Russians had seized in 1885. However, in return it gained a fairly stable border, which was further upheld by the Afghan-Soviet agreement of 1946 with some adjustments to compensate for changes in the course of flow of the Oxus River.[2] The Thalweg (mid-channel) of the river was defined with more precision as forming the borderline between the two countries. Following the original determination of the Oxus Line, the latter was extended eastwards to meet Chinese Turkestan, which created a short Afghan-Chinese border. Similarly, Great Britain played an overarching role in the determination of the Afghan-Persian border. To counter Tsarist Russia's ambitions and its growing friendship with Persia, and the latter's renewed designs to retake Afghanistan's western province of Herat, Britain found it strategically imperative to go to war with Persia in 1856. However, a year later when the two sides signed a peace treaty, the Afghan-Persian border was also determined as part of this treaty. Apart from periodic displeasure on the part of Tehran over the distribution of the waters of the Helmand River, the border remained by and large stable over the next century. In March 1973, Afghan Prime Minister Mohammed Mussa Shafiq, who was keen to see Afghanistan benefiting from Iran's oil wealth and reducing its dependence on the Soviet Union, decided also to settle the issue of water distribution and its associated complications. He signed an agreement with his Iranian counterpart to this effect, which was subsequently reaffirmed by President Mohammed Daoud (1973–1978), strengthening the permanency of the border between the two countries.[3]

While the northern and western borders endured with as much stability as could be expected, the determination of Afghanistan's southern and eastern border—the longest of all borders with a continuous length of 2,200 kilometers—with at first British India and then its successor Pakistan, from 1947, was to prove controversial and contentious. This border, commencing from the intersection of the border with China in the northeast and extending to the east, south and southwest across to where today Afghanistan, Pakistan and Iran intersect, was largely transfixed under an agreement which was signed in Kabul on November 12, 1893[4] by the Afghan ruler Amir Aburrahman Khan (1880–1901) and the head of the British Commission, Sir Mortimer Durand, who determined the course of the boundary that became known as the "Durand Line." This was done at the time when, under previous but largely British-imposed agreements, Britain had control over Afghan foreign policy and finances. The course of the Line was fixed more by the dictates of British strategic interests in competition with Tsarist Russia within the frame of the "Great Game" than by any serious consideration of how it could affect the future of Pathan or Pashtun tribes that populated the two sides of the border, and the economic life and nomads of landlocked Afghanistan with the British controlling all the border passes.[5]

Although Amir Abdurrahman Khan consented to Durand's demarcation and an Anglo-Afghan commission supervised its implementation, the Amir and many in his entourage remained dissatisfied with the whole development. The Amir's objection was that the Durand demarcation not only divided Pashtun tribes, who have historically constituted the largest ethnic cluster in Afghanistan but was a minority at the time within British India, but also deprived the Afghans of their historical claim over what is today Pakistan's Northwest Frontier Province and parts of its Baluchistan Province. Yet, while he had been a witness to Russian expansion in Central Asia during his stay in the area in the 1870s and had become very distrustful of them and mindful of their ambitions southward, he needed to maintain British goodwill and could not afford to antagonize them. The result was that he signed the Durand Line agreement under pressure, but possibly with an understanding that the borderline would be open to renegotiation when appropriate.[6] This was not, however, the understanding of the British side, which viewed the Anglo-Afghan agreement on the issue as final. Some from the Afghan side have also intimated that the 1893 agreement was to be valid for one century—that is, expiring in 1993. But again no documentary evidence exists to substantiate this claim and the Pakistanis have discounted it in its entirety.

Political Complexities

Whatever the basis of Afghan dissatisfaction and claims, the Durand Line was implicitly, if not explicitly, confirmed in the Anglo-Afghan treaty of 1921 that formally acknowledged Afghanistan's full independence from Britain, and the Anglo-Afghan treaty of 1933. Yet, like Aburrahman Khan, neither King Amanullah (1919–1929) nor King Nadir Shah (1929–1933) of Afghanistan was in a position to challenge the British on the border issue. They were both domestically and regionally weak, and therefore keen to maintain good relations with British India and Soviet Russia if they were to rebuff the two powers' traditional rivalry and secure the necessary opportunity to consolidate their power and generate a stable national order. This, however, did not mean that subsequent Afghan leaders would do the same. It was not just the question of physical and sociological problems arising from the Durand Line, but also the extent to which future political leaders on both sides of the Line would deem it expedient to exploit the border issue for domestic and regional purposes. The 1947 partition of the Indian subcontinent into two independent states—the Hindu-dominated India and Muslim-dominated Pakistan—opened the way for such a development. It came in the context of Pakistan's inheritance of the border issue with Afghanistan and the creation of serious Indo-Pakistan border disputes, especially over Kashmir, as well as a change of ruling guard within the Afghan royal family from 1953 against the backdrop of a new post-World War II international environment.

Encouraged by New Delhi, which was keen to see the newly created Pakistan remain regionally subordinate to "mother India," the Afghan monarchy found it appropriate to call for a resettlement of the border on the ground that Afghanistan's previous consent to the 1893 agreement with British India was under duress and that that agreement now had to be renegotiated with Pakistan. In the wake of Pakistan's independence, Kabul rapidly cast its net wider to include support for the right of the Pakistani Pashtuns to "self-determination" within an entity that it called "Pashtunistan" to be created out of Pakistan's Northwest Frontier and Baluchistan Provinces.[7] In this, Kabul found a very willing ally in New Delhi, which viewed the Afghan claim as an important assistance to its cause against Pakistan. To make its point sharply, Kabul initially withheld Afghanistan's endorsement of Pakistan's admission to the United Nations. Although it soon rescinded its opposition, its initial action caused deep concern on the part of the Pakistani leadership, which now had reason to believe that it was faced with two "hostile" neighbors. Afghanistan's action also contributed to serious tension and skirmishes along the Afghan-Pakistan border. This concern was further compounded by two other developments. One was the onset of the global Cold War. Another was the rise of the brother–in-law and rival cousin of Afghan King Mohammed Zahir, Mohammed Daoud, to the prime ministership. In the context of the first development and of Pakistan's problems with India, Pakistan drifted into the US orbit, while India gravitated towards the

Soviet Union. Meanwhile Afghanistan sought to maintain its traditional neutrality in world politics but leaned towards the Soviet Union and hardened its position on the border with Pakistan.[8]

Daoud was essentially an autocratic Pashtunist nationalist and reformer, with a serious interest in Afghanistan's modernization along socialist lines. Upon assuming the prime ministership in 1953, he was keen to achieve three objectives. One was to enhance the cause of a Pashtun-centered Afghan nationalism. For this, he considered as imperative Afghanistan's support for the right of Pashtuns in Pakistan to "self-determination," and a settlement of the Afghan-Pakistan border problems in favor of this and as a way of securing access to international waters for landlocked Afghanistan. Another was to engage in a speedy process of modernization of Afghanistan, somewhat along the lines that King Amanullah had attempted with only partial success in the 1920s. The third was to preserve Afghanistan's traditional neutrality in world politics and thus to avoid a complication of the country's relations with its powerful northern neighbor, the Soviet Union, and to deflect any pressure to join a regional pact in support of the US and its allies in the US-Soviet global Cold War.[9]

Yet he needed massive foreign financial, economic and military assistance to achieve these objectives. Lacking any interest in Marxism-Leninism and considering atheistic communist ideology as totally unsuitable for Muslim Afghanistan, he first turned to the US for help. However, the US rejected his request on the basis that Afghanistan was not strategically and economically important and had a border dispute with the US's new ally, Pakistan. His turn to the Soviet Union proved very fruitful. Moscow not only embarked on a generous program of economic and military aid, amounting to over $2 billion over the next two and half decades, but also sided with Afghanistan in its dispute with Pakistan. As Daoud's program of modernization took off, he also became increasingly assertive over the issue of "Pashtunistan" and receptive to closer ties with New Delhi. The US refusal to mediate a settlement of the Afghan-Pakistan dispute, as desired by Daoud, only pushed the Afghan leader more towards the Soviet Union. Meanwhile, Washington soon realized the weakness of its policy approach, and it set out to provide some economic assistance. But its aid, amounting to some $500 million over the next two decades, proved to be too little and no match to that of the Soviet Union.[10]

Afghan-Pakistan relations continued to deteriorate, resulting by 1961 in an increase in border skirmishes and border troop deployment, and a breakdown of diplomatic relations. As Pakistan blocked Afghan transit trade, the whole development turned out to be more costly than Daoud had anticipated. Not only did Afghan dependence on and therefore vulnerability to the Soviet Union increase, but also the economic impact of the crisis on Afghanistan became unsustainable. This finally prompted Daoud to resign his post in 1963. King Zahir Shah, whose role had been overshadowed by Daoud, took over and unleashed a series of domestic and foreign policy changes designed to deliver a limited experiment with democracy to Afghanistan on the one hand, and normalize relations with Pakistan and rationalize Afghanistan's dependence on the USSR on the other. The successive governments of the period of "New Democracy" (1964–1973) deemphasized the issue of Pashtunistan, with a call for a peaceful resolution of differences with Pakistan, and sought to diversify Afghanistan's foreign relations, albeit with a degree of care not to cause any major concern for the Soviet Union.[11]

The return of Daoud to power, with help from some pro-Soviet communist elements, in a bloodless coup in 1973, and his declaration of Afghanistan as a republic with good neighborly relations with the Soviet Union, but "a political difference over the Pashtunistan issue"[12] with Pakistan once again raised the specter of border tensions between the two sides. However, as he was above all an ardent autocratic nationalist, Daoud soon turned his back on his communist helpers and, as part of this, also sought to rationalize relations with the Soviet Union and normalize relations with Pakistan. He turned to pro-western Egypt and oil-rich Iran and Saudi Arabia for economic assistance. He also once more approached the US to assist in reducing his dependence on local communists and their Soviet patron, although to little avail as Washington under the "Nixon Doctrine" by now had relegated the responsibility for developments in the region to its staunchest and most powerful regional ally, Mohammad Reza, shah of Iran.[13]

If there was one recurring theme of Afghan-Pakistan relations, it was the two sides' use of the border dispute, although more so by Afghanistan than by Pakistan, for domestic and foreign policy purposes whenever required. With the successful pro-Soviet coup of April 1978, the subsequent Soviet invasion of Afghanistan 20 months later to maintain its long-built influence in the country, and the concurrent fall of the shah in a mass revolution, the turn came for Pakistan to seek a central role in determining the future of Afghanistan. As Pakistan assumed a "frontline state" position to defeat Soviet communism in Afghanistan, now with the active support of the US and its allies as well as many Muslim countries and China, one objective urgently gripped its military ruler, General Zia ul-Haq—to make sure that the border issue would never again be raised by Afghanistan as a point of contention. His support of the Afghan Islamic resistance forces, the mujahideen, was premised on helping primarily those Pashtun Islamist mujahideen groups who could enable Pakistan to secure a post-communist government in Afghanistan which would be receptive to Pakistan's wider regional strategic interests. These interests included a transformation of Afghanistan into a source of "strategic depth" against India.[14] As the Afghan-Pakistan border was wide open to traffic for mujahideen and their Pakistani and other international helpers, the Durand Line dispute became a thing of the past and its legitimacy as an international border was no longer questioned.

As post-Soviet Afghanistan plunged into domestic fighting between various mujahideen groups, with a predominantly non-Pashtun force under the celebrated resistance leader, Ahmed Shah Massoud, emerging as central to the operation of government in Kabul, Islamabad felt that it was once again failing in its objectives. The main Pashtun client of Pakistan's military intelligence (ISI), Gulbuddin Hekmatyar's Hezb-i-Islami, proved inadequate to take over power in Kabul. Weary of Massoud's strong nationalist Islamist stand, the ISI finally found it expedient in late 1994 to raise a fresh theocratic force—the Pashtun-dominated Taliban militia—to counter Massoud and his supporters. ISI also forged a close alliance between the Taliban militia and Al Qaeda as a means to bring in Arab money and fighters to support the Taliban rule. This development also led to the transformation of Afghanistan into the epicenter of international terrorism and all kinds of other illegal activities as the Taliban-Al Qaeda alliance, backed by the ISI, succeeded by 1996–1998 in pushing Massoud and his forces into the northeastern corner of Afghanistan.[15] This was a development with which Washington remained content as the Taliban's anti-Iranian posture and close ties with Pakistan and two Arab allies of the US—Saudi Arabia and United Arab Emirates—suited its wider strategic goals in the region.[16] For Pakistan, the rule of the Taliban enabled it to achieve what it had long sought—a receptive Afghanistan with an open boundary with Pakistan.

However, the events of September 11, 2001 swung the pendulum once again—this time against the Taliban, Al Qaeda and the ISI but in favor of the anti-Taliban forces within the predominantly non-Pashtun United Front or the so-called "Northern Alliance," which had been led by Massoud until his assassination by Al Qaeda agents on September 9. The US, which had scaled back its involvement in Afghanistan following the Soviet troop withdrawal by 1989, had left the country at the mercy of its warring factions and neighbors, most importantly Pakistan. The US, which had done little to stop Pakistan's support of the Taliban, was now prompted to act against the Taliban and Al Qaeda. While warning the regime of General Musharraf—who had seized power in 1999 and had described Pakistan's backing of the Taliban regime as a "security imperative" for Pakistan,[17] with repeated calls on the international community to recognize the Taliban as the legitimate government of Afghanistan (as Pakistan and two Arab allies, Saudi Arabia and UAE had done)—either to support the "war on terror" or become a target. The US also embraced the United Front as an ally. The latter's leaders were so incensed by the killing of Massoud and by Pakistan's "creeping invasion" of Afghanistan that they were more than willing to help the US and its allies to topple the Taliban, dismantle Al Qaeda, and end Pakistan's influence in Afghanistan. It was also their expectation that in the process the US would punish Pakistan for patronizing the Taliban and the Taliban-Al Qaeda alliance.

However, Musharraf's clever move to join the war on terror against Pakistan's clients not only spared Pakistan of any American recrimination, but also rendered the country once again a strategic asset for the US in overthrowing the Taliban and waging war against Al Qaeda and its associates within a wider arena. Despite their valuable assistance in the success of the US military campaign and subsequent contributions to Afghanistan's transition under a US-backed Pashtun opponent of the Taliban, Hamid Karzai, the Northern Alliance leaders' expectations were soon to be confounded. The Musharraf regime emerged stronger from Pakistan's Afghan fiasco, as the Bush Administration decided to buy it off as a critical ally. The Administration's thinking may have been that if it brings Pakistan within its orbit of influence, it would be able to achieve several objectives. One is to have Pakistan's cooperation to hunt down key Al Qaeda and Taliban figures and activists, including Osama Bin Laden and Mullah Mohammed Omar, who are at large, and to entice the Musharraf regime to change the political culture of many Pakistanis (especially in North West Frontier and Baluchestan) away from radical to moderate pro-US Islam. Another is to enable Musharraf, who has proved to be more receptive to the US than could have been expected, to help the US in whatever way necessary to secure the long and treacherous Afghan-Pakistan border against cross-border infiltrations by the remnants of the Taliban and Al Qaeda for operations in Afghanistan. Washington has considered these measures to be of paramount importance to its success in the transformation of Afghanistan and the war on terror. A further objective has been to bring about changes whereby a nuclear armed Pakistan would become a beacon rather than being a source of menace for regional, and for that matter, international peace and stability.

Whatever Washington's claim of success in other areas with Pakistan, Pakistan's past support of the Taliban and the Taliban-Al Qaeda alliance has added to the political complexities of the Afghan-Pakistan border. It has deeply concerned many Afghans about Pakistan's motives and ambitions, leading them to become highly distrustful of its leaders. Since the overthrow of the Taliban, the Musharraf government has declared full support for the Karzai government, and has repeatedly emphasized a resolve to do everything in its power to help Afghanistan's processes of stabilization and reconstruction, and to prevent illegal cross-border traffic. It has certainly taken a number of practical measures in this respect, including close intelligence and military cooperation with the US forces along the border and engaging, especially since early 2005, in a military campaign against the remnants of Al Qaeda on Pakistan's side of the border, to give substance to its changed policy behavior. It has also eased border restrictions for Afghan transit and has improved communications with Kabul.

Yet little has been achieved in terms of border security enhancement. Neither has the flow from Pakistan of the remnants of the Taliban and Al Qaeda fighters, as well as Hekmatyar's supporters, substantially diminished, nor has there been any noticeable drop in the volume of smuggling activities and drug trafficking across the border. Most of the evidence points to the contrary. Tension along the border, many parts of which are not clearly defined, has resulted in a number of exchanges of fire between the Afghan and Pakistani border guards, with Kabul accusing Pakistan of making a forward thrust into Afghan territory three times in 2003–2005. The most serious clash was reported on July 29, 2003, which caused anti-Pakistan demonstrations in Kabul and recriminatory exchanges between Kabul and Islamabad.[18] These developments have reinforced the view among many Afghans that Pakistan continues to harbor ambitions towards Afghanistan, and that the Musharraf government's policy attitude needs to be treated with caution and skepticism until such time as all border violations from the Pakistani side stop.

On the other hand, the Karzai Administration has remained weak, with only limited writ outside Kabul. It is essentially protected by a NATO-led International Security Assistance Force (ISAF) and US-led Coalition forces fighting the Taliban-led insurgency, especially in the areas along the border with Pakistan. It is therefore badly in need of all the cooperation it can acquire from neighboring states—Pakistan in particular—to stabilize and rebuild the war-torn Afghanistan. This, together with the Karzai government's almost total dependence on the US and Washington's treatment of Pakistan as a non-NATO ally, has left Kabul with little or no leverage to pressure Pakistan for improvement on the present situation along the border, let alone to renew Afghanistan's past concerns over the border. Even so, it has repeatedly complained that Pakistan has not done enough in relation to border security, resulting in incriminatory exchanges between Presidents Karzai and Musharraf in early 2006. This complaint was also echoed by Zalmay Khalilzad, presidential envoy and US ambassador to Afghanistan (2003–2005), drawing official protests from the Pakistani government.[19] An Afghan-Pakistan-US tripartite commission was established in early 2003 and since its first meeting on June 17, 2003 it has met a number of times to discuss how to improve border security and to deal with problems arising from it. However, the commission's meetings have focused mainly on how to "further coordinate their efforts for combating acts of terrorism."[20] They have not entailed a discussion of Afghanistan's traditional demand for a mutually acceptable border settlement.

Although the Musharraf government is certainly a lot better resourced than its Afghan counterpart to address some of Kabul's concerns, its ability to secure the border still remains limited, for a number of reasons. First, the border is long, rugged and full of treacherous terrain, with numerous primary and secondary points of crossing, and therefore not easy for any force to control. It is populated on both sides by a variety of Pashtun tribes who have traditionally been fierce in maintaining their individual sense of identity and autonomy. On the Pakistani side, they have historically lived within what has become known as the "free tribal belt." While maintaining a strong determination to oppose any outside encroachment, they have also shown flexibility whenever appropriate to make deals and counter-deals with one another and the Afghan and Pakistani authorities for pecuniary gains whenever they have found it opportune to support their autonomous existence. While successive Pakistani and Afghan governments may have controlled the main crossing points, such as at Torkham, Chaman, Parachinar and Quetta—the secondary crossing points have by and large remained within the sphere of tribal and nomadic influences. Neither British India nor their Pakistani successors nor Afghanistan and its Soviet invaders of the 1980s had ever been able to gain full control over this border.

Second, both sides of the border are awash with light and heavy weapons, and are the domain of goods smugglers and drug traffickers, some of whom have their own private militias. While this has been so traditionally, the Soviet invasion of Afghanistan and the US-led response to it terribly exacerbated the problem. With Afghanistan returning to be the largest poppy grower and heroin producer in the world, and with a lucrative weapon market thriving along the border—with involvement of some officials from the two sides of the border—many individuals and forces have now acquired a capacity to operate along the border with virtual impunity.[21] This is a development that cannot easily be reversed without well-coordinated and resourced political, economic and military strategies on the part of all governments involved.[22]

Third, the border region is infested with forces of Islamic radicalism, which today strongly support or sympathize with Al Qaeda and the Taliban. It is these forces that have also gained a controlling share, as a result of the late 2002 provincial elections, in the North West Frontier and Baluchestan provincial governments. Musharraf held these elections as part of a process of limited democratization to boost his own popularity, but they backfired as many voters sought to take revenge on him for being too closely allied with the United States. Al Qaeda, the Taliban and Hekmatyar's activists continue to enjoy sanctuaries along the border, with an ability to cross the border without much trouble to fight in Afghanistan, and to deflect search and destroy missions by the US forces and their allies.

Fourth, despite Islamabad's insistence that Pakistan is no longer involved in any hostile operations in Afghanistan, this does not seem to be entirely so. Some retired and active elements from Pakistan's ISI and military are reportedly still involved in support of the Taliban. These elements have been very disappointed over the "loss" of Taliban rule in Afghanistan, and are troubled by India's increased activities in Afghanistan since the fall of the Taliban. At the same time, they believe that the current level of involvement by the US and its allies in Afghanistan will not last very long and that ultimately the opportunity will come for Pakistan to renew its strategic involvement in the country. One influential figure who is often cited in this context is the former head of ISI, retired General Hamid Gul, who played a key role not only in orchestrating mujahideen resistance to the Soviets, but also in building Pakistan's support of the Taliban. It was reported that the ISI even had a role in the anti-US protests that swept Afghanistan in May 2005 over a claim in *Newsweek* magazine, which was subsequently confirmed by declassified FBI documents, that the US guards in Guantanamo Bay prison camp had desecrated a copy of the Koran and flushed it down a toilet.[23]

Options

To secure this border what is required is a large volume of human and material resources, and a mutual political acceptance of the border. In other words, two imperatives are needed at the minimum. One is to have a sufficient number of well-trained and appropriately armed border guards, adequately resourced border posts, and extensive ground and air surveillance, involving sophisticated electronic monitoring equipment as well as early warning and communication systems, back-up forces and extensive cross-border cooperation. Another is to re-determine those parts of the border that are not clearly defined and to secure a mutual declaration of the border by Afghanistan and Pakistan as their permanent international boundary.

Currently, Afghanistan is in no position to meet any of the resource requirements sufficiently. Several ministries, ranging from defense to interior are in charge of the border security, but without much coordination and effectiveness. Although Kabul has embarked on a program to raise an adequate border guard force and back-up military units, it is far from achieving this objective. Even when these forces are ready, it will not be able to resource such a force sufficiently and meet other border surveillance and control requirements. Yet it desperately needs to secure this border, and reach a final settlement with Pakistan.

On the other hand, Pakistan is better positioned than Afghanistan to enhance the security of the border from its side. But it is faced with severe limitations, for three important reasons. First, many of its military and border security resources are still tied up to its eastern frontiers with India. Although there has been some thaw in Indo-Pakistan relations since early 2005, their fundamental disputes are not resolved. As long as this remains the case, Pakistan cannot be expected to shift many of its resources across to its border with Afghanistan. Second, Islamabad cannot achieve progress on problems with India if it does not first generate the right domestic environment to enable it to make the foreign policy compromises required to reach a settlement with India. One way to improve the domestic situation is to move Pakistan on a path of genuine secular democratization, whereby a publicly mandated government would not need to use the disputes with India as a major foreign policy diversion and would not view Afghanistan as possible "strategic depth" against India. Only under such circumstances would a Pakistani government be in a position to strike a lasting historic deal with India. Third, despite its public expression of full support for Afghanistan's transition, Islamabad refuses to recognize the fact that, whatever the past claims and counter-claims over the Afghan-Pakistan border, there is a need for a final settlement of this border to be signed between the two sides in order to ease many Afghans' concerns and help them to shake off their negative perceptions of Pakistan.

The only power that can help to secure the border and mediate between the two sides to reach a final settlement is the United States. Washington has the necessary capacity, as well as leverage with both Kabul and Islamabad to achieve this objective. But its role too has remained circumscribed. The US involvement in Afghanistan is very much tied to its war on terrorism, with a commitment to assist Afghanistan only in proportion to what it takes to destroy Al Qaeda and prevent the return of the Taliban to power. As such, its contributions to securing, stabilizing and rebuilding Afghanistan have been limited. This has allowed it to divert many of the resources which should have been invested in

Afghanistan to Iraq. Its military and economic assistance has been enough to keep resurgent Taliban and Al Qaeda activities largely confined to the south and southeast, and to help the Karzai government to remain afloat in Kabul, but not much more than this to secure effectively Afghanistan's border with Pakistan.[24]

If Washington is genuinely committed, as it has repeatedly said it is, to Afghanistan's transformation into a viable state with a democratic order, then it needs to commit far more resources than it has so far to the country. It will need to do this without seeking to have a determining role in Afghan politics for no other reason than its own wider geostrategic reasons. Further, it needs to do whatever it takes to secure the historically troubled Afghan-Pakistan border and enable the two sides to reach a final settlement. If this means that it has to pressure Pakistan to become an effective party through both domestic reforms and foreign policy changes, then let it be the case. The problems of Afghanistan and Pakistan cannot be wished away. There may be lulls in the relations from time to time, but these should not hide the deeply troubled currents underlying relations between the two sides.

Notes

1. This chapter was originally published as "Securing Afghanistan's Border," *Survival,* vol. 48, no. 1 (Spring 2006): 129–141. It is reprinted by permission of Taylor and Francis. The journal is available online at http://www.informaworld.com.

2. For a detailed discussion, see Alastair Lamb, *Asian Frontiers: Studies in a Continuing Problem* (London: F. W. Cheshire, 1968), 86–89; Louis Dupree, *Afghanistan* (Princeton: Princeton University Press, 1980), Chapter 18.

3. Amin Saikal, *The Rise and Fall of the Shah* (Princeton: Princeton University Press, 1980), 173.

4. For the text of the agreement, see Ludwig W. Adamec, *Afghanistan 1900–1923: A Diplomatic History* (Berkeley: University of California Press, 1967), 176–177.

5. Vertan Gregorian, *The Emergence of Modern Afghanistan: Politics of Reform and Modernization, 1880–1946* (Stanford: Stanford University Press, 1969), 159.

6. For an Afghan perspective on the course of developments, see Mir Gholam Mohammad Ghobar, *Afghanistan in the Course of History,* vol. 2, translated by Sharif A. Fayez (Herndon: All Prints Inc., 2001), 189–196.

7. The Afghan case for Pashtunistan is made poignantly by Abdul Rahman Pazhwak, who was Afghan ambassador to the UN and president of the General Assembly in 1966, in his publication *Pakhtunistan: A New State in Central Asia* (London: The Royal Afghan Embassy, 1960). Also see Arnold Fletcher, *Afghanistan: Highway of Conquest* (Westport: Greenwood Press, 1965), Chapter 17.

8. For a detailed discussion, see Amin Saikal, *Modern Afghanistan: A History of Struggle and Survival* (London: I. B. Tauris, 2004), Chapter 5; Henry S. Bradsher, *Afghanistan and the Soviet Union* (Durham: Duke University Press Policy Studies, 1983), Chapter 2; Barnett R. Rubin, *The Fragmentation of Afghanistan: State Formation and Collapse in the International System* (New Haven: Yale University Press, 1995), Chapter 4.

9. For details, see Saikal, *Modern Afghanistan,* Chapters 5 and 7; and Dupree, *Afghanistan,* Chapter 23.

10. For a detailed discussion, see J. Bruce Amstutz, *Afghanistan: The First Five Years of Soviet Occupation* (Washington, DC: National Defense University Press, 1986), Chapter 2.

11. See Saikal, *Modern Afghanistan,* Chapter 6.

12. For the text of Daoud's speech, see "Mohammad Daoud Proclaims Afghanistan Republic," in Abdul Aziz Danishyar, ed., *The Afghanistan Republic Annual—1974* (Kabul: Government Press, 1974), 2–4.

13. Saikal, *Modern Afghanistan,* 180.

14. For a detailed discussion of Pakistan's objectives and role in the Afghan resistance, see William Maley, *The Afghanistan Wars* (London: Palgrave Macmillan, 2002), Chapter 3.

15. See Ahmed Rashid, *Taliban: Militant Islam, Oil and Fundamentalism in Central Asia* (New Haven: Yale University Press, 2001), especially Parts 1–2.

16. See Richard Mackenzie, "The United States and the Taliban," in William Maley, ed., *Fundamentalism Reborn?: Afghanistan and the Taliban* (London: Hurst and Co., 2001), Chapter 5.

17. Amin Saikal, *Islam and the West: Conflict or Cooperation?* (London: Palgrave Macmillan, 2003), 106.

18. BBC News, 24 July 2003.

19. For Khalilzad's criticism of Pakistan and a perspective on how Musharraf policies have revived a border problem that his successors had been trying to banish for 50 years, see Zia Sarhadi, "Pakistan Paying a High Price for Musharraf's Urge to Please the US," *Muslimedia International,* 16–31 August 2003.

20. *Daily Times,* 1 August 2004.

21. See Paul Watson, "The Lure of Opium Wealth Is a Potent Force in Afghanistan," *Los Angeles Times,* 28 May 2005.

22. For a detailed discussion of drug production and strategies to control it, see Amir Zada Asad and Robert Harris, *The Politics and Economics of Drug Production on the Pakistan-Afghanistan Border* (Hampshire: Ashgate, 2003).

23. Sarah Chayes, "With a Little Help from Our Friends," *New York Times,* 26 May 2005.

24. If two developments clearly illustrate the extent of US failures in Afghanistan, they are the decision in 2004 by Médecins sans Frontières (Doctors without Borders) to pull out of Afghanistan after 24 years of involvement in the country because of insecurity and use of humanitarian aid by Coalition forces for gathering intelligence on terrorism, and the warning by the US government to its citizens not to travel to Afghanistan. AFP, 24 July 2004; ABC Radio Australia News, 31 July 2004.

12

Islam and the Transformative Power of Tradition[1]

Anna Seleny

MOMENTOUS POLITICAL STRUGGLES EVERYWHERE HINGE partly but crucially on contenders' interpretations of what is "imaginable" and "doable."[2] In the Middle East, as in Europe prior to Westphalia, these interpretations have been forged and reshaped at the nexus of religion and politics.[3] Indeed, I argue that pragmatism, decentralization and pluralism—three attributes often associated with modern democracies—have long made Islam a political-cultural resource that is both powerful in its effect and available for use by a variety of competing groups.

More recently, the spread of madrassas, the dispersion of communication technologies (audio and video), and ironically, mass higher education all have made Islam's political-cultural resources accessible in novel forms to an increasingly complex pool of activists and aspirants to leadership and power. But while multiple anti-modernist groups exploit these resources, secular modernizers, in contrast, typically refrain from doing so. Authoritarian governments, moreover, restrict secular associations that could articulate alternative or complementary claims about the role of Islamic teachings in social and political life.

The political opportunity structure is thus distorted from different angles, often to the detriment of self-described moderns and their secular ideologies. The most obvious example, though by no means the only one, is the retreat by non-Islamist groups from political spaces that now seem lost to the religious "street." More generally still, the public voices of Islamist groups have become disproportionately prominent, especially those of puritanical and supremacist activists who attract adherents by simplifying or even warping Islam's message.

In sum, Islam's hallmark attributes and key actors' strategic choices have combined to produce a distorted opportunity structure and an exaggerated impression of Islamism's uniformity, scope and strength. But none of this is irreversible because, as we will see, liberal and pro-democratic Muslims are beginning to reclaim the transformative power of Islamic tradition.

Extant Explanations

Recent scholarly attempts to explain the apparent surge in Islamism have not been wholly satisfactory. Accounts that attribute Islamism's rise to the legacy of colonialism tend to focus on frustrated nationalist aspirations, weak and/or illegitimate state institutions, pervasive corruption, and acute economic dislocation. But then, why the rise of Islamism and not some other form of protest or concentrated attempt at political change? After all, the same underlying factors have been implicated in a range of revolutionary upheavals, from Russia, China, and Vietnam to Mexico and Cuba.

The argument that Islam itself generates a totalitarian blend of religion and politics is also flawed. Islamic law does rest on a theistic understanding of sovereignty.[4] But this does not necessarily entail a closed system of thought and action. Indeed, the classical lineage of Islamic juridical tradition was highly pluralistic, and thus not particularly conducive to monolithic constructs. Moreover, Muslim political actors have successfully opened up non-Islamist avenues to politics, so much so that the notable state-builders of the past century were, in the main, secular modernizers who collided rather than colluded with religious leaders.[5] Finally, it should be noted that a number of countries with Muslim majorities or substantial Muslim populations—Bahrain, Dubai, India, Indonesia, Jordan, Kuwait and Malaysia—have tended to become more cosmopolitan and less prone to Islamism.[6]

Even the Taliban's ascent in Afghanistan, which can be presented either as a case of culture run amok or as an extension of geopolitical disruptions, suggests a far more complex dynamic. Afghanistan was an increasingly pluralistic and relatively stable country prior to the murder of modernizer President Mohammed Daoud Khan in 1978 and the Soviet invasion of 1979.[7] But even then, the central government never exerted full control over the provinces, and the post-invasion governments, corrupt and repressive, built a political center so feeble it had virtually collapsed before the Soviet retreat.[8] The subsequent power vacuum intensified both the ambitions of domestic political entrepreneurs and Saudi Arabia's determination to encircle Iran, where Ayatollah Khomeini would soon lead the only fully Shia state on the Muslim map. The Saudi strategy, based on the export of Wahhabism to Pakistan and Afghanistan, undoubtedly worked to the Taliban's advantage. At the same time, however, the Taliban's identity, coherence and agenda—essential to their rise and dominance—all hinged on the political strength of their brand of extreme Islamism.

For some scholars, this strength has been historically associated with the ruptures of modernization, which is said to have severed the shared worldview that once tied Muslim rulers and subjects. Specifically on this view, as official power holders and subaltern groups increasingly diverged in their understandings of their respective duties and prerogatives, extremist variants of Islam seized the hearts and minds of the masses, particularly the uneducated and the poor.[9] But although modernization has wrought havoc on traditional state-society relations everywhere it has spread, including its European cradle, no predetermined or mechanical correspondence obtained between modernization's ruptures and the emergent predominance of a particular ideological or political force in the West. Similarly, modernization attempts in the Arab world from the 1950s through the 1970s stimulated the growth of organized leftist movements, for example, that were deeply secular.[10]

This last objection applies by extension to the claim that the growing strength of Islamism is best explained as a reaction to the loss of community and the spread of western individualism. Such reactionary sentiments, however, are not peculiar to the Muslim experience. Xenophobia and nostalgia remained pervasive in Russia on the eve of modernity's first communist regime—a regime which, it soon became obvious, was bent on subordinating national, tribal and even familial loyalties.

Islamism's power also has been said to stem from the special persuasiveness of Islamist activists, who are willing and able, in Eric Hoffer's words, to depict the present as merely "an interlude between past and future." But the recasting of historical time is part and parcel of any sweeping vision of a reconfigured world. On this point, a final parallel with communism may be useful, since like Islamism, it treated the present as an "aberration and a deformity."[11]

More convincing accounts of Islamism's new prominence stress shifts in state-society relations. Sheri Berman has demonstrated that in Egypt nearly every vacuum that an exhausted developmental state has left behind in civil society soon becomes an opportunity target for Islamist activists.[12] Similarly, Aquil Shah has shown that state actors' divide-and-rule strategies, and their deleterious effects on political society, contribute to Islamists' sway. For example, Pakistan's Islamist parties have managed to regain electoral ground in recent years in good measure because the military has sought to consolidate its hold on state power by splintering the opposition and sponsoring religious allies.[13] These changes in civil and political society, moreover, have a synergetic quality to them. Islamist groups, for instance, use mosques and madrassas as vehicles of ideological inculcation and political mobilization in civil society; and in political society, they deploy their enhanced organizational, institutional and electoral capabilities to press for the "Islamization" of public life.[14]

But shifts in state-society relations are only part of the story. Arabs, Persians and Turks long have struggled, competed, compromised and cooperated with reference to Islam. In fact, the role that the state today plays in the rise of Islamism resembles the role it once played in the early emergence of Islam in the public sphere. In eastern Iran between the ninth and eleventh centuries, for example, the changing strategies and preferences of ruling dynasties, as well as their rise and fall, ultimately enhanced the influence and raised the profile of the ulama, first among the Iranian peoples, then across the Asiatic lands that came under the domination of Turko-Persian empires.[15]

The importance of Islamic institutions in shaping state-society relations over time is not new, either. Consider the madrassas. Between the eleventh and thirteenth centuries, Sunni scholars used these centers of higher instruction and research to shape and consolidate internal consensus on matters of dogma. Indeed, the madrassas became the frame that united the Sunni ulama. And to the extent that the ulama developed some degree of unity, they were better positioned to endure the indifference and even the hostility of state actors. This was the case from the seventeenth to nineteenth centuries, a period when the Turko-Persian empires suffered debilitation, first by tribal wars and later by European encroachment. Foreign ideologies and institutional models, moreover, gained currency among the ruling class, and secularism displaced Islamic "perspectives and ideals" from the public sphere. But the Islamic perspectives and ideals that were shunted aside by secularism in the nineteenth century did not perish. Rather, they permeated and governed a less visible complex of "informal" relations.[16]

Unforeseen outcomes of this kind can be traced to other key points in the history of Islam. One such point came early on with the attempt by four successive caliphs to dispel the traditionalist claim that the Koran always existed, and to impose by decree the alternative belief that the Koran was "created." Perceived as doctrinal imposition, the caliphs' move provoked intense resistance, and its failure helped reassert the autonomy of the "religious public sphere" from the "official sphere of rulers."[17]

The ambiguity of this dual-sphere construct allowed for contestation and settlements subject to renegotiation and even displacement by hybrid alternatives. The case of the Ottoman Empire is especially illuminating on this count. Sultans claimed "perfect wisdom and knowledge," seized the mantle of religious leadership, and ultimately even reached for the title of caliph. And yet, by the seventeenth and eighteenth centuries, these sultan-caliphs had to contend with "the ulama and janissaries of Istanbul, who frequently challenged the Sultan's authority and severely restricted his room for maneuver, especially if he wanted to implement changes." Indeed, "central-despotism" became symbiotically entwined with both "secular and religious notables" and a "patchwork of local autonomies," so much so that the Ottomans eventually relied on de facto power sharing.[18]

Time and again, Islam's relation to the state has been contested; and time and again, these contestations have been settled in a variety of ways. Ottoman statecraft produced a hybrid that upheld the primacy of *sharia* but combined it with the innovation of *kanun,* or non-religious law (alternatively known as customary law and sultanistic law). That kanun was possible in the first place is intriguing, since it implied the possibility of the sharia's insufficiency. That the sultanate managed to integrate kanun and sharia so effectively is just as important. To begin with, kanun was intended to supplement the sharia in matters pertaining to criminal offense, land-tenure, inheritance, taxes, and the like. This allowed for a degree of legalistic differentiation. Yet the same courts administered both laws. The Sultan's jurists, the *kadis,* often decided on sharia cases, while the ulama could adjudicate kanun cases.[19] Most remarkably, this hybrid was embedded in a consensus of pragmatic opinion which said that "the Holy Law did not cover everything necessary for social order, the preservation of which was after all a basic postulate of Islam."[20]

Well-tolerated during the Ottomans' high noon, kanun proved keenly vulnerable to criticism at the dusk of empire. Nothing defends pragmatic arrangements from attack better than success; nothing exposes them more than failure. The ulama had been key participants in the Ottomans' hybrid legal system. But with the onset of imperial decline, it was the universities and academies controlled by the ulama that clamored for a return to a purer Islamic tradition. Changing conditions once again shaped Islam's relation to the state specifically and to politics more broadly. This was also the case, for example, with the formative alliances between Saudi rulers and Wahhabism. The terms and strengths of these alliances reflected shifting opportunities and challenges in the Arabian Peninsula and beyond—the enticing vision of a Saudi kingdom, the Ottomans' reversals, the advances of the British, and the potential threat that the Sauds perceived in the Hashemite monarchies.[21]

Modern Turkey further illustrates the potential for adaptive reconfigurations in the relationship between the official and the religious-public spheres. In the 1920s, republican leaders embarked on an unrelenting campaign to centralize state power and to secularize society—by reform if possible, by coercion if necessary. The decades that followed brought religious reaction, provincial alienation, and ultimately, a bifurcation whereby Kemalist doctrine guided official elites, while Islam showed the way for the people. The process of democratization in the 1980s closed this bifurcation, but only in the sense that civil society now brimmed with a plethora of causes, ranging from religious fundamentalism to postmodern issues.[22] By the 1990s, the context for the emblematic expression of pragmatism—unlikely political alliances—was provided partly by the formal rules of the political game, partly by the character of the groups in the game. The Islamist Welfare Party was one such group, and its electoral success in 1995 was due in good measure to its willingness to pool votes with left-leaning Kurdish groups.[23]

Islam's affinity with pragmatism also underlies political-religious debates, which in the 1990s revealed a basic consensus even among conservative elements of the Sunni Arab mainstream. Gudrun Kramer summarizes this consensus as follows: "The state is considered to be central to having Islamic law enforced; its form and organization are declared to be secondary, a matter not of substance but of technique." From this assertion, which reduces political form and organization to a technical question, the theoretical possibility of virtually any sort of government follows logically.[24] In this sense, Islamic political thought allows for significant political contestation. Indeed, it is arguable that Islam more than *allows* contestation; it *invites* it. Islamic law, for example, is divinely inspired and authorized. This means that, in theory, it is more important to determine accurately "what constitutes law" than it is to possess the means and capacity to impose it. There is a "gap between law and enforcement," a gap that pulls in contenders "who claim to understand the true meaning of the law over those who have the temporal power to enforce it." Further, the divine nature of the law compels society to intervene when voluntary compliance fails. "[B]y enforcing the law, society reinforces the law's authority."[25] Perhaps this is partly why Ayatollah Khomeini was once moved to remark that "Islam is politics or it is nothing."[26]

Among contenders, the hallmark of fundamentalists is their insistence on a dual return to the essentials of Islam and "to a fixed historic framework." The critical pieces of their argument are fairly obvious. First, because the Koran is immutable, and the *Sunna*[27] is the last word on the Koran, God and His Prophet have said everything that had to be said. Second, given that nothing remains to be said, all that matters henceforth is the rigorous execution of the divine will. With this argument in place, fundamentalist leaders move to claim the role of arbiters, and arrogate unto themselves the authority to render decisive judgment on the validity of positions. From this arrogation, in turn, flow momentous political consequences, such as the prerogative to establish and apply the distinction between true believer and heretic.[28]

These puritanical arbiters, however, are not without competition. The same pragmatism and decentralized structure that help account for their visibility and influence also enable a variety of new Islamists simultaneously to update traditional political discourse and selectively to adopt modern political practices. This discourse is traditional in the sense that it remains pledged to the delivery of Islamic justice and to the unimpeachable nature of Islamic law. The prerogative of interpretation, however, is less strictly defined. Mass higher education, a legacy of previous rounds of state-led modernization, allows emerging Islamist leaders and intellectuals to develop their interpretative competencies independently of traditional sources of knowledge and truth. Mass higher education, moreover, provides these leaders and intellectuals with audiences that are more open and responsive to novel forms of religious discourse.[29]

In this "renovated" tradition, Islamic justice and law remain the central referents, but the sacred texts are no longer the sole means of access to their wisdom. Instead, as Dale Eickelman has shown, publics are more likely to rely on Islamic practical manuals, audiocassettes and even martial chants, all of which marginalize the sacred texts and diminish the role of religious scholars. "Chemists, medical doctors, journalists, even garage mechanics," Eickelman reminds us, "can interpret 'Islamic' principles as equals with scholars who have graduated from the schools of the *ulama.* This multiplication of voices in public discussion of religious and political belief further erodes the boundaries between kinds or sources of authoritative speech."[30] These Islamic interpreters, though unqualified, can pose as authorities because the majority of Muslims, like their Christian counterparts, lack any real expertise in the history, development and even pillars of the faith.[31] Their target audience, in short, may have attained higher levels of formal education than previous generations, but in matters of religion, they are mostly in the dark.[32]

Decentralization and Pluralism

All members of the *umma,* or community of Muslims, stand in equal relation to God, or *Allah,* who is the only law-maker and whose divine law is embodied in sharia.[33] The state is mandated to preserve this law, but no explicit directions are given on how to organize the umma politically. Moreover, while the Koran and the Sunna, the primary sources of law, do have their learned scholars, the texts lend themselves to interpretation by virtually anyone who sets himself up as an expert. To further complicate matters, Islam has no final arbiter. The result is that disagreements among the ulama are commonplace, yet there is no central authority to which one can appeal for definitive answers.

Even in the glory days of Islamic civilization, the juristic class did not opt for assembly within an encompassing institution. Classical jurists, to echo Khaled Abou El Fadl, did possess the distinctive "insignia of investiture." But theirs was a pluralist tradition, at once a fountain of competing learned opinions and an anchor for tolerant conduct. As El Fadl puts it, this tradition "reveled in indeterminacy."[34] The Islamic hierarchies that later appeared in Turkey and Iran had no roots in this classical tradition, nor did its members assert powers comparable to those of Christian hierarchs.

Classical jurisprudence insisted on the multi-valance of orthodoxies, even though it was partly for this reason that puritanical movements emerged to contest the legitimacy of the juristic class. But tolerance had its limits. It stopped at the point where puritans began their violent attempts at imposing a single legitimate orthodoxy. Jurists viewed such extremists as enemies of society, and condemned their "crimes of terror" with the force of "religious imperative."[35] In this there was no indeterminacy, only a delicate balance between the exercise of tolerant pluralism and its vigorous defense.

That this balance was lost is a matter of significant consensus.[36] Agreement on the causes of imbalance and the relevant critical junctures is less substantial. For Bashir Ahmad Ansari, the lineage of Islamism can be traced back to the absolutist caliphs, from the Umayyads to the Ottomans, who weakened and distorted Islam's system of consultative government. On this account, the golden centuries were the crucial period, and voracious state actors were the unwitting originators of Islamism. The clergy were merely the enablers, who permitted the corruption of Islam.

For El Fadl, in contrast, the scales began visibly to tip in the mid-1970s under the newly combined pressure of Wahhabism and Salafism. Interestingly enough, however, El Fadl also suggests that more subtle shifts had been set in motion in the nineteenth century, when in an effort to produce Koranic interpretations compatible with the political ideals and institutions of western modernism, Salafism disregarded jurisprudential precedent and championed interpretative egalitarianism. Individuals were now equally suited to glean authoritative insights from the sacred texts. From this followed a further erosion of authority within Islam. Worse yet, for El Fadl, it was all for naught. The modernization project was truncated, and Salafism became enmeshed with Wahhabism in a web of puritanical theology, ahistorical idealization of the Prophet's time, and the supremacist repudiation of plural doxa.

Both of these accounts—one pointing to egalitarianism, the other to absolutism—are partially accurate because each points, from a different angle, to the fluctuations that stem from Islam's decentralization and pragmatism. In the practice of Islamic law, these fluctuations occur in good part because the legal structure provides a fixed, uncontestable premise for interpreters and upholders while simultaneously engendering highly complex divergences among their schools. To restate the claim in historical terms: although the Koran and Sunna were universally recognized early on as *the* primary sources of Islamic law, their ambiguities and silences also led to the accretion of supplemental legal sources.

These supplemental sources were perhaps the only practical way to cope with new questions and changing conditions after the Prophet's death. But they *also* stimulated disagreement. The four Sunni schools of jurisprudence have differed in their ranking, understanding and ad hoc application of such sources. Each school followed its own legal method, and each, as a result, reached its own conclusions. Furthermore, all schools of jurisprudence, particularly across the Sunni and Shiite divide, have varied in the degree of flexibility they deem appropriate in reading the Koran and the Sunna. The upshot of all this was that the complexities of the schools' methodologies, as well as their intricate debates and divisions, created a demand for "streamlined simplicity." As fundamentalist movements meet this demand, they grow increasingly popular.[37] In other words, neither despotism nor egalitarianism can wholly account for fundamentalism. Rather, the development of Islam has ushered in de facto pluralism, from which decentralization continues to flow and fundamentalism emerges endogenously.

Like the practice of the law, the practice of the faith has shown a tendency to generate difference and diffusion. Islam is practiced on two levels. One is formal, legal and scholarly. The other is more intuitive and mystical. Formal Islam is austere, devoid of sacraments, ordained priests and saints. The mosque is sparse, the *imam* is only a prayer leader, and public prayer is a disciplined act of submission to a remote God. These characteristics often have led the faithful to seek a more personal religious experience. In medieval Turkey, the faithful sought out Shiite sects, which many Sunni leaders deemed heretical. After the Mongol invasions, they turned to the dervish brotherhoods, which remained within the sphere of Sunni dogma and were thus tolerated better.[38]

The faithful found in the brotherhoods what they could not find in the mosque and the imams. The leaders of the brotherhoods played the role of pastors, saints played the role of intercessors, and mysticism offered the hope of a "union with the Godhead." Despite their rivalries, the brotherhoods provided community services, gained control of guilds and professional associations in the seventeenth and eighteenth centuries, and in the nineteenth century they even managed to penetrate the formal, orthodox institutions. By the early twentieth century, the brotherhoods were vibrant enough to be noticed by political parties and movements, which often instrumentalized them. But with the secular reforms of the 1920s, the dervishes demonstrated their capacity for independent opposition, even though the reforms were initially aimed not at them but at the ulama. Soon thereafter, the reformist state dealt severe blows to the brotherhoods. Moreover, when the state eventually turned to a more conciliatory religious policy, it reserved its benefits for the ulama. But by the 1950s, a religious revival was flowering in Turkey, and once again a wide range of voices emerged. The revitalization of the brotherhoods was only a matter of time.[39] In fact, they became increasingly important in key parts of the Muslim Middle East. Their renaissance generally conformed to the Turkish pattern. In Egypt, the Muslim Brotherhood seized the initiative in a wide range of civil society activities such as charitable works and university students' organization. By the 1990s, the Brotherhood had even gained electoral control of professional associations and syndicates.[40]

Looming Islamism and the Promise of Ijtihad

Islam's pragmatism and decentralization allow for a multiplicity of activisms without creating macro-coordination challenges. Moreover, activist groups evade the inertia that often seizes large, vertically-organized movements, whose rank and file can march full force only after higher-ups debate, resolve and issue directives.[41] This is not to say that pragmatism and decentralization necessarily entail the absence of discipline. Loosely-connected organizations, associations and movements, in fact, sometimes can better establish and enforce clear lines of authority because leadership and monitoring are both closer to the ground. Karmer observes that "forceful leadership, unity, strict loyalty and obedience is mirrored in the organizational structure of virtually all Islamist movements, from the relatively moderate Muslim Brotherhood to the militant underground, which in their internal affairs do not adhere to democratic principles."[42] At the same time, pragmatism and decentralization enable militant groups without any serious commitment to "doctrinal purity" to draw on Islam for symbolic power and for the necessary elements to craft an identity style.[43]

The aggregate effect of all this, again, is to amplify the sound and to raise the profile of Islamist groups while blurring important distinctions *among* the groups themselves. In this way, an undifferentiated Islamism looms disproportionately large. Looming Islamism, in turn, tests the mettle and strategies of secular political actors. The reformed Palestinian left of the 1990s, for example, competed ineffectually with puritanical religious forces for power in political society and for influence in civil society. Most crucially, on matters of social freedoms, both the Palestinian and the broader Arab left were loath to "alienate the religious street," and retreated.[44] Meanwhile, the Egyptian state responded to Islamists through a strategic blend of coercion and contestation. On the one hand, in the same way that the left abandoned the cause of social freedoms, the

Egyptian state abandoned the cause of secularism while simultaneously repressing violent and militant Islamists. On the other hand, as one writer points out, "a group of highly conservative Islamic scholars with close ties to Hosni Mubarak's regime" became key players "in the struggle over what practices are deemed justifiable in Islamic terms."[45]

That a group of conservative Islamic scholars would enter this fray is neither strange nor wholly explained by state cooptation. For if the terms of Islamism are left wholly uncontested, there could be especially deleterious consequences for those who identify themselves as learned interpreters and upholders of Islam but are not, or cannot be, doctrinal supremacists. Here they need only recall that the champions of Wahhabism—self-described Salafis—consider their dogmatic and methodological orientations not merely a school of Islam but Islam itself.[46] In this sense, conservatives have a specific incentive to protect their long-term prospects.[47] And yet, fearful of innovation and its attendant disruptions to the status quo, religious scholars (and authoritarian governments) have for decades restricted the contemporary practice of *ijtihad*—interpretation of and reasoning about the Koran and the Sunna—a practice which in its traditional incarnation was effectively "terminated" five centuries ago.[48]

Moderate and liberal Muslims in search of innovative flexibility now advocate ijtihad's revival, an idea that raises delicate issues, such as: what is the nature of ijtihad, who is qualified to practice it, and how should this be done? Moreover, ijtihad's revival must entail, among other things, a liberalized scholarly environment and a reformed educational system.[49] If these are exacting challenges, then the attainment of two related broader goals is bound to prove even more difficult. One is the restoration of Islam's ethical discourse to the public sphere. This strategic call, eloquently made by El Fadl, emphasizes the tradition at the core of Islam that is "tolerant toward the other and mindful of the dignity and worth of all human beings."[50] The other strategic call, made with equal eloquence by Radwan Masmoudi, emphasizes the resolution of the grave dilemma facing liberal and moderate Muslims: that is, while they cherish liberty, justice, consultation and rational interpretation, they find themselves wedged between a repressive state and religious extremists, and are thus unable to express these Islamic values freely. These liberal and moderate Muslims, Masmoudi laments, are "the silenced majority."[51]

Could electoral democracy give them back their voice? Vali Nasr, for one, argues in the affirmative, and points to the examples of Pakistan and Turkey (as well as Indonesia and Malaysia).[52] The big electoral winners, Nasr notes, have been neither secularists nor Islamists. Instead, those right-of-center forces that successfully integrate Muslim values, moderate Islamic politics, and non-religious concerns have been the ones to capture "the strategic middle."[53] But this still leaves a prior question unanswered: how is democracy to be established and sustained? For Nasr, a series of factors—military involvement in politics, an entrepreneurial private sector, and keen competition over votes—combine to create a structure of incentives and opportunities that favors pragmatic change.

Though intriguing, this argument is ultimately problematic on several counts. First, the triad of 1) military involvement in politics, 2) an entrepreneurial private sector, and 3) keen competition over votes, is a very specific product of complex historical struggles and political choices that cannot be replicated as a matter of strategy and/or sheer political will. Second, the triad's posited outcome (an incentive structure that favors *pragmatic* politics), represents in itself neither a modernist breakthrough nor necessarily a pro-democratic condition. Pragmatism, we have seen, can also be viewed as a traditional attribute that may or may not contribute to the pacification and democratization of nations. Third, the electoral allegiance of "the strategic middle"—the political prize sought by pragmatic Muslim politicians—may not be forthcoming because "the middle" cannot even begin to emerge when caught in a religious rift that dominates the political field. Fourth, and perhaps most importantly, electoral processes are neither isolated nor crowning events.

Conclusion

Rising Islamism, I have argued, is best understood as an exaggerated impression of a real trend, which is itself the result of a distorted political opportunity structure. The distorting forces stem from a combination of actors' strategic (non)choices and Islam's decentralized, pluralistic and pragmatic structure. But none of this is irreversible.

The political relevance of tradition in general and religious meaning in particular is becoming increasingly obvious to liberal and pro-democratic Muslims in the Near and Middle East, as well as in the United States and Europe. These scholars, clerics, jurists and activists now better appreciate the need to establish through reason, interpretation *and* practice a legitimate link between political agency and Islamic tradition.

The advanced industrial democracies can best serve their own interests and ideals by lending their full support to the groups and institutions that constitute this emerging interpretative force. The fact that many of them, as individuals, are exiled in the West highlights the depth of the challenge. But there is also good cause for optimism precisely because these exiles have a proven record of tolerance and independent thinking. Just as importantly, they seek to recapture the spirit of classical Islam. That this political-cultural enterprise is now within the realm of the imaginable is already a significant achievement. Open pluralism may yet replace the skewed alternative that has warped the public sphere of the Muslim world.

Notes

1. I would like to acknowledge the generous support of the Liechtenstein Institute on Self-Determination at Princeton University in the research and writing of this chapter. I am

also grateful to Hassan Abbas, Sheri Berman, Consuelo Cruz, Malik Mufti and Assaf Moghadam for their comments.

2. For "imaginable possibilities"—the thinkable and the doable—and political culture, see Consuelo Cruz, *Political Culture and Institutional Development in Costa Rica and Nicaragua: World-Making in the Tropics* (New York: Cambridge University Press, 2005), especially the Introduction and Chapter 1.

3. For a penetrating analysis of religious conflict and Westphalia, see Daniel Philpot, "The Religious Roots of Modern International Relations," *World Politics,* vol. 52, no. 2 (January 2000).

4. See Bernard Lewis, ed., *Islam: From the Prophet Muhammad to the Capture of Constantinople, vol. 1: Politics and War* (New York: Oxford University Press, 1987).

5. See Malik Mufti, *Sovereign Creations: Pan-Arabism and Political Order in Syria and Iraq* (Ithaca: Cornell University Press, 1996), especially Chapter 10.

6. Thoughtful observers, however, remind us that India's constitutional secularism remains vulnerable to political leaders' opportunistic disregard. Indira Gandhi's record illustrates the point. See Sumit Ganguly, "The Crisis of Indian Secularism," *Journal of Democracy,* vol. 14, no. 4 (2003): 11–25.

7. Dauod, along with most of his family members, was murdered in April of 1978 immediately after the start of a revolution led by the Marxist People's Democratic Party of Afghanistan, itself bitterly divided internally. Afghanistan's government under Adour had been an admixture of repression and increasing pluralism. Nevertheless, in the 1970s, the country was clearly moving towards a system of representative government that retained some indigenous political traditions. See, among others, Louis Dupree, *Afghanistan* (New York: Oxford University Press, 2002); Barnett Rubin, *The Fragmentation of Afghanistan* (New Haven: Yale University Press, 1995); and William Maley and Amin Saikal, eds., *Regime Change in Afghanistan: Foreign Intervention and the Politics of Legitimacy* (Boulder: Westview Press, 1991).

8. Even so, it should be noted that, ineffective and/or brutal as they were, the regimes of Nur Muhammad Taraki (March-December 1979), Hafizullah Amin (September-December 1979), Babrak Karmal (1979–1986), and Najibullah (1989–1992) did considerably better than the alliance of mujahideen in power from 1992–1994, to say nothing of the Taliban. Thanks to Hassan Abbas for his comments on this point.

9. One well-known exponent of this view is Elie Kedourie, *Democracy and Arab Political Culture* (London: Frank Cass and Co., 1994).

10. Salim Tamari, "Left in Limbo: Leninist Heritage and Islamist Challenge," *Middle East Report,* November/December (1992): 16–21.

11. Eric Hoffer, *The True Believer* (New York: Harper and Brothers, 1951).

12. Sheri Berman, "Islamism, Revolution, and Civil Society," *Perspectives on Politics,* vol. 1, no. 2 (2003): 257–272.

13. Some of the tactics include manipulation of the electoral process, opportunistic constitutional amendments, and abuse of executive orders. Aqil Shah, "Pakistan's Armored Democracy," *Journal of Democracy,* vol. 14, no. 4 (2003): 26–40.

14. Berman, "Islamism, Revolution, and Civil Society;" and Shah, "Pakistan's Armored Democracy."

15. Robert Canfield details how the Samanids' drive to differentiate themselves from their Shiite neighbors, the Buyids, led them to favor Sunnism, which in turn elevated the ulama above the other influential classes—the scribes, who staffed the bureaucracy, and the literati. Moreover, the decline of the Samanis and the rise of the Qarakhanids caused societal tremors that turned the network of recognized religious authorities into an institutional instrument of public order. Finally, the ulama's alliance with the Qarakhanids, as well as the latter's predilection for exercising control from outside the cities, rendered the ulama the de facto urban leaders, able to bring into their fold even the bureaucratic

class. See Robert L. Canfield, ed., *Turko-Persia in Historical Perspective* (New York: Cambridge University Press, 1991), 8–9.

16. Canfield, *Turko-Persia in Historical Perspective,* 14, 28.

17. Dale Eickelman and Jon Anderson, "Redefining Muslim Publics," in Eickelman and Anderson, eds., *New Media in the Muslim World* (Bloomington: Indiana University Press, 2003), 2. Eickelman and Anderson are referring to the period from 844–848. It is, of course, a key tenet of the Muslim faith that the Koran always existed and was revealed or "recited" by God, in Arabic, to Mohammed. Moreover, interpretations of the four caliphs' decrees vary, and many do not see them as "directly challenging the assertion that the Koran always existed in Heaven." Hassan Abbas, personal communication with author, January 2005, Medford, Mass.

18. Anthony Black, *The History of Islamic Political Thought: From the Prophet to the Present* (New York: Routledge, 2001), 203–204, 206–208. By comparison with Arab control, during the Umayyad and Abbasid periods, the caliphs used the ulama to legitimate their controversial policies.

19. And a degree of cooperation existed as well. Kadis also sought the expert opinion of ulama when adjudicating sharia. Thanks to Hassan Abbas for pointing this out.

20. Black, *The History of Islamic Political Thought,* 210–213.

21. Lewis, *Islam,* op. cit., 120–125.

22. Ayse Kadioglu, "The Paradox of Turkish Nationalism and the Construction of Official Identity," *Middle Eastern Studies,* April (1996): 177–193.

23. Jillian Schwedler, "Islamic Identity: Myth, Menace, or Mobilizer?," *SAIS Review,* vol. 21, no. 2 (2001): 1–17.

24. Gudrun Kramer, "Islamist Notions of Democracy," *Middle East Report,* July/August (1993): 5.

25. M. Cherif Bassiouni and Gamal M. Badr, "The Shari'ah: Sources, Interpretation, and Rule-Making," *UCLA Journal of Islamic and Near Eastern Law,* vol. 1, no. 2 (2002): 172.

26. Cited in Lewis, *The Crisis of Islam*, 7–8.

27. "Sunna" in this context are the traditional social and legal practices that constitute proper observance of Islam, which over time were codified as the Hadith by Abu 'Abd Allah Shaf'ii, and authenticated by later scholars.

28. Bassiouni and Badr, "The Shari'ah," 171.

29. Dale Eickelman, "Trans-State Islam and Security," in Susanne Hoeber Rudolph and James Piscatori eds., *Transnational Religions and Fading States* (Boulder: Westview Press, 1997), 28–29.

30. Dale Eickelman, "Communication and Control in the Middle East: Publication and Its Discontents," in Dale Eickelman and Jon Anderson, eds., *New Media in the Muslim World* (Bloomington: Indiana University Press, 2003), 42.

31. See, for example, R. Scott Appleby, "The Quandary of Leadership," in Khaled Abou El Fadl, *The Place of Tolerance in Islam* (Boston: Beacon Press, 2002), 85–90.

32. See El Fadl, "Islam and the Theology of Power," *Middle Eastern Report,* Winter (2002): 28–33; and *The Place of Tolerance in Islam,* 107.

33. See Reinhard Bendix, *Kings or People: Power and the Mandate to Rule* (Berkeley: University of California Press, 1980). For a more contemporary work see Patricia Crone, *God's Rule—Government and Islam: Six Centuries of Medieval Islamic Political Thought* (New York: Columbia University Press, 2004).

34. El Fadl, "Islam and the Theology of Power," 28–33.

35. Ibid.

36. El Fadl explains this loss with reference to several factors, most notably the importation of European systems of codified civil law at the expense of the "dialectical and indeterminate methodology of Islamic jurisprudence," and Muslim modernizers'

reshaping of jurisprudential tradition to fit the ideological exigencies of Third-World nationalism.

37. Bassiouni and Badr, "The Shari'ah," 140–144.

38. Bernard Lewis, *The Emergence of Modern Turkey: Studies in Middle Eastern History* (New York: Oxford University Press, 2001), 407–409.

39. Ibid., 407–409, 417–424.

40. Berman, "Islamism, Revolution, and Civil Society," 260–262.

41. For the complex connections among sectarianism, networked organization, insurgence, and terror, see the discussion among Daniel Byman, Michael Scheuer, Anatol Lieven, and W. Patrick Lang, "Symposium: Iraq, Afghanistan, and the War on 'Terror'," *Middle East Policy,* vol. 12, no. 1 (Spring): 1–24.

42. Karmer, "Islamist Notions of Democracy," *Middle East Report,* July/August, (1993): 6.

43. See, for example, Camille Pescataing in *Foreign Affairs,* January-February (2004): 156–157.

44. Salim Tamari, "Left in Limbo: Leninist Heritage and Islamist Challenge," *Middle East Report,* November/December (1992): 18, 20–21.

45. Schwedler, "Islamic Identity," 8.

46. El Fadl, "Islam and the Theology of Power," 32.

47. Even the Society of the Muslim Brothers in Egypt have suffered splintering. In fact, this may be the provenance of many Egyptian jihadi groups. See Byman, Scheuer, Lieven, and Lang, "Symposium," 14.

48. Ijtihad refers to the science of interpretation "developed by Muslim scholars in order to understand and apply the message of the Qur'an to varying needs and conditions," *The Muslim Democrat,* 2004, 2. See also "Ijtihad: Reinterpreting Islam for the Twenty-First Century," workshop co-sponsored by the United States Institute of Peace and the Center for the Study of Islam and Democracy, 19 March 2004, Special Report 125, accessible at http://www.islam-democracy.org; and the US Institute of Peace Special Report "Reinterpreting Islamic Principles for the Twenty-First Century," available at http://www.usip.org.

49. Radwan Masmoudi, one of the most prominent figures in the West advocating for the revival of ijtihad. Ibid.

50. El Fadl, "Islam and the Theology of Power," 33.

51. Radwan Masmoudi, "What is Liberal Islam: The Silenced Majority," *Journal of Democracy,* vol. 14, no. 2 (2002): 40–42.

52. Vali Nasr, "The Rise of Muslim Democracy," *Journal of Democracy,* vol. 16, no. 2 (2005): 13.

53. Ibid.

Epilogue

Wolfgang Danspeckgruber

AFTER DECADES OF CONFLICT IN a very traditional society, building state and security in Afghanistan is a unique challenge—for the Afghans but also for the international community. This undertaking might be compared to a "chicken and egg" situation, representing a critical conundrum. On the one hand, only a secure environment will allow for the creation and effective implementation of a working state and its economy. On the other hand, neither can there be true security nor stability without a functioning and effective state and a working economy. Security may be imposed from the outside for a certain period of time and national income may be substituted by international assistance, but eventually the state in question will have to be able to provide both independently.

The discussion in the above chapters brought to light some important conceptual insights: 1) general lessons for state- and security-building; 2) the factors of time, costs, stakes involved and perception; 3) the role of third/initially unrelated events; 4) the danger of spoilers; 5) the power and influence of the media; 6) the role of the economy and international assistance; and 7) the need for an overarching national and regional strategy, including consideration of larger geostrategic dimensions.

General Lessons for State- and Security-Building

First, successful state- and security-building demands a long-term commitment by a unified international community, with states, IOs and NGOs acting cooperatively according to a well-conceived plan for the target state and its region. Second, the negative interference of outside spoilers should be resolutely and effectively dealt with. Third, there has to be sufficient flexibility as well as time and resource allocation to adapt or alter involvement according to changes in the national, regional or international framework.

One of the most important lessons conveyed in this volume is that no two cases are alike. This is particularly true for an archaic society like Afghanistan, with different ethnic and religious groups, having experienced decades of war including horrendous internecine conflict. These factors demonstrate the importance of religious-cultural dimensions and societal particularities in postwar state- and security-building. Further predicaments become obvious if combined with the peculiar topographical and climatic context, lack of infrastructure, and the strategic interests from its neighbors in a state like Afghanistan.

The debate about centralization versus decentralization of state authority has to recognize these facts and accept some of the situational limitations against enforcing either one. The establishment of a working and legitimate justice system has to try to include the non-state legal system, which is critical in Afghanistan with its autonomous social cultures. Both have coexisted for decades and gradually merged over time. The more the state system became bankrupt and ineffective the more that informal system expanded and eventually spun out of control. Similarly, the formation of "security commissions" may be an effective way to use traditional forms of governance in order to make peace without arms.

Education and training for Afghanistan's youth and all those who are part of reintegration, following successful DDR, is essential. DDR will produce lasting effects only when accompanied by training and education programs, which in turn have to be followed by effective job creation. Disarmed and demobilized former combatants have to be able to earn a living and to trust in this opportunity. Creations of schools in rural areas will offer access to primary and secondary learning to a wider proportion of the Afghan population, while local school construction projects—with Afghan involvement—provide both jobs and a local feeling of ownership over the educational infrastructure. This too would help shape the meaningful perception that progress is indeed happening. An Afghan academy for public policy could offer critical training of civil servants in the development of a cohort of skilled public officials who are also informed about the workings of administration abroad while building on Afghan experience. Educational exchanges between Afghan and regional/international places of higher learning would serve to bolster positive relations and ties with the region and the wider international community.

The presence of more than 20,000 US forces in West, Central and South-Asia has been the most critical regional effect of 9/11. They, besides some 30,000 ISAF forces, are there to both assist state- and security-building in Afghanistan but also to fight terrorism and fetch senior terrorist leaders. Excessive and indiscriminate use of force in the conduct of such operations, typically causing serious civilian casualties and collateral damage, however, will not contribute to stability and security but to the loss of "the hearts and minds" of the civilian population, to hostility to their own armed forces—the ANA—involved in these operations, and to difficulties for the governing Afghan elites who depend on that international support. Security questions, such as those involving the eradication of poppy plants, should build on Afghan national experience, capability and involvement, rather than solely involving costly external contractors.

Effective "security sector" reform such as an adequate armed force and a responsive, non-corrupt police force can only be undertaken with sufficient international training personnel and material available. Also those participating ought to receive adequate pay, and the prestige of the newly formed units has to be kept as high as possible in order to make it an honor to serve and to put the onus on those who oppose them.

Moreover, effective PRTs as a state-building tool require sufficient manpower and the readiness to adapt their operations to actual local conditions, rather than being guided by distant national regiments which are more concerned with the legal-political reality in the sender state than the one existing in Afghanistan. An inappropriate and ineffective PRT however not only wastes resources and endangers people—both Afghans and internationals—but also ruins the repute of the others. The international contributors, state and non-state alike, ought to coordinate their PRTs and other security actions and adapt them while evaluating and recalibrating according to their military/security potential and political/psychological ramifications.

But security-building has to be concerned with yet another challenge: the fact that regional interdependencies still trump global interdependencies. When fighters adopt new tactics in one regional theater, others elsewhere will soon copy the example. Once the war in Iraq saw the emergence of new forms of urban warfare like the use of IEDs (improvised explosive devices), suicide bombings and kidnappings, all these hitherto unutilized tactics have come to influence the conduct of the conflict in Afghanistan. Many times such actions, especially suicide bombings, are not even carried out by Afghans.

Time, Costs, Stakes Involved and Perception

The various parties in the state- and security-building process operate from distinctly different perspectives and have different degrees of stakes involved. Members of the international community, especially governments based on democratic elections recurring every four or five years, carefully calculate their involvement in the target country, especially in terms of human, material and financial resources, as well as the potential and extent of threats to those, time involved and the possible public relations effects. International actors thus frequently look for state-building solutions which are expedient, cheap, rapid and effective in domestic politics—and hence produce "a quick bang for the buck"—while their effective implementation on the ground in a war-torn society may be much more tedious, longer and more costly than planned. On the other hand, this interest potentially offers savvy and shrewd leaders on the ground ways to manipulate and exploit the situation to their advantage. They can calculate long term with the eventuality that the international actors will withdraw, their engagement will become reduced, and thus they can once again prepare their ascent to power. For the population, however, this in effect necessitates leaving all options open and also possibly accepting having to deal with old foes again in the not so distant future.

"Perception forms reality" especially where hope and trust are critical to win the support of the population. Neither words nor promises, but deeds matter. Gaining popular trust for an effective state-building process and the central authority is ruined by the combination of sensationalized reporting of civilian deaths, kidnapping of international collaborators, and among other things, possible international departures. This combined with the experience of unfulfilled promises and economic/infrastructure projects which either do not work or do not exist as promised can obviously easily be exploited by those who yearn for power and want state-building to fail and the international community to leave. An effective dissemination of honest, positive, though not propagandistic, information has the potential to positively influence the local perception, to show that "things are moving" in the right direction and to instill hope.

The Role of Third/Initially Unrelated Events

Third, other, independent events while unrelated to the state and security exercise can have significantly challenging effects in our globalized interdependent world. Their effects may both be direct, as in affecting resources and capabilities, but also indirect, as having political and perceptive ramifications. Depending on the public opinion evaluation of the events, those who are supported by powers involved may suffer from related negative public relations.

For instance, the current Operation Iraqi Freedom and the atrocities reported in prisons have harmed the public image of the US and its forces in the Islamic world. Consequently, whether justified or not, this has also created a public relations problem for Afghanistan's current presidency which is seen to depend on continuous US support. Each time US and Coalition forces are involved in military operations in Afghanistan which cause excessive civilian casualties and collateral damages, Afghanistan's government is in an even worse situation in the public perception. In addition this can easily be manipulated and exploited by foes to the international involvement there.

Another example concerns a non-political crisis, the 2005 Tsunami. Albeit much needed by the victims and the region affected, the international financial assistance given in the wake of the tsunami diverted significant international funds originally earmarked for Afghanistan. In view of limited financial resources at the end of the fiscal year, many western governments accepted the shift of funds originally marked for the "Asian state Afghanistan" to the tsunami-stricken region. Moreover, both the war in Iraq and the tsunami managed to take Afghanistan out of the international media spotlight, with severe consequences—"out of sight, out of mind."

The Danger of Spoilers

Spoilers may be national actors who want to regain power, and/or who want the state-building effort to fail. But they may also be those regional neighbors who have a stake involved and/or try to influence or exploit developments to their advantage, or would like the international community to leave soon and without success. So too could they be international actors who want the same and hence try to negatively interfere in the state-building process. Possible spoilers have to be identified, anticipated and taken into consideration in the overall assessment of the situation. A strategy dealing with them should include three options: include and build them into the process under certain conditions, neutralize them, or ascertain that they are "out of the equation." To ignore them can have devastating consequences. The less there is a well-conceived overarching national and regional strategy for the state-building effort, the more spoilers could potentially be effective.

The Power and Influence of the Media

The media is of pivotal importance in a globalized world with access to real-time information, especially in the leading democracies. Whether to report or not to report at all, whether to show that progress is underway—"the glass is half-full"—or to lament that it is not, whether to dramatize the security situation or not, whatever news is reported produces a lasting effect over time. Unfortunately it is frequently overlooked that media reports, newspaper and television alike, are also followed by interested experts in the target country and the region. So not only are many of their leaders aware of the state of international involvement and the debates about the various intentions therein, but they may also be tempted to influence them by certain actions. For news corporations, reporting of negative, exciting, "big time" news creates serious (commercial) rewards. Good news, or regular forward development may be seen as dull to a reading, listening or viewing audience. There is hence a tendency toward sensational reporting, which may also be exploited by potential spoilers in the field. This cannot be to the advantage of the state-building process.

The Internet is of particular importance as it offers opportunities to transmit in real-time writings, images, sounds and videos, and to report, discuss and blog virtually unchecked facts that mix truth, fiction and interpretation. The outcome of all this can have significant ramifications on international involvement, the situation in the target state and the region, and the role of state and non-state actors alike.

The dissemination of information about reconstruction and economic development projects which truly work are crucial for a positive and constructive effort. This also has to happen in Afghanistan and the region. Public information about effectively held elections, progress in health and education initiatives, and even cultural and sporting events can also be used to show that progress is underway and garner the support of local populations as well as the increased interest and involvement of the international community. People within and outside Afghanistan and in the donor countries should receive objective information about the situation. Deliberate negative manipulation of the news and public perception is shortsighted and will neither serve national state-building nor the long-term international interest.

The Role of the Economy and International Assistance

When looking at economic development, sustainable and alternative job creation, sources of income must be put into place to effectively replace the income derived from poppy production and the drug trade. Poppy eradication programs will have little or no impact without viable economic alternatives and real sources of income. Besides that, poppy crop alternatives and financial support should effectively be delivered and their implementation and use verified and controlled jointly by Afghans and international actors. Afghanistan is blessed with numerous mineral and natural resources—from uranium to lapislazuli to natural gas—upon which myriad small and large scale industries could be based. This in combination with jobs to be created in manufacturing and other industries could also contribute to reverse the brain drain currently plaguing the country. The geographic location of Afghanistan, moreover, makes it uniquely positioned to become a crucial north-south, east-west transit point. All-year and all-weather workable infrastructure including regional roadways and railroads could facilitate intrastate village interconnectivity and market access, offer new sources of income, and incentive industrialization, employment and national pride. Direct foreign investment from regional investors, international financial institutions, and the EU is essential in the start-up of these industries and infrastructure projects, and necessary for building up the ability of Afghanistan's central authority to deliver basic human services. The country should be encouraged to participate in regional and international economic organizations so as to ease market access and to provide incentive for foreign direct investment.

It is perhaps here where regional security and economy most importantly mesh. As succinctly stated by US Lieutenant General Karl Eikenberry, "where the road ends, the Taliban begins." Security in Afghanistan depends largely on the sustained support of locals for both the government and reconstruction efforts—otherwise the population may well be tempted to trust those who criticize. Without tangible deliverables, without completed projects which work effectively, without the rule of law, without real alternatives for economic viability, without work for civilians and for those participating in the DDR process, without Afghans feeling they have a direct input and therefore a stake and ownership in the success or failure of village-level projects, neither the battle for security and against the Taliban, nor that for "hearts and minds" of Afghans can be won.

The Need for an Overarching National and Regional Strategy

It is imperative to delineate a long-term and all-encompassing strategy. There should be a preparation for the future role of the state in the region; the development of a regional compact also based upon the interaction of individual key states in the region; and their respective alliances with and the interest of out-of-area powers. Continued international attention to, presence in, and support of Afghanistan are all the more important in light of broader regional developments: the resurgence of the Taliban especially in the Afghanistan-Pakistan border region, the concomitant deterioration in the bilateral relations between Kabul and Islamabad, the possible problems in Pakistan, and the new India-US nuclear agreement. Iran's nuclear ambitions and role in the region harbor another problem, especially if they trigger an international military operation against Iran. Similarly, major shifts in regional strategic alliances like the India-US nuclear deal affect the behavior and strategic calculations of neighboring Pakistan, particularly as it concerns its strategic hinterland. It is important that Afghan leadership interacts closely with the leaders of its neighbors, and it is essential to create a new effective and possibly guaranteed regional compact between Afghanistan and its neighbors. This should also include India, Russia and China, the EU and US, and focus on security, stability, border issues, economic and infrastructure development, trade and energy, and law and order. A standing "Afghan Contact Group" comprised by representatives of these states and international organizations concerned can meet in follow-on sessions to deal with these issues and effective problem recognition, anticipation and solution.

Conclusion

Having followed the development of Afghanistan for nearly three decades—since the Soviet occupation in December 1979—one has to express admiration and amazement for the steadfastness, ingenuity and determination with which the individual man, woman and child in Afghanistan has faced decades of warfare and conflict, occupation and repression, and countless other security, health and economic difficulties. There exists a seemingly endless challenge of reconciling an ancient society with the requirements of a state in the twenty-first century. The story of Afghanistan, therefore, should always remain mindful of one dictum: Afghan ownership or "Afghanization." Namely it is the Afghans who ought to be the principal benefactors of the international efforts to assist in the establishment of a peaceful and viable Afghanistan. It is with and for them and their country that the international community acts, has to act, and must do so continuously.

There are already achievements in many dimensions of the state- and security-building endeavor in Afghanistan: a reduction of birth mortality; an increase in health services and housing; developments related to infrastructure, communication, road building and energy supply; and growth in the educational sector. Although overshadowed since 2003 by the ongoing operations in Iraq, the 2005 tsunami, and an increasingly challenged global system, the security and stability of Afghanistan remains the international community's litmus test in the post-9/11 world. As a historic first in that region and for a NATO out of area operation, the US and the EU has far more at stake in Afghanistan than just the country's fate and success in state-building. Success in Afghanistan is hence also critical for any future hopes of a globally engaged and active NATO presence in reconstruction and stability.

History, however, has already once demonstrated what can happen if after years of foreign presence in Afghanistan the country is suddenly left alone and at the mercy of its neighbors. Today a repeat of this would have catastrophic ramifications for Afghanistan, the region and the world. Thus, there remains no option other than to hold a steady course and to remain involved in the region to support the Afghans so that they can build a secure, just, stable and prosperous country.

Appendix I: Timeline of Key Events

1747
Ahmad Shah Abdali, the Durrani leader and Pushtun chief, seizes local power following the assassination of the Iranian king Nadir Shah Afshar. Durrani rule is extended to Peshawar as Ahmad Shah begins his 26 year rule under the Sadozai dynasty with Afghan tribes united.

1748
The Durranis move against Lahore. The Afghan empire extends to Baluchistan, Sind and Punjab. In November, Ahmad Shah invades India for the third time.

1752
Kashmir is conquered by the Durranis.

1757
Ahmad Shah is suzerain ruler of India. Coins are struck in his name.

1761
Afghans defeat the Hindu Mahratta confederacy in the Battle of Panipat. The Muslim Moghul ruler is restored to his throne in Delhi.

1769–1770
Ahmad Shah moves to Khorasan.

1772
Ahmad Shah dies, and Timur Shah moves the capital from Kandahar to Kabul.

1793
Zaman Shah begins his six year rule. Afghans lose areas around the Indus River basin.

1798
Britain begins a policy of containment against Afghanistan as Britain fears Afghan attacks on India. Britain seeks the support of Persia in containing Afghanistan.

1799
The Persian army invades Herat. Internal conflicts become apparent among the Sadozai Durranis.

1805
A Persian attempt to capture Herat fails. Afghan and Sikh struggles over Kashmir begin.

1809
The first British embassy is established in Peshawar as the British attempt to form an alliance against the French and the Russians. Shah Shuja receives the British ambassador, Mountstuart Elphinstone, and they sign the Anglo-Afghan treaty. However, Shah Shuja's defeat by Shah Mahmoud at Gandomak also meant the defeat of the treaty.

1818
Civil war results in the division of Afghanistan. Quasi-independent states form until 1835.

1819
Ranjit Singh conquers Kashmir.

1826
After the last of the Durrani kings is forced to abdicate, the Muhammadzai clan rises to prominence in Afghanistan. The first ruler of the dynasty, Emir Dost Muhammad Khan (1793–1863), ruler of Ghazni, reunifies most of the lands held by the Durranis and subdues the Sikhs during the first part of his reign.

1834
Dost Muhammad defeats Shah Shuja and captures Kandahar. The Sikhs annex Peshawar.

1838
Ranjit Singh, the British East India Company and Shah Shuja sign a tripartite treaty to restore Shah Shuja to the Afghan throne. Britain breaks relations with Dost Muhammad and declares war.

1839–1842
The first Anglo-Afghan War takes place. The British are able to overthrow Dost Muhammad in 1839, and he flees to Balkh, then Bukhara before eventually surrendering to the British. The British, however, are unsuccessful in fighting in the mountainous terrain of Afghanistan. They begin to retreat from Kabul in January 1842, and the British fight their last stand at Jagdalak. Dost Muhammad retakes the throne in December 1842. Shah Shuja is assassinated.

1855
An Anglo-Afghan agreement to prevent Persian and Russian incursions on Afghan territory is negotiated. This agreement leads to the Treaty of Peshawar, which reopens diplomatic relations between Britain and Afghanistan.

1857

Dost Muhammad signs a treaty with the British, pledging his support against their mutual foes, Russia and Iran. The Treaty of Paris is negotiated and becomes the agreement through which Iran recognizes Afghan independence.

1863

Dost Muhammad takes Herat and later dies. Sher Ali ascends to the Afghan throne.

1872

The Russians and British sign the Granville-Gorchakoff Agreement, which assures Britain that Afghanistan is outside Russia's sphere of influence. A British commission also begins work on marking a border between Afghanistan and Iran in Sistan. However, the work is not completed for another century.

1878

A Russian mission under General Stolietoff arrives in Kabul, raising British fears of Russian encroachment on Afghanistan. Britain invades Afghanistan to begin the Second Anglo-Afghan War. Sher Ali leaves Kabul and appoints his son Yaqub Khan as governor of Kabul.

1879

Sher Ali dies and Yaqub Khan ascends to the Afghan throne. On May 26, 1879, the Treaty of Gandomak is signed between Sir Louis Cavagnari and Yaqub Khan, giving British control of the Khyber Pass. General Roberts occupies Kabul as Yaqub Khan is forced to abdicate, and Britain takes control of the Afghan government.

1880

Britain recognizes Abdul Rahman Khan as Emir of Kabul. General Steward withdraws from Kabul as Abdul Rahman Khan moves in after his exile in Tashkent.

1881

As British troops withdraw from Kandahar, the Second Anglo-Afghan War comes to an end.

1883

Russia occupies the Tejend Oasis.

1884

Britain and Russia open negotiations on the northern boundary of Afghanistan. Britain begins work on a railroad in Quetta. Northern Afghanistan, including Maimana, is conquered by Kabul.

1887

Britain and Russia make a final settlement on the demarcation of the Afghan frontier with Bukhara.

1892

An uprising by Hazaras is severely suppressed.

1893

Britain's Sir Mortimer Durand negotiates Afghanistan's border with India along an artificial boundary that divides tribal homelands and causes problems with Pakistan to this day. Britain's subsidy to Abdul Rahman Khan is increased.

1896

Abdul Rahman Khan conquers Kafiristan and renames it Nuristan after the population's conversion to Islam.

1901–1919

Abdul Rahman Khan dies in 1901 and Habibullah Khan is elevated to emir. Emir Habibullah Khan pushes for modernization of his country. During his reign, the first colleges open, and hospitals, factories and roads are built. However, he is assassinated in 1919.

1907

The Anglo-Russian Convention of St. Petersburg defines British and Russian spheres of influence in the region, which each country agrees to respect. These borders currently define the present republics of Turkmenistan, Uzbekistan and Tajikistan.

1910

The first telephone lines are built between Kabul and Jalalabad.

1914

Habibullah declares Afghan neutrality in World War I.

1918

Afghan intellectual and poet Mahmud Tarzi introduces modern journalism into Afghanistan with the creation of several newspapers.

1919

Habibullah Khan is assassinated, and his son, Amanullah, is proclaimed emir of Kabul. Amanullah proclaims Afghan independence. The Third Anglo-Afghan War begins and ends in 1919 with an armistice in June and a preliminary Anglo-Afghan treaty signed at the Rawalpindi peace conference with the British beleaguered in the wake of World War I.

1921

Treaties of friendship are signed between Afghanistan and the Soviet Union, Turkey, Italy and Persia. The Anglo-Afghan Treaty of 1921 is signed. The Kabul Conference ends in December 1921 with Britain recognizing Afghan independence in internal and external relations, and diplomatic relations are established between the two countries.

1923

The first Afghan constitution is ratified. It is based on the Belgian, Turkish and Iranian models. A British-Afghan trade convention is also signed, and a criminal code is adopted.

1926
Amanullah adopts the title of shah (king) to replace emir (leader or prince). He launches a series of modernization plans and attempts to limit the power of the Loya Jirga, the National Council.

1928–1929
Tribal rebellion broadens as a result of Amanullah's secular policies. Amanullah flees after civil unrest over his reforms and goes into exile in Italy. On October 17, 1929, Nadir Khan is proclaimed king.

1929
Habibullah Kalakani, a Tajik with appeal to religious conservatives, declares jihad against Amanullah whom he considers an "infidel." He captures Kabul and declares himself Emir (rather than shah) Habibullah II Ghazi. However, he is pejoratively referred to as Bacha-i Saqao (son of the water carrier) and is defeated within nine months by General Nadir Khan. On October 17, 1929, Nadir Khan is proclaimed king.

1930
Nadir Shah confirms the validity of the 1921 and 1923 Anglo-Afghan Agreements as well as other international agreements.

1931
A second Afghan constitution is ratified that is more Islamic in nature though largely based on the first constitution. A new treaty of neutrality and mutual nonaggression is signed between Afghanistan and the Soviet Union.

1933
Zahir Shah becomes king following his father's assassination. The new king rules for the next four decades.

1934
The United States formally recognizes Afghanistan, and Afghanistan subsequently joins the League of Nations.

1937
The Saadabad Pact is signed by Afghanistan, Turkey, Iran and Iraq to withstand European political pressure and interference.

1940
Zahir Shah declares Afghan neutrality in World War II and reaffirms his position in July 1941 and November 1942.

1944
A treaty of friendship is signed between Afghanistan and China.

1947
Britain withdraws from India, setting the stage for the break between Islamic Pakistan and largely secular India. Afghanistan protests the entry of Pakistan to

the United Nations because of Afghanistan's refusal to accept the Durand Line as the international border.

1949

Afghanistan's Loya Jirga repudiates treaties with Britain regarding borders and tribal areas.

1950

A four year trade agreement is signed between Afghanistan and the Soviet Union. Afghan goods are permitted free transit through the Soviet Union and by 1952, trade doubles between the two nations.

1953

Mohammed Daoud Khan, cousin of the king, becomes prime minister and introduces a number of social reforms including allowing women a more public presence. By 1957, women are allowed to attend university and enter the workforce. Daoud also describes US military aid to Pakistan as a "grave danger to the security and peace of Afghanistan."

1955

Soviet Premier Nikita Khrushchev offers Afghanistan a development loan, secret military aid, Soviet support for a plebiscite on Pushtunistan, and a ten year extension of the 1931 friendship treaty. Diplomatic relations between Afghanistan and Pakistan deteriorate as trade and transit between the two countries is closed.

1960

Former King Amanullah dies. Soviet teams discover petroleum and natural gas deposits in northern Afghanistan.

1961

Afghanistan becomes a charter member of the Non-Aligned Movement at the Belgrade Conference. This status sets it apart from Turkey, Iran and Pakistan, all of which are states that established bilateral security arrangements with the US. As relations deteriorate once more, Afghanistan breaks diplomatic ties with Pakistan over tribal, trade and transit issues. Both states accept to have the shah of Iran mediate their dispute.

1963

Mohammed Daoud is forced to resign as prime minister and Dr. Muhammad Yusuf takes his place. Pakistan and Afghanistan reestablish diplomatic and commercial ties.

1964

The Loya Jirga approves a new Afghan constitution that calls for a bicameral legislature, independent judiciary, and freedom of speech, press and, although never enacted, political party formation.

1965

The People's Democratic Party of Afghanistan is established but breaks down into two factions, the Khalq (people's) party and Pacham (flag) party. The US and Soviet Union both provide development assistance, though the Soviets have a near monopoly on military aid.

1967

A protocol on the export of natural gas is signed between the Soviet Union and Afghanistan. The first direct telephone line is completed between Kabul and Herat.

1969

Student unrest in Kabul and a student boycott at Kabul University result in the closing of all primary and secondary schools in Kabul by the Afghan government.

1972

Kabul Radio broadcasts a demand for the creation of an independent Pushtun state to be carved from Pakistan territory.

1973

A treaty between Afghanistan and Iran is ratified which settles the Helmand River dispute. Muhammad Daoud Khan overthrows the last king, Mohammed Zahir Shah, in a military coup. Daoud's regime, the People's Democratic Party of Afghanistan, comes to power. Daoud abolishes the monarchy, dissolves Parliament and names himself president. The Republic of Afghanistan is established with firm ties to the USSR.

1975

A rebellion is mounted in the Panjshir Valley against the government by Islamic extremists. It is put down by the military but its leaders find refuge in Pakistan.

1976

Relations begin to sour between Soviet leader Brezhnev and Daoud, causing Daoud to turn toward Iran and the Arab world for development assistance.

1977

Daoud proposes a new constitution that grants women rights and works to modernize the economy. He also cracks down on opponents, forcing many suspected dissidents out of the government.

1978

Daoud is killed in a communist coup. Nur Mohammad Taraki, one of the founding members of the Afghan Communist Party, takes control of the country as president. Afghanistan proclaims itself to be "nonaligned and independent," and the party declares its policies to be based on Islamic principles, Afghan nationalism and socio-economic justice. Taraki signs a friendship treaty with the Soviet Union. A rivalry grows between Taraki and Hafizullah Amin, his second in command in the Khalq faction of the communist party. At the same time, conservative Islamic and ethnic leaders who objected to social changes introduced by Daoud begin an armed revolt in the countryside. In June, a guerrilla movement, the mujahideen, forms to battle the Soviet-backed government.

1979
American Ambassador Adolph Dubs is killed. The United States ends assistance to Afghanistan. A power struggle between Taraki and Deputy Prime Minister Hafizullah Amin results in Taraki's death on September 14. Amin assumes leadership of the Khalq party and the presidency. The USSR invades Afghanistan on December 24 to bolster the faltering communist regime. On December 27, Amin and many of his followers are executed. Deputy Prime Minister Babrak Karmal becomes prime minister. Widespread opposition to Karmal and the Soviets spawns violent public demonstrations. By early 1980, under Pakistan's sponsorship, the mujahideen have united against Soviet invaders and the USSR-backed Afghan army.

1980
US President Jimmy Carter authorizes a supply of weapons for Afghan resistance through Pakistan. The UN General Assembly adopts Resolution 35 that calls for the withdrawal of foreign troops from Afghanistan. Sixty countries, including the US, boycott the Moscow Olympic Games in protest over the Soviet invasion of Afghanistan.

1982
Some 2.8 million Afghans have fled from the war to Pakistan, and another 1.5 million have fled to Iran. Afghan guerrillas make gains in the rural areas, and Soviet troops hold urban areas.

1983
A first round of UN sponsored talks begin in Geneva on the withdrawal of troops in Afghanistan. They end without progress.

1984
Soviet shelling of Herat and Kandahar results in heavy civilian casualties and the widespread belief that the Soviets engaged in chemical warfare. The Soviet scorched-earth policy aims to kill off resistance fighters in the countryside.

1985
The US increases its assistance to the mujahideen fighters. Gulbuddin Hekmatyar, leader of a key party in the mujahideen alliance, refuses to meet with US President Ronald Reagan.

1986
The mujahideen receive increased arms from the United States, Britain and China via Pakistan. Mikhail Gorbachev announces the unilateral withdrawal of six regiments from Afghanistan by the end of the year.

1987

A meeting of mujahideen fighters in Ghor Province calls for a permanent council of resistance. A new constitution that is "Islamized" is ratified by the Loya Jirga in September.

1988

In September, Osama Bin Laden and 15 other Islamists form the group Al Qaeda, or "the base," to continue their jihad against the Soviets and others who stand in the way of the goal of a pure nation governed by Islam. With their belief that the Soviet's faltering war in Afghanistan was directly attributable to their fighting, they claim victory in their first battle, but also begin to shift their focus to the US, proclaiming that the remaining superpower is the main obstacle to the establishment of a state based on Islam. In June the Afghan Interim Government is formed in Peshawar under Pakistan's supervision.

1989

The Soviets complete their troop withdrawal as stipulated in the Geneva Accords signed the previous year. Following Soviet withdrawal, the mujahideen continue their resistance against the Soviet-backed regime of Dr. Mohammad Najibullah, who had been elected president of the puppet Soviet state in 1986. The mujahideen name Sibhatullah Mojadidi as head of their exiled government.

1991

Rabbani leads a delegation of mujahideen to Moscow in November to discuss the end of the war.

1992

The mujahideen and other rebel groups, with the aid of turncoat government troops, storm Kabul and oust Najibullah from power. Ahmad Shah Masood, legendary guerrilla leader, leads the troops into the capital. The UN offers protection to Najibullah. The mujahideen begin to fracture as warlords fight over the future of Afghanistan. In an agreed rotation, Burhanettin Rabbani assumes the position of president.

1993

Rabbani steps down as head of the Jamiat Party. Dostum and Masood agree to join forces against Hekmatyar.

1994

The Afghan civil war continues as Rabbani extends his mandate until the end of the year. In November, armed Afghan students, Taliban from Pakistan, capture parts of Kandahar. The Taliban head north toward Kabul. Rabbani again extends his mandate at the end of the year.

1995–1999

Continuing drought devastates farmers and makes many rural areas uninhabitable. More than one million Afghans flee to neighboring Pakistan, where they languish in squalid refugee camps.

1995

The Taliban rise to power on promises of peace. Most Afghans, exhausted by years of drought, famine and war, approve of the Taliban for upholding traditional Islamic values and, most importantly, for bringing civil order. The Taliban occupy Wardak Province and capture Herat, though they are unable to capture Kabul.

1996

Hekmatyar enters Kabul and is made prime minister. Hekmatyar forces are defeated at Sarobi and Pul-i Charkhi, and the Taliban capture Kabul. The Taliban publicly executes Najibullah after he is taken from the UN compound. The Taliban outlaw cultivation of poppies for the opium trade, crack down on crime, and curtail the education and employment of women. Women are required to be fully veiled and are not allowed outside alone. Islamic law is enforced via public executions and amputations. The United States refuses to recognize the authority of the Taliban.

1997

The Taliban defeat Masood and Dostum forces north of Kabul. Pakistani sponsored peace talks between the Taliban, Rabbani, Khalili and Dostum prove futile. Pakistan, Saudi Arabia and the UAE recognize the Taliban government.

1998

The Taliban issue orders that all television sets be destroyed and that individuals be tested on their knowledge of Islam. Iran accuses the Taliban of assassinating ten Iranian diplomats and one journalist. Following Al Qaeda's bombings of two American embassies in Africa, US President Clinton orders cruise missile attacks against Bin Laden's training camps in Afghanistan. The attacks miss the Al Qaeda leaders.

1999

By now considered an international terrorist, Bin Laden is widely believed to be hiding in Afghanistan, where he is cultivating thousands of followers in terrorist training camps. The US demands that Bin Laden be extradited to stand trial for the embassy bombings, but the Taliban refuses. The UN punishes Afghanistan with sanctions restricting trade and economic development to force Afghanistan to hand over Bin Laden for trial.

2000

Mullah Omar forbids the cultivation of poppy. In December, the UN imposes further sanctions on Afghanistan.

February 2001

The US orders that Taliban offices in New York be closed.

March 2001

Ignoring international protests, the Taliban carry out their threat to destroy Buddhist statues in Bamiyan, Afghanistan, saying they are an affront to Islam.

April 2001

Mullah Mohammad Rabbani, the second most powerful Taliban leader after the supreme commander Mullah Mohammad Omar, dies of liver cancer in Pakistan.

May 2001

In its annual terror report, the US State Department accuses Pakistan of providing military support to the Taliban. The Taliban order religious minorities to wear tags identifying themselves as non-Muslims, and Hindu women to veil themselves like other Afghan women.

June 2001

The Taliban caves in to international pressure when it revokes a rule that non-Muslims identify themselves with tags.

August 2001

Rashid Dostum, a leader in the opposition Northern Alliance, resumes his attacks on Taliban positions.

4 September 2001

A month after arresting them, the Taliban put eight international aid workers on trial for spreading Christianity. Under Taliban rule, proselytizing is punishable by death. The group is held in various Afghan prisons for months and finally released on November 15.

9 September 2001

Masood, leader of the opposition Northern Alliance, is killed by assassins posing as journalists.

11 September 2001

Suicide attacks on the US kill more than 3,000 people and destroy the two towers of the World Trade Center in New York City and part of the Pentagon in Washington, DC.

7 October 2001

Osama Bin Laden, held responsible for the September 11 attacks on America, is protected by the Taliban after demands for his capture. In response, the US and Britain, working with the forces of the United Front (UNIFSA) and NATO, launch Operation Enduring Freedom and air strikes against Afghanistan.

12 November 2001

The Taliban lose control of Mazar-i Sharif to Northern Alliance opposition forces, which within days also march into Kabul and other key cities.

5 December 2001

Afghan groups agree upon a deal in Bonn, Germany—the Bonn Agreement—for the establishment of an interim government, the Transitional Islamic Republic of Afghanistan, with Hamid Karzai as chairman. The International Security Assistance Force in Afghanistan (ISAF) is established under the leadership of the UK, with a mandate from the UN.

7 December 2001

The Taliban finally give up their last stronghold of Kandahar, but Mullah Omar remains at large. Two days later, Taliban leaders surrender the group's final Afghan territory, the province of Zabul. The move leads the Pakistan-based *Afghan Islamic Press* to declare "the rule of the Taliban in Afghanistan has totally ended."

22 December 2001

Pashtun royalist Hamid Karzai is sworn in as head of a 30 member interim power-sharing government, the Afghan Interim Authority.

January 2002

The first contingent of foreign peacekeepers are put in place. International donors convene at the International Conference on Reconstruction Assistance to Afghanistan in Tokyo, pledging $1.8 billion, and a total of $4.5 billion over five years.

18 April 2002

The former king, Zahir Shah, returns, but says he makes no claim to the throne.

May 2002

The UN Security Council extends the mandate of the International Security Assistance Force (ISAF) until December 2002.

June 2002

The Emergency Loya Jirga is convened by the UN. It elects Hamid Karzai as interim head of the Transitional Authority Government. Karzai picks members of his administration to serve until elections in 2004.

July 2002

Vice-President Haji Abdul Qadir, brother of Abdul Haq, is assassinated by gunmen in Kabul. A US air raid in the Uruzgan Province kills approximately 48 civilians, many of them members of a wedding party.

5 September 2002

President Karzai narrowly escapes an assassination attempt in Kandahar, his home town.

December 2002

President Karzai, Pakistani and Turkmen leaders sign a deal to build a gas pipeline through Afghanistan, carrying Turkmen gas to Pakistan. The first Provincial Reconstruction Team (PRT) is established.

January 2003

Reconstruction of the Kabul-Kandahar highway begins. The American army completes the formation of 400 recruits for the new Afghan army.

19 March 2003

The US launches war against Iraq.

May 2003
Reports of human rights violations at the American Guantanamo Bay detention center in Cuba begin to reach the general public.

18 May 2003
Afghanistan adopts a National Drug Control Strategy for the next five years.

6 June 2003
Six peacekeepers are killed in a Kabul blast.

11 August 2003
NATO takes control of security in Kabul, its first-ever operational commitment outside Europe. Aid agencies appeal for a UN resolution to expand the role of the multinational security force in Afghanistan.

October 2003
The disarmament, demobilization and reintegration (DDR) process begins.

November 2003
The UN says relief work in Afghanistan cannot continue on existing terms after a French aid worker is murdered by Taliban insurgents. Appointment of the NATO Senior Civilian Representative in Afghanistan occurs, who is responsible for advancing the political-military aspects of the alliance's commitment to the country, for working closely with ISAF, for liaises with the Afghan government and other international organizations, and for maintaining contacts with neighboring countries.

6 December 2003
A US bombing mistakenly kills Afghan children.

January 2004
The Loya Jirga adopts a new constitution following input from nearly 500,000 Afghans. The constitution provides for a strong presidency and three branches of government within a republican system. The official languages are Pashto and Dari, and the new constitution calls for equality for women.

March 2004
Afghanistan secures $8.2 billion in aid over three years at the International Conference on Afghan Reconstruction in Berlin. The conference also presents the Berlin Declaration on Counter-Narcotics, within the framework of the Kabul Good-Neighborly Relations Declaration.

April 2004
Reports of the abuse, rape and torture of prisoners at the US-run Abu Ghraib prison in Iraq, as well as graphic pictures showing American military personnel in the act of abusing prisoners, come to public attention.

14 April 2004
Osama Bin Laden offers Europe a truce if it "stops attacking Muslims."

May 2004

The Doha I Conference on regional police cooperation is held, focusing on Afghanistan's security and regional stability. The international community pledges $350 million through 2007 for rebuilding the Afghan police force and for regional police cooperation.

June 2004

NATO pledges to increase the number of peacekeeping forces in Afghanistan to strengthen security beyond Kabul and safeguard elections in September.

July 2004

Médecins sans Frontières pulls out of Afghanistan after 24 years due to security deterioration. NATO agrees to provide support for the presidential elections in Afghanistan.

August 2004

Activity is reported at Al Qaeda camps in Pakistan.

September 2004

A rocket fired at a helicopter carrying President Karzai misses its target. It is the most serious attempt on his life since September 2002.

October—December 2004

Presidential elections are finally held after being delayed twice. Hamid Karzai is declared the winner, with 55.4% of the vote, with over 10.5 million voters. He is sworn in, amid tight security, in December. Karzai's strongest challenger, Yunis Qanuni, comes in second with 16.3% of the votes. The elections are not without controversy. Allegations of fraud and ballot stuffing are brought up by many of the presidential candidates including Yunis Qanuni. A panel of international experts is sent in to investigate the matter. While finding evidence of voting irregularities, they find that these are not enough to affect the outcome of the elections.

26 December 2004

A 9.3 magnitude earthquake and subsequent tsunami in east Asia leave 229,866 people lost, including 186,983 dead, and 42,883 missing.

January 2005—August 2006

Afghan militants change tactics and follow the lead of suicide bomber Iraqi insurgents. Sixty-four suicide attacks are recorded, resulting in 181 deaths (not including suicide bombers).

29 January 2005

The Afghan Independent Human Rights Commission presents a report asking for further attention to human rights violations in Afghanistan.

February 2005

Several hundred people are killed in the harshest winter weather in a decade. Major advances in the disarmament process are announced. Afghanistan adopts the Counter-Narcotics Implementation Plan.

March 2005
Rashid Dostum is appointed as the chief of staff to the commander of the armed forces. Yunis Qanuni announces a new political alliance on March 31.

April 2005
President Karzai welcomes the formation of Qanuni's political alliance.

May 2005
Riots erupt in Afghanistan over reports of US desecration of the Koran at Guantanamo Bay. Details emerge of alleged prisoner abuse by US forces at detention centers.

June 2005
A suicide bomber in police uniform kills 20 in a Kandahar mosque. Osama Bin Laden is declared "alive and well." Fighting continues to intensify in southern Afghanistan.

July 2005
London terrorist attacks on the city's public transport system kill 52.

August 2005
Hurricane Katrina devastates the US Gulf Coast.

September 2005
The first parliamentary and provincial elections in more than 30 years are held. Over 6.2 million Afghans vote.

December 2005
The new National Assembly holds its inaugural session in Kabul.

January 2006
Afghanistan adopts the interim Afghanistan National Development Strategy (iANDS), to establish a strategy for security, governance, economic growth and poverty reduction.

February 2006
International donors at the International Conference on Afghanistan in London pledge more than $10 billion in reconstruction aid over five years. Violent protests occur over the publication of editorial cartoons satirizing the Prophet Mohammad.

28 February 2006
The Doha II Conference on Border Management in Afghanistan—a "Regional Approach"—is held. It aims at strengthening Afghanistan's borders by applying modern integrated border management, modernizing its border crossing points, and increasing cross-border cooperation.

March 2006
A Christian convert faces execution in Afghanistan.

May 2006
Violent anti-US protests in Kabul, the worst since the fall of the Taliban in 2001, erupt after a US military vehicle crashes and kills several people. Eighty are killed in an air strike in southern Afghanistan. An earthquake in Java, Indonesia, kills 6,000.

May-June 2006
Scores of people are killed in battles between Taliban fighters and Afghan and Coalition forces in the south during an offensive known as Operation Mountain Thrust.

26–28 June 2006
The Second Ministerial Conference on Drug Trafficking Routes from Afghanistan is held in Moscow.

July 2006
The Second Tokyo Conference on Consolidation of Peace in Afghanistan is held. Fighting erupts between Hezbollah forces in southern Lebanon and Israeli troops.

July 2006
NATO troops take over the leadership of military operations in the south of Afghanistan. Fierce fighting ensues as the forces try to extend government control in areas where Taliban influence is strong.

3 August 2006
Twenty-one are killed when a suicide car bomber rams a NATO convoy in Kandahar.

5 September 2006
A north Waziristan accord is signed between Pakistan and pro-Taliban militants on the Afghan border to end the unrest there. NATO kills 94 Taliban fighters in southern Afghanistan. NATO fails to meet the plea by commanders in Afghanistan for more troops. Poland vows to boost the NATO Afghan force.

October 2006
NATO assumes responsibility for security across the whole of Afghanistan, taking command in the east from a US-led Coalition force. Chancellor Merkel calls photos of German soldiers in Afghanistan playing with a skull "shocking and disgusting." Civilians are killed in NATO raids in southern Afghanistan.

19 November 2006
The Second Regional Economic Cooperation Conference on Afghanistan is held, and adopts the New Delhi Declaration to continue the fight against terrorism and to support the establishment of a broad-based, multiethnic and sovereign Afghan government.

November-December 2006
NATO eyes an Afghan handover in 2008, and signals Afghan reinforcements. Democrats take control of the US Congress after November midterm elections. Saddam Hussein is sentenced to death and later hanged.

January 2007
NATO declares from Belgium that it will "step up Afghan support."

30–31 January 2007
A Joint Coordination and Monitoring Board meeting at senior officials level is held in Berlin, where agreements are made to step-up efforts to build Afghan ownership of security, governance and socio-economic recovery. The conference results in pledges of $4.4 billion for 2007, and $8.2 billion over the next three years.

March 2007
Pakistan says it has arrested Mullah Obaidullah Akhund, the third most senior member of the Taliban's leadership council. NATO and Afghan forces launch Operation Achilles, said to be their largest offensive to date against the Taliban in the south. There is heavy fighting in Helmand Province. The UN announces the successful conclusion of the DDR process started October 2003, and the launch of the program of Disbandment of Illegal Armed Groups (DIAG).

May 2007
The Taliban's most senior military commander, Mullah Dadullah, is killed during fighting with US and Afghan forces. Afghan and Pakistani troops clash on the border in some of the worst violence in decades.

May-June 2007
NATO raids kill 46 civilians. Afghan police are hit by a suicide bomber, killing 35.

July 2007
The former king, Zahir Shah, dies. Two German hostages held by the Taliban are reported killed. The Taliban seizes 23 South Korean missionaries and holds them as hostages. Pakistan declares it will not tolerate a US attack against Bin Laden within its borders.

Timeline Sources

Adamec, Ludwig W. *Historical Dictionary of Afghanistan.* Oxford: Scarecrow Press, 2003.
http://usinfo.state.gov/sa/Archive/2006/Jan/26–44634.html.
http://www.afghanistanwatch.org/facts.html.
http://www.afghanweb.com/history/chron/index4.html.
http://www.eu2007.bmi.bund.de/nn_992442/Internet/Content/Themen/Police/DataAndFacts/Assistance__in__rebuilding__the__police__force__Afghanistan.html.
http://www.fco.gov.uk/servlet/Front?pagename=OpenMarket/Xcelerate/ShowPage&c=Page&cid=1050510189265.
http://www.guardian.co.uk/afghanistan/subsection/0,,884042,00.html.
http://www.mapreport.com/countries/afghanistan.html.
http://www.metmuseum.org/toah/ht/10/nc/ht10nc.htm (October 2004).

http://www.nato.int/issues/afghanistan/index.html.
http://news.bbc.co.uk/2/hi/south_asia/1839896.stm.
http://www.oxuscom.com/greatgame.htm.
http://www.pbs.org/newshour/indepth_coverage/asia/afghanistan/timeline/timeline7.html.
http://www.usaid.gov/press/factsheets/2003/fs031214.html.
Magnus, Ralph and Eden Naby. *Afghanistan: Mullah, Marx, and Mujahid.* Boulder: Westview Press, 1998.
Rasanayagam, Angelo. *Afghanistan: A Modern History.* London: I. B. Tauris, 2003.
Rashid, Ahmed. *Taliban.* New Haven: Yale University Press, 2000.
Saikal, Amin. *Modern Afghanistan.* London: I. B. Tauris, 2004.
Tanner, Stephen. *Afghanistan: A Military History from Alexander the Great to the Fall of the Taliban.* New York: Da Capo Press, 2002.
Vogelsang, Willem. *The Afghans.* Oxford: Blackwell Publishers, 2002.

Appendix II: UN Security Council Resolutions Related to Afghanistan

29 August 1946
Resolution 8: Recommends the admittance of Afghanistan to the UN. (Afghanistan is approved entry by the UN General Assembly on November 9, 1946, and Abdul Husain Aziz becomes Afghanistan's first representative to the UN on November 19, 1946).

31 October 1988
Resolution 622: Confirms the arrangement to send military officers from existing UN missions to Afghanistan and Pakistan to monitor the implementation of the Geneva Accords. (The accords call for Soviet troop withdrawal and the return of Afghan refugees.)

11 January 1990
Resolution 647: Extends UN operations in Afghanistan and Pakistan by two months.

22 October 1996
Resolution 1076: Calls for a cessation of armed hostilities in Afghanistan.

28 August 1998
Resolution 1193: Condemns attacks on UN personnel in Afghanistan and the Consulate-General of Iran in Mazar-i Sharif; calls on reconciliation between warring factions in Afghanistan to establish a broad-based, representative government.

8 December 1998
Resolution 1214: Demands that the Taliban stop providing sanctuary and assistance to international terrorists and that the Taliban halt the cultivation, production and trafficking of illegal drugs.

15 October 1999
Resolution 1267: Imposes economic and military sanctions on the Taliban should they refuse to surrender Osama Bin Laden; prohibits international flights of Afghan aircraft and freezes the financial assets of the Taliban.

19 December 2000

Resolution 1333: Broadens the sanctions regime imposed by Resolution 1267; reiterates the UN Security Council's call for the Taliban to close terrorist training camps, to hand over Osama Bin Laden, and for the Taliban to halt illegal drug activities.

30 July 2001

Resolution 1363: Creates a Monitoring Group and Sanctions Enforcement Support Team to implement the economic and military sanctions imposed by Resolutions 1267 and 1333.

12 September 2001

Resolution 1368: Condemns the September 11 terrorist attacks on the US; declares UN commitment to an immediate response.

28 September 2001

Resolution 1373: Encourages criminalizing, prosecuting and removing state links and funds to terrorism; establishes the UN Counter-Terrorism Committee.

12 November 2001

Resolution 1377: Renewal of support for the Counter-Terrorism Committee.

14 November 2001

Resolution 1378: Condemns specifically the Taliban and Al Qaeda for the September 11 attacks; supports the UN's role in the creation of a new transitional Afghan government that will lead to a permanent system; asks for international support in terms of security for Afghans and foreign actors, as well as in the eradication of Taliban power.

6 December 2001

Resolution 1383: Welcomes the Bonn Agreement of December 5, 2001 establishing a transitional government; asks for the full implementation of the agreements, Afghan support for international intervention, and for international funding.

20 December 2001

Resolution 1386: Establishes the International Security Assistance Force (ISAF) to assist the Afghan Interim Authority and UN officials for a period of six months; asks for international support in funding and resources of ISAF and for the removal of Afghan military from Kabul, to be replaced with ISAF troops; authorizes a funding system via a trust fund for ISAF.

16 January 2002

Resolution 1390: Condemnation of the Taliban, Al Qaeda and Osama Bin Laden; demands an assets freeze of said designated individuals and entities, a travel ban preventing the entry into or transit through state territories by the designated individuals, and an arms embargo preventing the direct or indirect supply, sale and transfer from state territories or by their nationals outside their territories, or using their flag vessels or aircraft, of arms and related materiel of all types, spare parts, and technical advice, assistance, or training related to military activities, to designated individuals and entities; asks for international information and support.

28 March 2002
Resolution 1401: Encourages the fulfillment of international donation promises from the Tokyo conference; establishes the UN Assistance Mission in Afghanistan (UNAMA) for one year to aid the Interim Government; urges fund and resource coordination via UN and Afghan Interim Authority channels.

23 May 2002
Resolution 1413: Extends the mandate of ISAF six months beyond June 20, 2002, and asks for further international funds, resources, and support.

26 June 2002
Resolution 1419: Congratulates the holding of the Emergency Loya Jirga June 11–19, and its large turnout, including by women; recognizes the election of Hamid Karzai as Interim President as well as the leader of the Afghan Transitional Authority; encourages further development and the resolution of security, narcotic and human rights issues; calls for fulfillment of financial aid promises from Tokyo; asks for further international support, especially concerning the refugee issue, and asks Afghans to continue their support of UN and humanitarian forces.

27 November 2002
Resolution 1444: Extends ISAF's mandate for one additional year; asking for additional international support in aiding ISAF and Afghan Transitional Authority efforts.

24 December 2002
Resolution 1453: Recognizes the Afghan Transitional Authority as the sole legitimate government and continues to pledge full support for the Bonn Agreement; supports the Kabul Declaration on Good-Neighborly Relations, signed December 22, 2002, by the Transitional Authority of Afghanistan, as well as China, Iran, Pakistan, Tajikistan, Turkmenistan and Uzbekistan.

17 January 2003
Resolution 1455: Reiterates condemnation of Al Qaeda and the Taliban; asks for further support in gaining information on and for the prosecution of these; enhances the influence of the Counter-Terrorism Committee within the Security Council and asks for further international cooperation with the committee and its monitoring group.

20 January 2003
Resolution 1456: Further condemns any supporters of terrorist factions as well as terrorists themselves; asks for the intensification of the Counter-Terrorism Committee in gaining international support and cooperation.

28 March 2003
Resolution 1471: Extends UNAMA for an additional year beyond March 28, 2003; asks for additional international support and funding for the Afghan Transitional Authority and through the Afghan Consultative Group Process; requests support for security, human rights and counter-narcotics activities wherever local officials deem it necessary.

13 October 2003
Resolution 1510: Extends ISAF's mandate for an additional year to ensure security for Afghan Transitional Authority and UN forces; asks for the continued cooperation of ISAF with the Afghan Transitional Authority, Special Representative of the Secretary-General Lakhdar Brahimi, and with the forces of the Operation Enduring Freedom Coalition.

30 January 2004
Resolution 1526: Reiterates the terms of Resolution 1390; strengthens the Counter-Terrorism Committee's mandate in informing the Security Council; establishes a New York-based Analytical Support and Sanctions Monitoring Team to aid the committee specifically in different areas relating to Al Qaeda and the Taliban.

26 March 2004
Resolution 1535: Establishes the Counter-Terrorism Committee Executive Directorate; expands the Counter-Terrorism Committee's activities to include visits to member states.

26 March 2004
Resolution 1536: Extends UNAMA's mandate for an additional year; encourages further efforts for voter registration and security for the upcoming national elections; recognizes the Loya Jirga's January 4, 2004 constitution; supports further efforts towards the disarmament, demobilization and reintegration (DDR) process; asks for continued counter-narcotic efforts; asks for the continued assistance to the Afghan Independent Human Rights Commission, especially for women's rights; supports the establishment of the Afghan National Army and Afghan National Police.

17 September 2004
Resolution 1563: Recognizes continuing problems in Afghanistan, as well as efforts of differing success (such as those of NATO's Provincial Reconstruction Teams); extends the mandate of ISAF for another year; asks for continued international support and cooperation.

24 February 2005
Resolution 1589: Extends the mandate of UNAMA for another year; encourages the establishment of a strong framework for free and fair elections; asks for international support and funds in ensuring a smooth election process, in supporting

ISAF and Provincial Reconstruction Teams, and in coordination with UNAMA and the Afghan government; welcomes the progress of the DDR process in disarmament, and that of the Government of Afghanistan in the implementation of a national drug control policy adopted May 2003 and in the launch of the 2005 Counter-Narcotics Implementation Plan in February 2005, further asking for international counter-narcotics support; welcomes the signing on April 1, 2004 of the Berlin Declaration on Counter-Narcotics within the framework of the Kabul Declaration on Good-Neighborly Relations of December 22, 2002; commends the Afghan Independent Human Rights Commission for its efforts to monitor respect for human rights in Afghanistan as well as to foster and protect these rights, and welcomes in this regard the commission's report of January 29, 2005 and the proposed national strategy for transitional justice, and requests international support for that endeavor.

29 July 2005
Resolution 1617: Reiterates Resolution 1390; defines association with a terrorist faction such as Al Qaeda or the Taliban; encourages closer UN cooperation with Interpol, especially concerning stolen travel documents that could be aiding Al Qaeda or Taliban international movement; extends the mandate of the New York-based monitoring team for 17 months.

13 September 2005
Resolution 1623: Extends ISAF's mandate for another year, and asks for further international support and strengthening of the force.

14 September 2005
Resolution 1624: Considers the issue of incitement to commit acts of terrorism; expands the Counter-Terrorism Committee's mandate to include monitoring its implementation.

15 February 2006
Resolution 1659: Supports the establishment of the Afghanistan Compact in London on January 31, 2006; welcomes the interim Afghanistan National Development Strategy (iANDS) presented by the Afghan government and the political, security and financial pledges made by participants at the London conference; encourages international support, including through contribution to the Counter Narcotics Trust Fund, for the updated National Drug Control Strategy presented by the Afghan government at the London conference; supports continued efforts by NATO and ISAF.

23 March 2006
Resolution 1662: Extends UNAMA's mandate for another year; asks for the completion of the DDR process by June 2006; welcomes the outcome of the Doha Conference on Border Management on February 28, 2006, the inauguration of the Afghan National Assembly, and the adoption of the Action Plan on Peace, Justice and Reconciliation on December 12, 2005.

12 November 2006

Resolution 1707: Extends ISAF's mandate for another year, and asks for continued international support and funds.

22 December 2006

Resolution 1735: Reiterates Resolution 1390 and asks for continued international counter-terrorism cooperation; suggests the creation of a consolidated list of information on known terrorist individuals and entities.

23 March 2007

Resolution 1746: Welcomes the New Delhi Declaration adopted at the Second Regional Economic Cooperation Conference on Afghanistan on November 19, 2006; extends the mandate of UNAMA for another year; acknowledges the central role played by the Joint Coordination and Monitoring Board in facilitating and monitoring the implementation of the Afghanistan Compact, stresses the role of the JCMB to support Afghanistan by inter alia coordinating international assistance and reconstruction programs, and encourages efforts to strengthen the JCMB Secretariat; welcomes the decision by the European Union to establish a mission in the field of policing with linkages to the wider rule of law and counter-narcotics, to assist and enhance current efforts in the area of police reform at central and provincial levels; welcomes the successful conclusion of the DDR process started in October 2003, as well as the launch of the program of disbandment of illegal armed groups (DIAG) and the commitments made in this regard at the Second Tokyo Conference on Consolidation of Peace in Afghanistan on July 5, 2006; calls for determined efforts by the Afghan government to pursue at all levels the timely implementation of the program throughout the country, including through the implementation of the newly adopted Action Plan; calls upon the Afghan government, with support from the international community, to begin planning and preparation for Afghanistan's next election cycle, including the establishment of a permanent Civil Voter Registry (CVR) as called for in the Afghanistan Compact, the passage and implementation of an updated election law, and financial and political support for the Independent Election Commission (IEC) to allow for free and fair elections; welcomes the outcome of the Second Ministerial Conference on Drug Trafficking Routes from Afghanistan organized by the Government of the Russian Federation in cooperation with the United Nations Office on Drugs and Crime held in Moscow from June 26–28, 2006, within the framework of the Paris Pact initiative; recognizes the importance of voluntary, safe, orderly return and sustainable reintegration of the remaining Afghan refugees for the stability of the country and the region; requests strong international aid and support in all of these contexts.

Bibliography

ABC News. "Despite Deep Challenges in Daily Life, Afghans Express a Positive Outlook (ABC News Poll)." 7 December 2005. http://www.tcf.org/afghanistanwatch/charneyresearchpoll.pdf.

Adamec, Ludwig W. *Afghanistan 1900–1923: A Diplomatic History.* Berkeley: University of California Press, 1967.

Afghan Civil Society Forum and Afghan Youth Coordination Agency. *Mapping Youth Organizations in Afghanistan.* Kabul: ACSF, 2005.

Afghan Civil Society Forum-swisspeace. "People Make the Constitution: Civil Society and Civic Education on the Constitution-Making Process." *Final Narrative Donor Report.* Kabul: ACSF-swisspeace, 2004.

AFP. "Afghan Peacekeeping Expansion 'Too Little, Too Late': Aid Agencies Warn." 7 October 2003.

Agency Coordinating Body for Afghan Relief. "Provincial Reconstruction Teams and the Security Situation in Afghanistan." (Kabul: Agency Coordinating Body for Afghan Relief, July 2003).

"Aid Workers: Afghanistan in Jeopardy." *USA Today,* 22 January 2004.

Akiner, Shirin. "Prospects for Civil Society in Tajikistan." In Amyn B. Sajoo, ed., *Civil Society in the Muslim World: Comparative Perspectives.* London: I. B. Tauris Publishers, 2002.

Amnesty International. *Afghanistan: Police Reconstruction Essential for the Protection of Human Rights.* ASA 11/003/2003, March 2003.

Amstutz, J. Bruce. *Afghanistan: The First Five Years of Soviet Occupation.* Washington, DC: National Defense University Press, 1986.

Andeshmand, Muhammad Akram. *Amrika dar Afghanistan* [The US in Afghanistan]. Kabul, 2005.

Appleby, R. Scott. "The Quandary of Leadership." In Khaled Abou El Fadl, ed., *The Place of Tolerance in Islam.* Boston: Beacon Press, 2002.

Archambeaud, Gait. *Le principe d'égalité et la Constitution de l'Afghanistan de janvier 2004.* Paris: L'Harmattan, 2005.

Asad, Amir Zada and Robert Harris. *The Politics and Economics of Drug Production on the Pakistan-Afghanistan Border.* Hampshire: Ashgate, 2003.

Asia Foundation. *Afghanistan in 2006: A Survey of the Afghan People.* Kabul: The Asia Foundation, 2006.

———. *Democracy in Afghanistan 2004: A Survey of the Afghanistan Electorate.* Kabul: The Asia Foundation, 2004.

Azarbaijani-Moghaddam, Sippi. *Technical Lessons Learned from the Afghan Civil Society Forum (ACSF/swisspeace) Civic Education for the Constitution Project.* Kabul: ACSF-swisspeace, 2003.

Azarbaijani-Moghaddam, Sippi, Conrad Schetter, and Susanne Schmeidl. "The Transition from Relief to Development from a Human Security Perspective: Afghanistan." New York: Commission on Human Security, 2002.

Bajpai, Kanti. "The Idea of Human Security." *International Studies,* vol. 40, no. 3 (July-September 2003): 195–228.

Barfield, Thomas. "Radical Political Islam in an Afghan Context." In *Political Transition in Afghanistan: State, Islam, and Civil Society.* Woodrow Wilson International Center, Asia Program Special Report, no. 122 (2004).

Barfield, Thomas, Neamat Nojumi, and J Alexander Thier. "The Clash of Two Goods: State and Non-State Dispute Resolution in Afghanistan." Washington, DC: United States Institute of Peace, 2006. http://www.usip.org/ruleoflaw/projects/clash_two_goods.pdf.

Barnard, Anne. "Afghan Projects Slow to Reach Villages." *Boston Globe,* 17 October 2004.

Barnett, Michael. *Eyewitness to a Genocide: The United Nations and Rwanda.* Ithaca: Cornell University Press, 2002.

Bassiouni, M. Cherif and Gamal M. Badr. "The Shari'ah: Sources, Interpretation, and Rule-Making." *UCLA Journal of Islamic and Near Eastern Law,* vol. 1, no. 2 (2002): 32–44.

BBC News. "NATO Seals Afghanistan Expansion Plan." 1 October 2004.

———. "Woman Singer Angers Afghan Judges." 14 January 2004.

Bêgî, Abd al-Raûf. *Afghânistân ba'd az pîrûzî-yi inqilâb-i islâmî tâ suqût-i shamâl ba dast-i Tâlibân, 1991–1998* [Afghanistan from the Victory of the Islamic Revolution until the Fall of the North to the Taliban, 1991–1998]. Peshawar: 2000.

Bellamy, Alex J. and Matt McDonald, "'The Utility of Human Security': Which Humans? What Security? A Reply to Thomas & Tow." *Security Dialogue,* vol. 33, no. 3 (September 2002): 373–377.

Bendix, Reinhard. *Kings or People: Power and the Mandate to Rule.* Berkeley: University of California Press, 1980.

Berman, Sheri. "Islamism, Revolution, and Civil Society." *Perspectives on Politics,* vol. 1, no. 2 (2002): 257–272.

Berntsen, Gary. *Jawbreaker: The Attack on Bin Laden and Al-Qaeda: A Personal Account by the CIA's Key Field Commander.* New York: Three Rivers Press, 2005.

Bhatia, Michael. "The Future of the Mujahideen: Legitimacy, Legacy and Demobilization in Post-Bonn Afghanistan." *International Peacekeeping,* vol. 14 (2007): 90–107.

Bhatia, Michael, Kevin Lanigan, and Philip Wilkinson. "Minimal Investments, Minimal Results: The Failure of Security Policy in Afghanistan." Kabul: Afghanistan Research and Evaluation Unit, Briefing Paper, June 2004.

Bieber, Florian. "Power Sharing after Yugoslavia: Functionality and Dysfunctionality of Power-Sharing Institutions in Post-War Bosnia, Macedonia, and Kosovo." In Sid Noel, ed., *From Power Sharing to Democracy: Post-Conflict Institutions in Ethnically Divided Societies.* Montreal and Kingston: McGill-Queen's University Press, 2006.

Black, Anthony. *The History of Islamic Political Thought: From the Prophet to the Present.* New York: Routledge, 2001.

Bradsher, Henry S. *Afghanistan and the Soviet Union.* Durham: Duke University Press Policy Studies, 1983.

Brancati, Dawn. "Decentralization: Fueling the Fire or Dampening the Flames of Ethnic Conflict and Secessionism." *International Organization,* vol. 60, no. 3 (2006): 651–685.

Brennan, Geoffrey and Alan Hamlin. *Democratic Devices and Desires.* Cambridge: Cambridge University Press, 2000.

Brown, MacAlister and Joseph J. Zasloff. *Cambodia Confounds the Peacemakers 1979–1998.* Ithaca: Cornell University Press, 1998.

Burke, Edmund. *Select Works of Edmund Burke,* vol. I. Indianapolis: Liberty Fund, 1999.

Byman, Daniel. *Deadly Connections: States that Sponsor Terrorism.* Cambridge: Cambridge University Press, 2005.

Byman, Daniel, Michael Scheuer, Anatol Lieven, and W. Patrick Lang. "Symposium: Iraq, Afghanistan, and the War on 'Terror'." *Middle East Policy,* vol. 12, no. 1 (Spring 2005): 1–24.

Byrd, W. and C. Ward. *Drugs and Development in Afghanistan.* Washington, DC: World Bank, Social Development Papers, no. 18, 2004.

Canfield, Robert L., ed. *Turko-Persia in Historical Perspective.* New York: Cambridge University Press, 1991.

Caplan, Richard. *International Governance of War-Torn Territories: Rule and Reconstruction.* Oxford: Oxford University Press, 2005.

Center for the Study of Islam and Democracy (Washington, DC). *The Muslim Democrat,* vol. 5, no. 1 (2004).

Chayes, Sarah. "With a Little Help from Our Friends." *New York Times,* 26 May 2005.

Chesterman, Simon. *You, The People: The United Nations, Transitional Administration, and State-Building.* Oxford: Oxford University Press, 2004.

Chopra, Jarat. "The UN's Kingdom of East Timor." *Survival,* vol. 42, no. 3 (Autumn 2000): 27–39.

Clarke, Richard A. *Against All Enemies: Inside America's War on Terror.* New York: Free Press, 2004.

Congressional Research Unit (US). "Afghanistan: Post-War Governance, Security, and U.S. Policy." Washington, DC: The Library of Congress, 17 March 2006.

Cordesman, Anthony. *Iraq: What Is to Be Done.* Washington, DC: Center for Strategic and International Studies, 2004.

Cotton, James. *East Timor, Australia and Regional Order: Intervention and Its Aftermath in Southeast Asia.* London: Routledge Curzon, 2004.

Counterpart International. *Afghanistan Civil Society Assessment.* Washington, DC: CPI, 2005.

Crone, Patricia. *God's Rule—Government and Islam: Six Centuries of Medieval Islamic Political Thought.* New York: Columbia University Press, 2004.

Cruz, Consuelo. *Political Culture and Institutional Development in Costa Rica and Nicaragua: World-Making in the Tropics.* New York: Cambridge University Press, 2005.

Dallaire, Roméo. *Shake Hands with the Devil: The Failure of Humanity in Rwanda.* Toronto: Random House, 2003.

Danishyar, Abdul Aziz., ed. *The Afghanistan Republic Annual—1974.* Kabul: Government Press, 1974.

Deutsche Welle. "US Blames Europe for Failures in Afghanistan." 30 September 2004.

Dodge, Toby. *Iraq's Future: The Aftermath of Regime Change.* New York: Routledge, 2005.

Dorronsoro, Gilles. *La révolution Afghane,* Paris: Karthala, 2000.

———. *Revolution Unending: Afghanistan, 1979 to the Present.* New York: Columbia University Press, 2005.

Doyle, Michael W. *UN Peacekeeping in Cambodia: UNTAC's Civilian Mandate.* Boulder: Lynne Rienner, 1995.

Dupree, Louis. *Afghanistan.* New York: Oxford University Press, 2002.

Eickelman, Dale. "Communication and Control in the Middle East: Publication and its Discontents." In Dale Eickelman and Jon Anderson, eds., *New Media in the Muslim World.* Bloomington: Indiana University Press, 2003.

———. "Trans-State Islam and Security." In Susanne Hoeber Rudolph and James Piscatori, eds., *Transnational Religions and Fading States.* Boulder: Westview Press, 1997.

Eickelman, Dale and Jon Anderson. "Redefining Muslim Publics." In Eickelman and Anderson, eds., *New Media in the Muslim World.* Bloomington: Indiana University Press, 2003.

Eisenstadt, S. N. *The Political Systems of Empires: The Rise and Fall of the Historical Bureaucratic Societies.* New York: The Free Press, 1969.

El-Affendi, Abdelwahab. "What is Liberal Islam? The Elusive Reformation." *Journal of Democracy,* vol. 14, no. 2 (2003): 37–38.

El Fadl, Khaled Abou. "Islam and the Theology of Power." *Middle Eastern Report,* Winter (2001): 28–33.

European Union. "Afghanistan: The EU Keeps Its Promises," EU Press Release, Memo/07/34, 26 January 2007.

Evans, Anne and Yasin Osmani. *Assessing Progress: Update Report on Subnational Administration in Afghanistan.* Kabul: Afghanistan Research and Evaluation Unit, 2005.

Evans, Anne, Nick Manning, Yasin Osmani, Anne Tully, and Andrew Wilder. *A Guide to Government in Afghanistan.* Washington, DC, and Kabul: The World Bank and the Afghanistan Research and Evaluation Unit, 2004.

Evans, Anne, Nick Manning, and Anne Tully, with Yasin Osmani and Andrew Wilder, *Subnational Administration in Afghanistan: Assessment and Recommendations for Action.* Kabul and Washington, DC: The World Bank and the Afghanistan Research and Evaluation Unit, 2004.

Farley, Lawrence T. *Plebiscites and Sovereignty: The Crisis of Political Illegitimacy.* Boulder: Westview Press, 1986.

Feinstein International Famine Center. "Human Security and Livelihoods of Rural Afghans, 2002–2003." Medford: Feinstein International Famine Center, Tufts University, 2003.

Fielden, Matthew and Johnathan Goodhand. "Beyond the Taliban: The Afghan Conflict and United Nations Peacemaking." *Conflict, Security and Development,* vol. 1, no. 3 (December 2001): 5–32.

Findlay, Trevor. *Cambodia: The Legacy and Lessons of UNTAC.* Oxford: Oxford University Press, 1995.

Fletcher, Arnold. *Afghanistan: Highway of Conquest.* Westport: Greenwood Press, 1965.

Fukuyama, Francis. *State-Building: Governance and World Order in the 21st Century.* Ithaca: Cornell University Press, 2004.

Gall, Carlotta. "At Border, Signs of Pakistani Role in Taliban Surge." *New York Times,* 21 January 2007.

Ganguly, Sumit. "The Crisis of Indian Secularism." *Journal of Democracy,* vol. 14, no. 4 (2003): 11–25.

Gardiner, Beth. "World Pledges $10.5B for Afghanistan Aid." *Washington Post,* 1 February 2006.

Gellner, Ernest. *Conditions of Liberty, Civil Society and its Rivals.* London: Hamish Hamilton, 1994.

Ghani, Ashraf. "Afghanistan—XI. Administration." In *Encyclopedia Iranica,* vol. I. New York: Columbia University Center for Iranian Studies.

Ghani, Ashraf, Clare Lockhart, and Michael Carnahan. "An Agenda for State-Building in the Twenty-First Century." *The Fletcher Forum of World Affairs,* vol. 30, no. 1 (Winter 2006): 101–123.

———. *Closing the Sovereignty Gap: An Approach to State-Building.* London: Working Paper no. 253, Overseas Development Institute, September 2005.

Ghobar, Mir Gholam Mohammad. *Afghanistan in the Course of History,* vol. 2 (translated by Sharif A. Fayez). Herndon: All Prints Inc., 2001.
Gill, Graeme. *The Nature and Development of the Modern State.* London: Palgrave Macmillan, 2003.
Giustozzi, Antonio. "The Demodernization of an Army, 1992–2001." *Small Wars and Insurgencies,* vol. 15, no. 1: 1–18.
———. *Genesis of a "Prince": The Rise of Ismail Khan in Western Afghanistan, 1979–1992.* London: Crisis State Research Centre Working Paper no. 4, London School of Economics, 2006.
———. *"Good State" vs. "Bad" Warlords?: A Critique of State-Building Strategies in Afghanistan.* London: Crisis State Programme Working Paper 51, London School of Economics, 2004.
———. *The Missing Ingredient: Nonideological Insurgency and State Collapse in Western Afghanistan 1979–1992.* London: Crisis State Research Centre Working Paper no. 11, London School of Economics, 2007.
———. *Respectable Warlords?: The Politics of Statebuilding in Post-Taleban Afghanistan.* London: Crisis States Programme, London School of Economics, 2003.
———. *Respectable Warlords?: The Transition from War of All Against All to Peaceful Competition in Afghanistan.* London: Crisis State Programme Seminar Paper, London School of Economics, 2003.
———. "War and Peace Economies of Afghanistan's Strongmen." *International Peacekeeping,* vol. 14 (2007): 75–89.
———. *War, Politics and Society in Afghanistan, 1978–1992.* Georgetown: Georgetown University Press, 2000.
Giustozzi, Antonio and Noor Ullah. *"Tribes" and Warlords in Southern Afghanistan, 1980–2005.* London: Crisis State Research Centre Working Paper no. 7, London School of Economics, 2006.
Glasius, Marlies. "Civil Society" (2002). Fathom Knowledge Network. http://www.fathom.com/feature/122536/index.html.
Goodson, Larry. *Afghanistan's Endless War.* Seattle: University of Washington Press, 2001.
—. "Afghanistan's Long Road to Reconstruction." *Journal of Democracy,* vol. 14, no. 1 (2003): 82–99.
Government of Afghanistan. *Afghanistan National Development Strategy: An Interim Strategy for Security, Governance, Economic Growth and Poverty Reduction.* Kabul: Islamic Republic of Afghanistan, 2006.
———. *Interim Afghanistan National Development Strategy.* Kabul: Islamic Republic of Afghanistan, 2006.
Government of Afghanistan and UNAMA. "Implementation of the Afghanistan Compact." Biannual JCMB Report, November 2006.
Government of Afghanistan et al. *Securing Afghanistan's Future: Accomplishments and the Strategic Path Forward.* Kabul: Government of Afghanistan, Asian Development Bank, United Nations Assistance Mission to Afghanistan, United Nations Development Programme, and The World Bank Group, 17 March 2004.
Great Negotiator 2002: Lakhdar Brahimi. Documentary Film. Cambridge: Harvard Law School Program on Negotiation, 2004.
Gregorian, Vertan. *The Emergence of Modern Afghanistan: Politics of Reform and Modernization, 1880–1946.* Stanford: Stanford University Press, 1969.
Grevemeyer, Jan-Heeren. *Afghanistan: Sozialer Wandel und Staat im 20. Jh.* [Afghanistan: Social Change and State in the 20th Century]. Berlin: Express Edition, 1987.
Harpviken, Kristian Berg, Arne Strand, and Karin Ask. *Afghanistan and Civil Society.* Peshawar and Bergen: Chr. Michelson Institute, 2002.

Hashim, Ahmed S. *Insurgency and Counter-Insurgency in Iraq.* Ithaca: Cornell University Press, 2006.
Hayek, F. A. *The Constitution of Liberty.* London: Routledge and Kegan Paul, 1960.
Hendrickson, Dylan. "Cambodia's Security-Sector Reforms: Limits of a Downsizing Strategy." *Conflict, Security and Development,* vol. 1, no. 1 (2001): 67–82.
Hersh, Seymour. "The Other War." *New Yorker,* 12 April 2004.
Higgins, Andrew. "U.S. Ambitions Run Into Reality on an Afghan Road." *Wall Street Journal,* 6 February 2004.
Hippler, Jochen. "Nation-States for Export?: Nation-Building Between Military Intervention, Crisis Prevention and Development Policy." In Jochen Hippler, ed., *Nation-Building: A Key Concept for Peaceful Conflict Transformation.* London: Pluto Press, 2005.
Hobbes, Thomas. *Leviathan.* Cambridge: Cambridge University Press, 1996.
Hoffer, Eric. *The True Believer.* New York: Harper and Brothers, 1951.
Human Rights Watch. *Afghanistan's Bonn Agreement One Year Later: A Catalog of Missed Opportunities,* December 2002.
———. *Killing You Is a Very Easy Thing for Us,* July 2003.
———. *On the Precipice: Insecurity in Northern Afghanistan,* July 2002.
Hussain, Rizwan. *Pakistan and the Emergence of Islamic Militancy in Afghanistan.* Aldershot: Ashgate, 2005.
Ibrahimi, Niamatullah. *The Failure of a Clerical Proto-State: Hazarajat, 1979–1984.* London: Crisis State Research Centre Working Paper no. 6, London School of Economics, 2006.
International Crisis Group. *Afghanistan: Getting Disarmament Back on Track.* Kabul and Brussels: ICG Asia Briefing, 23 February 2005.
———. *Afghanistan: The Problem of Pashtun Alienation.* Kabul and Brussels: ICG Asia Report no. 62, 2003.
———. *Afghanistan's Flawed Constitutional Process.* Kabul and Brussels: ICG Asia Report no. 56, 2003.
———. *Elections and Security in Afghanistan.* Kabul and Brussels: ICG Asia Briefing, 30 March 2004.
________. *Iraq's Transition: On a Knife Edge.* Baghdad and Brussels: ICG Middle East Report no. 27, 2004.
Jackson, R. *Quasi-States: Sovereignty, International Relations and the Third World.* Cambridge: Cambridge University Press, 1990.
Jenning, John. "Afghanistan: The Gulf Between Report and Reality." *Middle East Intelligence Bulletin,* no. 6 (January 2004).
Jennings, R. S. *The Road Ahead, Lessons in Nation Building from Japan, Germany and Afghanistan for Postwar Iraq.* Washington, DC: United States Institute of Peace, April 2003.
Johnson, Chris, William Maley, J Alexander Thier, and Ali Wardak. "Afghanistan's Political and Constitutional Development." London: Overseas Development Institute, 2003. http://www.odi.org.uk/hpg/papers/evaluations/afghandfid.pdf.
Jones, Seth G. "Averting Failure in Afghanistan." *Survival,* vol. 48, no. 1 (Spring 2006): 111–128.
Kadioglu, Ayse. "The Paradox of Turkish Nationalism and the Construction of Official Identity." *Middle Eastern Studies,* April (1996): 177–193.
Kakar, Muhammad Hasan. *Afghanistan: A Study in International Political Developments, 1880–1896.* Lahore: Panjab Educational Press, 1971.
———. *Government and Society in Afghanistan: The Reign of Amir 'Abd al-Rahman Khan.* Austin: University of Texas Press, 1979.
Kamali, Masoud. "Civil Society and Islam: A Sociological Perspective." *Archives Europeenes De Sociologie,* vol. 42, no. 3 (2001).

Kamali, Mohammad Hashim. "Islam and its Shari'a in the Afghan Constitution 2004 with Special Reference to Personal Law." In Nadjma Yassari, ed., *The Shari'a in the Constitutions of Afghanistan, Iran and Egypt—Implications for Private Law,* 23–43. Tübingen: Mohr Siebeck, 2005.

———. *Law in Afghanistan.* Leiden: E. J. Brill, 1985.

Karokhail, Masood and Susanne Schmeidl. "Integration of Traditional Structures into the State-Building Process: Lessons from the Tribal Liaison Office in Loya Paktia." In *Publication Series on Promoting Democracy under Conditions of State Fragility,* Issue 1: Afghanistan. Berlin: Heinrich Böll Foundation, 2006. http://www.boell.de/downloads/asien/afghanistan_en.pdf.

Katib, Fayz Muhammad. *Kabul Under Siege* (translated by R. D. McChesney). Princeton: Markus Wiener Publishers, 1999.

Kedourie, Elie. *Democracy and Arab Political Culture.* London: Frank Cass and Co., 1994.

Kerr, Pauline, William T. Tow, and Marianne Hanson. "The Utility of the Human Security Agenda for Policy-Makers." *Asian Journal of Political Science,* vol. 11, no. 2 (December 2003): 89–114.

Khalilzad, Zalmay. "How to Nation-Build: Ten Lessons from Afghanistan." *The National Interest,* Summer (2005): 19–27.

King, Charles. *Ending Civil Wars.* Oxford: Oxford University Press, for the International Institute for Strategic Studies, Adelphi Paper no. 308, 1997.

King, Laura. "Pakistani City Serves as Refuge for the Taliban." *Los Angeles Times,* 21 December 2006.

Kramer, Gudrun. "Islamist Notions of Democracy." *Middle East Report,* July/August (1993): 2–8.

Krasner, Stephen D. *Sovereignty: Organized Hypocrisy.* Princeton: Princeton University Press, 1999.

Kuran, Timur. *Private Truths, Public Lies: The Social Consequences of Preference Falsification.* Cambridge: Harvard University Press, 1995.

Lamb, Alastair. *Asian Frontiers: Studies in a Continuing Problem.* London: F. W. Cheshire, 1968.

Lee, Jonathan L. *The "Ancient Supremacy": Bukhara, Afghanistan and the Battle for Balkh, 1731–1901.* Leiden: E. J. Brill, 1996.

———. *Water Resource Management on the Balkh Ab River and Hazhda Nahr Canal Network: From Crisis to Collapse.* Mazar-i Sharif: UNAMA and Central Asian Free Exchange, December 2003.

Lee, Jonathan L. and Mervyn Patterson. *Water Resource Management and Conflict in Northern Afghanistan.* Mazar-i Sharif: Oxfam, March/April 1996.

Lewis, Bernard, ed. *The Crisis of Islam: Holy War and Unholy Terror.* New York: The Modern Library, 2003.

———. *The Emergence of Modern Turkey: Studies in Middle Eastern History.* New York: Oxford University Press, 2001.

———. *Islam: From the Prophet Muhammad to the Capture of Constantinople,* vol. 1: Politics and War. New York: Oxford University Press, 1987.

Liechtenstein Institute on Self-Determination at Princeton University. "Creating Security and Stability in Afghanistan and the Region" (Summary Report). Princeton: Liechtenstein Institute on Self-Determination at Princeton University, October 2006. http://www.princeton.edu/lisd/publications/AfghSummary_2006.pdf.

———. "Stability and Viability in Afghanistan: Building a Viable and Effective Afghan State" (Policy Brief). Princeton: Liechtenstein Institute on Self-Determination at Princeton University, April 2003. http://www.princeton.edu/lisd/publications/Afghanistan_April_2003.pdf.

Lister, Sarah. "Caught in Confusion: Local Governance Structures in Afghanistan." Kabul: Afghanistan Research and Evaluation Unit, 2005.

Lister, Sarah and Hamish Nixon. "Provincial Government Structure in Afghanistan: From Confusion to Vision." Kabul: Afghanistan Research and Evaluation Unit, 2006.

Lister, Sarah and Adam Pain. "Trading in Power: The Politics of 'Free' Markets in Afghanistan." Kabul: Afghanistan Research and Evaluation Unit, Briefing Paper, June 2004.

Ludin, Jawed. "Civil Society in Afghanistan." Background Paper for the Second Afghan Civil Society Conference. Kabul, 15–19 May 2002.

Machiavelli, Niccolò. *The Prince.* Harmondsworth: Penguin, 1978.

Macintyre, Andrew. *The Power of Institutions: Political Architecture and Governance.* Ithaca: Cornell University Press, 2003.

Mack, Andrew, ed. *Human Security Report 2005: War and Peace in the 21st Century.* Oxford: Oxford University Press, 2005.

Mackenzie, Richard. "The United States and the Taliban." In William Maley, ed., *Fundamentalism Reborn?: Afghanistan and the Taliban.* London: Hurst and Co., 2001.

Maley, William. *The Afghanistan Wars.* London: Palgrave Macmillan, 2002.

———. "Democratic Governance and Post-Conflict Transitions." *Chicago Journal of International Law,* vol. 6, no. 2 (Winter 2006): 683–701.

———. "Institutional Design and the Rebuilding of Trust." In William Maley, Charles Sampford, and Ramesh Thakur, eds., *From Civil Strife to Civil Society: Civil and Military Responsibilities in Disrupted States,* 163–179. New York and Tokyo: United Nations University Press, 2003.

———. "International Force and Political Reconstruction: Cambodia, East Timor and Afghanistan." In Albrecht Schnabel and Hans-Georg Ehrhart, eds., *Security Sector Reform and Post-Conflict Peacebuilding,* 297–312. Tokyo: United Nations University Press, 2005.

———. "Peace, Needs and Utopia." *Political Studies,* vol. 33, no. 4 (December 1985): 578–591.

———. "The Reconstruction of Afghanistan." In Ken Booth and Tim Dunne, eds., *Worlds in Collision: Terror and the Future of Global Order,* 184–193. London: Palgrave Macmillan, 2002.

———. *Rescuing Afghanistan.* London: Hurst and Company, 2006.

———. "The UN and East Timor." *Pacifica Review,* vol. 12, no. 1 (February 2000): 63–76.

Maley, William and Amin Saikal. "Civil Society and Reconstruction: Some Reflections." *Afghanistan Info,* vol. 52, nos. 7–8 (2002).

———, eds. *Regime Change in Afghanistan: Foreign Intervention and the Politics of Legitimacy.* Boulder: Westview Press, 1991.

Maley, William and Daoud Yaqub. *A Long Hot Summer: Crisis and Opportunity in Afghanistan* (Policy Brief). Sydney: Lowy Institute for International Policy, March 2007.

Mansûr, Abdul Hafîz. *Nuhzat-i Islamî-yi Afghânistân: barrasî-yi intiqadî-yi guzashta, hâl-u âyanda* [Islamic Revival in Afghanistan: A Critical Appraisal of the Past, Present and Future]. s.l. 2001.

Manuel Anja and P. W. Singer. "A New Model Afghan Army." *Foreign Affairs,* vol. 81, no. 4 (July/August 2002).

Marten, Kimberly Zisk. *Enforcing the Peace: Learning from the Imperial Past.* New York: Columbia University Press, 2004.

Martin, Ian. *Self-Determination in East Timor: The United Nations, the Ballot, and International Intervention.* Boulder: Lynne Rienner, 2001.

Masmoudi, Radwan. "What is Liberal Islam: The Silenced Majority." *Journal of Democracy,* vol. 14, no. 2 (2002): 40–42.
McChesney, Robert D. *Waqf in Central Asia: Four Hundred Years in the History of a Muslim Shrine,* 1480–1889. Princeton: Princeton University Press, 1991.
McRae, Rob and Don Hubert, eds. *Human Security and the New Diplomacy: Protecting People, Promoting Peace.* Montreal and Kingston: McGill-Queen's University Press, 2001.
Mearsheimer, John J. *The Tragedy of Great Power Politics.* New York: W. W. Norton, 2001.
Middlebrook, P. J. and S. M. Miller. "Lessons in Post Conflict Reconstruction from the New Afghanistan Compact." *Foreign Policy in Focus Policy Report,* 27 January 2006. http://www.fpif.org.
Migdal, Joel S. *Strong Societies and Weak States: State-Society Relations and State Capabilities in the Third World.* Princeton: Princeton University Press, 1988.
———. "The State in Society: An Approach to Struggles for Domination." In Joel S. Migdal, Atul Kohli, and Vivienne Shue, eds., *State Power and Social Forces: Domination and Transformation in the Third World,* 7–34. Cambridge: Cambridge University Press, 1994.
Miller, Linda B. *World Order and Local Disorder: The United Nations and Internal Conflicts.* Princeton: Princeton University Press, 1967.
Mohan, C. Raja. "India and Afghan Railroads." *The Hindu,* 20 February 2003.
Montesquieu, Baron de. *The Spirit of the Laws.* New York: Hafner Press, 1949.
Moore, Robin. *The Hunt for Bin Laden: Task Force Dagger.* New York: Random House, 2003.
Mufti, Malik. *Sovereign Creations: Pan-Arabism and Political Order in Syria and Iraq.* Ithaca: Cornell University Press, 1996.
Murray, Tonita. "Police-Building in Afghanistan: A Case Study of Civil Security Reform." *International Peacekeeping,* vol. 14, no. 1 (January 2007): 108–126.
Nasr, Vali. "The Rise of Muslim Democracy." *Journal of Democracy,* vol. 16, no. 2 (2005): 13–27.
"NATO Flirts with Failure in Afghanistan." *International Herald Tribune,* 21 May 2004.
"NATO's Incredibility; Its Real Challenge Lies in Afghanistan, not Iraq." *Financial Times,* 26 June 2004.
Naylor, Sean. "The Waiting Game: A Stronger Taliban Lies Low, Hoping the U.S. Will Leave Afghanistan." 31 March 2006. http://72.14.203.104/search?q=cache:wZGqk8JCp7IJ:www.armedforcesjournal.com/story.php%3FF%3D1404902_0206+Sean+Naylor+Securing+the+Future+Afghanistan&hl=en&ct=clnk&cd=1&client=safari.
Newell, Richard. *The Politics of Afghanistan.* Ithaca: Cornell University Press, 1972.
Niland, Norah. "Justice Postponed: The Marginalization of Human Rights in Afghanistan." In Antonio Donini, Norah Niland, and Karin Wermester, eds., *Nation-Building Unraveled?: Aid, Peace and Justice in Afghanistan,* 61–82. Bloomfield: Kumarian Press, 2004.
Nojumi, N. *The Rise of the Taliban in Afghanistan.* New York: Palgrave, 2002.
Organization for Economic Co-Operation and Development. *Financial Action Task Force on Money Laundering: Annual Report 2001–2002.* Paris: Organization for Economic Co-Operation and Development, 2002.
Orvis, Stephen. "Civil Society in Africa or African Civil Society?" *Journal of Asian and African Studies,* vol. 36, no. 1 (2001).
Ottaway, M. "Rebuilding State Institutions in Collapsed States." *Development and Change,* vol. 33, no. 5 (November 2002): 1001–1023.
Oxhorn, Philip. "Making Civil Society Relevant (Again)." *Focal Point: Spotlight on the Americas,* vol. 2, no. 3 (2003).

Packer, George. *The Assassins' Gate: America in Iraq*. New York: Farrar, Straus and Giroux, 2005.

Paffenholz, Thania and Christopf Spurk. "Civil Society/Civic Engagement and Peacebuilding." Research Paper Commissioned by the Social Development Department of the World Bank, 2006.

Pain, Adam. *Opium Trading Systems in Helmand and Ghor.* Kabul: Afghanistan Research and Evaluation Unit, Issues Paper Series, 2006.

Pakulski, Jan. "Eastern Europe and 'Legitimacy Crisis'." *Australian Journal of Political Science,* vol. 25, no. 2 (November 1990): 272–288.

Pazhwak, Abdul Rahman. *Pakhtunistan: A New State in Central Asia.* London: The Royal Afghan Embassy, 1960.

Peimani, Hooman. "Iran Stakes a Claim to the Silk Road." *Asia Times,* 14 August 2003.

Pelton, Robert Young. *Licensed to Kill: Hired Guns in the War on Terror.* New York: Three Rivers Press, 2007.

Peou, Sorpong. *Conflict Neutralization in the Cambodia War: From Battlefield to Ballot-Box.* Kuala Lumpur: Oxford University Press, 1997.

Pescataing, Camille. "The Secret Agents: Life Inside an al Qaeda Cell." *Foreign Affairs,* vol. 83, no. 1 (January/February 2004): 156–157.

Phillips, David L. *Losing Iraq: Inside the Postwar Reconstruction Fiasco.* Boulder: Westview Press, 2005.

Philpot, Daniel. "The Religious Roots of Modern International Relations." *World Politics,* vol. 52, no. 2 (2000): 206–245.

Poggi, Gianfranco. *The Development of the Modern State: A Sociological Introduction.* London: Hutchinson, 1978.

———. *The State: Its Nature, Development and Prospects.* Stanford: Stanford University Press, 1990.

Polk, William R. *Understanding Iraq.* New York: HarperCollins, 2005.

Poullada, Leon. *Reform and Rebellion in Afghanistan, 1919–1929: King Amanullah's Failure to Modernize a Tribal Society.* Ithaca: Cornell University Press, 1973.

Rashid, Ahmed. *Taliban: Militant Islam, Oil and Fundamentalism in Central Asia.* New Haven: Yale University Press, 2001.

Raum, Tom. "Analysis: Osama Haunts Bush in Afghanistan." Associated Press, 2 March 2006.

Reus-Smit, Christian. *The Moral Purpose of the State: Culture, Social Identity, and Institutional Rationality in International Relations.* Princeton: Princeton University Press, 1999.

Reynolds, Andrew. "The Curious Case of Afghanistan." *Journal of Democracy,* vol. 17, no. 2 (April 2006): 104–117.

Reynolds, Andrew and Jorgen Elklit. "Jordan: Electoral System Design in the Arab World." In *The International IDEA Handbook of Electoral System Design,* 53–54. Stockholm: International IDEA, 1997.

Reynolds, Andrew and Andrew Wilder. *Afghanistan: From Presidential to Parliamentary Elections.* Kabul: Afghanistan Research and Evaluation Unit, 2004.

———. *Free, Fair or Flawed: Challenges for Legitimate Elections in Afghanistan.* Kabul: Afghanistan Research and Evaluation Unit, 2004.

Rigby, T. H. "Introduction: Political Legitimacy, Weber, and Communist Mono-Organisational Systems." In T. H. Rigby and Ferenc Fehér, eds., *Political Legitimation in Communist States,* 1–26. London: Macmillan, 1982.

Rossi, Simonetta and Antonio Giustozzi. *Disarmamanet, Demobilisation and Reintegration of Ex-Combatants (DDR) in Afghanistan: Constraints and Limited Capabilities.* London: Crisis States Research Centre Working Paper no. 2, London School of Economics, 2006.

Rotberg, Robert I. "Renewing the Afghan State." In Robert I. Rotberg, ed., *Building a New Afghanistan,* 1–21. Washington, DC: Brookings Institution Press, 2007.
Rousseau, Jean-Jacques. *The Social Contract and Discourses.* London: J. M. Dent, 1973.
Roussel, Frédéric and Marie-Pierre Caley. *The Mantiqas: The Underground Puzzle of Afghanistan.* Kabul and Peshawar: ACTED, 1994.
Roy, Olivier. *Islam and Resistance in Afghanistan.* Cambridge: Cambridge University Press, 1985.
Rubin, Barnett. "Crafting a Constitution for Afghanistan." *Journal of Democracy,* vol. 15, no. 3 (July 2004): 5–19.
———. *The Fragmentation of Afghanistan.* New Haven: Yale University Press, 1995.
———. "(Re)Building Afghanistan: The Folly of Stateless Democracy." *Current History,* April (2004): 165–170.
———. "Saving Afghanistan." *Foreign Affairs,* vol. 86, no. 1 (January-February 2007): 57–78.
———. *The Search for Peace in Afghanistan: From Buffer State to Failed State.* New Haven: Yale University Press, 1995.
Rubin, Barnett and Helena Malikyar. "The Politics of Center-Periphery Relations in Afghanistan" (Draft Paper). New York: New York University Center on International Cooperation, March 2003.
Saikal, Amin. *Islam and the West: Conflict or Cooperation?* London: Palgrave Macmillan, 2003.
———. *Modern Afghanistan: A History of Struggle and Survival.* London: I. B. Tauris, 2004.
———. *The Rise and Fall of the Shah.* Princeton: Princeton University Press, 1980.
———. "Securing Afghanistan's Border." *Survival,* vol. 48, no. 1 (Spring 2006): 129–142.
Sanderson, John M. and Michael Maley. "Elections and Liberal Democracy in Cambodia." *Australian Journal of International Affairs,* vol. 52, no. 3 (November 1998): 241–253.
Sanfilipo, John R., et al. "Coal Mining in Afghanistan: Third World Problems and Opportunities." Geological Society of America 2006 Philadelphia Annual Meeting, Paper no. 33–11.
Sarhadi, Zia. "Pakistan Paying a High Price for Musharraf's Urge to Please the US." *Muslimedia International,* 16–31 August 2003.
Schmeidl, Susanne. "The Emperor's New Cloth: The Unravelling of Peacebuilding in Afghanistan." *Friedens-Warte—Journal of International Peace and Organizations,* 1–2 (2007): 69–86.
———. "(Human) Security Dilemmas: Long-Term Implications of the Afghan Refugee Crisis." *Third World Quarterly,* vol. 23, no. 1 (2007): 7–29.
———. "Understanding Civil Society in Non-Western Countries: Some Initial Thoughts on Afghanistan." Kabul: ACSF-swisspeace, 2003.
Schetter, Conrad. *Kriegsfürstentum und Bürgerkriegsökonomien in Afghanistan* [Warlordism and Civil War Economies in Afghanistan]. Cologne: Lehrstuhl für Internationale Politik, 2004.
———. "Wiederaufbau zwischen allen Stühlen: Die Internationale Intervention zwischen Staat, Zivilgesellschaft und traditionellen Eliten." In *Schriften zur Demokratieförderung uner Bedingungen fragiler Staatlichkeit,* Issue 1: Afghanistan. Berlin: Heinrich Böll Sitftung, 2006.
Schetter, Conrad and Susanne Schmeidl. "Afghanistan: Aktuelle Situation und Möglichkeiten der Befriedung." In Erich Reiter, ed., *Jahrbuch für internationale Sicherheitspolitik 2004.* Hamburg: Mittler, 2004.

Schiewek, Eckart. "State and Human Security in the Age of Terrorism: Security Sector Reform in Afghanistan." In *State and Human Security,* 71–92. Geneva: UNOG-DCAF, 2004.

Schroen, Gary. *First In: An Insider's Account of How the CIA Spearheaded the War on Terror in Afghanistan.* New York: Presidio Press, 2005.

Schwedler, Jillian. "Islamic Identity: Myth, Menace, or Mobilizer?" *SAIS Review,* vol. 21, no. 2 (2001): 1–17.

Scott, James C. *Seeing Like a State: How Certain Schemes to Improve the Human Condition Have Failed.* New Haven: Yale University Press, 1998.

Sedra, Mark. *Challenging the Warlord Culture: Security Sector Reform in Post-Taliban Afghanistan.* Bonn: Bonn International Center for Conversion, 2002.

———. "Security Sector Reform in Afghanistan: The Slide Towards Expediency." *International Peacekeeping,* vol. 13, no. 1 (March 2006): 94–110.

Shah, Aqil. "Pakistan's Armored Democracy." *Journal of Democracy,* vol. 14, no. 4 (2003): 26–40.

Shahrani, M. Nazif. "Resisting the Taliban and Talibanism in Afghanistan." *Perceptions: Journal of International Affairs,* vol. 5, no. 4 (December 2000–February 2001): 121–140.

———. "State Building and Social Fragmentation in Afghanistan: A Historical Perspective." In Ali Banuazizi and Myron Weiner, eds. *The State, Religion and Ethnic Politics: Afghanistan, Iran and Pakistan,* 23–74. Syracuse: Syracuse University Press, 1986.

Shahrani, M. Nazif and Robert L. Canfield, eds., *Revolutions and Rebellions in Afghanistan.* Berkley: University of California Press, 1984.

Shehab, Sophie. "Physique d'ours, le padishah-général Dostom reçoit dans son palais de Sheberghan." *Le Monde,* 28 December 2001.

Sipress, Alan. "Peacekeepers Won't Go Beyond Kabul, Cheney Says." *Washington Post,* 20 March 2002.

Sitafi, Muhammad Hasan. *Yâdnâma-yi Muhammad Tâhir Badakhshî* [Memorial of Muhammad Tahir Badakhshi]. Kabul: 1991.

Skocpol, Theda. "Bringing the State Back In: Current Research." In Peter Evans, Dietrich Rueschemeyer, and Theda Skocpol, eds., *Bringing the State Back In.* New York: Cambridge University Press, 1985.

Smith, Michael G. with Moreen Dee. *Peacekeeping in East Timor: The Path to Independence.* Boulder: Lynne Rienner, 2003.

Spector, Regine A. "The North-South Transport Corridor." *Analyst* (Central Asia-Caucasus Institute), 3 July 2002.

Spin Giri: The White Beards. Documentary Film. Berlin: Heinrich Böll Foundation.

Stallard, Dawn. *Speaking Out: Afghan Opinions on Rights and Responsibilities.* Kabul: Human Rights Research and Advocacy Consortium, 2003.

Stapleton, Barbara J. "A British Agencies Afghanistan Group Briefing Paper on the Development of Joint Regional Teams in Afghanistan." London: British Agencies Afghanistan Group, January 2003.

Starr, S. Frederick. "A 'Greater Central Asia Partnership' for Afghanistan and its Neighbors." Baltimore: Johns Hopkins School of Advanced International Studies, Central Asia-Caucasus Institute, March 2005.

———. "Sovereignty and Legitimacy in Afghan Nation-Building." In Francis Fukuyama, ed., *Nation-Building: Beyond Afghanistan and Iraq,* 107–124. Baltimore: The Johns Hopkins University Press, 2006.

Stedman, Stephen John. "Spoiler Problems in Peace Processes." *International Security,* vol. 22, no. 2 (Fall 1997): 5–53.

Stewart, Richard W. *The United States Army in Afghanistan: Operation Enduring Freedom, October 2001–March 2002.* Washington, DC: Defense Department, Army Center of Military History, 2004.

Stockton, Nicholas. "Strategic Coordination in Afghanistan." Kabul: Afghanistan Research and Evaluation Unit, 2002.

Suhrke, Astri. "The Limits of State-Building: The Role of International Assistance in Afghanistan." Paper Presented at the Annual Meeting of the International Studies Association. San Diego, 21–24 March 2006.

———. "Peacekeepers as Nation-Builders: UN Dilemmas in East Timor." *International Peacekeeping,* vol. 9, no. 4 (Winter 2001): 1–20.

———. *When More is Less: Aiding Statebuilding in Afghanistan.* Madrid: Working Paper no. 26, Fundación para las Relaciones Internacionales y el Diálogo Exterior, 2006.

Suhrke, Astri, Kristian Berg Harpviken, Are Knudsen, Arve Ofstad, and Arne Strand. *Peacebuilding: Lessons for Afghanistan.* Bergen: Chr. Michelsen Institute, 2002.

Tamari, Salim. "Left in Limbo: Leninist Heritage and Islamist Challenge." *Middle East Report,* November/December (1992): 16–21.

Tarzi, Amin. "The Judicial State: Evolution and Centralization of the Courts in Afghanistan, 1883–1896." Ph.D. diss., New York University, 2003.

Taylor, Telford. *Munich: The Price of Peace.* New York: Doubleday, 1979.

Trives, Sébastien. "Afghanistan: Tackling the Insurgency—The Case of the Southeast." *politique étrangère,* vol. 1 (2006).

UNDP, Civil Society Development and Governance Division. *Civil Society Sourcebook: Participatory Organizational Evaluation Tool.* CSOPP Resource Center: Toolbox, 2000.

United Nations. *Report of the Panel on United Nations Peace Operations.* A/55/305–S/2000/809, 21 August 2000.

———. *Report of the Secretary-General on the Situation in Afghanistan and Its Implications for International Peace and Security,* S/2002/278, 18 March 2002.

———. *Report of the Secretary-General on the Situation in Afghanistan and Its Implications for International Peace and Security,* S/2002/737, 11 July 2002.

———. *Report of the Secretary-General on the Situation in Afghanistan and its Implications for International Peace and Security,* S/2002/1173, 21 October 2002.

———. *Report of the Secretary-General on the United Nations Mission of Support in East Timor.* S/2004/333, 19 April 2004.

United States, General Accountability Office. *Afghanistan Reconstruction: Deteriorating Security and Limited Resources Have Impeded Progress; Improvements in U.S. Strategy Needed.* Washington, DC: United States General Accountability Office, GAO-04–403, 2004.

United States, House of Representatives. *Afghanistan Security: Efforts to Establish Army and Police Have Made Progress, but Future Plans Need to Be Better Defined* (Report to the Committee on International Relations). Washington DC: United States Government Accountability Office, GAO-05–575, June 2005.

United States, National Commission on Terrorist Attacks Upon the United States. *The 9/11 Commission Report: Final Report of the National Commission on Terrorist Attacks Upon the United States.* Washington, DC: National Commission on Terrorist Attacks Upon the United States, 2004.

United States Institute of Peace, and the Center for the Study of Islam and Democracy (workshop co-sponsors, 19 March 2004). "Ijtihad: Reinterpreting Islam for the Twenty-First Century," Special Report 125. http://www.islam-democracy.org.

van Creveld, Martin. *The Rise and Decline of the State.* Cambridge: Cambridge University Press, 1999.

Vile, M. J. C. *Constitutionalism and the Separation of Powers.* London: Oxford University Press, 1967.

von Einsiedel, Sebastian. "Policy Responses to State Failure." In Simon Chesterman, Michael Ignatieff and Ramesh Thakur, eds., *Making States Work: State Failure and the Crisis of Governance,* 13–35. Tokyo: United Nations University Press, 2005.

Walsh, Declan. "Frustrated US Forces Fail to Win Hearts and Minds." *The Guardian,* 23 September 2004.

Walter, Barbara F. *Committing to Peace: The Successful Settlement of Civil Wars.* Princeton: Princeton University Press, 2002.

Watkins, C. "Provincial Reconstruction Teams (PRTs): An Analysis of Their Contribution to Security in Afghanistan." M.Sc. Thesis, Oxford Brookes University, 2003.

Watson, Paul. "The Lure of Opium Wealth Is a Potent Force in Afghanistan." *Los Angeles Times,* 28 May 2005.

———. "On the Trail of the Taliban's Support." *Los Angeles Times,* 24 December 2006.

Weber, Max. *Economy and Society: An Outline of Interpretive Sociology,* vol. I. Berkeley and Los Angeles: University of California Press, 1978.

———. "Politics as a Vocation." In H. H. Gerth and C. Wright Mills, eds. *From Max Weber: Essays in Sociology,* 77–128. New York: Oxford University Press.

Weinbaum, Marvin G. "Afghanistan: Nonparty Parliamentary Democracy." *The Journal of Developing Areas,* vol. 7, no. 1 (October 1972): 57–74.

———. "Afghanistan and Its Neighbors: An Ever Dangerous Neighborhood." Washington, DC: United States Institute of Peace, Special Report 162, June 2006.

———. "Legal Elites in Afghan Society." *International Journal of Middle East Studies,* vol. 12 (1980): 39–57.

Wilder, Andrew. "A House Divided." Kabul: Afghanistan Research and Evaluation Unit, 2006.

———. *The 2005 Elections in Afghanistan: Case Studies from Herat and Kandahar.* Kabul: Afghanistan Research and Evaluation Unit, 2006.

Wilder, Andrew, Christina Bennett, and Shawna Wakefield. "Afghan Elections: The Great Gamble." Kabul: Afghanistan Research and Evaluation Unit, Briefing Paper, November 2003.

Wimmer, Andreas and Conrad Schetter. "State-Formation First: Recommendations for Reconstruction and Peace-Making in Afghanistan," ZEF Discussion Paper, no. 45, 2002. http://www.zef.de/publications.htm.

World Bank. *Afghanistan—State Building, Sustaining Growth, and Reducing Poverty.* Washington DC: The World Bank, 2005.

Wulwaljî, Asadullah. *Âyâ quwâ-yi nizâmî-yi ittihâd-i shûrâwî az Afghânistân khârij sâkhta shud?* [Was the Military Force of the Soviet Union Pushed Out of Afghanistan?]. Peshawar: 2001.

———. "Can Jumbish-i Milli-i Islami Afghanistan Survive in Alliance with Shura-i Nazar?" *Central Asia,* Special Issue (2001).

———. "Junbish-i millî-yi Islâmî-yi Afghânistân mêtawânist dar ittihâd bâ sâzmân-i shûrâ-yi Nazâr bâqî bamânad?" [Could the National Islamic Movement of Afghanistan Continue in an Alliance with the Supervisory Council?]. In *Andesha* (Private Journal Published in Mazar-i Sharif 1992–1998 and collected by Patterson & Schiewek), nos. 4, 6, 7, 8 (1374/1995–1996).

———. *Khurûj-i Jinrâl Dôstum wa suqût-i Dâktar Najîbullah* [The Emergence of General Dostum and the Fall of Dr. Najibullah]. Kabul: 2003.

Xinhua Net. "Anti-US Resentment on Rise in Southeast Afghanistan." Kabul: 15 March 2004.

Zahab, Mariam Abou and Olivier Roy. *Islamist Networks: The Afghan-Pakistan Connection.* London: Hurst and Company, 2004.

Contributors

WOLFGANG DANSPECKGRUBER is the founding director of the Liechtenstein Institute on Self-Determination at Princeton University and has been teaching on issues of state, security, self-determination and diplomacy at Princeton's Woodrow Wilson School of Public and International Affairs and Department of Politics since 1988. He is also founder and chairman of the Liechtenstein Colloquium on European and International Affairs, a private diplomacy forum. His current work focuses on security problems in Afghanistan, Iran, and Central Asia.

Danspeckgruber was educated at the Universities of Linz and Vienna, Austria (D.Laws) and the Graduate Institute of International Studies, Geneva, Switzerland (Ph.D.). Following his Austrian military service, he served as special assistant to the commander of the Austrian National Defense Academy. Danspeckgruber was a visiting scholar at the Fletcher School of Law and Diplomacy, and held research fellowships at the Center of Science and International Affairs at the Kennedy School of Government at Harvard University, and at Princeton's Center of International Studies. His books include *Self-Determination of Peoples: Communities, Nations, and States in Global Interdependence; Self-Determination and Self-Administration: A Sourcebook* (edited with Sir Arthur Watts); *The Iraqi Aggression against Kuwait* (edited with Charles R. H. Tripp); and *Emerging Dimensions of European Security Policy.* Danspeckgruber is the editor of the forthcoming *Princeton Encyclopedia of Self-Determination.*

ROBERT P. FINN is currently Senior Research Associate at the Liechtenstein Institute on Self-Determination and Lecturer in the Department of Near Eastern Studies at Princeton University. From 2003–2005, he was the Ertegun Visiting Professor of Turcology at Princeton University. He served as the first US ambassador to Afghanistan in more than 20 years, from March 2002 until August 2003. He served as US ambassador to Tajikstan from 1998–2001 and his other diplomatic postings include Istanbul, Ankara and Izmir, Turkey; Lahore,

Pakistan; and Zagreb, Croatia. He opened the US embassy in Azerbaijan in 1992.

Among other publications, Finn is the author of the book *The Early Turkish Novel,* which has been published both in English and Turkish. His poems and translations have appeared in the US, Turkey, France and Pakistan. He reads in more than ten languages. He holds a B.A. in American Literature and European History from St. John's University, a M.A. in Near Eastern Studies from New York University, and a M.A. and Ph.D. in Near Eastern Studies from Princeton University. He was a Peace Corps volunteer in Turkey and a Fulbright scholar at Istanbul University.

SARAH LISTER is currently civil society and governance advisor at UNDP's Oslo Governance Center. From 2003–2006, she was senior researcher in governance and political economy at the Afghanistan Research and Evaluation Unit where she specialized in issues of subnational governance. Prior to that, she was a research fellow in governance at the Institute of Development Studies, UK. Working in Asia, Central America, and East Africa, she has consulted for the UK Department of International Development, the World Bank and other donors, as well as a number of international NGOs.

Lister is the author and co-author of numerous papers, articles, and book chapters. She holds M.Sc. and Ph.D. degrees in Social Policy from the London School of Economics, and a B.A. in History from Cambridge University.

WILLIAM MALEY is professor and director of the Asia-Pacific College of Diplomacy at the Australian National University. He has served as a visiting professor at the Russian Diplomatic Academy, a visiting fellow at the Centre for the Study of Public Policy at the University of Strathclyde, and a visiting research fellow in the Refugee Studies Programme at Oxford University.

A regular visitor to Afghanistan, Maley is author of *Rescuing Afghanistan, and the Afghanistan Wars;* co-author of *Regime Change in Afghanistan: Foreign Intervention and the Politics of Legitimacy,* and *Political Order in Post-Communist Afghanistan;* editor of *Fundamentalism Reborn?: Afghanistan and the Taliban;* and co-editor of *The Soviet Withdrawal from Afghanistan,* and *From Civil Strife to Civil Society: Civil and Military Responsibilities in Disrupted States.* He has published numerous articles and chapters on Afghanistan in a wide range of international journals and books.

RANI D. MULLEN is assistant professor of Government at the College of William and Mary in Williamsburg, Virginia, where she is also a faculty participant in the Program on the Theory and Practice of International Politics. She received her Ph.D. from Princeton University in 2007. While a Ph.D. candidate, Mullen directed the Liechtenstein Institute on Self-Determination's Asia Program. Her dissertation, "Does Local Governance Matter?" focused on the relationship between village government and social welfare in selected Indian states. Mullen is a contributing author to Atul Kohli, Chung-in Moon, and Georg Sørensen, eds., *States, Markets, and Just Growth: Development in the Twenty-First Century.*

ANDREW REYNOLDS is associate professor of Political Science at the University of North Carolina at Chapel Hill. He received his M.A. from the University of Cape Town and his Ph.D. from the University of California, San Diego. His research and teaching focus on democratization, constitutional design and electoral politics. He has worked for the United Nations, the International Institute for Democracy and Electoral Assistance, the UK Department for International Development, the US State Department, the National Democratic Institute, the International Republican Institute, the Organization for Security and Cooperation in Europe, and the International Foundation for Election Systems. He has also served as a consultant on issues of electoral and constitutional design for Afghanistan, Angola, Burma, Fiji, Guyana, Indonesia, Iraq, Jordan, Kenya, Liberia, Netherlands, Netherlands Antilles, Northern Ireland, Sierra Leone, South Africa, Yemen and Zimbabwe, most recently in Kabul reporting on election preparations in Afghanistan and in Rangoon, Burma. He has received research awards from the US Institute of Peace, the National Science Foundation, and the Ford Foundation.

Among Reynolds' books are *The Architecture of Democracy: Constitutional Design, Conflict Management, and Democracy; Electoral Systems and Democratization in Southern Africa; Election '99 South Africa: From Mandela to Mbeki;* and *Elections and Conflict Management in Africa* (co-edited with T. Sisk). He is currently working on a book titled "First Do No Harm: Applying the Lessons of Medicine to the Art of Constitutional Design." His articles have appeared in numerous journals, and he has published opinion pieces in the *Washington Post, Chicago Tribune, Christian Science Monitor* and *San Diego Union Tribune.* His work has been translated into French, Spanish, Arabic, Serbo-Croat, Albanian, Burmese and Portuguese.

AMIN SAIKAL is director of the Centre for Arab and Islamic Studies (the Middle East and Central Asia) and professor of Political Science at the Australian National University. He is a specialist in the politics, history, political economy and international relations of the Middle East and Central Asia.

Saikal has been a visiting fellow at Princeton University, Cambridge University, and the Institute of Development Studies at the University of Sussex, as well as a Rockefeller Foundation Fellow in International Relations (1983–1988). He is a member of many national and international academic organizations, and is the author of numerous works on the Middle East, Central Asia and Russia, including monographs, articles in international journals, and feature articles in national and international newspapers. He is a frequent commentator on these issues on radio and television. He was awarded the Order of Australia as Member of the Order (AM) in January 2006 for his services to the international community, as well as an advisor and author.

SUSANNE SCHMEIDL is an Afghanistan specialist and in 2007 started an appointment as a senior researcher at the Key Centre for Ethics, Law, Justice and Governance at Griffith University in Australia. Prior to this she worked for nine years with swisspeace in the areas of early warning, conflict prevention and peace-building. Between 2002 and 2005 she managed the swisspeace office in Afghanistan and supported civil society development and peace-building mainly through working with two Afghan organizations that she helped set up: the Afghan Civil Society Forum and the Tribal Liaison Office. She also advised and supported other civil society organizations and served on the Board of Rights and Democracy, an organization funding women's projects in Afghanistan.

Schmeidl received her M.A. and Ph.D. in sociology from the Ohio State University (1989 and 1995) and worked at the Centre for Refugee Studies (York University, Canada) as a postdoctoral researcher (1995–1996), coordinator of the Prevention/Early Warning Unit (1996–1997), coordinator of the interim secretariat of the Forum on Early Warning and Early Response (1996–1997), and technical consultant for the food and statistics unit of the UN High Commissioner for Refugees (1997). She has published in the areas of Afghanistan, civil society, refugee migration, conflict early warning and peace-building, and human security.

ECKART SCHIEWEK is currently political advisor to Tom Koenigs, the Special Representative of the Secretary-General, UNAMA. After working as a rapporteur at the civil society conference in Bonn in November-December 2001 and as a monitor of the Emergency Loya Jirga in May–June 2002, he joined UNAMA as political affairs officer in August 2003. Following deployments as political representative in Herat and Mazar-i Sharif, he became responsible for planning and supervising the elections to the Constitutional Loya Jirga, and handled protocol, floor management and the conduct of voting at the event itself. In 2004, he was briefly seconded to assist UNAMI in the holding of the interim parliament elections in Baghdad.

In January 2000, Schiewek started as a civil affairs officer for UNSMA. He was in charge of setting up and managing several regional offices of the mission, among them Mazar-i Sharif, Herat, Jalalabad, and was the liaison to the United Front in Faizabad. From 1995–1998 he worked with research institutions in Iran, Italy, Uzbekistan and Tajikistan. He joined the French NGO ACTED in 1997 and later worked for ACTED in Afghanistan on the delivery of humanitarian aid in joint programs with WFP and other UN agencies. Schiewek studied in Germany and Iran and graduated in 1995 from Bamberg University in auxiliary historical sciences, modern history and Iranian studies.

ANNA SELENY is professor of the Practice of International Politics at Tufts University's Fletcher School. Her research focuses on political economy, political and legal-institutional development, political culture and post-socialist and developing countries. She is the author of *The Political Economy of State-Society Relations in Hungary and Poland: From Communism to the European Union.* Her articles have appeared in numerous journals, including *World Politics, Comparative Politics, Perspectives on Politics, International Studies Quarterly, Journal of Democracy* and *Law & Policy.*

Seleny received a M.A. from The Johns Hopkins School of Advanced International Studies, and a Ph.D. in political science from the Massachusetts Institute of Technology. She was previously assistant professor of politics at Princeton University, a fellow at the Institute for Advanced Studies, and the recipient of fellowships from the American Council of Learned Societies, IREX, and the German Marshall, Fulbright and MacArthur Foundations. Seleny has also worked in international banking and in international development in Latin America and Central Asia (including nearly two years in Afghanistan).

BARBARA J. STAPLETON is currently political advisor to the European Union Special Representative for Afghanistan and has been based in Kabul since October 2002. Previously, she was advocacy and policy coordinator of the Agency Coordinating Body for Afghan Relief (ACBAR). In addition to speaking at numerous conferences on political and security developments in Afghanistan, she addressed NATO's North Atlantic Council on Provincial Reconstruction Teams and Best Practice in 2005. She studied at SOAS (Middle East history and politics) and has a LL.M. in the international law of human rights from the University of Essex. She co-wrote and was senior consultant to the BBC's flagship human rights program "Human Rights, Human Wrongs" from 1992–1998 following which she worked as lead consultant on media and democratization projects for Amnesty International and the EC amongst others.

Having worked in Eritrea, Burma, the Thai-Cambodian border and Iranian Kurdistan during the 1980s, her experiences in Iraq led to an extended period of involvement in Iraqi politics. Her report on "The Shias of Iraq" was researched in southern Iran following the first Gulf War and was published by the British Parliamentary Human Rights Group and the Al Khoei Foundation in 1992. In 1996, she traveled extensively in northern Iraq to research the effects anticipated by Iraqis linked to the implementation of the UN Security Council Resolution 986 (commonly known as the "Food for Oil" Resolution), her subsequent report was published by Christian Aid. She is the author of a chapter on Iraq for a global report on freedom of religion and belief published by Routledge.

J ALEXANDER THIER is senior advisor in the Rule of Law Program at the United States Institute of Peace. Previously, he was director of the Project on Failed States at Stanford University's Center on Democracy, Development and the Rule of Law. From 2002 to 2004, Thier was legal advisor to Afghanistan's Constitutional and Judicial Reform Commissions in Kabul, where he assisted in the development of a new constitution and judicial system. Thier worked as a UN and NGO official in Afghanistan during the civil war from 1993 to 1996, where he was the officer-in-charge of the UN Office for the Coordination of Humanitarian Assistance to Afghanistan in Kabul. He also worked for the United Nations in Iraq, Rwanda and New York, and served as a graduate fellow at the US National Security Council's Directorate for Near-East and South Asia. Thier has appeared as an expert commentator on NPR and the BBC, and in the *New York Times, Washington Post,* and *Los Angeles Times,* among others. He holds a B.A. from Brown University, a master's in Law and Diplomacy from the Fletcher School at Tufts University, and a J.D. from Stanford Law School.

MARVIN G. WEINBAUM is professor emeritus of political science at the University of Illinois at Urbana-Champaign. From 1999–2003 he served as an analyst for Pakistan and Afghanistan in the US State Department's Bureau of Intelligence and Research. He is currently a scholar-in-residence at the Middle East Institute in Washington, DC. He is the author of numerous articles and books. Among his recent publications are studies and book chapters for edited volumes dealing with Afghanistan's regional relations, the US-Pakistan strategic partnership, state- and economy-building in Afghanistan, and the politics of human rights in Turkey, Iran and Afghanistan.

ANDREW WILDER is a research director at the Feinstein International Center at Tufts University, where he leads the Center's research on "Politics and Policy" in countries affected by conflict. His areas of interest include state-building, governance, and aid-effectiveness, with a specialization on Afghanistan and Pakistan. Prior to joining the Center he worked in Afghanistan where he established and was the director of Afghanistan's first independent policy research institution, the Afghanistan Research and Evaluation Unit (AREU). Between 1986 and 2001, Wilder worked for several different international NGOs managing humanitarian and development programs in Pakistan and Afghanistan, including for six years as the director of the Pakistan/Afghanistan program of Save the Children (US).

Wilder is the author of *The Pakistani Voter,* a co-author of *A Guide to Government in Afghanistan,* and the author of several book chapters, journal articles and briefing papers. His recent research and publications have looked at police reform policies in Afghanistan, Afghan refugee education policy in Pakistan, the politics of civil service reform in Pakistan, electoral politics and policies in Pakistan and Afghanistan, and the politics of subnational administration in Afghanistan. Wilder has a B.S.F.S. degree from Georgetown University, and a M.A.L.D and Ph.D. from the Fletcher School of Law and Diplomacy at Tufts University.

Index